A Noble Crusade

The History of Eighth Army
1941 to 1945

A NOBLE CRUSADE

THE HISTORY OF EIGHTH ARMY
1941 TO 1945

by

Richard Doherty

*For all those from many nations who answered the call to fight
for peace with justice and served under the sign of the
Crusader's Cross in Eighth Army*

SPELLMOUNT
Staplehurst

British Library Cataloguing in Publication Data:
A catalogue record for this book is available
from the British Library

Copyright © Richard Doherty 1999
Maps copyright © Spellmount Ltd

ISBN 1-86227-045-7

First published in the UK in 1999 by
Spellmount Limited
The Old Rectory
Staplehurst
Kent TN12 0AZ

1 3 5 7 9 8 6 4 2

Typeset in Palatino by MATS, Southend-on-Sea, Essex
Printed in Great Britain by
Clays Ltd, St Ives plc

Contents

List of Maps

List of Plates

1. A troop of 25-pounders of an unidentified field regiment open up on enemy positions in March 1942. The 25-pounder was the standard field gun of the Royal Artillery and was an excellent weapon. (*IWM: E9535*)
2. British tanks move up towards Knightsbridge during the battles of June 1942. (*IWM: E12699*)
3. Far from being the golden sands portrayed so often on celluloid the desert varied in terrain. This is the Knightsbridge area, scene of the Cauldron battles of May/June 1942. The land is hard and stony with many small rocks making the going difficult for any vehicle but especially so for ambulances carrying wounded. The thin black line in the distance is a Bedouin with his flock of goats. (*Stuart Hamilton, MC*)
4. The desert could also be barren land with thorny scrub, as in this photograph at Tamar. The ground is covered with loose pebbles and there are tank tracks in the foreground. (*Stuart Hamilton, MC*)
5. Not all tanks damaged in battle were lost. Both sides went to great lengths to recover tanks that had been knocked out. Here a tank recovery team loads a Crusader onto a transporter under enemy fire during the Knightsbridge/Gazala battles. (*IWM: E13082*)
6. The courage and tenacity of the French Foreign Legion at Bir Hakeim in June 1942 became legendary. Here Colonel Amilakvari, commanding 13th Regiment, FFL, is seen in conference with battalion commander Puchois and other officers at Bir Hakeim. (*IWM: E13274*)
7. One of the greatest scourges of the desert soldier was the fly. This photograph shows how a 'brew-up' by a Bofors 40mm LAA gun crew became the centre of attention for a swarm of flies. Even more could be expected when food was present and they brought with them the risk of serious infection. (*Author's collection*)
8. Another scourge for the desert soldier was the khamsin or sandstorm which could last for two days. The heat was unbearable, the breath seemed to be sucked out of an individual and sand got everywhere. (*Author's collection*)
9. General Sir Claude Auchinleck, C-in-C Middle East and Commander Eighth Army, visits troops along the Alamein line in July 1942. He is driven in a 'peep' by his ADC, Captain Cunningham. (*IWM: E14782*)

fierce fighting around Croce. These knocked-out Shermans are evidence of the price paid by Eighth Army in Operation OLIVE. (*Stuart Hamilton, MC*)

20. The Germans also paid a heavy price in the Gothic Line battles. This self-propelled gun was one of the victims of Eighth Army's tanks or artillery. (*Stuart Hamilton, MC*)

21. Vickers machine guns firing on German positions at Monte Gemmano in the Gothic Line defences. (*Stuart Hamilton, MC*)

22. The crew of *Mohawk*, a Sherman of 4 Troop, A Squadron Warwickshire Yeomanry, rest beside their tank in the Apennines in September 1944. The Troop had just spent a night trapped on an Apennine hillside when the track along which they had passed fell away behind them. They had been supported by Indian troops of the Frontier Force Rifles and by an elderly Italian, Angelo Rossi. (*Len Trinder*)

23. Tank regiment in strength. A photograph of a tank park of the Warwickshire Yeomanry in Italy. The regiment was equipped with M4 Shermans. (*Len Trinder*)

24. In the final operations in Italy Eighth Army was faced with many water obstacles. Here a Churchill tank crosses the river Senio using a Churchill AVRE bridging tank of the Royal Engineers on 10 April 1945. (*IWM: NA23920*)

25. One of the largest water obstacles in northern Italy was Lake Comacchio. The Germans extended the lake by blowing a hole in the dyke on its south-west side, thereby flooding a wide area of countryside. To overcome the problem presented by this Eighth Army used American 'Fantails' to carry infantry across the flooded areas. Here men of 2/5th Queen's cross the flooded landscape in American-manned 'Fantails'. (*IWM: NA23949*)

26. First into Austria. Soldiers of 6 Troop, 56th Reconnaissance Regiment in their M8 Greyhound armoured cars were the first members of Eighth Army to cross the frontier into Austria. The customs' barrier on the Plockau Pass has been lifted for the cars. (*Walter Falconer*)

Photographs credited to Stuart Hamilton, MC are to be found in his book *Armoured Odyssey*. From the above list nos 3, 4, 19, 20 & 21 are numbered as 21, 20, 39, 41 and 40 respectively in *Armoured Odyssey*.

Acknowledgements

Writing a history of an army, especially one as famous as Eighth Army, is a task that requires much guidance, advice and assistance from a variety of sources. It was not a task that I could have undertaken alone and I must therefore record my gratitude to the many individuals and organisations whose co-operation made this book possible.

A great many Eighth Army veterans from locations stretching from the United States to New Zealand were generous with their time in supplying information and answering questions. My initial intention had been to write a book that was largely based on such individuals' experiences but this proved impossible and, although much of the information I received is within the covers of this book, I would have needed at least two more volumes to do justice to all of it. I hope that, in the near future, much more of that material may find its way into a companion volume to this present work. I am most grateful to all the veterans who provided information to me; their great pride in having served in Eighth Army was clear to me from their writings.

Several institutions were invaluable to my research and I thank them for their help: the staff of the Public Record Office, Kew, Richmond, Surrey were always patient, helpful and efficient, even in the throes of re-organisation.

At the Imperial War Museum the staffs of the Departments of Printed Books and of Photographs helped to identify published references to, and photographs of, Eighth Army, while the Reading Room staff at the National Army Museum, Chelsea were equally helpful.

The Central Library, Foyle Street, Londonderry enabled me to track down a number of important books and, for similar assistance, I also record my thanks to Lieutenant Carol Liles, RHQ Royal Irish and the Prince Consort's Library, Aldershot.

I also readily acknowledge permission to use quotations from various publishers: Crown copyright material from HMSO books is reproduced with the permission of the Controller of Her Majesty's Stationery Office; The Trustees of The Imperial War Museum (*Black Cats at War* by David Williams); B T Batsford Ltd (*El Alamein* by Michael Carver; *Rommel as Military Commander* by Ronald Lewen); Cassell Ltd (*Approach to Battle* by General Francis Tuker; *The History of the Green Howards* by Geoffrey

Powell; *Tobruk: The Great Siege Reassessed* by Frank Harrison); Leo Cooper (*Crusader* by Richard Humble; *Princess Patricia's Canadian Light Infantry 1914-1984* by Jeffery Williams; *Dance of War* by Peter Bates); Tom Donovan Publishing Ltd (*Armoured Odyssey* by Stuart Hamilton); Greenhill Books, Lionel Leventhal Ltd (*The Desert Rats* by Maj-Gen G L Verney, DSO, MVO); Greystone Books, W & G Baird Ltd (*Front of the Line* by Colin Gunner); Hamish Hamilton Ltd (*Monty: Master of the Battlefield* by Nigel Hamilton; *The Desert War* by Alan Moorehead); HarperCollins Ltd (*The Desert Generals* by Correlli Barnett; *The Turn of the Tide* by Arthur Bryant; *Bitter Victory: The Battle for Sicily* by Carlo D'Este; *Alanbrooke* by David Fraser; *The Memoirs of Field Marshal The Viscount Montgomery of Alamein* by Viscount Montgomery); A M Heath & Company (*The Monastery* and *Cassino* by Fred Majdalany); Hodder and Stoughton Ltd (*Tug of War; the battle for Italy, 1943-45* by Dominick Graham and Shelford Bidwell); Colonel John Horsfall, DSO, MC and Bar (*Fling Our Banner To The Wind* by John Horsfall); Macmillan Publishers Ltd (*An Army in Exile* by Lt-Gen W Anders; *Chink: A Biography* by Lavinia Greacen; *A History of the 17th/21st Lancers* by Lt-Col R V L Ffrench-Blake); Oxford University Press and the estate of Sir Howard Kippenberger (*Infantry Brigadier* by Sir Howard Kippenberger); The Pentland Press (*The History of the 51st (Highland) Division* by J B Salmond); The Trustees of The Queen's Royal Surrey Regiment Museum (*The Surreys in Italy: 1943-45* by G L A Squire and P G E Hill); The Royal Artillery Institution (*Anti-Aircraft Artillery, 1914-1955* by Brigadier N W Routledge, published by Brassey's); Secker & Warburg (*The Italian Campaign* by John Strawson); Tabb House (*Now the Dust has Settled* by Freddie de Butts).

Crown copyright material in the Public Record Office is reproduced by permission of the Controller of Her Majesty's Stationery Office.

Quotations from *The Register of the Victoria Cross* are used by permission of This England Books, Cheltenham.

Material from *And We Shall Shock Them* (published by Hodder and Stoughton) is reprinted by permission of The Peters Fraser and Dunlop Group Ltd on behalf of General Sir David Fraser.

A quotation from *With Prejudice: The War Memoirs of Marshal of the Royal Air Force Lord Tedder* (Cassell & Co. Ltd, 1965) is reprinted with the permission of Simon and Schuster.

The extract from Keith Douglas' poem *'Elegy for an 88 Gunner'*, originally entitled *'Vergissmeinnicht'*, from *The Complete Poems of Keith Douglas* edited by Desmond Graham, appears by permission of Oxford University Press. Keith Douglas served with The Sherwood Rangers in Eighth Army.

Quotations from Stephen Brooks' *Montgomery and the Eighth Army*, published by the Army Records Society are reproduced by kind permission of Viscount Montgomery of Alamein, CBE and the Montgomery

ACKNOWLEDGEMENTS

Collections Committee of the Trustees of The Imperial War Museum.

Material from the *Accounts of the Service of The Irish Brigade* written by Brigadiers Nelson Russell and Pat Scott are reproduced by kind permission of the Trustees of The Royal Irish Fusiliers' Museum.

Material relating to Captain J J B Jackman, VC, is reproduced by permission of The Fusiliers' Museum of Northumberland.

Mrs Elizabeth Ray kindly gave permission for the use of quotations from *Algiers to Austria, The History of 78 Division 1941–1946*, by her late husband, Cyril Ray.

In a number of cases it has not proved possible to trace current copyright owners but the author and publisher are prepared to make the necessary arrangements to rectify this at the earliest opportunity.

Richard Doherty

April 1999

Introduction

In the history of the British Army several field armies have performed with such distinction that they have become almost part of the national consciousness. The first such was Marlborough's army with its famous battles at Blenheim, Ramillies, Oudenarde and Malplaquet, followed a century later by Wellington's army of the Peninsular War, one of the greatest armies of history. In this century one army has come close to equalling the fame of Wellington's force with a level of public awareness that is arguably the highest accruing to any British army ever: that army was Eighth Army, born in the sands of North Africa, which carried its Crusader's Cross from the waters of the Nile, across North Africa to Tunisia, over the sea to Sicily and Italy and, finally, into Austria.

There were other armies deserving of public acclaim: Second Army in North-West Europe in 1944-5; Fourteenth Army in Burma; and First Army, the truly forgotten army, in Tunisia. Somehow, however, the greatest degree of publicity seemed to attach itself to Eighth Army. Some might argue that this was due to the penchant for publicity of General Sir Bernard Montgomery, but there were other factors, and Winston Churchill predicted the lasting fame of Eighth Army when he spoke to its soldiers at Tripoli on 3 February 1943 and summed up their elan by saying: 'When the war is over it will be enough for a man to say, "I marched and fought with the Desert Army"'. The fact that Eighth Army had won that great victory at El Alamein in 1942, a victory seen as a turning point in the war, must have been a very powerful factor in the building of the Army's lasting reputation.

One of the men who listened to Churchill that February day in 1943 was my father. And therein lies my special interest in Eighth Army, for my father served in the Desert before Eighth Army was born, was one of those who became the first members of that Army, and one of those who proudly wore the Africa Star with Eighth Army clasp in later years. Today that medal is in my possession and is perhaps one of the spurs behind the writing of this book.

Many books have been written about Eighth Army's achievements, its commanders and its constituent formations. Yet there is no single volume which attempts to tell the story of the Army from its beginnings until it was renamed British Troops Austria and to do so by giving the soldier in the ranks a voice. That is understandable in many ways for Eighth Army, although officially British, was a highly cosmopolitan formation: its soldiers, its divisions and its corps came from throughout the British Commonwealth and Empire as well as from the occupied countries of Europe. Thus there were Australians, Indians, Canadians, New Zealanders, South Africans, all from countries which gave their allegiance to the British Crown; Frenchmen, Poles, Czechs and Greeks, whose countries had been overrun by Germany; Jews who fought in a Jewish Brigade, men who counted Gideon and his chosen warriors as their predecessors; and the hardy little Gurkhas from the Kingdom of Nepal. Nor did that end the list of countries represented in Eighth Army: Cypriots and Rhodesians were also Imperial troops, as were Sudanese, while neutral Irishmen served in the ranks of the British Army's Irish regiments and many other units besides. It would, therefore, be very difficult, if not impossible, to put together a one-volume historical record of Eighth Army in which all nationalities in its ranks were represented by personal accounts and I have not attempted to do so. I have, however, tried to give an overall picture of Eighth Army's record that allows officers and men to tell of their experiences and, in so doing, to represent their comrades from all the nations that fought together under the sign of the Crusader's Cross.

The late A J P Taylor once wrote of the Second World War: 'No English soldier who rode with the tanks into liberated Belgium or saw the murder camps at Dachau and Buchenwald could doubt that the war had been a noble crusade'. Eighth Army's soldiers, with their Crusader's Cross, were truly part of that noble crusade.

CHAPTER I

The Opening Shots 1940-41: From COMPASS to CRUSADER

We are but warriors for the working day.

North Africa is a land of sand seas and pyramids, of dry heat and flies, of khamsins and mirages, of romance and history. British armies had defeated the Turks there during the Great War and before that had beaten Napoleon's troops. Those campaigns had left an impression that the British soldier survives and fights well in desert conditions, an impression strengthened during the Second World War as Eighth Army's soldiers adapted to desert life and fought, with ultimate success, against Germans and Italians.

But why fight in North Africa at all? It was neither a natural nor an obvious choice of battleground between Britain and Germany. The catalyst in bringing conflict to North Africa was Germany's ally, Italy: war in that region began between Italy and Britain in June 1940; Germany entered, to support Italy, in early 1941.

The kingdom of Italy, created from a collection of states in 1861, had, with the addition of Venetia in 1866 and Rome in 1870, become the modern state of Italy, uniting the country for the first time since the Romans. The glory that had been Rome inspired the new nation-state to seek greatness; and one measure of greatness for a late-19th century European nation was the possession of overseas colonies.

Other European countries sought colonies leading to a scramble for a 'place in the sun' with Italy competing against, amongst others, Britain and another new nation-state, Germany, which had also achieved unification in 1870. Short on muscle, Italy's gains were limited to Eritrea and Italian Somaliland (the southern part of modern Somalia). An attempt to annex Abyssinia was defeated at Adowa in 1896. However, in the early years of the 20th century, Italy increased its presence in Africa as the Ottoman Empire crumbled. Italian troops invaded Tripolitania and Cyrenaica; this Italian foothold on the Mediterranean's southern shores was ratified after the Great War.

The Fascist leader, Benito Mussolini, became Italy's prime minister in

1

1922 and implemented an aggressive expansionist foreign policy, coupled with modernisation at home. In North Africa, punitive action was taken against any opposition to Italian colonial rule; communications were improved and an excellent road was constructed from Tripoli along the coast to the Egyptian border. As with the great Roman roads this artery was intended to help control the country and assist future expansion in the region. In January 1935 Tripolitania, Cyrenaica and Fezzan were merged under the common name of Libya with Tripoli as its capital, while the colonies of Eritrea and Somaliland became Italian East Africa.

In October 1935 Mussolini attacked Abyssinia (modern Ethiopia) from Italian East Africa. On this occasion Italy overran Abyssinia in spite of strong resistance. Only Egypt and Sudan were free of Italian rule in north-eastern Africa. West and south of Libya lay the French territories of Tunisia, Algeria and Chad.

Egypt had been part of the Ottoman Empire but the ruling dynasty, established by the Ottoman viceroy, Mehemet Ali (1769-1849), bank-rupted the country in the late 19th century. Egypt was occupied by Britain, a principal creditor, in 1882 and a British protectorate was established. Although Egypt became independent in 1936 a British presence remained: the Anglo-Egyptian Treaty gave Britain control of the Suez Canal for a further twenty years with bases in Egypt to defend the canal and the sea route to India.

The Italian presence in Africa led to the strengthening of Britain's Middle East forces since Mussolini and Hitler had created an alliance known as the Rome-Berlin Axis. Thus when war broke out between Britain and Germany in September 1939 there was every possibility that Italy would soon join the conflict on Germany's side. Although there was no immediate Italian involvement, reinforcements were sent from the United Kingdom to the Middle East where the garrison increased training and readiness levels.

In May 1940 German forces attacked the French and British armies through the Low Countries. The brief campaign that followed, leading to the collapse of the French army and the evacuation of the British Expeditionary Force from France, inspired Mussolini to declare war on Britain and France on 10 June 1940. *Il Duce* had hoped that Italy might annex some of both countries' territories, but his entry into the war had been delayed by Hitler until the French air force had been completely destroyed. Nonetheless, Mussolini sent Italian troops into southern France; the French were forced to sign an armistice with Italy on 24 June, and demilitarised zones were established in France, Tunisia and Algeria.

Mussolini's best remaining imperial expansion option lay with wresting territory from Britain. That Egypt was independent, and neutral, did not concern him. Mussolini saw a prize beyond compare: Egypt and the Anglo-Egyptian Sudan would extend the Italian empire over all of north-east Africa.

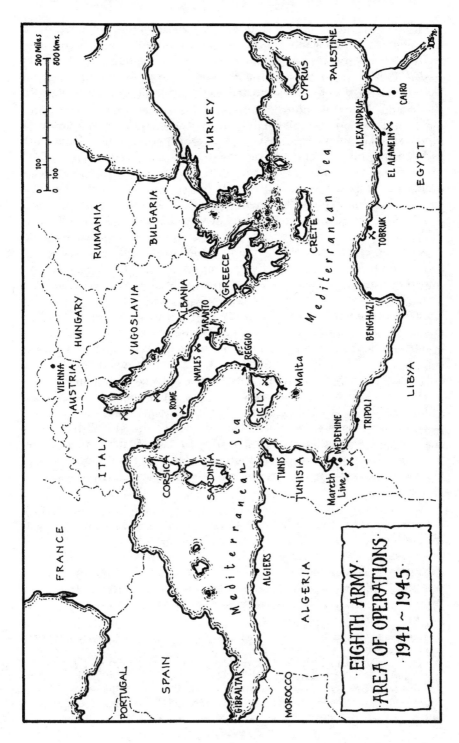

EIGHTH ARMY.
AREA OF OPERATIONS.
·1941 ~ 1945·

Libya's governor, Marshal Italo Balbo, was ordered to invade Egypt. One of many Italian senior officers who were not convinced that Britain was beaten and that Egypt would fall like a ripe plum, Balbo was fated not to direct an invasion of which he did not approve. On 28 June 1940, at Tobruk, Italy's most famous airman died when his aircraft was shot down by Italian anti-aircraft gunners.

Balbo's successor was Marshal Rodolfo Graziani, another senior officer who was not enamoured of the plan to invade Egypt. Not until September did Graziani judge that his forces could attack Egypt although his field army vastly outnumbered the tiny British force in Egypt,* which was scarcely of corps strength. Italy also had a large air arm and a navy that promised to dominate the Mediterranean.

While the Italians waited, the British were busy: on 11 June, the day after Italy declared war, British patrols from 7th Armoured Division crossed into Libya while RAF aircraft bombed the Italian industrial city of Turin. Reinforcements were arriving in Egypt for Middle East Command and preparations were underway to deal with the expected onslaught from Libya.

On 13 September Graziani's Tenth Army crossed into Egypt. British troops had withdrawn from the frontier area, mining roads and salting water supplies to hamper the invaders. Earlier British raids had made the Italians wary; their advance stopped on 16 September at Sidi Barrani, only fifty miles inside Egypt, where defensive positions were prepared.

The Italians had used the one good all-weather road, the Via Balbia, which ran along the coast. They were reluctant to move far from it which gave British troops a morale advantage. Before the war, British commanders in Egypt had trained their soldiers in desert warfare, while Royal Engineers had explored the southern sand seas in Egypt and Libya to produce excellent maps indicating where 'good going' for vehicles could be found.

The area over which this war was to be fought was totally alien to most Europeans. Along the Mediterranean littoral a strip of fertile land accommodates most of the settlements; otherwise there were no civilians to get in the way of the warring armies. The desert war of 1940-43 was fought mostly from El Alamein to El Agheila, a huge, almost empty, land with no food and little water, thus demanding great logistic effort to supply an army. From east to west this area stretches for almost 400 miles with its

---

* Middle East Command, under General Sir Archibald Wavell, covered not only Egypt but also Palestine, Aden, the Sudan and the British possessions in East Africa. The defence of Egypt was the responsibility of British Troops Egypt (BTE), commanded by Lieutenant-General Sir Henry Maitland Wilson. The fighting element of BTE was Western Desert Force, commanded by Lieutenant-General Richard O'Connor. This force disposed an armoured division and the equivalent of two infantry divisions.

southern limits, at Jarabub and Siwa oases, 150 miles from the coast. Farther south, the great Sand Sea is 'a scorching waste where only Bedouin or British can live and move'.[1]

What appeared at first sight to be a featureless waste became, with familiarity and experience, a rock ocean, with many features that allowed easy navigation with map and compass.

> There is one dominating natural feature: the five-hundred-foot escarpment, facing north to the coastal plain, that leads down from the limestone plateau which is the arena of the desert battles. It is like the wall of a terrace . . . broken only by a few flights of steps. It is everywhere a barrier to wheeled vehicles and in most places even to tanks. The gaps that are passable by *all* vehicles became therefore immensely important – Fuka, Halfaya and Sidi Rezegh.[2]

Britain's Middle East commander, General Sir Archibald Wavell, had anticipated a further Italian advance against which a defence line, anchored on Mersa Matruh, was established. Lieutenant-General Richard O'Connor, commanding Western Desert Force, hoped that Graziani would push on towards Matruh where O'Connor could use the open southern flank to launch attacks on the long, vulnerable Italian columns.

Deprived of the opportunity to attack the Italians en route to Matruh, O'Connor's Western Desert Force would tackle them effectively before the year ended. Reinforcements in men and equipment, including three tank regiments, forty-eight anti-tank guns, twenty light anti-aircraft guns and forty-eight 25-pounder field guns, were sent from the United Kingdom, at a time when the home defences could least afford them.[3] Thus reinforced, Wavell planned strikes in the desert and East Africa.

The desert attack, Operation COMPASS, was to be launched in December 1940. Although intended as a raid in strength by O'Connor's force of some 30,000 men to undermine Tenth Army's morale, Wavell considered that COMPASS might have further strategic possibilities, including the opportunity for 'converting the enemy's defeat into an outstanding victory'.[4] That is exactly what happened: the 'raid' at Barrani was handled so brilliantly by O'Connor that it led to the rout of the Italians and the conquest of Cyrenaica.

COMPASS was carried out by a force anticipating the make-up of the future Eighth Army. As well as 7th Armoured Division, Western Desert Force included 4th Indian Division and two brigades of 6th Australian Division, the third brigade of which joined after the opening stages of the operation. Thus the Force, commanded by an Irishman, drew its manpower from the United Kingdom, the Commonwealth and the Empire.

On 8 December 1940 Western Desert Force was concentrated some ten miles from the Italian fortified camps protecting Sidi Barrani. Those camps, Tummar East, Tummar West and Nibeiwa, were about twenty miles south of Barrani itself. Nibeiwa was assaulted by 4th Indian Division at dawn on 9 December; Tummar West fell to 4th Indian just hours later, while Tummar East surrendered next morning. Sidi Barrani fell within four hours of being attacked by 16 Brigade on 10 December. Some 20,000 Italians were captured.

COMPASS had achieved its first objective: Tenth Army's morale had been well and truly undermined. O'Connor now had the opportunity to convert the Italian defeat into 'an outstanding victory' although his force was reduced by the withdrawal of 4th Indian for operations in East Africa.

Although driven from Egypt, the Italians could be expected to defend the fortified Libyan coastal towns of Bardia, Tobruk and Derna. Before attacks on those towns took place, Western Desert Force was renamed, becoming XIII Corps on 1 January 1941. O'Connor sent a mobile force down the escarpment to cut the coast road west of Bardia, assigning the assault on Bardia to the Australians who opened their attack on 3 January and took the town, with 40,000 prisoners, after two days' hard fighting.

O'Connor's sights then turned to Tobruk, some eighty miles westward. Tobruk, which was to become synonymous with the desert war, was an important port which could be used to shorten the logistical tail of O'Connor's command. By 9 January Tobruk was under siege; twelve days later it was attacked by 6th Australian Division. After bitter fighting the port fell and another 27,000 Italian soldiers passed into captivity, bringing to over 100,000 the number taken prisoner since the opening of COMPASS.

With Tobruk in British hands and what remained of Tenth Army scattered over central and western Cyrenaica, O'Connor decided to push his mobile forces south of the Jebel Akhdar, the Green Mountain, to cut off Tenth Army before it could retreat safely into Tripolitania, while pressing the remainder of his command along the coast road to take Derna, Barce and Benghazi. The latter was an important port, just south of which the mobile force would reach the coast.

In a twin-pronged advance, 6th Australian Division moved on Derna and 7th Armoured Division on Mechili. Those two objectives represented, respectively, the northernmost and southernmost points of a line of Italian defensive positions. At Mechili, a junction of desert tracks, O'Connor also hoped to entrap an Italian armoured force, thus preventing its withdrawal towards the Jebel.

That latter hope was dashed when British troops found Mechili empty on 27 January. On 29 January, after some hard fighting en route, the Australians reached Derna and found it, too, to have been evacuated. By 3 February it was clear that the Italians were evacuating Cyrenaica. Although O'Connor's mobile force needed a rest to ensure their vehicles were fully fit for the dash across the Cyrenaican bulge, it became vital to push on to trap Tenth Army. Since the difficult terrain south of the Jebel Akhdar made for slow movement, with many stoppages caused by punctures, mechanical breakdowns and sumps split by grounding on rocks, part of 7th Armoured Division was sent ahead of the remainder. This advance force was led by the division's armoured-car regiment, 11th Hussars,

> the same indefatigable armoured-car regiment that had first ranged the Libyan frontier in June. It was appropriate that they should be the first to see the Gulf of Sirte and the coastal road running south from Benghazi, which they reached at midday on 5th February, ten miles south of Beda Fomm.[5]

Beda Fomm was to be the nemesis of Graziani's army. Soon after reaching the coast, 11th Hussars were joined by infantry from 7th Support Group and by some artillery; the road was blocked and a line established. Half an hour later the first Tripolitania-bound Italians came down the road from Benghazi. Over the next two days the Italians made repeated attempts to break the British line. Although Graziani still had many operational tanks, the British were constantly being reinforced as further elements, including tanks, arrived from the east; over the course of the battle the Italians lost 100 tanks. By dawn on 7 February Tenth Army had had enough. White flags were flown from scores of vehicles as the Italians gave up the fight. Tenth Army had been destroyed; over 20,000 prisoners joined those already in captivity. Meanwhile Benghazi was falling to the Australians.

Since the beginning of COMPASS, O'Connor's 30,000-strong force had advanced some 500 miles, destroyed Tenth Army's nine-and-a-half divisions, taken 130,000 prisoners, captured some 400 tanks and almost 1,300 artillery pieces while losing fewer than 2,000 casualties, of whom 500 had been killed (1,373 were wounded and 55 missing).[6]

XIII Corps had lost much equipment, however, due as much to wear and tear as to enemy action. This was another factor in which desert warfare differed from north-west Europe. Some four-fifths of Western Desert Force's original vehicles were now unusable; most of the remainder needed maintenance. It was, therefore, time for re-organisation but O'Connor, having achieved his 'outstanding victory' wanted to push on to the logical final objective: the destruction of all Italian forces in Libya. With elements of 2nd Armoured Division arriving in Egypt from Britain, O'Connor believed that he could advance into Tripolitania and seize Tripoli, the only port through which the Germans could reinforce their Italian allies. Such a move could prevent any such reinforcement and thus end the North African campaign.

But it was not to be. In London the Chiefs of Staff had agreed that XIII Corps' advance should stop at Benghazi after which British troops in

Cyrenaica would go over to the defensive while the force would be stripped of all available troops for operations in Greece. On 12 February 1941 orders to that effect reached O'Connor. That same day Major-General Erwin Rommel arrived in Tripoli to be followed, on 14 February, by the first two units of Hitler's reinforcements for the Italians: these were the leading elements of the *Deutsches Afrika Korps*. Almost two years would pass before British troops, of Eighth Army, would finally enter Tripoli.

O'Connor, now a sick man, was admitted to hospital in Cairo. His achievements were recognised by a knighthood and he was appointed to command British Troops Egypt; XIII Corps was no longer an effective formation. The Cyrenaica garrison was reduced to the minimum necessary to repel an attack from Tripolitania, which was not expected for several months, and renamed Cyrenaica Command under Lieutenant-General Sir Philip Neame, VC.

Neame's command included 2nd Armoured Division, 7th Armoured having been withdrawn to Egypt to re-equip, and 9th Australian Division, two brigades of which had been replaced by two raw, partially-trained formations, which was hopelessly short of the transport needed in the desert. Nor was 2nd Armoured Division capable of meeting the demands that might be placed on it. One of its two brigades, with some divisional support troops, had gone to Greece leaving Neame with only 3 Armoured Brigade. The problems did not end there: two of the brigade's three tank regiments were equipped with light tanks and captured Italian M13s while the third had cruiser tanks, of which only twenty-three were runners. None of the vehicles was in top condition; neither the division itself nor its commander, Major-General Gambier-Parry, had desert experience and lacked the depth of training that 7th Armoured Division had undergone under Percy Hobart.

Rommel was a believer in speed as the essence of war. On arriving at Tripoli he flew to the front to assess the terrain and situation and ordered his own Afrika Korps troops to move eastwards on their arrival in Tripoli. He planned to attack into Cyrenaica at the earliest opportunity. Not for him the lengthy wait while adequate forces were built up: he would use speed and surprise to defeat Neame. A quick victory would also bring support from Hitler and further reinforcements.

The first German division to arrive in North Africa was 5th Light Division* with about 120 tanks and strong anti-tank units, including some 88mm guns. Fittingly, 5th Light was the first German division to go into

---

* 5th Light Division was formed from elements of 3rd Panzer Division and included that formation's Panzer Regiment 5. The division was later restyled 21st Panzer Division.

action in North Africa. Rather more prosaically, it received this distinction because Rommel did not await the promised arrival of 15th Panzer Division before launching his first attack at Mersa Brega on 31 March 1941 in which 5th Light was supported by three Italian divisions.

Against the Axis tanks, 2nd Armoured Division deployed only forty-seven tanks which mechanical defects and enemy action reduced to fewer than ten in a matter of days; the divisional commander reported the loss of one tank for every ten miles of movement. Fuel was also a problem while the division's scattered tanks were receiving orders from many sources. Not surprisingly, 2nd Armoured Division had ceased to be an effective fighting force by 3 April. Rommel had virtually a clear path through Cyrenaica.

Trying to restore the balance of the situation in Cyrenaica, Wavell sent O'Connor from Egypt to assume command. The Irishman persuaded the CinC that it would be unwise to change commanders in mid-battle but agreed to give Neame whatever help he could. On 7 April O'Connor and Neame were taken prisoner by a German reconnaissance unit south of Derna. Gambier-Parry, most of his divisional HQ, and 3 Indian Motor Brigade were captured at Mechili. East of Derna a column of 5th Light Division reached the coast in a mirror image of 7th Armoured Division's dash to Beda Fomm.

From all this chaos some order and normality was being restored: 9th Australian Division, having withdrawn east of Derna, was moved into Tobruk whither a fourth Australian brigade and a tank regiment were being sent by sea from Egypt. Western Desert Force was re-formed under command of Lieutenant-General Beresford-Peirse to include 6th Division, albeit understrength, and a mobile force commanded by Brigadier 'Strafer' Gott which deployed in small columns, each of an infantry company with some field guns and light tanks, to harass enemy columns as they approached the Libyan frontier.

On 10 April Rommel noted that he could chase his foe as far as the Suez Canal although his own troops were tiring while the opposition was regaining composure.[7] As well as attacking eastwards he resolved to capture Tobruk, on which he made his first attack on 13 April. That attack was beaten off by the Australians as was a further, Italian, attack on the 16th. Rommel settled down to the business of a siege.

By now 15th Panzer Division had arrived in Tripoli and moved forward to cover the frontier, allowing the formations which had taken part in Rommel's advance to rest and refit. Both sides were licking their wounds although, on 15 May, Western Desert Force attacked in the Sollum-Capuzzo area to clear the escarpment above the Halfaya Pass. Operation BREVITY met with only limited success and on 26 May a German attack returned the Pass to Axis control.

*

Rommel's first offensive in Cyrenaica had been a major success. He had staved off any possible British incursion into Tripolitania and, although his force was not strong enough to push on for the Nile delta, he had given the Axis air forces the Cyrenaican airfields which menaced both Egypt and Malta, and Benghazi port was an important strategic gain. The attack had also had considerable psychological effects, especially for the Italians who saw some of the slur of the loss of Tenth Army wiped out. Italian territory had been regained and German soldiers had had their first taste of desert war. And the legend of the *Desert Fox* had been born.

That legend took root in the British forces. A great British success, the first of the war, had been wiped out in weeks by this German general. Chaos and disorder seemed to have been the order of the day as British forces fell back before him. In contrast to Rommel's speed and incisiveness, British commanders, with O'Connor gone, appeared rank amateurs. And the enemy was much better equipped: his tanks and anti-tank guns were vastly superior as was their tactical deployment. Coupled with defeats in Greece and Crete, it was small wonder that British troops in North Africa suffered a drop in morale.

Not only the morale of the troops in North Africa was suffering: the British public wondered how the victors of Operation COMPASS could be defeated in such a manner. Public opinion was mirrored by the government which wanted an early counter-attack on the Egyptian-Libyan frontier as did Middle East Command. The tools for that counter-attack were soon at hand.

Churchill had ordered a convoy to be sent through the Mediterranean with reinforcements for the Desert Army. That convoy, codenamed TIGER, arrived at Alexandria on 12 May 1941 to unload its cargo, including 220 tanks, dubbed 'Tiger cubs' by Churchill, to re-equip 7th Armoured Division. Wavell was then pressed to attack, in spite of the need to make the tanks desertworthy and train reinforcements in desert conditions. But the strength of the forces at his disposal had increased: 4th Indian Division had returned from East Africa, although it was only one brigade strong; it was strengthened by the addition of 22 Guards Brigade. Both divisions were assigned to Beresford-Peirse's Western Desert Force which was ordered to undertake an offensive in June: Operation BATTLEAXE.

Beresford-Peirse was to attack in the frontier region, secure the Halfaya Pass, engage and destroy the enemy armour and advance to relieve Tobruk after which Western Desert Force was to exploit to the line Derna-Mechili. Beresford-Peirse planned an attack on his right flank by 4th Indian Division, supported by the I-, or infantry, tanks of 4 Armoured Brigade from 7th Armoured Division. The Indians were to take the Halfaya Pass and Fort Capuzzo with two thrusts in this opening phase, the right thrust aimed at both ends of the Pass with the left targeted on

Point 206 and Fort Capuzzo. At the same time, 7th Armoured Division was to advance towards the Hafid Ridge, deploying 7 Armoured Brigade with its faster cruiser tanks to engage Rommel's main tank force. It was hoped that the two brigades could link up, once 4th Indian Division no longer needed the I-tanks, so that the cruisers could lure the enemy armour onto the hull-down I-tanks.[8] Support Group, 7th Armoured Division would advance on the British left.

It took only two days for BATTLEAXE to be added to the litany of failure. Although 4th Indian Division, with 22 Guards Brigade and 4 Armoured Brigade's tanks, took Capuzzo and saw off a counter-attack, the tanks supporting 11 Indian Infantry Brigade drove into 88mm anti-tank guns at Halfaya Pass; all but one were knocked out. It was 88s which also wrote *finis* to 7 Armoured Brigade's attack on Hafid Ridge. By nightfall on 15 June, more than half of Beresford-Peirse's armour was no more. By noon next day Western Desert Force had fewer than forty tanks from the 200 with which it had started the battle.

Rommel had known of the British attack plans through intercepted radio messages and had brought the refitted 5th Light Division forward for a counter-attack. On the 16th he made his move, with 15th Panzer attacking Capuzzo from the north as 5th Light swept around the outer flank of 7th Armoured Division. This attack led to the armour-versus-armour battle that had been BATTLEAXE's objective but the battle was resolved in favour of the Germans. Although 15th Panzer met firm opposition at Capuzzo, losing some tanks to British 25-pounders, 5th Light had a field day as they pushed across the British axis of advance. Rommel then ordered 15th Panzer to disengage at Capuzzo and join 5th Light. With the enemy weight now shifted from left to right, all Western Desert Force was threatened. The commander of 4th Indian Division decided to abandon Capuzzo rather than lose his men there and 7th Armoured Division drew back to the frontier. Wavell, who had flown up to the front, ordered BATTLEAXE to be called off and the attacking troops withdrawn. Western Desert Force had lost ninety-one tanks against twelve German tanks destroyed, some of which were later repaired. (The Germans also salvaged some British tanks.)

The offensive failed for several reasons. Beresford-Peirse's 'laborious and pedestrian' plan was partly to blame; British equipment was inferior and training in armoured warfare inadequate. The tank-versus-tank battle was a serious mistake. Although sometimes inevitable, it was not a German concept. They preferred to draw enemy armour onto anti-tank guns, preferably powerful weapons with long range, which were their principal killers of tanks; German armour was used, whenever possible, for exploiting the soft areas of an enemy's defensive dispositions in accordance with the philosophy that a tank's engine was as much a weapon as its gun.

11

BATTLEAXE's failure cost Wavell his command. He was moved to India as Commander-in-Chief in a straight exchange with the previous holder of that post, General Sir Claude Auchinleck.

No sooner was the latter installed in Cairo than he came under pressure from London to mount an offensive, not solely because of the failure of Wavell's operation but also on account of the new direction the war was taking. On 22 June Hitler had attacked the Soviet Union in Operation BARBAROSSA and the feeling in London was that the British Army should become involved in a much wider scope of action. From a London perspective there were valid grounds for such a feeling: the bulk of the new Army was in the United Kingdom with much of the old Regular Army in India and the Far East. Since the evacuation of France in June 1940 only two British divisions, 2nd and 7th Armoured, had operated against the Germans with another handful of detached brigades fighting in North Africa, Greece and Crete. Much of the fighting had been undertaken by Commonwealth or Imperial troops.

Additional British formations were on their way to North Africa. The Territorial Army's 50th Division was the first although it was initially sent to Cyprus, and then Syria and Palestine, leaving Australian, Indian, New Zealand and South African troops with the major burden in any fresh desert offensive. The Australian government wanted their troops relieved from Tobruk; Canberra was concerned that the port might fall and the four Australian brigades there, plus support troops, be captured. Those wishes were acceded to: between August and October 1941 the Australians were relieved in a seaborne operation by 70th British Division, which included the Polish Carpathian Brigade and Czechoslovak Infantry Battalion 11-East. Locking 70th Division in Tobruk added to the impression that there were few British formations in the desert although all the tank units, most of the medium and heavy artillery and the base units were British. The paucity of British fighting divisions irked Churchill considerably.

Auchinleck stoutly resisted pressure to undertake a fresh offensive before his troops were ready and his apparent reluctance to move made him unpopular in London. Unfortunately the Auk and Churchill could not work well together. Although a superb leader, admired and respected by his men, Auchinleck lacked the ability needed to humour the prime minister whose persistent telegrams and interference annoyed him considerably and he made his feelings clear to the prime minister. In spite of his abilities, therefore, Auchinleck could never gain the confidence of his political master.

During the Great War Auchinleck had served in Mesopotamia where the chaos surrounding the siege at Kut Al Amara had convinced him that troops should never be asked to fight until properly trained and with all aspects of their logistic support seen to. In London, however, this attention to preparation and planning was not fully understood. There it was felt that a battalion was fit for action on disembarkation, and that equipment was ready once unloaded. The example of Rommel's Afrika Korps was held up to British commanders; but London, and Churchill himself, did not appreciate that German army training standards outstripped those in the British Army while German equipment was more reliable, and more robust, than the British.

While Auchinleck waited, a steady flow of men and equipment arrived in Egypt. During summer and early autumn 600 tanks and some 800 artillery pieces were unloaded. Manpower increased to the point where a second corps could be created. Western Desert Force would once again become XIII Corps; its new sister was to be a specialised armoured corps, to be known, initially, simply as the Armoured Corps but soon to receive the designation XXX Corps.[9]

This was Auchinleck's creation, although Montgomery was to claim the credit: it was designed to engage and destroy the Afrika Korps; it would harry Rommel's panzers, reduce their freedom of movement and draw them off XIII Corps' infantry.* The new corps included 7th Armoured Division, 22 Armoured Brigade Group, 1st South African Division, less a brigade group, and 22 Guards Brigade. Corps HQ was established on 25 September and mobilisation began at Pirbright Camp, Abbassia on 2 October. Three days later an air crash killed the corps commander, Lieutenant-General Vyvyan Pope, and two of his staff, Brigadiers Russell and Unwin. To succeed the unfortunate Pope, Major-General Willoughby Norrie, DSO, MC was appointed.

Corps HQ staff were selected for their experience (Pope had been Director of Armoured Fighting Vehicles at the War Office) in the Royal Armoured Corps and the HQ was allotted eight armoured command vehicles, trained signallers and additional operators.

The creation of a second corps demanded an intermediate level of command between Headquarters, Middle East and corps HQs. This was to be an army command and accordingly:

HQ Western Army was formed in Cairo on the 10th of September 1941, with Lt-Gen Sir A Cunningham† being appointed to command.

The CinC had already announced his intention of driving the enemy out of North Africa and charged Gen Cunningham with the execution of this task. It was anticipated that the offensive would begin on or about 1st November.[10]

---

* The slow-moving I-tanks would remain with XIII Corps to provide close support for the infantry while the faster cruiser tanks would be concentrated in XXX Corps.
† Cunningham was appointed to the command of Western Army on 9 September 1941.

Auchinleck had re-organised Middle East Command radically: an East Africa Command, based on Sudan, was created under Beresford-Peirse, while Syria and Iraq's security were entrusted to another new army, Ninth, under General Sir Maitland Wilson, with its base area in Palestine and Transjordan.

From Cairo, Headquarters Western Army moved to Ma'aten Baggush on 25 September and from midnight on the 26th, as Headquarters, Eighth Army, assumed command of all troops in the Western Desert west of a line from, and including, Bahig to El Maghra. Tobruk Fortress came under command at the end of October and Western Desert Force, now under Major-General A R Godwin-Austen, became XIII Corps.

Planning continued for the forthcoming offensive with intelligence on enemy dispositions being built up. King's Dragoon Guards reconnaissance patrols

> frequently penetrated into enemy territory to a depth of 40-50 miles west of frontier as Army Commander particularly wanted information on extent to which enemy used the area south of Trigh Capuzzo. This information had an important bearing on degree of surprise which could be introduced into plan. Patrols brought back information that enemy maintained nothing more formidable than light . . . recce elements south of Trigh Capuzzo. Area north of Trigh Capuzzo thoroughly covered by aerial recce.[11]

Eighth Army had 118,000 men with 126 light, 529 cruiser and 205 medium tanks, 849 medium, field and anti-tank guns, and support from 512 aircraft. Cunningham's command included two Corps HQs, an armoured division, an armoured brigade group, an army tank brigade, two lorried infantry divisions, a motor brigade, an infantry brigade group and a further infantry division. Another infantry division was held in reserve while, in Tobruk, Cunningham also had an infantry division, an infantry brigade and about 100 tanks.[12]

The operation in which Eighth Army was to be blooded was codenamed CRUSADER which also inspired the Army's Crusader's Cross badge and provided the title of its weekly newspaper. It was to be the first step in Auchinleck's plan to drive the enemy out of North Africa and preparations were thorough. Patrolling into Libya, in accordance with Eighth Army Instruction No.2, had been carried out '. . . to discover how much the enemy uses this area without . . . disturbing him to the extent of causing undue suspicion'[13] and to ascertain Axis strength and dispositions.

> Most of enemy army in North Cyrenaica, most in NE corner. Apart from 3 attacks on Tobruk and a recce into Western Desert in mid-September

he had spent his time [April-September] re-organising and preparing.[14]

German forces included 15th and 21st Panzer Divisions and one infantry division (90th Light*) which, with the Italian Savona Division, constituted Afrika Korps. The Italians had an armoured division and a motorised division (XX Armoured Corps), and four infantry divisions (XXI Corps) with a second motorised division en route to Cyrenaica. Three Italian infantry divisions, 'stiffened by German infantry', were investing Tobruk; the fourth, also supplemented by some German infantry, manned the line of newly-built frontier fortresses. Afrika Korps and XXI Italian Corps had, since 15 August, made up Rommel's Panzergruppe Afrika. The lorried infantry regiment of 21st Panzer Division had yet to arrive and both divisions of the Italian XX Corps appeared to be in the Jebel Akhdar.

Axis strength in Cyrenaica, under the Italian Marshal Bastico, totalled 102,000 men with 380 medium tanks,[†] 1,140 medium and anti-tank guns plus a strong air support element which was, however, smaller than the Desert Air Force. Thus Eighth Army was significantly superior in manpower and in numbers of tanks and artillery pieces.

> . . . these figures are misleading since we were soon to discover that the German armour was superior to ours in almost every aspect: mechanical reliability, armour and gunnery, quite apart from the skill and dash with which it was used.[15]

Given the element of surprise there was every reason to anticipate an Eighth Army victory.

There would be no head-on assault on the Sollum/Halfaya/Capuzzo sector. Two options were planned for. The first envisaged a main striking force jumping off from Jarabub Oasis, on the edge of the southern sand sea, via Jalo, to cut off the enemy retreat from Cyrenaica while maintaining pressure and advancing along the coast against whatever opposition was offered; this would isolate the enemy in the Cyrenaican bulge and lead to a re-enactment of Beda Fomm. The second option was for a main attack in the coastal sector south of the escarpment with a feint further south. Auchinleck was clear that the course chosen was to be the first of two phases: the recapture of Cyrenaica 'followed by the conquest of Tripolitania'.

* 90th Light Division had been created to meet the need for motorised infantry to accompany the panzer divisions. The Division was formed by using German units in Africa to establish three motorised infantry regiments as the *Afrika* Special Purpose Division. The nomenclature 90th Light was adopted later.
† Brigadier Freddie de Butts, then a G2 (Major) in XIII Corps notes in his book, *Now the Dust has Settled*, 550 German and Italian tanks.

The second option was chosen. Axis positions at Sollum, Halfaya and Capuzzo were

> to be engulfed by XIII Corps in a bypassing advance through the Frontier Wire south of Sidi Omar, north to Sidi Azeiz, then west to Gambut and Tobruk. . . . the Tobruk garrison would . . . enter the fray at the earliest possible moment and turn their besiegers into besieged. To this end the 32nd Army Tank Brigade was built up within the Tobruk perimeter . . . to spearhead the breakout attack . . . which, in conjunction with the westward approach of XIII Corps from Gambut, was intended to catch Rommel's infantry divisions between hammer and anvil.[16]

Although Auchinleck had suggested that CRUSADER might be launched on or about 1 November he regarded mid-November as being more realistic. Although Churchill saw this as further delay, intensive preparations were underway: newly-arrived tanks, including some American M3 Stuarts, or Honeys, were being made desertworthy; three huge forward supply dumps* with about 30,000 tons of ammunition, fuel and other stores, were being established; the Western Desert Railway had been extended seventy-five miles westwards from Mersa Matruh; a water pipeline had been built from Alexandria to near the railhead; and water 'dumps' were created using *Sporta* (or Sporter) pools at Bir Ziqdin Abyad and Bir Ziqdin el Ahbir. Dummy positions, dumps and railway lines were constructed in an elaborate deception plan.[17]

A fortnight's slippage in delivering 150 tanks and personnel from the UK prompted Auchinleck to inform Churchill that 15 November was the earliest possible start date, but that had to be changed when General Norrie warned that transport shortages had restricted 1st South African Division's training. Auchinleck flew immediately to Eighth Army Headquarters to meet General Brink, the South African commander who said that, although ready to go into battle, he would not have full confidence in his division. Auchinleck decided to delay CRUSADER until 18 November.

In the meantime Rommel went to Rome to seek permission to attack Tobruk between 15 and 21 November. His trip had a dual purpose: his 50th birthday fell on 15 November and his 25th wedding anniversary on the 27th; he arranged for his wife, Lucie, to meet him in Rome for a celebration. Since Rommel would never have gone to Italy had he known that a major offensive was imminent, his trip indicates how effective was the security surrounding CRUSADER.

---

* One of these dumps, No.2 FMC (Forward Maintenance Centre) covered an area of 96.5 sq miles (250 sq km) and held some 20,000 tons of stores of which 50% was petrol. (WO201/418)

NOTES

1. Barnett: *The Desert Generals*, p.23
2. ibid
3. Fraser: *And We Shall Shock Them*, p.120
4. ibid
5. ibid, p.124
6. Raugh: *Wavell in the Middle East 1939-1941*, p.130
7. Fraser: *Knight's Cross: A Life of Field Marshal Erwin Rommel*, p.241
8. Verney: *The Desert Rats*, p.56
9. PRO, Kew: WO169/996, War Diary, Advance HQ, Eighth Army Sep-Dec 1941.
10. PRO: WO201/358, Report of Operations, Eighth Army Sep-Nov 1941.
11. ibid
12. ibid
13. PRO: WO169/996, op cit
14. PRO: WO201/358, op cit
15. de Butts: *Now the Dust has Settled*, p.30
16. PRO: WO201/358, op cit
17. ibid

CHAPTER II

Operation CRUSADER, *November – December 1941*

Our hearts are in the trim

As dawn brushed the horizon on the morning of 18 November, Eighth Army began its surge into Libya. The previous night's heavy rain had ceased but desert hollows held small rainwater lakes as 7th Armoured Division and 4 Armoured Brigade Group raced north-westwards to seek the enemy. Ahead of them loomed wide, empty horizons with no sign of enemy troops.

> . . . we rose at four in pitch dark, and at first streak of dawn are off. And so apparently are all the other units of our armoured division, as though released in some gigantic race. . . . As far as the eye can reach over the desert face are dust-reeking lines of vehicles – pennanted tanks and armoured cars, guns and limbers, carriers, trucks and lorries – all speeding along in parallel course westwards to Libya.[1]

The only contact made with Axis forces that day was with reconnaissance elements which rapidly withdrew. With no real resistance the rumour spread in 4th Indian Division 'that the panzers were bogged down in their harbours along the coast'.[2] Well ahead of schedule, XXX Corps' armour reached its battle positions around Gabr Saleh, the occupation of which was intended to entice the enemy armour into battle.

Meanwhile, XIII Corps had made its initial moves with Freyberg's New Zealanders and Messervy's 4th Indian Division creating a strong block against the Axis frontier defences. Halfaya, bombarded during the night by the cruisers *Euryalus* and *Naiad*, was invested by 11 Indian Infantry Brigade; 7 Indian Brigade, with 1 Army Tank Brigade's I-tanks in support, was south of the enemy frontier strongpoints at Sidi Omar; Central India Horse armoured cars patrolled the fifteen miles held by the Savona Division between Halfaya and Sidi Omar while the New Zealand Division had crossed the Wire some ten miles farther south, near Sherferzen, and halted five miles west of the frontier.

This lack of opposition caused uncertainty at Eighth Army Headquarters where no one could be expected to know that Rommel, who had returned on the 17th, believed that the British move was only a reconnaissance in force. He continued to plan his attack on Tobruk, the capture of which he hoped would bring more active support from Berlin for the North African campaign as well as shortening his supply lines.

Cunningham decided to change his plan: 7th Armoured Division would now destroy the Italian units at Bir el Gubi before driving for Sidi Rezegh, immediately south of Tobruk; 4 Armoured Brigade Group would cover 7th Armoured's right flank and XIII Corps' left flank. Norrie had always taken the view that provoking reaction demanded a deeper thrust than that first planned. The drive for Sidi Rezegh was almost certain to bring reaction since that position threatened Rommel's east-west lines of communication. That drive also widened the gap between Eighth Army's two corps as it took 7th Armoured Division farther from 4 Armoured Brigade, which was still charged with covering XIII Corps' left flank.

When 7th Armoured Division advanced on 19 November there began an extremely confused period of fighting, especially in XXX Corps' case, aptly described as 'some of the most extraordinary and complex movements in the history of the war'.[3] Much of that fighting pivoted around Sidi Rezegh ridge and airfield, and if one name stands out from the CRUSADER battles to lend a focus to the fighting then that name is Sidi Rezegh, where battles raged furiously from the 19th until the end of the month. In the course of those battles three Victoria Crosses were won, two posthumously, while a further two VCs, including another post-humously, were gained near El Duda just over ten miles from Sidi Rezegh in the breakout from Tobruk.

On the first day of battle all three British armoured brigades in XXX Corps saw action with mixed fortunes. At Bir el Gubi 22 Armoured Brigade was repulsed by the Italian Ariete Division with heavy losses, while 7 Armoured Brigade captured Sidi Rezegh airfield. The third brigade, 4 Armoured, having dispersed its armoured-car screen and sent an armoured regiment off to engage an enemy transport column, became engaged in a savage encounter battle with a German battlegroup near Gabr Saleh. British losses in this, CRUSADER's first major tank-to-tank engagement, were much heavier than the German, although the latter were overestimated by 4 Armoured Brigade, and XXX Corps regarded the battle as having been drawn.

The three armoured brigades finished the day disposed in a roughly triangular formation with some forty miles between 4 Armoured at Gabr Saleh and 7 Armoured at Sidi Rezegh. Each faced a different direction, emphasising the fluid nature of desert warfare.

*

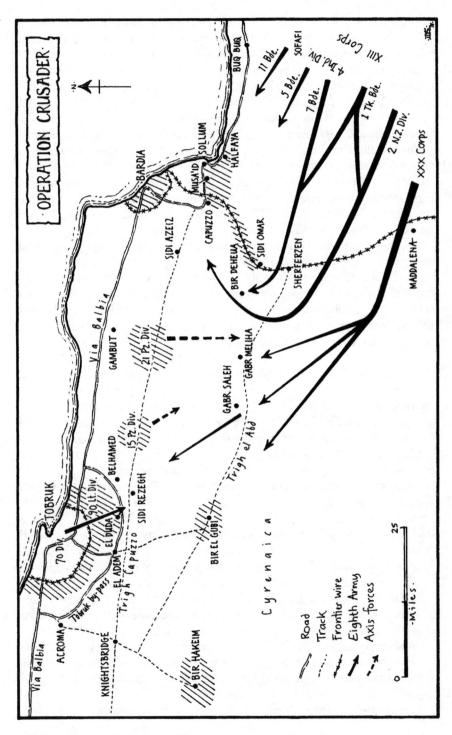

OPERATION CRUSADER.

XIII Corps

SOFAFI
11 Bde.
4 Ind. Div.
5 Bde.
7 Bde.

1 Tk. Bde.

2 N.Z. Div.

XXX Corps

BUQ BUQ

SOLLUM
HALFAYA
MUSA'ID
BARDIA
SIDI AZEIZ
CAPUZZO
SIDI OMAR
BIR DEHEUA
SHERFERZEN
MADDALENA

Via Balbia
GAMBUT
21 Pz. Div.
GABR MELIHA
GABR SALEH
BELHAMED
15 Pz. Div.
SIDI REZEGH
Trigh el Abd
TOBRUK
90 Lt. Div.
EL DUDA
70 Div.
EL ADEM
Trigh Capuzzo
BIR EL GUBI

Cyrenaica

Via Balbia
ACROMA
KNIGHTSBRIDGE
Tobruk by-pass
BIR HAKEIM

Road
Track
Frontier wire
Eighth Army
Axis Forces

25
Miles.
0

Rommel, still unconvinced of the seriousness of British intentions and determined to attack Tobruk, ordered Crüwell, Afrika Korps' commander to concentrate his armour between the British and Egypt to cut off the incursion.

Crüwell, however, was beginning to appreciate British intentions and ordered 15th and 21st Panzer Divisions to attack the British right flank. On 20 November German tanks moved against Gabr Saleh. As that move became clear, 22 Armoured Brigade was ordered to reinforce 4 Armoured. However, the Germans first went off on another wild goose chase during which 21st Panzer Division ran out of fuel. Thus only 15th Panzer hit 4 Armoured Brigade about an hour before sunset. Neumann-Silkow, commanding 15th Panzer, took his tanks far to the west to attack out of the setting sun, a new tactic for XXX Corps' men but one they would soon find familiar.

Darkness brought a quick end to the battle in which twenty-six British tanks were destroyed or damaged while, in spite of initial claims to the contrary, the Germans lost none. The late hour at which the attack was launched, plus the Honeys' speed and 22 Armoured Brigade's arrival from Bir el Gubi combined to save 4 Armoured Brigade from heavier losses. Both British brigades concentrated for the night with almost 200 tanks, about twice 15th Panzer's effective strength.

Sidi Rezegh had become pivotal. At the airfield 7 Armoured Brigade had beaten off two uncoordinated German attacks before 7th Support Group's leading elements arrived. Based on information from Gott, at Sidi Rezegh, and already outdated Desert Air Force reconnaissance, Cunningham saw the possibility of enclosing and destroying most of Panzergruppe within a British cordon from Tobruk to east of Sollum. He ordered 70th Division to break out from Tobruk at dawn on 21 November.

Thus the link-up was ordered before Eighth Army had destroyed Panzergruppe's armour, which had been considered essential before 70th Division's breakout. Far from destroying the German armour, XXX Corps had narrowly avoided having its own armour wiped out by Afrika Korps.

> Cunningham had been obliging enough to scatter the 7th Armoured Division all over the desert, and we had failed to exploit his generosity. If Afrika Korps had concentrated at Gabr Saleh on the morning of the 20th, it could have wiped out the 4th Armoured Brigade; on the other hand, if it had moved towards Sidi Rezegh it could have inflicted a crushing defeat on the British forces there. In that case we would have won the CRUSADER battle very easily, for the whole Eighth Army had been dispersed in a gigantic arc . . . from Sollum to Bir el Gubi.[4]

Rommel now finally realised that he faced a major offensive, postponed his attack on Tobruk and ordered Afrika Korps to move rapidly towards Sidi Rezegh. This they did on the morning of 21 November. At the same time 4 and 22 Armoured Brigades, believing Afrika Korps to be withdrawing, were heading, in the same direction, towards 7 Armoured Brigade and Support Group. At Sidi Rezegh, 7 Armoured prepared to move off to meet up with 70th Division which had begun its attack at dawn.

The plan for the Tobruk breakout to link up with 7th Armoured Division had been predicated on 70th Division, supported by armour and artillery and known as TOBFORCE, punching through the centre of the Italian Bologna Division. But 90th Light Division had redeployed to supplement Bologna and the attackers met stronger opposition than anticipated. Anti-tank guns inflicted severe casualties on 7 Armoured, and on Brigadier Willison's 32 Army Tank Brigade (1st, 4th and 7th Royal Tank Regiments with 1st Essex, Z Company, 1st Northumberlands and an anti-tank battery under command), which, with 2nd Black Watch, had struck south-east from Tobruk. Although, after four hours' fierce fighting and heavy casualties, 70th Division had pushed a salient some four miles deep into the Axis line and reached El Duda, the planned break-in had not occurred and the division needed a rest. Major-General H M Scobie, ordered a halt.

Some of the fiercest fighting of the campaign took place on the Sidi Rezegh-El Duda corridor. Afrika Korps' attack on Sidi Rezegh left 7 Armoured Brigade fighting a life-or-death struggle on the ridge. Thirty minutes before the break-in force, under Lieutenant-Colonel Peter de Sallis, was due to attack, 7 Armoured learned that Afrika Korps' divisions were approaching rapidly from the south-east. Brigadier Davy resolved that he must still support 70th Division's attack and, ordering Brigadier Jock Campbell, of 7th Support Group, to assume command of the attack northwards, turned his reserve, 7th Hussars and 2nd Royal Tanks, around to face the panzers.

One Greenjacket company of Support Group was pinned down as it advanced

by heavy fire at point blank range from the front and flank and on the flat and open ground of the aerodrome. All the officers but one of the Company, and many of the Other Ranks had been either killed or wounded. On his own initiative, and when there was no sort of cover, Rifleman Beeley got to his feet carrying a Bren gun and ran . . . towards a strong enemy post containing an anti-tank gun, a heavy machine gun and a light machine gun. He ran 30 yards and discharged a complete magazine at the post from a range of 20 yards, killing or wounding the entire crew of the anti-tank gun. The post was silenced and Rifleman

23

Beeley's platoon was enabled to advance, but Rifleman Beeley fell dead across his gun, hit in at least five places.

. . . His courage and self sacrifice was a glorious example to his comrades and inspired them . . . to reach their objective which [they] eventually captured . . . together with 700 prisoners.[5]

Enemy positions were subjected to heavy fire from 60th Field Regiment's guns after which the Greenjackets took the positions with fixed swords. By noon the escarpment had been captured but Colonel de Sallis, realising that his small force could not hold the entire captured position, consolidated his companies around Point 167. Although the infantry had opened the door for 6th Royal Tanks to cross the Trigh Capuzzo the tanks were forced to withdraw by enemy artillery fire from Belhammed ridge

In the tank battle between 7 Armoured Brigade and Afrika Korps, a storm of fire virtually destroyed 7th Hussars within minutes. The commanding officer, Colonel Byass, was killed by a direct hit on his turret and the Regiment was reduced to twelve tanks. Not until the next day did the survivors rejoin their brigade

Some fifty German tanks attacked 2nd Royal Tank Regiment while others struck Battalion HQ and S Company of 2nd Rifle Brigade to be repulsed by 2-pounder anti-tank guns from 3rd Regiment, Royal Horse Artillery, under Lieutenant Ward Gunn, and 60th Field's 25-pounders. The panzers then drove on to the escarpment and began replenishing fuel and ammunition. They were now east of Support Group preparing for a fresh attack which was preceded by heavy artillery fire and dive-bombing.

All that was left to resist the panzers were two 2-pounder portee anti-tank guns, under Ward Gunn, and a single Bofors anti-aircraft gun under Lieutenant Pat McSwiney. No match for the German armour, they quickly became the target for concentrated enemy artillery, tank, mortar and machine-gun fire. The gunners fought desperately, scoring hits on several panzers before the Bofors was knocked out and one 2-pounder destroyed. The remaining gun was damaged but

Together with Major B. Pinney, the Battery Commander, and with Sergeant Gray acting as loader, Lieutenant Ward Gunn got this last gun into action again. Despite the flames from the burning vehicle which might have exploded the ammunition at any moment, they went on fighting. After firing a few more rounds, Lieutenant Ward Gunn was killed and the gun so badly damaged as to become unusable. Gunner Turner drove the portee out of action with the gun still in flames, and the dead and wounded on the back of his vehicle. Another gun was fitted and the portee then drove back into action.[6]

Ward Gunn became Sidi Rezegh's second posthumous VC. Bernard

Pinney, M Battery's commander, was killed in action the following day.

The terror and confusion of that day's battles were summed up by a gunner of J Battery, RHA*

> We all met Mr Death that day at Sidi Rezegh. There was courage classed with [that of] the men of the Light Brigade. . . . We were being blown to pieces a bit at a time by the enemy and we could not do a thing about it. We had our faithful anti-tank guns, 2-pounders, against the German 88s. Our shells tried so hard to penetrate his armour. We had only peashooter, but we fought on. Men died by their guns . . . [of the] wounded some of us were captured but [were rescued] a week later by the New Zealanders.[7]

As the desperate fighting continued, Gott ordered 4 and 22 Armoured Brigades to assist the badly mauled 7 Armoured. Both were delayed by anti-tank guns and confused orders and, between 3 and 4pm, another German attack reduced 7 Armoured Brigade to about forty battleworthy tanks.

Around 5 o'clock, as daylight faded, Support Group HQ was heavily shelled. With the enemy within 1,000 yards, Campbell led 6 RTR's surviving tanks against the enemy

> riding in an open unarmoured staff car . . . hanging on to its windscreen, . . . he shouted, 'There they come. Let them have it'. When the car began to fall behind, he leaped on to the side of a tank . . . and directed the battle from there. He turned aside through the enemy barrage to his own twenty-five pounder guns and urged the men on to faster loading and quicker firing. He shouted to his gunners, 'How are you doing?' and was answered, 'Doing our best, sir.' He shouted back, grinning, 'Not good enough.'[8]

> Advanced HQ was still at the SE end of the L[anding] G[round] with Battle HQ, 7 Support Group. The whole of this area then became a tank battleground. Our own and enemy tanks were engaging each other at short range, 25-pounders were firing over open sights and 2-pounders on Portees were being switched from place to place to meet the nearest threat. Fine work was done by the Gunners and great gallantry displayed. . . . Brig Campbell . . . was away performing the most brilliant deeds of gallantry leading various tank squadrons into battle, himself standing up in his open staff car holding a blue flag in the air as a signal for them to follow. For these actions he was awarded the Victoria Cross.[9]

*J Battery was subsequently awarded the Honour Title of Sidi Rezegh to become J (Sidi Rezegh) Battery, Royal Horse Artillery.

Campbell's efforts checked the German advance although seven of the dozen tanks that he led were knocked out within five minutes. Afrika Korps had failed to shake Support Group off Sidi Rezegh although the east end of the escarpment was German-held.

The battles of 21 November are among the most complicated in military history with the official historians commenting that the situation would have been rejected as 'the setting of a training exercise . . . for the reason that in real life these things simply could not happen'.[10] But they had happened, creating confusion on both sides. Crüwell, believing Afrika Korps to have major problems, withdrew north of the Trigh Capuzzo to prepare to smash 7th Armoured Division next day. In Eighth Army HQ there was a perception that all had gone well although 7 Armoured Brigade had only twenty-eight battleworthy tanks from the 141 with which it had started the day.

While Crüwell planned to destroy 7th Armoured Division on the 22nd, Gott intended 7th Support Group to hold Sidi Rezegh aided by 22 Armoured Brigade, plus the remains of 7 Armoured Brigade with 4 Armoured Brigade providing mobile cover; 5 South African Brigade was to take the escarpment south of the airfield. The thrust to Tobruk was to resume as soon as possible.

Early on 22 November, XIII Corps, believing Afrika Korps to be withdrawing westwards, attacked Bardia, Capuzzo and Sidi Omar. The Corps' infantry had already achieved several successes and their operations continued thus on the 22nd although their supporting I-tanks suffered heavily from German 88s. Spearheading the New Zealanders' westward advance, 6 NZ Brigade was delayed until 2pm by the late arrival of 8 RTR's supporting Valentines. After Brigadier H E Barraclough, commanding 6 Brigade, had learned of the latest crisis at Sidi Rezegh, the Brigade marched twelve miles in six hours before resting for a meal, after which the march recommenced in darkness and brought 6 Brigade, through a navigational error, to Bir Chleta at first light. There they found themselves among Afrika Korps' command vehicles and narrowly missed capturing Crüwell who had left, minutes before, to join 15th Panzer.

A 21st Panzer Division attack on Sidi Rezegh ridge from the north forced the defenders to withdraw leaving the entire position in German hands by the morning of the 23rd. Reduced to ten tanks, 7 Armoured Brigade effectively ceased to exist while the combined strength of 4 and 22 Armoured Brigades was about 150 tanks, with the former's tanks scattered. Afrika Korps still had over 170 tanks. On the 22nd a chance pincer movement by Afrika Korps had not only taken Sidi Rezegh but had smashed through 4 Armoured Brigade's HQ area, scattering 8th Hussars with the loss of fifty tanks and 267 prisoners. For the 23rd, Rommel planned to repeat the pincer movement, destroy XXX Corps and relieve his frontier garrisons.

Wrong assessments persisted on both sides: Cunningham still believed that XXX Corps could wear down the enemy armour while collaborating with the New Zealanders to effect the link with 70th Division; Rommel thought he had destroyed 4 Armoured Brigade completely rather than simply scattering it.

Rommel now intended to deploy 15th and 21st Panzer Divisions and Ariete, with the Afrika Korps' divisions advancing towards the Italian division and the three smashing all between them. Thus began a disastrous day for Eighth Army. Although 4th (SA) Armoured Car Squadron reported sighting 15th Panzer as it set off to rendezvous with Ariete, this information was dismissed: XXX Corps HQ believed that the South Africans had really spotted 4 Armoured Brigade. Crüwell had further luck when 15th Panzer ran into 7th Support Group's transport and 5 South African Brigade. Although considerable chaos was caused, Crüwell did not divert to mop up the opposition and rendezvoused with Ariete around noon; 5th Panzer Regiment, detached from 21st Panzer, joined soon after. Crüwell commanded the greatest tank concentration yet seen in Africa in one attack. Over 250 tanks advanced against the British. With 21st Panzer behind the British, Crüwell intended that there could be no British reforming the following day.

At 3pm the Axis phalanx attacked. Elements of 7th Support Group, 22 Armoured Brigade, 2nd Scots Guards (4 Armoured Brigade's motor battalion) and 5 (SA) Brigade faced them. The British had had insufficient time to organise effective all-round defence and the northern flank was scarcely covered. Although the defenders inflicted heavy losses on Axis tanks and infantry, two panzer regiments smashed into the South African positions, killing over 200 South Africans, wounding almost 400 and capturing most of the brigade. But the British armour, though badly mauled, had still not been eliminated and Jock Campbell's guns had knocked out seventy-two panzers, reducing Crüwell's strength to ninety tanks.

Afrika Korps had suffered the worst German tank loss in a single day on this November Sunday which, ironically, was *Totensonntag*, the day on which Germany remembered her dead of past wars. Afrika Korps' tank strength was reduced to less than that of its foes.

Rommel had had problems himself. Setting out from Panzergruppe HQ to join Crüwell, he was caught up in 6 NZ Brigade's advance from Bir Chleta to Point 175 where the New Zealanders took over 400 casualties before being stopped six miles east of Sidi Rezegh airfield. At the end of the day Rommel and Crüwell were still not in contact.

In the Tobruk corridor, TOBFORCE had taken the position known as 'Dalby Square'. Before the attack, by 32 Army Tank Brigade, had been launched reports had been received of up to 100 enemy tanks approaching Tobruk from the south with another thirty located south of El Adem. Since Scobie had been expecting friendly forces to approach from this direction, and had planned that the day's attack would move on to a second objective, known as 'Bondi', if Eighth Army had reached the escarpment, this threw the plans into disarray. Willison, however, decided that 32 Tank Brigade's attack on 'Dalby Square' would go ahead as planned with the aim of straightening out one flank of his corridor.

As the armour made ready for its advance a message was received that two armoured cars had been hit badly near the 'Wolf' position. The CO of 4 RTR relayed the news to Major Pritchard, commanding C Squadron, who ordered two Matildas to go to the aid of the armoured cars, a patrol from the King's Dragoon Guards sent out to look for the South Africans. Commanding one of the tanks was Captain Philip 'Pip' Gardner, MC who located the armoured cars, about 200 yards apart 'being heavily fired on at close range and gradually smashed to bits'.[11] Gardner went forward under covering fire from the other Matilda to bring out the cars or their crews. Thinking that he could tow one car out, he dismounted from his tank but found that he could not release the tow rope on the side. He was able to release the rope on the back of the Matilda but had to signal to his driver to turn the tank around so that the rope could be used. As this was happening, Trooper Richards, the wireless operator, put his head out of the turret hatch to see what was happening and was killed as he did so. Bullets and shells were whistling around Gardner as he attached the rope to one of the cars.

Lieutenant Beames, one of the armoured car commanders, was lying on the ground, wounded in both legs, and Gardner lifted him into the car before ordering the Matilda driver to move off with the car in tow. Unfortunately, the rope snapped. At much the same time, Gardner was hit in the leg. He

> now gave up the attempt to tow the car away and he lifted Beames out of it, carried him to the tank and got him up on its rear louvres. He made a last visit to the car to make sure there was no one left alive in it, and then climbed up beside Beames. As he did so he was hit again, this time in the arm.[12]

With supporting fire from the other Matilda and two troops of 1 RHA, Gardner's tank beat a speedy and safe exit from action. Shortly afterwards Willison, who had listened to reports of the action, left his ACV to salute the tank and its surviving crew members. Gardner was subsequently awarded the Victoria Cross while his gunner, Lance-Corporal McTier, received the DCM; Trooper Richards received a posthumous Mention in Despatches but the driver, Trooper Robertson, received no official recognition on the grounds that he had already been gazetted for a

Military Medal a month earlier.[13] Tragically, Lieutenant Beames of the King's Dragoon Guards died before his wounds could be attended to.

That evening Cunningham's optimism was disappearing as he realised his true tank losses. In a chaotic situation Eighth Army was unprepared to meet any possible Axis invasion of Egypt. Rommel saw the same picture and wrongly concluded that the British were beaten and that a thrust into Egypt would finish them off.

Refusing to accept Godwin-Austen's assurances that all was well on XIII Corps' front, and that XXX Corps could still provide support from south of Sidi Rezegh, Cunningham asked Auchinleck to fly up from Cairo to decide CRUSADER's fate. Auchinleck arrived at Eighth Army HQ at Maddalena as darkness fell on the 23rd. Cunningham painted for him a picture of German superiority, and since he believed that British armour could no longer guarantee the security of the infantry, Cunningham was concerned that troops east and south of Sidi Rezegh might be cut off, leaving Eighth Army with no reserves to meet a thrust into Egypt.

Although accepting that Cunningham could be correct, Auchinleck decided to continue the offensive

> The enemy, it is true, had temporarily succeeded in seizing the local tactical initiative, but the strategical initiative remained with us: we were attacking, he was defending. This general initiative it was at all costs essential to retain.[14]

Auchinleck's assessment cut through the confusion of battle to the strategic possibilities that still existed for Eighth Army for the Auk realised that the enemy also had problems. His decision was arguably one of the most important of the desert campaign. In contrast to Rommel, who wrote to his wife on the 23rd that the battle had passed its crisis, Auchinleck informed London that it was moving to its climax.[15]

Next morning (24 November) Rommel took personal command of Afrika Korps and led its panzer divisions in what has been dubbed 'the dash to the wire' which Ronald Lewin has described as Rommel's most controversial act ever.[16] This German move caught almost everyone off balance and reports verging on panic flooded into Eighth Army HQ. But Auchinleck was unperturbed, and when Cunningham returned to Maddalena from 7th Armoured Division HQ, he found that the CinC had completed a detailed directive including the instruction that Eighth Army would continue to 'attack the enemy relentlessly using all your resources even to the last tank'. Cunningham was reminded that his main immediate objective was to destroy the enemy tank forces with his ultimate object the conquest of Cyrenaica followed by an advance on Tripoli.[17] And Tobruk would be relieved.

Rommel's plan quickly came unstuck. With Rommel and Crüwell both giving orders there was, inevitably, confusion. Logistics, always a weakness with Rommel, had not been properly worked out: the panzers ran out of fuel, ammunition and water. And they ran into British artillery, 'always a far more deadly matter than running into British tanks – and suffered heavily'.[18] Afrika Korps reached Bardia where the two divisions replenished:

> To carry out the operation at all was a considerable feat immediately after the heavy fighting of the last few days. It bore witness to the high mechanical reliability, the communications and the morale of the Afrika Korps. But it was a failure. It brought little relief to the German frontier garrisons. It did not cause a British withdrawal.[19]

As Rommel made his dash, the New Zealand Division, supported by 1 Army Tank Brigade, headed for Tobruk. Infantry and armour worked well together and, by the 25th, Freyberg's men had occupied Sidi Rezegh airfield. That night they attacked westwards towards Belhamed and El Duda. On the 26th, El Duda fell to TOBFORCE while the New Zealanders, after tough fighting, cleared the entire Sidi Rezegh ridge although there was still opposition in the area. In the course of that fighting Captain James Jackman, of 1st Royal Northumberland Fusiliers, who had already distinguished himself in the attack on the 'Dalby Square' position three days before, earned TOBFORCE's second Victoria Cross.

Jackman's Z Company of the Northumberlands, which was a machine-gun battalion, was under command of 32 Tank Brigade together with a squadron of King's Dragoon Guards, an anti-tank battery and 1st Essex Regiment. Z Company had carried out a special training programme during which Jackman had excelled himself and 'created a mobile force from nothing, which he lived to see achieve all that was planned and more and with few losses'.[20] On 26 November, two of 32 Tank Brigade's regiments were leading the attack on El Duda with Jackman's Company following up. When the tanks were stopped by heavy shell and mortar fire, Jackman brought Z Company forward, disregarding the enemy's fire. Each platoon debussed quickly and came into action, with the vehicles moving off under cover. From their positions the platoons were able to pour fire on to the Trigh Capuzzo, the enemy's main supply route. All the while Jackman drove around the positions to co-ordinate the defences and encourage his soldiers. In the course of visiting one machine-gun position, his luck ran out and he was killed by a mortar burst. The citation for his posthumous Victoria Cross sums up the gallantry of this Irish officer who had brought his guns into action

> as calmly as though he were on manoeuvres, and so secured the right

flank. Then standing up in front of his truck, with calm determination he led his trucks across the front between the tanks and the guns – there was no other road – to get them into action on the left flank.

Most of the tank commanders saw him, and his exemplary devotion to duty regardless of danger not only inspired his own men, but clinched the determination of the tanks crews never to relinquish the position which they had gained.[21]

That Jackman's example was inspiring is proved by the decorations won by his group that day: chief among those was his own posthumous Victoria Cross, but there were also three Distinguished Conduct Medals as well as several Military Crosses and Military Medals, a total of twelve gallantry awards in all.

By the end of that day, 70th Division and the relieving force were linked by a narrow corridor, east of which was 90th Light Division which had taken considerable punishment from Freyberg's men. Of Rommel's armour there was no sign. The British armour had had a brief and welcome respite: with 7 Armoured Brigade withdrawn from the battle its few surviving tanks and crews were handed over to 4 and 22 Brigades, now concentrated south of Sidi Rezegh ridge.

And there had been a change in command of Eighth Army. In his report on its operations from 26 November to 10 December, General Auchinleck wrote: 'At about midday on 26 November I assumed command of the Eighth Army'.[22]

The decision to dismiss Cunningham was not taken easily. Auchinleck was aware that the army commander had many fine qualities: his success in Ethiopia had been followed by his excellent preparation of Eighth Army for the offensive. Cunningham had imbued Eighth Army with a high sense of purpose and excellent morale. His departure was due to his 'not having the mental resilience to cope with the built-in crises of Desert warfare'.[23]

On the evening of the 26th Rommel realised that his mission with Afrika Korps had been futile. With the situation around Tobruk becoming perilous for the Axis forces due to the New Zealanders, he ordered Afrika Korps to return from Bardia along the Trigh Capuzzo at best speed. Next morning armoured car patrols informed 4 and 22 Armoured Brigades that German columns were approaching from the east.

Returning from Bardia the two panzer divisions drove into a British position but the clash was inconclusive: the Germans lacked cohesion with both divisions still operating independently and the British broke off the engagement as darkness fell. In fact, the Germans lost an excellent opportunity not only to improve their own supply position but to recover almost 1,000 PoWs

. . . reports came in from all quarters that the area was thick with the enemy. Enemy tanks overran No. 50 FMC; but, thanks to the dispersal of the centre, they did little damage and failed to locate the 900 enemy held captive there.[24]

About eight miles south-west of Sidi Omar some thirty tanks attacked 1st Field Regiment from the south. 'The Regiment fought lustily and drove the enemy off with a loss of seven tanks. But an equal number of British guns were damaged'.[25]

With only forty-three tanks left, 15th Panzer attacked the New Zealanders on the 27th. The panzers moved west of Sidi Rezegh and the New Zealanders defending the ridge.

27 November was disastrous for 5 NZ Brigade. . . . As the Brigade was widely deployed enemy columns were free to pass in and out of Bardia at will. At about 0900 hours the Brigade HQ at Sidi Azeiz was overrun by about 35 tanks. The whole staff of the HQ with those of the artillery regiments and of the MG battalion were captured. In the afternoon the 23rd Battalion was attacked at Capuzzo where the enemy reached the transport lines. A counter-attack with the bayonet, however, restored the situation. In the evening the B Echelon of the 28th Battalion was captured by an enemy column operating with tanks.[26]

Two days later attacks were made by all three Axis armoured divisions against the New Zealanders and 70th Division at El Duda. The Germans reached Belhamed and Freyberg's division was cut in two; the British armour failed to break through an Axis screen of anti-tank guns and Ariete Division. Following this, on 1 December, the New Zealanders were withdrawn eastward. Once again Tobruk was surrounded but with XIII Corps HQ now inside the perimeter. Subsequent Axis thrusts towards the frontier and an attack on El Duda failed.

Exhaustion was overtaking both sides but the British were receiving personnel and material reinforcements. Rommel had few reserves and his casualties had been severe. He knew that he would have to abandon his positions at Tobruk: after sharp attacks against Bir el Gubi on 4 and 5 December, Afrika Korps was down to about forty tanks against 140 British tanks and the British were preparing to renew the offensive.

Rommel made his decision on 6 December. Axis forces on the frontier would be abandoned; Afrika Korps would cover the retreat of as much of Panzergruppe Afrika as possible. The German armour put up such a show of tenacity that Norrie decided against an immediate tank pursuit: 90th Light moved back to Agedabia while the other surviving divisions moved to defensive positions at Gazala.

With Tobruk finally relieved and the first phase of CRUSADER at an end, thirteen days later than planned, XXX Corps was deployed to the frontier area to deal with the enemy garrisons still holding out at Bardia and Halfaya; XIII Corps continued operations west of Tobruk.

South of the main battlefield the planned feint had been carried out successfully by Brigadier D W Reid's E Force, which included 2nd South African Field Regiment, 6th SA Armoured Car Regiment, 7th SA Recce Battalion, 6 LAA Battery, RA, 3/2nd Punjab, and sapper, transport and signal elements as well as an RAMC detachment. This multi-national force, composed of South Africans, Englishmen, Irishmen and Indians, made good progress in spite of being harassed by enemy aircraft and meeting bad going which caused mechanical problems with the vehicles. Axis positions were engaged and overrun although the defenders of Jikara proved doughty. During the attack there, the field guns became bogged down some distance away and enemy guns brought the attacking column to a halt. However, the Bofors guns of the Irish 6 LAA Battery went into action against the Italian artillery and soon brought about an enemy surrender.[27] By 28 November E Force had done all that had been asked of it, and Brigadier Reid received a message of commendation from General Auchinleck for his work.

Eighth Army now had a new commander. On sacking Cunningham Auchinleck had sent for Major General Neil Ritchie from Cairo to take temporary command. Ritchie was a strange choice: apart from having formed the new 51st (Highland) Division in 1940 to replace that captured at St Valery, he had commanded nothing larger than a battalion. He was a competent staff officer and it seems that, in appointing him, Auchinleck intended to keep close personal control of the battle. Certainly for his first ten days in post Ritchie effectively acted as deputy to Auchinleck.

Auchinleck probably intended Ritchie's to be a stop-gap appointment until someone more suitable could be found. Ritchie himself suggested bringing out a new man from England. But why did Auchinleck not appoint one of the corps commanders? The answer is probably because that would have caused similar problems at corps level, trying to find a suitable replacement in the course of a battle. Unfortunately, Auchinleck's temporary appointment of Ritchie became permanent when the prime minister announced it to the House of Commons without indicating its temporary nature.

NOTES

1. Fielding: *They sought out Rommel,* p.45
2. Stevens: *Fourth Indian Division,* p.90
3. Fraser: *And we shall shock them,* p.167
4. Mellenthin, Major General F W, *Panzer Battles,* quoted in Humble, p.108
5. PRO: WO201/355
6. Verney: *The Desert Rats,* pp.72-73
7. Les Wood: J Bty, RHA, notes to author
8. Moorehead: *The Desert War,* pp.94-95
9. PRO: WO201/355
10. Playfair: *The Mediterranean and the Middle East, vol iii,* p.46
11. Victoria Cross citation
12. Harrison: *Tobruk, The Great Siege Reassessed,* p.227
13. ibid, p.228
14. Quoted in Parkinson, *The Auk,* p.128
15. Parkinson: *The Auk,* p.128
16. Lewin: *Rommel as Military Commander,* p.73
17. ibid, p.129
18. Fraser: op cit, p.171
19. ibid, p.171
20. Obituary: St George's Gazette, 28 Feb 1942
21. VC citation
22. PRO: WO201/359
23. Humble: *Crusader,* p.143
24. PRO: WO201/359
25. ibid
26. ibid
27. Doherty: *Wall of Steel,* p.185

CHAPTER III

The Benghazi Stakes:
December 1941 – May 1942

Marching in the painful field

On 15 December 1941 XIII Corps launched an attack intended to evict Axis forces from the Gazala position and trap them, allowing the destruction of the enemy armour. Corps strength approximated to two divisions plus one armoured brigade.

But the British plan was thwarted when 15th Panzer Division counter-attacked, demonstrating that the enemy had plenty of fight left. When, however, British armour swept out on a wide outflanking manoeuvre, Rommel decided to abandon the Gazala position and withdraw from Cyrenaica. There was to be no re-run of Beda Fomm in spite of efforts to cut off the Axis withdrawal.

By Christmas Rommel had brought his surviving forces back to the Agedabia area. It seemed that CRUSADER had achieved its aims: most of Cyrenaica was in British hands with the airfields there available to support the invasion of Tripolitania. But the enemy armour had not been destroyed and two convoys that had docked in Tripoli brought Afrika Korps' tank strength up to about sixty tanks.* With this reinforcement, albeit small, Crüwell was confident enough to launch two concentrated attacks on Eighth Army around Agedabia on 28 and 30 December. Opposing him was a re-equipped 22 Armoured Brigade, which had just replaced 4 Armoured Brigade in the forward area. Those clashes cost sixty British tanks lost against fourteen German.

Following these engagements Rommel withdrew to El Agheila whence he had started almost a year before. Once again British troops stood on the threshold of Tripolitania but, once again, deployed too lightly in the Mersa Brega-Agedabia area, the covering position for Cyrenaica that needed least force; but Godwin-Austen's dispositions were simply too

---

* Some tanks had been landed at Benghazi docks before the city fell to the British. Failure to detect the German tank build-up cost the Director of Military Intelligence in Cairo his job.

economical of force. At the front were two brigades, each of only two battalions: 200 Guards Brigade and 1st Armoured Division's Support Group. Echeloned to the left rear was 1st Armoured Division's 2 Armoured Brigade with about 130 tanks; 22 Armoured Brigade had been sent back to Tobruk after the battles of late-December. General 'Gertie' Tuker's 4th Indian Division held the Via Balbia and Benghazi. With supply, fuel and ammunition stocks being built up through Benghazi, Auchinleck reckoned that the offensive could be resumed between 10 and 15 February:

> . . . it was generally expected that Rommel could not possibly attack for some time, and that if he did it must be local and containable. The dramatis personae had all changed since Wavell, Neame, and Gambier-Parry had first experienced contact with the Afrika Korps in March 1941. Only the illusions remained.[1]

Expecting Rommel to remain quiescent for any length of time was certainly an illusion. With further reinforcements arriving in Tripoli, his armoured strength had increased to over eighty German tanks by mid-January, with almost ninety Italian tanks as well. Thus the Axis armour now outnumbered the inexperienced British brigade that faced them. For Rommel it was an open invitation to attack which he did on 21 January 1942* in spite of a crucial fuel and supply situation: the opportunity to knock the British off balance, forestalling an attack on Tripolitania, could not be ignored. And British fuel and supply dumps could restock his force.

Rommel's intention was to cut through the British front and encircle the armour, followed by a short easterly advance into Cyrenaica coupled with a vigorous left hook to take Benghazi. Intended as a limited offensive with limited aims, the outcome was radically different.

Afrika Korps gained complete surprise, cutting through the British front as planned and then, rather than encircling the British armour, met 2 Armoured Brigade en route to Msus on 25 January. This clash resulted in the total rout of the British brigade which, although it disposed about eighty Crusader and over fifty Honey tanks, thus outnumbering Afrika Korps by almost two-to-one, was summarily defeated and driven in confusion from the battlefield. Afrika Korps had a goodly opportunity to acquire hastily-abandoned stores and vehicles. The rout left 1st Armoured Division with little strength; what survived of the division could do little

---

* The next day Rommel's command was renamed Panzer Armee Afrika to include Crüwell's Afrika Korps (15th and 21st Panzer and 90th Light Divisions); X and XXI Italian Corps totalling five infantry divisions and XX Italian Corps with Ariete Armoured and Trieste Motorised Divisions.

to support Tuker's Indians. Godwin-Austen therefore proposed to withdraw XIII Corps towards Mechili and ordered 4th Indian Division to abandon Benghazi.

Ritchie, however, ordered a halt to the withdrawal, took 4th Indian Division under direct Army command and instructed it to continue defending Benghazi. The Army Commander planned, by offensive action, to stop the Axis advance on Benghazi and in the Jebel. His corps and divisional commanders disagreed: they could see no comparison, as Ritchie apparently did, with Auchinleck's decision back in November for, this time, Eighth Army's armour was in considerable disarray while Afrika Korps had been virtually unscathed and the Italian armour had seen little action. Rommel might have a fuel problem but everything else favoured him.

Auchinleck, who had believed that Ritchie could stop the German advance, became concerned enough to fly to the front to assess the situation. He did not assume command of Eighth Army nor did he interfere with any of Ritchie's decisions, including the countermanding of the order to abandon Benghazi.

Although Ritchie was acting positively, both Godwin-Austen and Tuker felt that he should have done so much earlier. Tuker had been urging a counter-attack for two days but Godwin-Austen would not authorise one, partly because of the state of 1st Armoured Division but also due to the absence of firm orders from Army HQ. Tuker later wrote:

> Godwin-Austen had asked for bread and been given a stone. The one thing he did not get out of Army was a positive, definite plan.[2]

In spite of Ritchie's efforts, the initiative remained with Rommel who launched a fresh assault on the 27th. In a two-pronged move, 90th Light Division, supported by Italian troops, advanced along the coast road while Rommel led another force through the hills south-east of Benghazi. A simultaneous feint attack was made towards Mechili to divert British attention. Rommel's attack was over extremely tough terrain where no activity had been expected and the Desert Fox succeeded in unsettling Ritchie.

The Eighth Army commander was completely outsmarted while Auchinleck, still refraining from interference, reposed too much confidence in his subordinate whom he felt had 'the situation very well in hand'. But Ritchie had never taken a firm grasp of the battle and now ordered the re-organised 1st Armoured Division to meet the enemy at Mechili. With the remnants of the armour chasing a non-existent German force, 4th Indian Division was left unsupported at Benghazi. Tuker had no option but to abandon the city, having first demolished vital installations.

Thereafter, events overtook Ritchie and the campaign simply became a retreat to Gazala where Eighth Army found itself on 4 February. Rommel, still suffering severe supply problems, did not press hard after the retreating British. Cyrenaica, along with its airfields, was once more in Axis hands. Morale in Eighth Army had taken a severe blow and the soldiers coined their own laconic description for the ebb and flow of the desert war: the Benghazi Stakes.

Godwin-Austen, aggrieved at Ritchie's taking 4th Indian Division under his personal command, asked to be relieved of command of XIII Corps, stating that the Army Commander had shown no confidence in his abilities. Auchinleck accepted his resignation and appointed 'Strafer' Gott, previously 7th Armoured Division's commander, to lead XIII Corps. Although, later in February, his Chief of Staff, Eric Dorman-Smith, suggested removing Ritchie, Auchinleck demurred on the grounds that he could not go on sacking Eighth Army commanders. In any case, the Auk felt that should Ritchie be removed then Montgomery would be sent from England to command Eighth Army. As there had been antipathy between Auchinleck and Montgomery since 1940, when the pair had worked together in England, Monty would never have been the Auk's choice as army commander.

Dorman-Smith recommended many changes in Eighth Army. In a report to Auchinleck he condemned

> the use of amateur Jock Columns and the widespread desert jargon and old-boy familiarities. Eighth Army was 'more of a club than a strictly disciplined entity', he cautioned, and recommended immediate action. 'Chink was not the most tactful of men', de Guingand would agree later, 'but from the talks he had with me on his return [from Eighth Army HQ to investigate command and control] I can say without any doubt that he had arrived at some extremely sound deductions. He was particularly critical of the way the Army was being handled, which of course reflected on some of the commanders concerned'.[3]

Auchinleck considered sidelining Ritchie by creating a GHQ Reserve, with Ritchie commanding, which would provide better back-up for Eighth Army. It would take Ritchie out of the desert, although it would probably bring Montgomery out to command the Army. The idea came to naught because manpower and equipment resources were now stretched even further by the Japanese invasions of Malaya and Burma. Formations intended for the Middle East had been diverted to the Far East while formations under Auchinleck's command were to be transferred to meet the Japanese threat: among those was 70th Division while the Australian government recalled its troops from the Middle East; artillery and aircraft were also transferred.

Eighth Army had now to prepare to meet a possible fresh Axis offensive which Auchinleck reckoned might happen in mid-February. The Army had established itself from Gazala to Bir Hakeim, doglegging through Alem Hamza using, in some places, positions that Rommel's troops had held only seven weeks earlier. As Eighth Army faced westward its losses had to be made good: since 21 January these had been 1,400 dead, wounded or missing with forty-two tanks destroyed, another thirty damaged or abandoned, forty field guns lost and forty-five aircraft shot down.[4] The worsening situation in the Far East did not help. Singapore fell on 15 February and Brooke, the CIGS, informed Auchinleck that, as well as losing three or four divisions, he would 'not receive more than a division from UK during the next six months'.[5]

Brooke appreciated that the reinforcement situation might force the abandonment of plans to retake Cyrenaica. That, however, did not save Auchinleck from pressure from Churchill for a renewed offensive to ease pressure on Malta by providing the RAF with forward bases in Cyrenaica from which to protect Malta-bound convoys. On 27 February Auchinleck signalled his intentions to Churchill. He planned:

1. To continue to build up armoured striking force in the Army forward area as rapidly as possible. 2. Meanwhile to make Gazala-Tobruk and Sollum-Maddalena positions as strong as possible and push railway forward towards El Adem. 3. To build up forward area reserves of supplies for renewal of offensive. 4. To seize first chance of staging limited offensive to regain landing grounds in area Derna-Mechili provided this can be done without prejudicing chances of launching major offensive to recapture Cyrenaica or safety of Tobruk base area.[6]

However, the numerical superiority required for a major offensive would not prevail before June; any such offensive before then would risk defeat and imperil Egypt. As Auchinleck's signal made its way to England another, from the Chiefs of Staff, was en route to him emphasising the need to be able to cover a substantial convoy to Malta by the April dark period. Eventually, after refusing to travel to London, Auchinleck met with Sir Stafford Cripps, the Lord Privy Seal, and General Robert Nye, the Vice-CIGS, in Cairo. In the course of the meeting he brought forward his earliest target date for an offensive to 15 May while stressing that the date should not be considered as definitive.

Since Brooke had guaranteed that no more forces would be withdrawn from the Middle East and the number of medium tanks should have increased to 450 by mid-May, Auchinleck felt that the risk of renewing the offensive could be taken about then. He also had to worry about the possibility of a German attack through the Caucasus as well as the enemy on the Cyrenaican front. Ritchie, on the other hand, had only to worry about holding the Gazala line and building up Eighth Army for the renewal of the offensive. Priority, however, was given to preparing for the offensive and thus the line was far from being a satisfactory defensive system.

The Gazala Line, really a loose system of defended localities, and the area around Tobruk was held by XIII and XXX Corps. The former was now composed of 50th (Northumbrian) Division, a Territorial Army formation, together with 1st and 2nd South African Divisions with the support of 1 and 32 Army Tank Brigades with Valentine and Matilda I-tanks. Two armoured divisions, 1st and 7th, made up XXX Corps: 1st Armoured Division included 1 and 22 Armoured Brigades with 201 Guards Brigade (formerly 200 Guards Brigade); 7th Armoured Division had lost 7 Armoured Brigade to the Far East and now was composed of 4 Armoured Brigade, 7 Motor Brigade (formerly Support Group), 3 and 29 Indian Brigades; General Messervy, the divisional commander, also had 1 Free French Brigade under his command. The armoured divisions' equipment included Crusaders, Honeys and the new American Grants which mounted a 75mm gun but, unfortunately, had that gun fitted in a side-mounted sponson, thus denying it all-round traverse. Finally, in Eighth Army reserve, Ritchie had 5th (Indian) Division. Of the Army's six divisions, three, plus the two army tank brigades, were British.

The northern part of the system was held by XIII Corps with 1st South African Division deployed from Gazala to Alem Hamza where 50th Division assumed responsibility to south of the Trigh Capuzzo. Each was supported by an army tank brigade; 50th Reconnaissance Battalion of the Northumbrian division was under 22 Armoured Brigade's command in XXX Corps. Tobruk itself was protected by 2nd South African Division. Barbed wire and minefields formed part of the defences.

Norrie's XXX Corps had the task of meeting and dealing with Rommel's armoured thrust which could come in one of two ways: Afrika Korps might exploit an attack on XIII Corps' positions, perhaps along the Trigh Capuzzo, or it could attempt to outflank the southern defences at Bir Hakeim. Wherever it came, the attack would take time and would require the German armour to refuel. Norrie should, therefore, have sufficient time to concentrate forces to meet the threat. If the attack came on Norrie's right, through the British centre, there should be adequate time for the armour to concentrate as the Germans had to breach the minefields. The left, a sweep around Bir Hakeim, was another story and, accordingly, the armoured brigades were deployed in positions from which they could concentrate as quickly as possible. Thus 2 Armoured Brigade was located astride the Trigh Capuzzo, west of El Adem and eight miles north-east of 22 Armoured which was near Bir El Harmat, north of the Trigh el Abd, and about fifteen miles north-west from 4 Armoured which deployed some dozen miles east of Bir Hakeim. In battle this concentration would mean one or more armoured brigades passing from command of one division to another, thus creating the undesirable situation of divided command.

Infantry from XXX Corps held defensive positions at Retma (7 Motor Brigade), twenty miles east of Bir Hakeim where 1 Free French Brigade was deployed; at Knightsbridge (201 Guards Brigade), a track crossing-point on the Trigh Capuzzo, behind 50th Division's left centre junction; at Bir el Gubi (29 Brigade), on the Trigh el Abd almost forty miles south of Tobruk; and in the desert five miles south of Bir Hakeim (3 Indian Motor Brigade). Defensive 'boxes' were established around which armour could manoeuvre and into which it could withdraw to refuel, replenish ammunition and undertake general maintenance. Each 'box' was held by infantry, artillery and anti-tank guns. Typically an armoured brigade would operate from three such boxes: 22 Armoured Brigade's boxes each included a battery of 107th Medium Regiment, two troops of 102nd Anti-Tank Regiment and a company of 50th Reconnaissance Battalion. There were large gaps in the Gazala system through which Eighth Army's armour was to advance in the forthcoming offensive; between Bir Hakeim and its northern neighbour stretched a massive thirteen-mile gap.

Not everyone was convinced of the value of the Gazala system. Tuker felt particularly strongly about it and urged

the Corps Commander to exchange the linear Gazala position for a fortress defence of the Tobruk area, creating a secure base from which mobile forces might sally in a battle of manoeuvre. To this end he urged that Fourth Indian Division should be entrusted with a role similar to that of 90 Light Division in Afrika Korps, with employment as lorryborne troops in close support of tank operations.[7]

This eminently sensible advice was not taken. That was unfortunate as Tuker showed a clearer appreciation of the demands of desert warfare than almost anyone else in Eighth Army. Had his ideas been implemented the story of the summer battles of 1942 might have been very different indeed. Instead Tuker and his division were moved to Palestine and Cyprus. When Tuker returned to Cairo in May he found that his comments on the indefensibility of Bir Hakeim had been heeded.

He was entrusted with command of the Eighth Army forces which held the desert flank, consisting of a Free French brigade under General Koenig, 29 Indian Infantry Brigade, 7 Motor Brigade of 7 Armoured Division, 3 Indian Motor Brigade, comprising three mechanized cavalry units and 2 Field Regiment, Indian Artillery. He hurried to the desert with one dominating idea – to get his command on wheels, and by making it mobile to save it from destruction. Thereafter it would operate as a threat to the Axis flank and rear.[8]

Tobruk was garrisoned principally by 2nd South African Division but it had never been intended to defend it against siege for a second time. The Royal Navy had made it clear that they would not be prepared to supply Tobruk by sea, as in 1941, in the event of another siege. Auchinleck had ordered Ritchie to hold a line that would cover the port and prevent it being invested. As a result the port's defences had been allowed to deteriorate.

Originally Tobruk had been defended by two concentric perimeters but, due to insufficient manpower, the inner perimeter was not manned.

> The outer perimeter was only garrisoned by a series of isolated section posts, whose positions were clearly identified by the belts of concertina wire which surrounded them. The outer perimeter originally had been covered by an extensive minefield. Many gaps now existed owing to mines having been raised for use at Gazala. Moreoever, the majority of the mines laid around Tobruk had been of the simple 'soup-plate and plunger' type which tended to deteriorate and to silt up rapidly.[9]

Anti-tank ditches had filled up with sand and there were insufficient anti-tank guns in Tobruk to provide adequate defence against any determined armoured attack. The siege of Tobruk had captured the imagination of the British public, and of Winston Churchill himself, in 1941 but it could not, in the conditions prevailing in 1942, be repeated.

Auchinleck was under considerable pressure from Churchill to launch his offensive. Since the date suggested at the meeting with Cripps, 15 May, was no longer possible as Eighth Army's build-up and training were not yet complete, Churchill became quite impatient and considered dismissing Auchinleck. An offensive to allow a Malta convoy through the Mediterranean in the June dark period was promised by the Auk who assured the prime minister that it would be a full-scale operation rather than simply a diversion to assist the convoy. This would mean an attack in early-June but, warned Auchinleck, the enemy might launch an offensive before this which would affect his own timings. Indeed an Axis attack was expected as a result of information from Ultra, the decrypting of German signals, but the exact date was unknown.

In the meantime Eighth Army waited. Large supply dumps to support an offensive were built up at Tobruk and the Western Desert Railway's railhead at Belhamed. Eighth Army enjoyed numerical superiority over Panzer Armee Afrika in manpower, armour and artillery while the air forces were of almost equal strengths. Ritchie had a total of 849 tanks: 573 equipped his two armoured divisions while the army tank brigades had a further 276. Rommel had 560 tanks, over half of which were German;

some were the new PzKw IIIs with a long-barrelled 50mm gun. Eighth Army had 167 new American Grants equipped with a 75mm gun, more powerful than anything used against the Germans before and capable of firing high-explosive as well as armour-piercing rounds so that anti-tank guns could be engaged at longer range.

Rommel had forty-eight 88mm anti-tank guns, the most powerful such weapon on the battlefield, which had no British equivalent, even though the 3.7-inch mobile anti-aircraft gun could have been deployed as a stop-gap anti-tank weapon and the development of a dedicated anti-tank carriage for the 3.7 would have produced a superior anti-tank weapon. As it stood, Eighth Army's principal anti-tank gun was still the 2-pounder although 112 of the new 6-pounders had recently arrived in Egypt and had been issued to a few units to replace the 2-pounder. Thus the two armies stood, almost evenly matched, although the British had a three-to-two advantage in tank numbers, ready for the clash of arms that had to come. German training and tactics were still superior, however, and although, on 8 February 1942, Auchinleck had emphasised the need for training to achieve better co-operation in battle,[10] there had been insufficient time and, in many units it seemed, a lack of willingness to change the way things were done.

On 26 May Rommel attacked.

NOTES

1. Fraser: *And We Shall Shock Them*, p.178
2. Tuker: *Approach to Battle*, p.65
3. Greacen: *Chink*, p.192
4. Playfair, *The Mediterranean and the Middle East, vol iii*, pp.150-153
5. Connell: *Auchinleck*, p.454
6. Butler: *Grand Strategy, vol iii*, p.450
7. Stevens: *Fourth Indian Division*, p.162
8. ibid, p.165
9. ibid, p.167
10. PRO: WO201/538, Co-operation in Battle

CHAPTER IV

From Knightsbridge to Alamein: The Summer Retreat, 1942

The greater therefore should our courage be.

Rommel's offensive opened in the early afternoon of 26 May with a diversionary attack by infantry in the Gazala-Sidi Muftah area, at the northern end of the British line. Most of the infantry who attacked 1st South African Division were Italian; the bulk of the attacks fell on 2 and 3 Brigade Group areas, with some on 1 Brigade Group. The attackers were engaged by South African artillery, machine guns and mortars and withdrew after suffering heavy casualties. The overall plan was for Afrika Korps, now commanded by General Walter Nehring, to strike at the French in Bir Hakeim while Ariete and Trieste Divisions pushed through the gap north of Koenig's position.

Surprise was lost when British reconnaissance elements spotted the dust cloud raised by the Bir Hakeim-bound thrust. Confusion then entered Rommel's plans when he decided that the Italian divisions, rather than Afrika Korps, should take Bir Hakeim. His orders never reached Trieste which continued on its original axis of advance, leaving Ariete to strike alone at the French. Afrika Korps ran into much tougher opposition than anticipated as it tried to flank round the south of the British line and ran into the new Grant tanks and 6-pounder anti-tank guns. Rommel's intelligence staff had failed to detect the presence of either of these new weapons; both provided shocks for the panzer crews.

Confusion was the order of the day for the 27th with neither side gaining an advantage. Rommel had planned to take Tobruk within four days, a timetable that was clearly not going to be adhered to. At Bir Hakeim, 1 Free French Brigade was holding out against Ariete whilst Crüwell was being contained to the north. Afrika Korps had been split with 90th Light detached, allowing British columns to strike through the gap and hit Rommel's supply columns. The two panzer divisions had advanced across the Trigh Capuzzo and were met by piecemeal British attacks. In spite of all the plans for concentration

Ritchie had thrown his armour into the battle piecemeal and thus given

45

us the chance of engaging them in each separate occasion with just about enough of our own tanks. This dispersal of the British armoured brigades was incomprehensible.[1]

The failure to concentrate the British armour had arisen from a misreading of the situation. Auchinleck had suggested to Ritchie that the enemy might attack through Eighth Army's centre. That never happened but, since Ritchie and his staff knew that Auchinleck was privy to highly secret sources of information, it was given particular credence at Army HQ. By the time the truth had been grasped, that the southern thrust was the main Axis effort, it was too late to concentrate the armour and the British tanks were doomed to fight at a disadvantage. Had they been able to concentrate, Rommel would surely have been trounced on the first day as he later was at Alam Halfa.

Rommel's attack caught 7 Motor Brigade totally unbalanced at the unfinished Retma box. The defenders had been given no warning of Afrika Korps' approach. In fact, 7th Armoured Division HQ had allowed half the garrison to go to Tobruk to swim. The brigade commander, Renton, who arrived back at his HQ on the morning of the 27th found that there were not even enough men to man all the guns. When Rommel hit Retma he went through 7 Motor Brigade like a knife through melting butter. A similar fate befell 3 Indian Motor Brigade. The command structure of 4 Armoured Brigade also suffered heavily when 15th Panzer fell on the brigade as it was preparing to move; there were also heavy tank losses. Rommel drove on northwards to overrun 7th Armoured Division's HQ. General Messervy was taken prisoner but his incarceration was only temporary as he passed himself off as a private soldier and escaped twelve hours later. In spite of these successes, Rommel did not have things entirely his own way.

> . . . the instinctive courage of the British soldier saved the day. Without any very definite plan, they closed through the smoke, dust and heat haze on to Rommel's columns and fought them to a standstill. The heavy Grants, in battle for the first time, shook the German tank crews. Fresh armoured brigades unknown to German intelligence joined the fight. Rommel and his commanders began to be anxious; the British armour, supposedly destroyed in the morning, was fighting with a violence never seen before. Their blind advances were now falling into a wide gap that existed between Rommel's armour at Knightsbridge and his supply trucks at Bir el Harmat. When night fell, Rommel's as well as Ritchie's battle was slipping out of control.[2]

By nightfall the situation was still fluid. Although commonsense should have made Rommel pull back to protect his logistic tail, he decided on

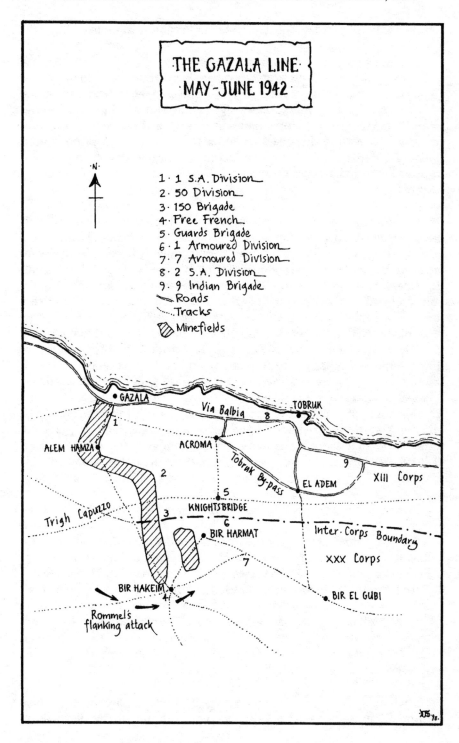

THE GAZALA LINE·
MAY-JUNE 1942·

·N·

1 · 1 S.A. Division
2 · 50 Division
3 · 150 Brigade
4 · Free French
5 · Guards Brigade
6 · 1 Armoured Division
7 · 7 Armoured Division
8 · 2 S.A. Division
9 · 9 Indian Brigade
— Roads
···· Tracks
Minefields

GAZALA

Via Balbia

TOBRUK

8

1

ALEM HAMZA

ACROMA

Tobruk By-pass

2

9

EL ADEM

XIII Corps

5

Trigh Capuzzo

3

KNIGHTSBRIDGE

6

BIR HARMAT

Inter·Corps Boundary

XXX Corps

7

BIR HAKEIM

BIR EL GUBI

Rommel's
flanking attack

another attempt to reach Tobruk. Thus battle continued on the 28th:

> As long as I live I will never forget the morning of May 28th. At first
> light we had fanned out from our closed leaguer positions to our battle
> positions, and, once again, I was on the extreme right flank of the
> Squadron. There was nothing in sight at all to my right or behind me
> and the Troop to my immediate left was spread out and a long way
> away as we were dispersed covering as much ground as possible. I
> could see that my Troop was in a very slight depression so I left my
> three tanks and walked forward about 100 yards or so to look over the
> rim.[3]

What Lieutenant Stuart Hamilton saw was the desert crammed with
tanks, artillery, troops and all their vehicles. At first he thought it was the
entire Afrika Korps but it was only 21st Panzer against which were
arrayed the sixteen tanks of Hamilton's B Squadron, 8th Royal Tank
Regiment. Shortly afterwards a German aircraft spotted the British tanks
and dropped flares to alert the panzers. Hamilton returned quickly to his
tank as some forty panzers left the enemy column to engage B Squadron.

In the battle that followed C Squadron came to B's aid and both fought
fiercely to repel the Germans. Hamilton had drilled his troop in a rapid-
fire technique whereby, once the tank commander had ascertained that
the tank's shots were landing near the target, further rounds would be
loaded as quickly as possible with little or no correction. This allowed the
rate of fire to almost double to about fifteen-plus rounds per minute. It
was very effective in keeping enemy heads down especially as it gave the
impression that there were more British than was the case. Sergeant
Tilford, of Hamilton's troop, won the Military Medal that day for 'his
accurate and rapid fire which prevented enemy tanks from outflanking
us'.[4]

However, the Germans had their redoubtable 88s and the

> sheer weight of numbers of the German Tanks plus their artillery with
> 88s firing airbursts right over our heads, eventually forced us to give
> ground and fall back. The damned 88s . . . firing time-fused shells which
> burst about 20 feet above ground showering red-hot shrapnel in all
> directions . . . caused Tank Commanders to keep well down in the turret
> as we had previously lost several chaps with wounds to head and
> shoulders . . . from this type of attack. Our delaying action did, however,
> give our Column a chance to pull back and regroup in more favourable
> positions – at a price though as we lost 16 tanks out of 32 here.[5]

This action is typical of the tank battles which were occurring and which
caused Rommel to make his caustic comments about the dispersal of

British armour. For Stuart Hamilton and his comrades it was the beginning of six weeks of fighting which ended when 8 RTR was pulled out of the line at the Alamein positions on 13 July. Allowing for occasions when the Regiment had to withdraw to receive new tanks and crews, which happened two or three times in this period, its soldiers saw about five weeks of continuous action. Such lengthy periods in action led to men becoming exhausted and acting like automatons; the Intelligence Office of 4th County of London Yeomanry noted how, on the night of 30/31 May

> at the Colonel's conference in the back of his truck, I noticed with a shock how worn and tired the Officers present looked. Red-eyed, haggard, bearded men, with matted hair huddled round the map I had marked . . . . Lack of sleep had sharpened features and lined every face into a sad caricature. Eye lids felt dry and sore, limbs ached with the longing for rest.[6]

On the 28th, Rommel had pushed Afrika Korps past Knightsbridge towards the coast with 90th Light near El Adem. While the two panzer divisions were racing forward, the supply columns lay back at Bir el Harmat with XX Italian Corps. Rommel's supply position was serious, one division having run out of fuel, but the Desert Fox himself led one supply column past Bir Hakeim through a khamsin on the 29th. Tanks clashed with tanks again that day as XXX Corps ordered 1st Armoured Division to attack Rommel from the east. Hard fighting failed to break Afrika Korps which was able to concentrate at nightfall.

The two panzer divisions were now in the area between Trigh Capuzzo and Trigh el Abd known as 'The Cauldron', a depression in the desert measuring about four miles by two and situated some five miles west-south-west from Knightsbridge. As Rommel had lost 200 tanks he was now outnumbered by the British by a higher margin than heretofore. But Rommel now changed tactics: he planned to break through the British minefields between Bir Hakeim and Sidi Muftah from the British side to shorten his communications. As he pulled back, Eighth Army made no real effort to engage Afrika Korps which was soon inside the minefields, protected by anti-tank guns. German engineers cleared two corridors for supply convoys and Rommel's armour was able to refuel and replenish ammunition stocks. However, as Afrika Korps created this bridgehead east of the line, Ritchie believed that it signified a German defeat.

Ritchie had already been planning an attack by XIII Corps, Operation LIMERICK, in which 50th Division would capture Tmimi and 5th Indian Division would then advance to the area Derna-Martuba-Carmusa. However, by the evening of 31 May, Ritchie felt that he had a better appreciation of the enemy situation and believed that the Axis armour had to be destroyed before XIII Corps could go on the offensive. Since he thought that the enemy were retreating, Ritchie must have considered that he had the tactical advantage.

While Ritchie tried to devise a plan to exploit the German retreat, Rommel was attacking 150 Brigade's box, which menaced one of his supply routes through the minefields. The attack commenced on 29 May and lasted until 1 June. Against bitter resistance, Afrika Korps triumphed and 150 Brigade was destroyed.

Ritchie's counter-stroke, Operation ABERDEEN, was not launched until 5 June. It started well, with an infantry attack before dawn which took a number of objectives but infantry/armour co-ordination broke down and a German attack caused heavy losses to the British infantry. The main enemy positions had escaped the full weight of British artillery fire as they had been farther west than had been believed. This, the Battle of the Cauldron, can only be described as a significant German success, although Ritchie suggested that the Germans had suffered heavy losses and that their position was not good. In fact, 22 Armoured Brigade had lost sixty tanks. Four field regiments were also lost.* The second prong of ABERDEEN, an army tank brigade attack, was foiled when 21st Panzer took the brigade in the flank and drove it into a minefield covered by anti-tank guns. The German counter-attack had also made Messervy a prisoner for the second time, but, once again, he quickly escaped.

Next day Messervy tried to rescue those British troops still within the Cauldron. It was another day of confusion, of orders and counter-orders and the initiative passed to the Germans. By nightfall ABERDEEN was over, having cost Eighth Army over 200 tanks, four artillery regiments and an infantry brigade.

At Alem Hamza 1st South African Division had also been engaged with the enemy and it was on that day that Sergeant Quentin George Murray Smythe of 1st Royal Natal Carabineers won the Victoria Cross. Smythe's platoon had been attacking a heavily defended strongpoint when his officer had been wounded severely; he

> took command of the platoon although he himself had been wounded in the head; when our troops came under enfilade fire from a machine-gun nest he attacked it with hand grenades, capturing the crew. Though weak from loss of blood he continued to lead the advance and on encountering an anti-tank gun position he again attacked single-handed and captured it, killing several of the enemy by rifle fire and the bayonet. When finally ordered to withdraw he did so successfully, defeating skilfully an enemy attempt at encirclement.[7]

---

* For an excellent account of the actions of one field regiment in this battle, see Peter Hart's *To The Last Round*, a record of 107th (South Notts Hussars) Fd Regt, published by Leo Cooper (1996).

Smythe not only survived to receive the Victoria Cross but was later commissioned into his own regiment.

Thus ended the second phase of the Gazala battles, leaving Rommel in a much stronger position than at any time since he had opened his offensive. The armoured battle had been fought at great speed 'over an undeveloped country, a great area lacking in landmarks',[8] and had been marked by confusion, the piecemeal nature of the fighting, and the exhaustion and losses of both sides. However, Afrika Korps was concentrated, confident and with its supply route secure. By contrast Eighth Army's morale had taken another hammering, having suffered several 'swift retreats and some disasters'; its infantry began to look distrustfully at their armour:

> Too many stories circulated of armoured formations arguing against orders setting them on the move towards battle and thus (or so the tale would run) leaving less protected soldiers in the lurch. It was the old cry from Waterloo: 'Where are our Cavalry?' The fault lay not with the brave soldiers of the tank units themselves so much as with the commanders who had become accustomed more to discussion than obedience; and lost time and initiative thereby. It also lay with inadequate tactical doctrine, and an habitual failure to grasp the best methods of attack.[9]

Rommel now turned his attention to the Free French at Bir Hakeim which had endured ferocious attack for ten days. The French garrison had probably given Rommel his hardest fight of the entire battle. With the Desert Fox's full attention turned on it, the strongpoint came under sustained artillery bombardment and aerial attack as well as assaults by the Panzer Armee. Once again, in spite of the fortress's importance to the British positions, no attempt at relief was made. If Bir Hakeim fell, Rommel would be able to roll up the British line as far as Knightsbridge. Losing Bir Hakeim would mean losing the Gazala battle. And that is exactly what happened.

General Koenig wanted his soldiers evacuated and thus refused resupply. He believed that his men's resistance had been futile:

> While the German attack grew closer and closer to the web of foxholes, barbed wire and mines, and the French soldiers, stunned by endless bombardment and lack of sleep, fought on, the indecision continued. Koenig pleaded that he had no water or ammunition; finally Ritchie ordered the garrison to break out on the night of 10th/11th June.[10]

On the morning of the 11th, XIII Corps, save for 150 Brigade, was still

51

intact. Ritchie turned its left flank back to the line of the Trigh Capuzzo; it was now at ninety degrees to the surviving part of the Gazala line and parallel to Eighth Army's main lines of communication. To the east of XIII Corps, and continuing the defensive line, were the strongpoints at Knightsbridge, El Adem and Belhamed which covered Tobruk, the garrison of which provided a left flank to the overall British position. In spite of their recent losses, 1st and 7th Armoured Divisions still had some 200 tanks, and there were eighty I-tanks in the tank brigades, against Afrika Korps' 150, and sixty Italian tanks. A rational assessment of the situation would have indicated that Eighth Army was numerically holding its own. Indeed a Rommel at the head of Eighth Army would have taken the opportunity to attack to prevent the Army being pinned against the coast and shattered. But no such effort was made. Rommel was allowed to resume his offensive.

That evening 15th Panzer, 90th Light and Trieste moved out of the Cauldron towards El Adem while 21st Panzer and Ariete deployed northwards towards Acroma. Eighth Army's plans to rebuff the enemy advance included a southwards attack on 15th Panzer which Rommel pre-empted when he sent 21st Panzer into the rear of 7th Armoured. Lumsden, commanding 1st Armoured, arrived with his division and was told to take 7th under his command, Messervy having been lost (he was hiding in a dry well after running into 90th Light while travelling to Army HQ). Although Lumsden felt that the armour should withdraw into the Knightsbridge box, Norrie insisted that it should break through 15th Panzer.

The battle raged between Knightsbridge, still held by 201 Guards Brigade, and El Adem throughout the afternoon of 12 June. The result was the sharpest defeat ever inflicted on the British armour with the German anti-tank guns taking a terrible toll. By evening the surviving British armour was east of Knightsbridge and virtually incapable of any immediate action. About 120 British tanks had been lost. Not only had the armour been reduced to a shadow of its earlier strength but the inferiority of British equipment and tactics had again been highlighted: although the Grant, in spite of its sponson-mounted main gun, was a match for the German Mark IIIs and IVs, the Crusader, with its 2-pounder, needed to outnumber the MkIIIs by three-to-one to hold its own while the Valentine, also 2-pounder armed, was very slow; the Stuart was considered only to be 'a very good armoured reconnaissance vehicle'. Those regiments which deployed one Grant and two cruiser squadrons had also failed to create a common battle drill.[11]

Auchinleck had spent the 12th at Ritchie's HQ, returning to Cairo on 13 June. He had not attempted to interfere in the running of Eighth Army but had accepted Ritchie's assessments, believing, correctly, that Ritchie had not lost his nerve and felt that Ritchie would continue to hold Rommel.

But the assessments and situation reports given to the Auk at Gambut had been out of date even before being presented to him. Matters were actually worsening at the front.

During the 13th Rommel pressed the Guards in Knightsbridge hard; that evening the garrison was evacuated on Gott's orders. Eighth Army was being forced northwards and the threat of being cut off and destroyed between Tobruk and Gazala loomed large. XXX Corps was down to fifty tanks while only about twenty I-tanks were still in action. Ritchie realised that he could no longer prevent Rommel from cutting off XIII Corps and, in the early hours of the 14th, ordered Gott to take his corps eastwards to the frontier.

> Some brigades were able to comply. Some drove west out of the Gazala positions and round the south. Rommel, despite vigorous efforts, failed to cut off the withdrawal. Some resolute rearguard actions were fought, and, like Eighth Army, Panzer Armee Afrika was exhausted; but they were masters of the field. Within Tobruk itself 2nd South African Division of three brigades, reinforced by the remaining troops of 32nd Army Tank Brigade and 201st Guards Brigade, prepared for the fourth phase of the Battle of Gazala.[12]

During this confused and bloody period there had been some striking examples of cool courage and perhaps none more so than that of the CO of 7 RTR, Lieutenant-Colonel Henry Foote. On 6 June Foote

> although wounded, had continued to lead his regiment from an exposed position on the outside of a tank. By dusk Lieut.-Col Foote had defeated the enemy's attempt to encircle two of our divisions.[13]

Seven days later, on the 13th, Foote

> again displayed outstanding leadership, when a number of our tanks had been destroyed, in going from one tank to another encouraging the crews under intense artillery and anti-tank fire. By his magnificent example the corridor was kept open and the brigade was able to march through.[14]

Foote was recommended for the Victoria Cross, although the award was not gazetted until 18 May 1944.

In the previous chapter it was noted that there had been no intention to hold Tobruk against a second siege due to the downgrading of the port's defences and the Navy's reluctance to carry out resupply. This remained Auchinleck's long-term policy but Ritchie appears to have had other ideas, as suggested in Eighth Army Operational Instruction No.78

> Tobruk garrison will take every opportunity to act offensively against the enemy with a view to forcing him to detach large forces for its investment and prevent him concentrating his forces on the Frontier. Such offensive action will however be subject to the overriding consideration that the security of Tobruk will not thereby be prejudiced.[15]

However, circumstances dictated that Tobruk was invested for the second time. On 15 June General Klopper, commanding 2nd South African Division and Tobruk garrison, told his subordinate commanders that they must be prepared for a siege of up to three months. Three days later he informed Ritchie of his confidence and told him that all was well. Churchill believed that Tobruk would once again defy the Axis and shine a beacon of British defiance to the world. It was not to be.

The survival of Tobruk in June 1942 depended on strong support for the garrison from a force operating in the El Adem-Belhamed area but the existence of such support died with Eighth Army's final tank battle of the Gazala actions. On 17 June the tanks of 4 Armoured Brigade, pennants fluttering in cavalry tradition, were ordered by Messervy to charge the German armour concentration between Sidi Rezegh and El Adem. Ninety British tanks drove forth to battle with the two panzer divisions of Afrika Korps. Over thirty tanks were lost in this desperate action, which cost Messervy his command. The brigade retired to Egypt; Eighth Army's tank arm was no longer in being. Auchinleck had, however, ordered HQ X Corps and 2nd New Zealand Division to move from Syria while 10th Armoured Division was ordered to the front.

By 18 June Rommel's forces surrounded Tobruk. Two days later, in the early morning, the might of the Axis air forces was turned on the town. Then infantry and engineers began working their way towards the south-east perimeter. At 8.30am Afrika Korps' tanks moved forward and, shortly after noon, high ground overlooking the harbour was taken. Later that afternoon 21st Panzer began an advance towards the town and, at 6pm, German troops were in Tobruk. Klopper's HQ was threatened and an order was issued to disperse, depriving the garrison of effective overall command. On the perimeter some battalions continued to hold out even though the enemy was now behind them. Others broke out from Tobruk, heading westwards at first and then turning east to rejoin Eighth Army.

Tobruk held out for less than twenty-four hours. Shortly after 6am on the 21st, Auchinleck's birthday, Klopper sent representatives to the German HQ to negotiate a surrender. A total of 32,000 prisoners, of whom 19,000 were British soldiers, passed into Axis hands.

And yet there had been some outstanding acts of heroism in the defence of Tobruk. The gunners of 68th HAA Regiment, part of 4 AA Brigade, had been in action against enemy aircraft on the morning of the 20th. They later faced another foe and showed how shortsighted was the British failure to employ the 3.7 as an anti-tank gun:

> The 3.7s had been deeply dug in for protection from dive-bombing attacks but found themselves faced, at short notice, with a duel with Mark III and Mark IV tanks. Stripping the walls of their emplacements to obtain low-angle fire, the positions engaged with armour-piercing and high explosive rounds until overrun and mopped up by swarms of enemy infantry. The 3.7s, in this brief action, emulated the German 88mm, one position held up an armoured battalion for four hours and killed four tanks. The outcome was inevitable; Tobruk was isolated, co-ordinated defence collapsed and the South African force commander gave up the struggle. HQ 4th AA Brigade and 68th HAA Regiment were wiped from the AA Order of Battle. . . .[16]

The fall of Tobruk was a deep psychological blow to Winston Churchill. He was given the news by President Roosevelt in the White House and described himself as the most unhappy Englishman in America since Cornwallis at Yorktown. There was, however, one beneficial side effect: Roosevelt ordered the release of 300 of the new Sherman tanks to Britain from US Army stocks; the Sherman would play an important part in the final phase of the war in North Africa.

Ritchie now planned to hold Egypt on a line pivoted on the coastal resort of Mersa Matruh with delaying actions being fought on the frontier to enable Eighth Army to prepare the Matruh line. This proposition was unrealistic. Although Matruh had once been considered the final point at which Egypt could be defended, the vulnerability of defences there to a southflanking movement had been recognised in Wavell's time and a new last-ditch position identified.* This latter was based on the railway halt of El Alamein and ran southwards for almost forty miles to the Qattara Depression: it could not easily be outflanked.

Ritchie's Matruh defences were similar to those at Gazala and relied on minefields, barbed wire and defensive boxes stretching south from Matruh for some thirty miles. Beyond lay open desert and Eighth Army no longer had the armour to deter an outflanking move.

Rommel's capture of Tobruk was rewarded with promotion to Field Marshal: it seems that the port had enthralled Hitler as much as Churchill.

---

* In a pre-war map exercise, Auchinleck had himself identified the El Alamein-Qattara line as the last possible line of defence for the Nile delta

Continuation of the offensive into Egypt was also authorised. To obtain that permission Rommel had to appeal over the heads of his military commanders to Hitler and Mussolini. A sensible analysis of the situation would have demanded that, before renewing the offensive, Rommel should re-organise and build up his army's strength. But the Desert Fox believed that the gamble of an immediate attack, while the British were still off balance, was worth taking. It was a gamble that would fail.

There was little organised opposition on the frontier. Rommel swept south of the defences towards the coast east of Sidi Barrani which he reached at dusk on 24 June. In twenty-four hours he had covered 100 miles.

> Eighth Army retreated in a final state of rout and dissolution; one observer said he did not see a formed unit of any kind. Eighth Army losses in the Gazala battles had now reached about eighty thousand, mostly in prisoners.
> By nightfall on 25th June, Rommel was in front of the Matruh defences. Ritchie had failed to 'put distance' between himself and the *Panzerarmee*. The final battle for the Middle East was at hand.[17]

That battle was not to be in Ritchie's hands. He had determined that there would be no more retreating: Eighth Army would stay at Matruh, it would offer battle there, and it would win or die. On the afternoon of 25 June, Auchinleck arrived at Eighth Army HQ, relieved Ritchie of his command and, once again, took control of Eighth Army. The Auk had signalled Brooke that he felt reasonably confident of turning the tables on Rommel in time, although he suggested that the CIGS might wish to relieve him of his command.

Auchinleck had obtained tank reinforcements from throughout his Middle East command and 1st Armoured Division now numbered 159 tanks, of which sixty were Grants. The Division was located in open desert south of Minqar Qaim and was part of XIII Corps which had become the Army's mobile, striking element. In Mersa Matruh, Ritchie had deployed X Corps, brought in from Syria, with 10th Indian and 50th Divisions. Freyberg's New Zealanders were at Minqar Qaim as their commander had refused to be shut up in Matruh while 29 Indian Brigade held the Sidi Hamza box. Two battlegroups, Gleecol and Leathercol, held the Army's centre.

There was to be no last stand at Mersa Matruh. Auchinleck had already decided that he would order a withdrawal to the Alamein positions being prepared by XXX Corps. That withdrawal order was issued at 4.15am on the 26th. Auchinleck proposed

> to keep all troops fluid and mobile, and strike at enemy from all sides.

Armour not to be committed unless very favourable opportunity presents itself. At all costs and even if ground has to be given up intend to keep 8th Army in being and to give no hostage to fortune in shape of immobile troops holding localities which can be easily isolated.[18]

He signalled to Brooke that the:

Plan of defence is based on deploying maximum amount of <u>artillery</u> kept fully mobile with minimum quantity of infantry required for local protection. Armour in reserve only to be used if circumstances so favourable as to make success reasonably certain. Matruh . . . is not essential and will not be allowed to become a trap . . . . Intention is to keep Army in being at all costs and this entails fullscale mobility and readiness to fight fluid battle unimpaired by necessity for defending fortified positions . . . .[19]

Rommel made his move before dawn that morning, thrusting 21st Panzer and 90th Light into the centre of what he thought to be a continuously held front line. In a matter of hours both divisions were pushing through the gap between 10th Indian and 2nd New Zealand Divisions; by evening units of 90th Light were swinging north for the coast east of Matruh.

Confused fighting continued throughout the following day with Gott attempting to conduct mobile defence as Auchinleck had ordered. The Axis met stubborn resistance at many points with infantry and artillery anti-tank gunners showing doughty courage as they strove to slow the advance of the enemy armour. South of Mersa Matruh, 9th Durham LI came under attack on the morning of the 27th. At one point a DLI company position was covered by a 2-pounder anti-tank gun on a forward slope in front of the position. Two enemy light guns were brought forward to bombard the 6-pounder and they succeeded in killing or wounding all the crew. One man, Private Adam Wakenshaw, lost his left arm above the elbow but

despite the intensity of the fire he crawled back to his gun, loaded it with one arm and fired five more rounds. He succeeded in damaging one of the enemy guns and setting its tractor on fire. He was then knocked over by a shell and again severely wounded. Undeterred, he dragged himself back to his gun, placed a round in the breech and was about to fire when a direct hit killed him and destroyed the gun. But by engaging the enemy's guns and sacrificing his own life Private Wakenshaw had prevented them from engaging an infantry company which was in the act of embussing.[20]

Wakenshaw's outstanding gallantry and self-sacrifice was recognised with the posthumous award of the Victoria Cross in September 1942.

Other battalions of the Durhams were also engaged with enemy armour that day: at 5.30pm 8 DLI were attacked from the south-west by captured Stuart tanks which were driven off with the loss of five. An hour later two enemy SPGs and several armoured cars attacked HQ Company and B Company of 6 DLI and a two-hour battle ensued during which the Durhams destroyed one SPG, an armoured car and two other vehicles but had lost fourteen dead, a similar number wounded and fifty-three missing.

Gott had already issued orders for his corps to withdraw eastwards which it did against heavy opposition during the night. Confusion still prevailed: the New Zealanders were cut off for more than twenty-four hours and suffered some 800 casualties during fierce fighting; X Corps HQ was out of touch with Army HQ for nine hours and only became aware of XIII Corps' withdrawal when communications were restored at 4.30am on the 28th. When X Corps did slip out that night with the aim of turning east on high ground and rallying at El Daba, Auchinleck told Holmes, the Corps' commander, that XIII Corps would provide cover for them. But that cover never materialised because of further communication breakdowns and X Corps became badly scattered in the course of the night. 'Nearly every column ran across an enemy leaguer at one point or another and the confusion on both sides was indescribable'.[21]

Auchinleck, however, was not confused. He was clear in his intention that Eighth Army would prepare for battle at El Alamein. His leadership was invigorating. Tedder, commanding the air forces in the Middle East, had noted this almost as soon as the Auk took over from Ritchie and, later, wrote:

> I was much impressed by the contrast between his calm authority and Ritchie's fumbling. Auchinleck had grasped the essentials of a most confused situation in about two hours . . . I felt that passive bewilderment was being replaced by active command.[22]

As Eighth Army poured back to El Alamein, order began to be built out of the chaos of retreat. Auchinleck aimed to fight the Panzer Armee with balanced forces that would stop Rommel in his tracks and, having stopped him, to prepare for a further offensive. Eighth Army Operations Order No.83 stated the Auk's intention 'to stop the enemy's Eastward advance and defeat him in the area Matruh-El Alamein-Naqb Dweiss-Ras El Qattara'.[23]

In the early hours of the morning of Wednesday 1 July Afrika Korps' tanks reached the front before El Alamein and Axis artillery opened fire on Eighth Army's forward positions. The first battle of El Alamein had begun.

As the guns roared at Alamein, GHQ in Cairo was busily burning confidential documents. The smoke rising from the chimneys 'was an amazing sight' and bits of burnt or charred paper floated through the air. The day came to be known as Ash Wednesday. GHQ and RAF HQ personnel were told to prepare for evacuation to Palestine; the Mediterranean fleet abandoned Alexandria harbour due to the proximity of Axis forces and British civilians were evacuated. Amid all this confusion, one man stood firm: General Sir Claude Auchinleck.

NOTES

1. Lewin: *Rommel as Military Commander*, p.115
2. Barnett: *The Desert Generals*, p.148
3. Hamilton: *Armoured Odyssey*, p.40
4. ibid, p.45
5. loc cit
6. PRO: CAB44/97, p.82
7. Smyth: *The Story of the Victoria Cross*, p.367
8. PRO: CAB44/97, intro
9. Fraser: op cit, p.220
10. Barnett: op cit, p.153
11. PRO: CAB44/97, p.11
12. Fraser: op cit, p.222
13. Smyth: op cit, p.366
14. ibid
15. PRO: CAB44/97, p.169
16. Routledge: *Anti-Aircraft Artillery, 1914-1955*, p.140
17. Barnett: op cit, p.169
18. Playfair: *The Mediterranean and the Middle East, vol iii*, p.286
19. PRO: CAB44/98
20. Smyth: op cit, pp.367-368
21. Playfair: op cit, p.295
22. Tedder: *With Prejudice*, p.304
23. PRO: CAB44/98

CHAPTER V

Rommel is Stopped: The July Battles

In bloody field doth win immortal fame

Rommel's attack on the El Alamein line on 1 July was brought to a standstill by 1st South African Division at El Alamein itself and by 18 Brigade of 8th Indian Division at Deir el Shein whose stalwart resistance, commented Auchinleck, provided valuable time for the consolidation of the Alamein defences.

The Indians, two battalions of whom had never before seen action, fought valiantly at Deir el Shein against tanks of Afrika Korps. Although the unfinished position had to be abandoned because there was no supporting British armour, the enemy attack was well and truly blunted by Robcol, an ad-hoc column of infantry from 1/4th Essex Regiment and 11th Field Regiment:

> The casualties of 18 Indian Infantry Brigade during this hard fought action were severe. The whole of Brigade HQ was lost as was 2/5 Essex, save for a dozen men. 4/11 Sikh Regt lost 7 British officers and 509 men, 2/3 GR 1 officer and 228 men. 21 25-pdr guns, 21 6-pdr and 14 2-pdr were lost, three, five and seven of these natures respectively managing to get clear. It later however became apparent that the Brigade had in fact delayed for a day almost the whole of the remaining German armoured forces, amounting to some 55 tanks.[1]

At El Alamein, 90th Light, having gone off course in the darkness, blundered too close to the defences and were pinned down by heavy fire from the South Africans. The German division extricated itself from the Alamein defences around noon, only to come under further, and unexpected, intensive fire from mobile South African brigade groups to the south-east; 90th Light was brought to a standstill. By evening both German thrusts had been stopped in very exposed positions.

The blocking of the Axis attack had followed Auchinleck's battle plan: that part of the Army should hold defensive positions to channel an enemy advance, while the remainder of the Army, maintaining as much mobility as possible, would hit at the rear and flank of the attack. El Alamein was one of the defensive positions and there were two other principal localities: Bab el Qattara was fifteen miles south of El Alamein and just south of 'the evil brown whaleback'[2] of Ruweisat Ridge (Deir el Shein was forward of this feature); Naqb abu Dweis was north of the escarpment above the Qattara Depression.

Defending north of Ruweisat was XXX Corps, still commanded by Norrie,* including 1st South African Division and 18 Indian Brigade, while Gott's XIII Corps covered to the south; X Corps had been withdrawn to the Delta to reform. Gott's command included 6 New Zealand Brigade in the Bab el Qattara area, 9 Indian Brigade farther south and 7 Motor Brigade as a mobile force between the two; 1st Armoured Division was slightly to the rear while 4 Armoured Brigade lay near El Alamein's south-east defences and 22 Armoured on the eastern extremity of Ruweisat Ridge. Eighth Army HQ was co-located with HQ XXX Corps north of Alam el Halfa ridge.

In the morning of 2 July, 11th Field began bombarding enemy transport in the Deir el Shein area. An enemy attack with lorried infantry, followed by an artillery bombardment and a tank assault failed to shift Robcol.

> The panzers followed forward to mount the high ground. They were beaten back. As they swung to flank the steady fire of the 25-pounders followed them. The Essex in their covering positions sat tight all day under continuous bombardment. Casualties mounted. By nightfall 7 guns had been knocked out and ammunition was all but exhausted. But for the first time since Tobruk, Rommel's armour had broken off action and had retired into the west.[4]

Rommel's attacks on the 2nd foundered on Auchinleck's achievement of creating, from Eighth Army's scattered formations, a force capable of fighting a determined defensive battle, as well as on the rock of Ruweisat. In an interview with Roger Parkinson, Auchinleck described his achievement: 'It worked all right. But it was against all rules and regulations. It was pretty desperate really'.[5]

Rommel and Auchinleck had squared up like heavyweight boxers, with the former's renewed assault and the latter's counterstroke almost coinciding. Near El Alamein, 90th Light struck at 1 South African Brigade which held out with the close support of the Desert Air Force, the co-operation of which was a vital factor in these battles, while, around Ruweisat, 1st Armoured Division and Afrika Korps locked in combat. In the tank battle, 4 Armoured Brigade clashed with 15th Panzer Division and 22 Armoured fought 21st Panzer.

---

* Norrie had considered that the British armour, although 'out-gunned, out-ranged and out-telescoped' had reduced the German armour 'to a fragment of its former self' in the Gazala battles.[3]

The tank fighting, which lasted until dark, left Eighth Army's armour solidly in possession of the disputed ground. Auchinleck's dictum, that the armour should stand firm and draw the German tanks on to British guns, had been adhered to and Afrika Korps, having been fed a strong dose of their own medicine, suffered considerably as did all Rommel's forces that day. Panzer Armee's losses might have been greater had XXX Corps' formations made more progress against 90th Light's flank. Although the day's fighting appeared to have been drawn, the foundation of British victory had been laid. Auchinleck had swung the balance to Eighth Army and, henceforth, the Axis forces would be at an increasing disadvantage. Major General von Mellenthin later commented that Rommel's command had been drawn into a battle of attrition when their one chance of success had been to outmanoeuvre Eighth Army. With a logistic tail stretching back to Tripoli, and receiving the Desert Air Force's full attention, Rommel could not now hope to smash through to the Nile delta. And Auchinleck continued to demonstrate his mastery of the flexible battle on the 3rd.

During that Friday the scales tilted clearly in Auchinleck's favour. He transferred 1st Armoured Division to XXX Corps command, bringing the armour closer to his direct control and, as the day wore on, ordered blows to be struck in a variety of locations, hitting Axis forces at one point before switching quickly to strike at another. Thus the enemy was kept off balance while Eighth Army maintained firm balance. In the north, XXX Corps was ordered to accelerate its counter-offensive while XIII Corps threatened the Axis rear near Deir el Shein. Eighth Army's armour was concentrated to meet enemy attacks: 1st Armoured Division sat on Ruweisat Ridge and slammed shells into Afrika Korps' panzers as they advanced up the slopes. The Desert Air Force flew about 900 missions, bombing enemy troops and transport at the rate of ten tons per hour.[6] To the south, the New Zealanders overran part of Ariete Division, capturing some 350 Italians with over forty guns. Afrika Korps' strength was now down to twenty-six runners while 1st Armoured Division had almost 120 tanks. Rommel's divisions were reduced to no more than 1,500 men each; stocks of artillery ammunition were critically low. Rommel was forced to signal OKW* in Berlin that he would have to go on the defensive for a fortnight at least.

The Desert Fox had met his match: he later commented that Auchinleck had handled his forces

with very considerable skill and tactically better than Ritchie had done. He seemed to view the situation with decided coolness, for he was not allowing himself to be rushed into accepting a second best solution by any moves we made.[7]

* OberKommando der Wehrmacht, the German high command.

On the 4th, Auchinleck continued to press Rommel hard, pushing north-wards and, for a time, thought that the Desert Fox might be considering retreat. However, Rommel was regrouping with Afrika Korps, 90th Light and XX Corps being replaced by the Italian X and XXI Corps. In spite of continued heavy attack from the air, this regrouping was carried out over the following few days. By nightfall on the 4th, all but the western extremity of the much-fought-over Ruweisat Ridge was in Eighth Army's hands.

Although Auchinleck was still hoping for XIII Corps to outflank the Axis positions and attack northwards against the enemy lines of communication, his soldiers were exhausted and unable to make significant progress on either 4 or 5 July. On the night of the 4th he had stressed to his commanders the necessity of giving the enemy no rest, and although XIII Corps had formations move into forming-up positions for a renewal of the British offensive, the deployment was too slow. Auchinleck realised that his corps commanders were themselves worn out: Norrie was relieved of command of XXX Corps by Ramsden, who had been commanding 50th Division, although Gott remained with XIII Corps.

This slow reaction by the British worked to Rommel's advantage: on 6 July he managed to increase his tank strength to forty-four, his troops laid down more minefields and ammunition arrived for his artillery.

Appreciating that Eighth Army lacked the strength needed to sweep round the enemy's south-west flank, Auchinleck decided, during the 6th and 7th, on a modified and less ambitious offensive. The New Zealanders were pulled back from the Bab el Qattara box during the night of 8 July, leading Rommel to assume that Eighth Army was again retreating. Accordingly, the German ordered Littorio Division to occupy the Bab el Qattara area in readiness for a general advance scheduled to begin on 10 July. By so doing Rommel was spreading his forces out too thinly at the same time as Auchinleck was concentrating his to the north. The latter was being reinforced: in addition to 8th Indian Division, 9th Australian Division had been moved to XIII Corps' area from Alexandria; a fresh armoured division, 8th, had also arrived in the Middle East and 10th Armoured Division had arrived from Palestine; 44th (Home Counties) Division was en route from the UK whence also 51st (Highland) Division was due in August. But Auchinleck, as CinC Middle East, had to worry about his northern flank as well and the possibility of a German attack through the Caucasus on the Persian oilfields. Only Russian resistance at Stalingrad, it seemed, was preventing such a southward movement by the German armies in the Soviet Union.

Ever the gambler, Rommel had told General von Bismarck of 21st Panzer that his tanks would soon be driving into the Nile delta. This assessment he made after visiting Bab el Qattara on 9 July to supervise preparations for his armoured attack from the southern sector of the front. But, the day before, Auchinleck had ordered Ramsden to plan the seizure of Tel el Eisa and Tel el Makd Khad, two Italian-held features west of El Alamein. Plans for the operation, to be carried out by 9th Australian Division in concert with 1st South African Division, with mobile groups preventing enemy reinforcement from the south, were complete by the evening of the 9th: the operation was to begin with an artillery bombardment at 3.30am on the 10th.

When Rommel first became aware of what was happening he rushed northwards with a battlegroup from 15th Panzer to assist the Italians. By 7.30am, Australian troops had cleared positions east of the railway and the South Africans had gained their first objective near Tel el Makd Khad which fell at about 10.30am. Italian soldiers panicked and fled and, in so doing, almost brought about the capture by Eighth Army of Panzer Armee HQ. Von Mellenthin, the officer commanding that HQ, had a narrow escape in what he described as Italian rout and panic.

The Australians had a tougher nut to crack at Tel el Eisa where 15th Panzer's battlegroup put in a successful counter-attack during the evening; the feature finally fell into Australian hands in the early hours of 11 July.

Auchinleck had introduced a new tactic in this phase: as well as making the most economical use of his forces, he was also, as he later described to Roger Parkinson, ascertaining the locations of Italian formations and hitting them as hard as possible; as Italian morale was 'obviously deteriorating' such a policy of attrition aimed at them specifically lowered morale even more and thus reduced overall Axis strength.[8] The tactic worked: Rommel hurriedly moved German troops north to bolster the Italians on 11-12 July.

Auchinleck and his Deputy Chief of General Staff, Major-General Eric Dorman-Smith, noted Rommel's reaction and set in motion plans for a further attack on Italian troops to the south: this attack would focus on Pavia and Brescia Divisions with the aim of breaking through the Axis centre and destroying their forces east of the El Alamein-Abu Dweis track and north of Ruweisat Ridge. The attack was to be launched on 15 July by 5 Indian Brigade and the New Zealanders but, in the meantime, Rommel made two further efforts against the South Africans in the El Alamein box. On the afternoon of the 13th he attacked the box during a sandstorm: he was beaten off by doughty South African resistance, as was an attack on the 14th.

At 4.30am on 15 July the New Zealanders and Indians moved forward in their attack on Pavia and Brescia Divisions. Progress was good at first as Brescia broke but the attack faltered as the day wore on: lack of artillery support and armoured back-up contributed to this; the lessons of infantry/armour co-operation had still to be absorbed by the British armoured units.* The attack, temporarily, gave Eighth Army possession of the entire Ruweisat Ridge before 4 and 5 New Zealand Brigades were overrun; the New Zealanders and Indians had created heavy loss in the Italian ranks before being assaulted by battlegroups from 15th and 21st Panzer Divisions. Fighting raged for three more days and cost the New Zealand division over 1,400 casualties; 4 Brigade would not see action again in North Africa. Ruweisat's western end had been retaken by the Axis but, on 17 July, a company of 4/6th Rajputana Rifles of 5 Indian Brigade, moved forward into position less than a mile west of Point 64 to be followed, next day, by 2nd West Yorkshires, the remnants of 9 Indian Brigade, who, supported by a troop of 1st Light AA Regiment, a battery of 149th Anti-tank Regiment and a machine-gun company of 6th Rajputana Rifles, recaptured the feature and then repulsed a counter-attack that included ten tanks.

In these battles, two Italian divisions had been removed from the Axis order of battle and the enemy line had been broken at Deir el Shein where the attacking troops had penetrated the box, overrunning German flak batteries and forcing Rommel to bring down 21st Panzer from Alamein, thus abandoning its attack there. And the New Zealanders had earned two Victoria Crosses, one of which was unique: Captain Charles Hazlitt Upham of the 20th Battalion (The Canterbury Regiment) had already won the VC in Crete a year before and now gained a Bar to his decoration; his was the only double award of the Cross in the Second World War:

> On 14/15 July 1942 at El Ruweisat Ridge . . . Captain Upham, in spite of being twice wounded, insisted on remaining with his men. Just before dawn he led his company in a determined attack, capturing the objective after fierce fighting; he himself destroyed a German tank and several guns and vehicles with hand grenades. Although his arm had been broken by a machine-gun bullet, he continued to dominate the situation and when at last, weak from loss of blood, he had his wounds dressed, he immediately returned to his men, remaining with them until he was again severely wounded and unable to move.[10]

The other New Zealander to win the VC in this operation was Sergeant Keith Elliott of 22nd Battalion who won his Cross on 15 July. Sergeant

---

* Auchinleck had established a higher-war course at Sarafand to train officers likely to become divisional commanders as part of his efforts to improve the effectiveness of leadership and training and to bring about closer co-operation on the battlefield. The Staff College at Haifa had been expanded and an RAF element added to ensure closer inter-service co-operation. All tactical and weapon training schools in ME Command were ordered 'to ensure that a uniform doctrine, which took account of the characteristics of all three arms [artillery, armour and infantry] and was attuned to modern conditions, was taught under a single direction'.[9]

Elliott had been leading his platoon in an attack against heavy and sustained machine-gun and mortar fire when he was wounded in the chest. However

> he carried on and led seven men in a bayonet charge which resulted in the capture of four enemy machine-gun posts and an anti-tank gun, killing a number of the enemy and taking fifty prisoners. Although badly wounded in four places Sergeant Elliott refused to leave his platoon until he had reformed them and handed over his prisoners, who by then amounted to 130.[11]

(After the war this outstandingly brave soldier chose to enter the Church and was ordained as a clergyman.)

Auchinleck now planned another attack against the Italians, targeting Italian troops at Deir el Shein. This attack went in on the night of 20/21 July after a 200-gun bombardment of the enemy positions. Although 161 Indian Brigade and 23 Armoured Brigade failed to obtain lodgements in the Italian-held sector, 6 New Zealand Brigade reached the El Mreir depression to the south where they came under attack from German armour on the 21st and suffered heavy casualties due to lack of armour support. On the 21st also, 23 Armoured Brigade renewed its advance but lost many tanks when they blundered into a minefield and were picked off by Axis gunners; others were knocked out as a result of 21st Panzer Division counter-attacks. In all ninety-three British tanks were lost that day as well as 2,000 infantrymen.

In further fighting on 22 July at Tel el Eisa, Australia gained its first Victoria Cross of the Desert War. Private Arthur Stanley Gurney of 2/48th Battalion (South Australia), Australian Imperial Force earned a posthumous VC when his company was held up by intensive machine-gun fire which caused heavy casualties including all the officers. Gurney, a 33-year old soldier

> realizing the seriousness of the situation, charged the nearest machine-gun post, silencing the guns and bayoneting three of the crew. He bayoneted two more at a second post, and was then knocked down by a grenade but picked himself up and charged a third post. Nothing more was seen of him until later, when his body was found by his comrades, whose advance he had made possible.[12]

Auchinleck continued to believe in Eighth Army's capacity to produce the effort that would lead to a breakthrough. Rommel was, however, exhausted and showing signs of pessimism. In a letter to his wife on 17 July he had written:

Things are going bad for me at the moment. The enemy is using his superiority, especially in infantry, to destroy the Italian formations one by one, and the German formations are much too weak to stand alone.[13]

The following day he was even more gloomy about his prospects:

Yesterday was a particularly hard and critical day. We pulled through again, but it can't go on like this for long, otherwise the front will crack.[14]

But, although Rommel was concerned, the front was not going to crack immediately. Auchinleck was determined to keep the pressure on the Axis and issued a Special Order of the Day to Eighth Army on 25 July congratulating his soldiers on having wrenched the initiative from the enemy and exhorting them not to slacken but to stick to it so that the Axis army would be broken. This order preceded Operation MANHOOD, Eighth Army's final attempt to smash Rommel's army in the first battle of El Alamein.

MANHOOD, launched on 26 July, aimed to disrupt and disorganise the enemy army to the point of destruction. Plans for the operation included extensive deception and the use of a sonic unit to simulate tank movement in XIII Corps' area: that Corps was to make a feint in the south, to draw enemy forces from the north, while the true attack was launched by XXX Corps in the northern part of the line to seize Miteiriya Ridge. But a time difference of only ninety minutes between the diversionary attack and the real attack allowed very little time for the enemy to react and move forces.

The main attack was to be carried out by troops of 9th Australian Division and 69 Brigade of 50th Division with armour support from 2 Armoured Brigade and 4 Light Armoured Brigade; the latter, with light tanks, armoured cars and motorised infantry, was intended to come round the enemy rear and cause chaos there. South African sappers were to provide gaps in the minefields. Herein lay a problem for there were two parties of sappers, one each from 1 and 2 South African Brigades:

For reasons that remain obscure, the two groups were instructed to begin their work from opposite ends of the proposed gap, which meant that if they were unable to finish there would be not one but two gaps, and these might well be two gaps that were too small rather than one that might be adequate had they worked out from the centre, and it was this that led to confusion.[15]

This was not the sole source of confusion: there was unhappiness with the artillery fireplan, some elements of which were cancelled as 69 Brigade's commander considered that they posed too great a risk to the South

Africans covering his men. In addition, both attacking infantry formations were to advance from widely separated start lines and on differing axes of advance, with ninety degrees between them. As a result no mutual support would be possible until both objectives had been reached: success in Operation MANHOOD depended, therefore, on the Australians and 69 Brigade gaining initial success. After that, the role of the armour was crucial: 2 Armoured Brigade had to be through the gap in the minefields in time to give support against an enemy dawn counter-attack.

The Australians of 2/28th Battalion reached their objective although they had suffered casualties from mines and more than a dozen ammunition and stores trucks had been shot up by a German 50mm anti-tank gun. With the Australians holding a precarious salient they needed 69 Brigade and the armour to move up quickly to secure their positions. But that brigade's leading units, a composite battalion of Durham Light Infantry and 5th East Yorks, went astray in the minefield gap and then discovered the South African sappers still at work.

The advance became disorganised with the East Yorks overtaking the DLI: the confusion that already prevailed continued throughout the day. For the isolated Australians, confusion became disaster as a German counter-attack hit them. Valentines of 50 RTR, on stand by in case 2/28th needed them, were ordered forward but ran into a ring of anti-tank guns as they crossed a ridge north of the infantry. Twenty-two tanks were knocked out by the enemy gunners; the rest of the regiment withdrew. After 10 o'clock that morning the Australians were being attacked by tanks from three sides. The CO radioed his brigade HQ that he had no option but to surrender. Last-ditch resistance at 2/28th Battalion HQ had included a Bren gunner dashing out to fire his machine-gun at approaching panzers.

By noon a similar fate had overtaken 69 Brigade. Isolated in their forward positions, with no armour support – 6 RTR had been stopped by heavy anti-tank gun fire after passing through the minefield gap at 11am – the Northumbrians were attacked by 90th Light and then by tanks and armoured cars that faced nothing more lethal than machine-gun fire.

The tanks of 6 RTR, still being held back by the anti-tank gunners, were then attacked by eleven panzers. A static tank battle lasted the rest of the day. At 3pm an order to retire at dusk was issued to the British tanks who halted another German attack just before they withdrew. In the course of the fighting 6 RTR had lost three Grants from its complement of forty-one tanks. But the battle had ended in another rebuff for Eighth Army: according to Rommel he took 1,000 prisoners and had knocked out thirty-two tanks; he was now confident that he could continue holding the front.

For Auchinleck, this was the moment when he decided to move to the defensive. Once again Eighth Army had shown itself defective in the proper co-ordination of infantry and armour. That weakness, which the

Auk had identified in January 1942, had cost the British success on more than one occasion at Alamein. Now they would have to fight against an enemy who was regaining his confidence and his poise although, in those closing days of July, that enemy had come close to withdrawing to the Egyptian frontier. In addition, Eighth Army's soldiers were simply exhausted, having been under constant strain since late-May. On occasions the black humour of the front-line soldier appears even in official records as on 18 July when the war diary of 9th Lancers notes that 'for once we had sausages instead of AP shot for breakfast'.[16] However, the same diarist wrote five days later that:

> It is apparent that the length of time which the regiment has now been in the desert (seven months), combined with the constant battles and lack of sleep, is having its effect: most of us are at the extreme limit and it is getting hard to even think clearly. Yesterday three men – all normal, stout-hearted men – went temporarily out of their minds and others were showing the same signs of mental and physical strain.[17]

There are so few references in such documents to the fatigue endured by the troops that 'it is a factor which is easily forgotten'.[18]

But Auchinleck and the redoubtable Dorman-Smith were preparing for the future offensive. The latter proposed a re-organisation, approved by his commander, in which armour and infantry would always fight under one commander: training would be improved, tank strengths increased, transport and ammunition shortages made good and positions strengthened from Alamein southwards. Although Eighth Army would be prepared to fight a defensive battle in the El Alamein-Hamman area, inducing the enemy to strike prematurely in mid-August, it was to make itself ready to renew the offensive. Dorman-Smith's assessment was that, reinforced by two armoured and two infantry divisions, Eighth Army would be ready to attack the enemy in late September and break through the Axis positions around El Alamein. It was a remarkably accurate forecast of events, although the breakthrough at El Alamein would take place a month later than predicted. By then, however, both the Auk and Dorman-Smith would be gone, falsely accused of being defeatists. For all its travails and its problems, Eighth Army still held the initiative.

In London, Brooke had misread the situation in Egypt. Believing matters were not improving, he resolved to travel to the Middle East to see events at first hand. Seeking Churchill's approval, he was dismayed when the prime minister decided to accompany him. The pair left for Egypt on Sunday 2 August, arriving there just after dawn on the Monday.

Auchinleck gave Churchill a detailed explanation of the prevailing military situation that afternoon. Brooke had already had a meeting with General Corbett, Chief of General Staff in Cairo, while Churchill had talked with Field Marshal Smuts who had flown in from Pretoria. That evening Churchill suggested to Brooke that Strafer Gott should take command of Eighth Army, a suggestion with which the CIGS was not happy as he believed Gott to be tired. The prime minister also suggested that Brooke himself might take over but Brooke pushed his own choice: Montgomery.

Matters were confused somewhat when Churchill had a meeting with Corbett, at the latter's request, and discovered that Auchinleck favoured Corbett taking command of Eighth Army. This had been suggested by Auchinleck in signals to Brooke but the CIGS appears not to have informed Churchill. Corbett's candidature was, therefore, short-lived and that of Gott continued to be pressed by the prime minister. Meanwhile Brooke had discussed with Auchinleck the possibility of Montgomery taking over Eighth Army and was surprised when Auchinleck accepted this idea.

> [Brooke] had absolute faith in Montgomery's tactical ability. He knew that he was self-confident to a fault, thoroughly resilient and ruthless in getting his own way. Eighth Army needed such a man. Brooke was dubious as to whether Auchinleck and Montgomery could work together – and with the Germans at the gates of the Delta the eyes of both Commander-in-Chief and Army Commander would, for the while, be on the Western Desert. Auchinleck, he felt, would try excessively to steer a subordinate – as he clearly, though perhaps necessarily, had done with Ritchie. Montgomery would not take to such treatment.[19]

Next day Brooke visited Eighth Army. Meeting Gott confirmed his belief that the corps commander needed a rest rather than promotion to command an army. However, he was unimpressed by Army HQ, deciding that Auchinleck was too much under the influence of Dorman-Smith, whom Brooke had long distrusted. The CIGS felt that Dorman-Smith's ideas needed objective analysis, of which he did not believe Auchinleck was capable. That visit to Eighth Army HQ sealed the Auk's fate as Commander-in-Chief. Until then, Brooke had not made his mind up about Auchinleck's future: he now decided that the Auk should go. Churchill had also been unimpressed by a visit to Auchinleck's spartan headquarters on Ruweisat Ridge where, he complained, he had been surrounded by 'flies and important military personages' in a 'wire-netted cube'.[20] Auchinleck had made no special preparations for the visit; nor did his refusal to be moved on an early offensive endear him to Churchill.

Further discussion between Churchill and the CIGS brought the suggestion that Brooke himself should succeed Auchinleck, who would be transferred to a new Persia-Iraq command, with Montgomery as Army Commander. Brooke declined even though Smuts also tried to talk him into accepting the command. Finally, Alexander was suggested and the combination of Alexander as CinC with Gott as Eighth Army's commander was signalled to the War Cabinet on 6 August.

As the War Cabinet discussed the proposals on Friday 7 August, two further telegrams were received from the Middle East. The first reported that Gott had been shot down and killed while travelling to Cairo; the second recommended Montgomery to take command of Eighth Army and that he should be sent out as soon as possible by special plane.

Strafer Gott had died when the Bombay aircraft in which he had been travelling was shot down by Luftwaffe Bf109F fighters. With both engines on fire, the pilot managed to land the aircraft on a sand plateau but its brakes were not working and it ran on for several miles during which the German fighters attacked. As the Bombay raced along the ground, the fuselage began blazing, and although the crew and one wounded soldier escaped through a hatch in the cockpit floor, those in the rear of the aircraft, including Gott, were trapped and perished in the inferno

Claude Auchinleck, the man who had outfought the Desert Fox, learned of his dismissal as CinC Middle East not from the prime minister, nor from Brooke, but from a letter written by Churchill and delivered by Colonel Ian Jacob of Churchill's staff. He declined to accept the new appointment offered to him and returned to India where he later played a vital role in the Allied success in south-east Asia. Dorman-Smith was also dismissed and his Army career destroyed on that August day. And so the men who had stopped Rommel and saved Egypt left the desert.

Eighth Army had faced another enemy in the Alamein positions: the omnipresent fly which Winston Churchill had noted on his visit to Army HQ. Flies found their way into nostrils, mouths and eyes and on to food and drink. Although flies had plagued troops throughout the desert campaign the problem seemed to be worse at Alamein:

> Owing to the heat and to the fact that the area occupied by [Eighth Army] was congested with troops, flies bred rapidly and became a serious menace to health. To control the plague of flies No. 1 Fly Control Unit started work in [the] area on 6 August, assisted by 7 Field Hygiene Section.[21]

This unit was formed from 1502 Mauritius Pioneer Company and soldiers from an infantry base depot, the Mauritians representing another of the many nations to be found in Eighth Army. No.1 Fly Control Unit cleaned up areas, particularly those previously occupied by Arabs, to prevent the breeding of flies.

On 9 August General Alexander arrived in Cairo to succeed Auchinleck as CinC from 15 August. Then, on 12 August 1942, Lieutenant-General Bernard Law Montgomery landed in Egypt and arrived at Middle East HQ in Cairo at about 10 o'clock that morning.

NOTES

1. PRO: CAB44/98, p.340
2. Stevens: *Fourth Indian Division*, p.315
3. PRO: CAB44/97, p.11
4. Stevens: p.182
5. Parkinson: *The Auk*, p.208
6. Playfair: *The Mediterranean and the Middle East, vol iii*, p.343
7. Lewin: *Rommel as Military Commander*, p.135
8. Parkinson: op cit, pp.208-209
9. PRO: CAB44/97, p.10
10. *Register of the Victoria Cross*, p.319
11. Smyth: *The Story of the Victoria Cross*, pp.368-369
12. *Register of the Victoria Cross*, p.133
13. Playfair: op cit, p.360
14. ibid
15. Bates: *Dance of War*, p.219
16. PRO: CAB44/98, p.390n
17. ibid
18. ibid
19. Fraser: *Alanbrooke*, p.283
20. Churchill: *The Second World War, vol viii*, p.46
21. PRO: CAB44/99

CHAPTER VI

Monty Arrives: Alam el Halfa and the Planning for El Alamein

The signs of war advance

When Montgomery arrived in Egypt he was not the man who carried Churchill's hopes for victory in North Africa: that distinction fell on the new CinC, General Alexander, who was Churchill's favourite general and in whom the prime minister reposed infinite trust. Alexander, he thought, would take the reins and guide Eighth Army to success. Brooke knew otherwise: that Montgomery would be the man conducting the battles; but in Alexander and Montgomery the War Cabinet had selected an ideal team as Alexander would certainly never try to interfere with his subordinate's operations and would support him all the way.

Montgomery met with Auchinleck on his first day in Egypt and the account of that meeting in Montgomery's subsequent memoirs makes clear the animosity which existed between the pair. Auchinleck gave Montgomery a briefing on the situation in Egypt and on his plan of operations. According to Montgomery this was

> based on the fact that at all costs the Eighth Army was to be preserved 'in being' and must not be destroyed in battle. If Rommel attacked in strength, as was expected soon, the Eighth Army would fall back on the Delta; if Cairo and the Delta could not be held, the army would retreat southwards up the Nile, and another possibility was a withdrawal to Palestine. Plans were being made to move the Eighth Army H.Q. back up the Nile.[1]

It was hardly an accurate reflection of the situation. Auchinleck was planning to fight Rommel, as he had already done, whenever the German chose to attack again. There was no intention of pulling Eighth Army back from engagement with Panzer Armee Afrika, but contingency plans to deal with a possible Axis breakthrough did exist which Montgomery later claimed to have scrapped. It is interesting, therefore, to note that such plans were still in place under Montgomery: 51st (Highland) Division, which arrived in Egypt after he became Army Commander, was deployed as South Delta Force to protect Cairo in the event of an Axis attack around the right flank of Eighth Army.[2]

Nor was this the only formation involved in such duties. HQ Middle East was aware that the danger

remained of penetration or airborne attack to sabotage and cause panic. GOC, BTE (Lt-Gen R G W H Stone) arranged to strengthen BARFORCE about Faiyum and to carry out daily aircraft and air recce of approaches to Delta from SW. From 25 Aug onwards the defences of the Delta were fully manned and when the Egyptian Government decided that Egyptian Army units would not oppose enemy raiders, a number of guards on VPs* in the Delta were taken over by British troops, who relieved Egyptian personnel of their duties.[3]

That such precautions were necessary was demonstrated on 4 September when a

party of 105 Provost Company assisted by an Arab officer and 5 men of No.1 Coy Libyan Arab Force captured a party [an officer and 13 men] of 34th Bn San Marco Marines south of the Bahig-Alexandria road. An NCO [was] also captured near K39 on Alexandria-Mersa Matruh road.[4]

The Italian commandos had intended to destroy the water pipeline and the railway near the coast. They managed to do some damage but this had been repaired by noon that same day.

Montgomery also decided that morale in Eighth Army needed improving:

From what I had learnt the troops had their tails down and there was no confidence in the higher command. This would have to be put right at once, but until I had actually got the feel of things myself I could not decide how to set about it.[5]

That Montgomery in his *Memoirs* was being unfair to Auchinleck was shown when his publishers inserted a note at the front of further editions of his book, with Montgomery's agreement, to the effect that the latter accepted that Auchinleck had successfully halted Rommel's advance at El Alamein in July 1942 and that it was Auchinleck's intention, when Eighth Army had rested and been re-organised, to launch an offensive from the El Alamein line.

Montgomery was later to claim that he was solely responsible for creating a *corps de chasse*, as he described it, to provide Eighth Army with

* Vulnerable, or Vital, Points.

its equivalent of the Afrika Korps. This new corps would be formed from units already in the Middle East, and its armoured divisions equipped with the 300 Sherman tanks due to arrive from the United States on 3 September, with Major General (later Field Marshal Lord) John Harding in command. Again it was not a new idea but one that had been implemented under Auchinleck. Dorman-Smith's *Appreciation of the situation in the Western Desert*, dated 27 July 1942 included a plan for a reserve mobile corps under Eighth Army command. Monty's reserve corps, actually X Corps returned to Eighth Army's order of battle, was to consist of 1st, 8th and 10th Armoured Divisions, each of one armoured brigade, an infantry brigade and divisional troops, plus 2nd New Zealand Division of two infantry brigades and an armoured brigade.

In assessing Eighth Army's morale, Montgomery was right in one respect: soldiers on the ground had little confidence in the higher command. This was something he intended to put right by building the Army's confidence in himself as its commander. Realising that Rommel was better known to the average British soldier than was any British general, he resolved to change that situation. His chosen method was simple: he undertook to visit as many units as possible and talk to the soldiers. When doing so, he often chose to stand on a platform, or the bonnet of a car, and tell the soldiers to gather around; he would frequently tell them to remove their headgear thus emphasising the air of informality. Then he would outline his plans and impress upon them the importance of their own part in those plans. In so doing he quickly captured the hearts of his soldiers to whom he became affectionately known as Monty.

Even in the more formal setting of a parade, Montgomery adopted a different attitude from most senior officers, being less concerned with the attention given to polishing boots than with the way in which the soldier bore himself. He would look into a man's eyes with an intensity that was almost unnerving but which left men with the strong impression that this little general meant business, knew what he was doing and could be trusted.

Montgomery's image-building did not end there. He chose to make himself distinctive by adopting a style of headdress radically different from that normally worn by a general officer. At first his choice was an Australian bush hat, liberally decorated with cap badges from various units under his command, which he wore at the time of the Battle of Alam el Halfa. However, the bush hat proved an awkward item to wear, and perhaps even a little bit too theatrical, and so Monty eventually settled for a much simpler piece of headgear, the black beret of The Royal Tank Regiment. On this he retained the regimental badge but added his own general's badge. This proved to be one of the outstanding public relations exercises of the war. Among the most popular images of the conflict for the British public was that of the general with the black beret and two badges. Montgomery later told the King that his headgear was worth at least a corps in morale terms.

One of Montgomery's senior staff wrote that Monty became the dynamo of Eighth Army. It is an apt description as its new commander imbued his Army with his own great sense of purpose and confidence, much like a powerful electric charge.

Montgomery began planning for an offensive but, at the same time, had to consider the probability of another Axis attack. This had been expected by Auchinleck and Dorman-Smith and alluded to in the latter's *Appreciation of the situation in the Western Desert* on 27 July: Dorman-Smith suggested that an enemy attack was unlikely before the end of August for only then would Rommel have any hope of success.

This proved an accurate assessment: Rommel was preparing an attack which was due to be launched in the closing days of August. Eighth Army was alerted in late August that

> Evidence [is] accumulating that enemy intend to attack within 2/3 days South of the New Zealanders by the open South flank. To meet this 8 Army is standing to as from 2400 24 August. From this day everyone will be constantly ready. As it is confidently expected the attack will only take place by night, by day units may relax somewhat unless concentrations are seen by recce.[6]

Rommel's armour strength had been rebuilt and Afrika Korps now had 200 tanks, of which twenty-six were Panzer Mark IVs fitted with a new, long-barrelled, 75mm gun. He had four armoured divisions from a total force of seven Italian and four German divisions. However, his fuel situation was critical: promises of additional fuel were not being honoured and time was running out. True to form, the Desert Fox gambled on attacking with a very low margin of fuel stocks in the hope of knocking out Eighth Army and punching his way through to the Delta. In reality, had he beaten Eighth Army on the El Alamein line, he would have met extremely powerful opposition in the Delta and, with his chronic fuel state, it is unlikely that he could have maintained any momentum.

Montgomery was sitting at El Alamein with a secure base behind, thanks to the efforts of his predecessors, although he never gave them credit, and he could afford to devote his attention to Rommel's planned attack. Eighth Army was being strengthened by the arrival of new equipment and fresh personnel: the first 6-pounder-armed Crusaders were due to arrive on 25 August; troopships disembarked thousands of troops to swell the Army's ranks. The artillery strength was increased and there were even plans to adapt the 3.7-inch HAA gun to a field role: the

Brigadier, AA stated that 'special scotches [were] being made so that 3.7s could fire from their wheels against ground targets'.[7]

Monty knew about Rommel's plans: like all senior Allied commanders, he had access to Ultra through which he was almost able to read Rommel's mind. The famous story of Monty keeping a photograph of Rommel in his caravan and saying that he was thus able to see what his adversary was thinking was a cover for the 'most secret' information to which he was privy. He now knew that Rommel was planning an attack that could be expected about the time of the August full moon.

Montgomery inherited Auchinleck's plans for meeting a German attack but decided to modify them in some respects. Since enemy deployments, and laying of minefields in the northern sector of the line, seemed to indicate an attack in the south, Monty decided to bolster his forces there. Identifying the Alam el Halfa ridge as crucial, he had the newly-arrived 44th (Home Counties) Division moved up almost immediately to relieve 21 Indian Brigade there; 132 Brigade of 44th Division was, however, placed under New Zealand command to complete their defences on Bare Ridge. Additional artillery and armour was brought up to the line: 10th Armoured Division and 8 Armoured Brigade deployed in the Alam el Halfa area.

Alam el Halfa ridge was important since it could hold the key to a battle in that area:

> If the Germans could bypass it quickly to the east, then they would have a clear run to the places on which they intended to meet and destroy the British armour. If Montgomery could hold Rommel from the Ridge then the battle was his, for the German commander would not dare to move eastwards towards the Nile so long as the undefeated Eighth Army was in a position to sever his lines of communication.[8]

Montgomery had also appointed a new commander to XIII Corps: Lieutenant General Brian Horrocks; Ramsden continued to command XXX Corps.

To mislead Rommel, deception plans were implemented by 25 August; it was hoped that, by giving the impression of great British strength in the southern sector, through dummy armoured and infantry formations, the enemy might even postpone his planned attack. Other measures included the deliberate loss of a 'going' map in the forward area which showed an area of quite soft sand south of Alam el Halfa as good going while the real good going was shown as bad. However, much of this effort was in vain; there is no evidence that Rommel ever became aware of the fake formations or of the map, although when the full moon came on the 26th and then began to wane without an attack, the deception experts started to believe that they had succeeded. Then, on the night of 30 August,

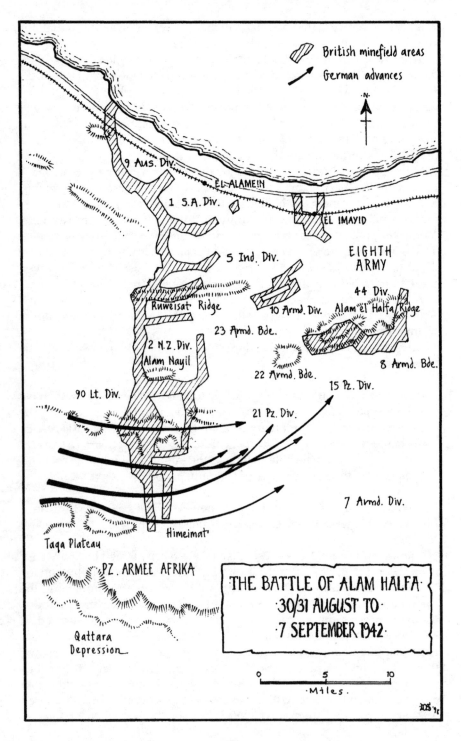

British minefield areas

German advances

·N·

9 Aus. Div.

EL ALAMEIN

1 S.A. Div.

EL IMAYID

5 Ind. Div.

EIGHTH
ARMY

44 Div.

Ruweisat Ridge

10 Armd. Div.

Alam El Halfa Ridge

23 Armd. Bde.

2 N.Z. Div.
Alam Nayil

22 Armd. Bde.

8 Armd. Bde.

90 Lt. Div.

15 Pz. Div.

21 Pz. Div.

7 Armd. Div.

Himeimat

Taqa Plateau

PZ. ARMEE AFRIKA

THE BATTLE OF ALAM HALFA·
·30/31 AUGUST TO·
·7 SEPTEMBER 1942·

Qattara
Depression

0   5   10

·Miles·

Panzer Armee Afrika began to move towards the British southern sector.

Rommel's plan was a rerun of that which had brought him success at Gazala. During the night of 30/31 August, there would be a rapid thrust round what was believed to be Eighth Army's southern flank, north of Himeimat, to place Afrika Korps' 15th and 21st Panzer Divisions south of Alam el Halfa and at the rear of Eighth Army's position. To Afrika Korps' right was a group created from all the Axis reconnaissance units while on the left were the Italian Ariete and Littorio Armoured Divisions. If all went to plan, the attacking forces would be in position, facing north, by 3.30am on the 31st; at first light Afrika Korps would attack northwards to the coast with the left-flank units hitting the rear of British positions about Ruweisat Ridge. Thus Eighth Army would be cut off from supply and annihilated; the British armour would be defeated and Rommel's formations would race for Alexandria and Cairo and then pursue the fleeing British up the Nile valley. That was the plan. And Montgomery was aware of it.

The British commander had prepared well to meet the expected attack. Although the Axis advance was slower than anticipated due to the southern minefields being stronger than expected, and thus taking longer to clear, and Afrika Korps and the Italian armour struck northwards earlier than planned, west of Alam el Halfa, Monty was not caught wrong-footed. He adjusted his armour positions and reinforced that armour so that he had 500 tanks in three brigades deployed between Bare Ridge and Alam el Halfa. The armour was to fight from static positions, with the tanks acting effectively as anti-tank guns. Montgomery was determined not to allow Rommel a battle of movement. In this respect the topography of the area helped the British.

Rommel failed to obtain even local surprise. German supply columns moving up to Gebel Kalakh were bombed by the Royal Air Force before the first ground clash and the minefields proved a greater obstacle than expected: at the time when Afrika Korps' panzers were scheduled to be lined up facing north from Alam el Halfa to Bare Ridge, ready and refuelled for the attack to the coast, they had still to pass through the first minefield.

Even before that, the first contact had occurred on the ground with anti-tank guns of 2nd Battalion, The Rifle Brigade near Deir el Munassib, south of Bare Ridge, and guns of F Battery, RHA driving back an attack, the first of a series that made Axis intentions clear to the defenders.

By 8 o'clock, Rommel knew that his plan had faltered and that his forces were suffering heavy air attack. General Nehring, commanding Afrika Korps, had been wounded in an air attack while General von Bismarck, 21st Panzer's commander, had been killed by a mine. Rommel considered calling off the attack but decided to let its future depend on the progress of Afrika Korps, now under command of Colonel Bayerlein, its chief of staff. However, instead of flanking east of Alam el Halfa, Bayerlein's command would now have that feature as its objective.

While a gloomy picture was being presented to Rommel, his counterpart was receiving much pleasanter reports. Apart from an attack by the Ramcke Parachute Brigade on Ruweisat, in which 2nd West Yorks lost a company, and some other actions involving Australians, South Africans and New Zealanders, XXX Corps had had a relatively peaceful night; any setbacks were made good at dawn. On XIII Corps' front there had been three enemy thrusts: north of Himeimat, at Munassib and south of the New Zealanders. What was not immediately clear was the enemy strength; one panzer division and 90th Light were certainly involved and, possibly, XX Corps. The picture became clearer as events unfolded.

Afrika Korps' attack from Himeimat was the main effort that morning, involving some 100 tanks. With the minefields behind and the Reconnaissance Group pushing 4 Light Armoured Brigade off the escarpment to the south, the panzers' eastward advance caused concern in 7 Motor Brigade and especially in 10th Hussars even though it did not create much pressure on that brigade's front. The brigade commander, Brigadier Bosvile, ordered his units back to the area of his reserve battalion, 7th Rifle Brigade; this manoeuvre had been completed by about 9.30am. At much the same time, Afrika Korps was about seven miles east of Himeimat, having reached the final minefield in 4 Light Armoured Brigade's area.

Horrocks quickly countermanded the order for 7 Motor Brigade to withdraw, making it clear that 7th Armoured Division should hold the line of the final minefield, which had already been abandoned. To redress the situation, 10th Hussars were sent forward again and deployed in the Muhafid depression north-east of Munassib; 23 Armoured Brigade was transferred to XIII Corps from XXX Corps, leaving a squadron from each regiment with the latter corps, and took up positions between the New Zealanders and 22 Armoured Brigade.

By noon Rommel's attack had made little progress. There had been constant air attacks although a sandstorm, which had begun to blow up from the south about thirty minutes earlier, grounded British aircraft for a time and added to an already confused situation.

After a refuelling stop, Afrika Korps moved off again at one o'clock, with the storm at its worst, in a north-easterly direction which led to contact with 3rd County of London Yeomanry and 1st King's Royal Rifle Corps. In a brief battle a number of Grants were knocked out but British anti-tank gunners also accounted for several German tanks. With elements of 4 Light Armoured and 7 Motor Brigades engaged against Afrika Korps and the sandstorm still blowing, there was still confusion on the battlefield and 10th Hussars, concerned that they might be cut off, sought permission to withdraw. After conflicting orders had been received the regiment was eventually pushed back against the Alam el Halfa minefields. It was by now late in the afternoon and 22 Armoured Brigade, which had been stood to since before dawn, was about to join the fray.

The brigade's positions were around Point 102, west of Alam el Halfa, although elements had been ordered south in the morning to a ridge some three miles distant. From there, during the afternoon, Brigadier Roberts, commanding 22 Armoured, had ordered patrols from 4th CLY and 2nd Gloucestershire Hussars to probe farther south to obtain information on enemy movements. Those patrols were soon in action against German tanks but quickly withdrew to send back the information that over 100 enemy tanks were moving south of 22 Armoured Brigade. Not long after this incident, 120 enemy tanks, Mark IIIs with some of the new Mark IVs, were spotted approaching a line of telegraph poles which ran at an angle across the front of 22 Armoured Brigade's positions and about 1,000 yards forward of those positions. The tanks, believed to be 21st Panzer Division, stopped as they reached the poles, where thirty tanks turned to the east. Soon afterwards the remainder moved off northwards but then made an eastward turn which would take them across the front of the County of London Yeomanry's positions. However, the panzers were out of effective range of the Yeomanry's guns and apparently unaware of 22 Armoured Brigade's presence. Since the sandstorm was still blowing, although beginning to subside, this was understandable but the axis of advance of the German tanks would take them straight for 44th Division's positions at Alam el Halfa.

Roberts opted to use a German tactic against the panzers, ordering 5 RTR and the CLY to show themselves and prepare to take on the enemy from the flank should their eastward movement continue. Just after 6pm Roberts' armour carried out the order and the Germans, finally aware of the presence of British tanks, shook themselves into a fighting formation and turned towards the tanks of the CLY:

> The dust was subsiding and visibility improving. There was only an hour's daylight left, and the light was in favour of our gunners, being slightly behind them and in the faces of the enemy. The German ... right came directly against the northern Grant squadron of the Yeomanry, A Squadron, while their left came straight towards B Company of the 1st Rifle Brigade. When the leading tanks were less than 1,000 yards from them, the Yeomanry opened up. The Germans halted and fired back, their guns being concentrated on A Squadron. In a short time all 12 of their tanks were knocked out ... [9]

The Grants suffered from a basic design fault: the sponson-mounted main armament was on the side of the hull which made it virtually impossible for the tank to take a hull-down position. Since the Grant was fuelled by high-octane petrol it was also liable to explode or rapidly combust. Major Cameron, A Squadron's leader, noted how tank after tank in his squadron, including his own, went up in flames or was otherwise put out of action, while 'German tanks seldom go on fire'.[10] However, B Squadron had also engaged the enemy; their attention made the Germans pull back.

The loss of A Squadron, CLY opened a gap in 22 Armoured's position which Roberts quickly strove to plug by ordering the Royal Scots Greys to move over the crest of Point 102 and deploy on the right of the Yeomanry. As the Greys began their move another German advance began. The panzers moved more slowly this time, making for the gap in the British positions. The Rifle Brigade's anti-tank guns opened fire at 300 yards, claiming a number of victims, but, although the advance was checked for a time, the Germans moved forward again. With the Greys still to arrive, Roberts exhorted their CO to get out the whips. Artillery engaged the advancing panzers which came inexorably onwards. Then, at last, the Greys came over the crest and charged downhill for the panzers. Light was fading as they clashed with the Germans, bringing the latters' advance in the centre to an end.

On the left flank, those thirty tanks which had detached themselves from the main body had been advancing towards 133 Brigade where they were engaged over open sights with armour-piercing shot by B Battery, 1st Royal Horse Artillery. Crusader tanks from the CLY were sent to support 133 Brigade as soon as the Greys had closed the gap in 22 Armoured Brigade's front. The Germans withdrew as darkness fell, although several of their tanks remained close to 133 Brigade throughout the night. British casualties had been remarkably light: although the CLY had lost twelve Grants and a Crusader, only one man had been killed with fifteen wounded; other units in 22 Armoured Brigade had been almost unscathed with 1st Rifle Brigade being the only other to suffer fatalities, of which there were two. The brigade claimed almost seventy enemy tanks destroyed but actual German losses for the entire day came to just over twenty.

The short battle at Point 102, the major action of the latter part of the day, marked the turning point of the Battle of Alam el Halfa. That night the German and Italian tanks went into leaguer and British aircraft and artillery bombarded enemy positions; the Reconnaissance Group was hit particularly hard by the bombers.

There was little action on 1 September. Montgomery, seeing that the possibility of an enemy outflanking move around Alam el Halfa had virtually disappeared, concentrated his three armoured brigades between the New Zealanders and 44th Division. Although 21st Panzer attempted to move round Roberts' left flank soon after daybreak, their move was stopped by Roberts' tanks and threatened on their right flank by 8 Armoured Brigade, two regiments of which, the Sherwood Rangers and Staffordshire Yeomanry, were in action for the first time since mechanisation. These regiments, plus 3 RTR, took the pressure off 22 Armoured Brigade and moved forward south of the minefield in front of 44th Division. As they were to be ready to counter-attack the enemy's northern flank in the event of a thrust around Alam el Halfa, the brigade commander, Custance, was ordered not to become too deeply involved in action or to take needless casualties. He did, however, advance when heavy artillery bombardment forced enemy tanks to withdraw.

The tank losses of the day indicate how light the fighting was: Afrika Korps lost thirteen tanks, three less than 8 Armoured Brigade. The greatest activity was in the air with RAF aircraft harassing enemy communications and supplies; seven officers were killed when Afrika Korps HQ was bombed. Although Rommel again considered abandoning his offensive he deferred a decision until the morning of the 2nd, by which time his command had suffered another night of heavy aerial bombardment, when the attempted breakthrough was finally called off. As his main reason for abandoning what turned out to be his final offensive in the Western Desert, Rommel quoted the shortage of fuel and specifically the failure to keep him supplied with sufficient fuel: half the petrol promised by 3 September had already been lost when the tankers carrying it had been sunk en route to Libya. At 10.30pm (German time) on the night of 2 September he signalled to Oberkommando des Heeres:

> The non-arrival of the petrol, oil and lubricants requested, which was the condition laid down for the successful carrying out even of limited operations, forbids a continuation of the attack.[11]

There was little ground activity that day, although air activity continued at a high level, as Rommel's attacking forces began to pull back. By the morning of the 3rd, Axis troops were in positions from below the New Zealand Division eastward to Muhafid and then around Ragil and thus in a salient south of Alam el Halfa. Montgomery was determined to cut them off and proposed mounting the only setpiece infantry attack of the battle with the New Zealand Division, including the British 132 Brigade, thrusting south towards the Munassib Depression to seal the British minefields behind Rommel's men and trap the erstwhile attackers in front of Alam el Halfa ridge.

Throughout 3 September Montgomery ordered that only patrols would operate from the British battle positions as Horrocks made ready for the attack, Operation BERESFORD, which was to be launched that night; operations by 7th Armoured Division were to follow next morning. In

BERESFORD, 5 New Zealand Brigade was to attack on the east flank with 132 Brigade on the west; 6 NZ Brigade was to mount a diversionary attack on 132 Brigade's right. The Division was to attack on a 5,000-yard front to a depth of 6,000 yards and take the enemy positions on the northern edge of Munassib. But the attack did not go according to plan.

The diversion alerted the German defenders who were ready when two battalions of Queen's Own Royal West Kents went in. The West Kents' attacks were to have been without artillery support and therefore 'silent'; but this was not the case and when the delayed attack finally went in after midnight it was brightly lit up by blazing lorries and by flares dropped by Luftwaffe aircraft. Neither battalion, the 4th on the left nor the 5th on the right, could make serious inroads into the Munassib defences. The brigade commander, Robertson, was wounded and communications broke down. It was left to the brigade major to re-organise 132 Brigade some 1,000 yards short of their intended objectives: 4th West Kents had suffered 250 casualties while the 5th also lost heavily; Brigade casualties totalled 700.

Brigadier Kippenberger's 5 NZ Brigade had been more successful but the Maori Battalion, on the right, had veered westwards while 21st Battalion, on the left, had moved to the east. A gap was thus created in the centre into which Valentine tanks of 50 RTR, believing they were following lamps to mark a way forward, drove too far and came to grief on mines and from anti-tank guns; twelve tanks were lost and the squadron commander was killed. The 'lamps' were really German Verey lights. The attack cost Kippenberger's brigade 124 casualties. In their diversionary attack 6 NZ Brigade lost 159, including their brigade commander, George Clifton, who was captured. Clifton escaped from a latrine that evening but was recaptured some days later by several German officers on a gazelle-hunting expedition.

BERESFORD had failed to achieve its objectives. Rommel continued his withdrawal throughout the next day and put in several counter-attacks against the New Zealanders' new positions, on an exposed forward slope. All that had been gained was under two miles of desert.

Montgomery decided against any further moves to close the gap in the south and Freyberg was ordered back to his original positions. Should the enemy pull back then the British armour was to follow up with patrols. Although there was some further enemy withdrawal, Rommel did not return to his original positions: Panzer Armee had advanced its front slightly to include the British January and February minefields which were now incorporated into the Axis defences; some high ground was also retained by the Germans and Italians from which they could observe the British lines.

Losses in this battle for Alam el Halfa, the second battle of El Alamein, had been fairly evenly balanced. In manpower the Axis had lost some 3,000 men against Eighth Army's 2,000 while losses in tanks were almost equal, under forty in each case. But the battle had been a British success: Rommel had failed in his drive for the Nile while Eighth Army had achieved its objective of holding that thrust. For Eighth Army's morale the success was an important boost as it helped to build up that morale for the long-term objective of smashing Rommel's command when Montgomery was ready. The Eighth Army's new commander had also improved his image throughout the Army; his men began to see him as someone who could be trusted to deliver success. And he had also given himself a hands-on introduction to conducting battle in the desert.

Preparations now began for the new offensive. Alam el Halfa had convinced Montgomery that his Army needed to be retrained: the various arms had to be better able to work together; the distrust between infantry and armour and the friction between infantry and gunners had to be eliminated if the Army was to work as a successful team. Retraining thus became one of Monty's priorities but he was able to build on the work already initiated by Auchinleck. The other priorities were consolidation of the present positions as the start line for the new offensive and re-organising Eighth Army's formations into the order of battle for the offensive:

> I had decided that in building up the Eighth Army . . . I would concentrate on three essentials: leadership, equipment and training. All three were deficient. The equipment situation was well in hand and I knew that Alexander would see that we got all that we needed. Training was receiving urgent attention. I soon realised that although the Eighth Army was composed of magnificent material, it was untrained; it had done much fighting, but little training. We had just won a decisive victory, but it had been a static battle; I was not prepared to launch the troops into an all-out offensive without intensive prior training.[12]

Changes in command were also made. Horrocks had already taken over XIII Corps and 'had proved himself in the Battle of Alam Halfa'[13] and now Montgomery decided to relieve the commanders of X and XXX Corps. Sir Oliver Leese, later to command Eighth Army, succeeded Ramsden in XXX Corps but Alexander overruled Montgomery's desire to replace Lumsden in X Corps although, in his *Memoirs*, the latter suggests that he gave X Corps to Lumsden after long consultation with the CinC. John Harding was brought in from GHQ, Cairo to command 7th Armoured Division while a new artillery commander, Brigadier Sidney Kirkman, was brought out from England for Eighth Army. Many other changes were made until Monty felt that he had the team he needed for what lay ahead.

Training continued as Eighth Army's strength built up and the composition of formations was adjusted. To the two surviving infantry brigades of the New Zealand Division was added 9 Armoured Brigade (3rd Hussars, Royal Wiltshire Yeomanry and Warwickshire Yeomanry) from 10th Armoured Division; 44th Division lost 133 Brigade to X Corps as lorried infantry but gained 151 Brigade, the surviving brigade of 50th Division and 1st Greek Independent Brigade; 7th Armoured Division lost 7 Motor Brigade to 1st Armoured Division. There were, of course, other changes and new formations came into the line: 51st (Highland) Division relieved 44th Division while 4th Indian Division took over from 5th Indian Division. The heavy losses of men and equipment since June were being put right although the manpower shortage was more serious. In order to build up front-line units

> dilution of British military personnel in the rear areas was already in progress. Additional Indian and African Pioneer Battalions arrived during [August] while recruitment of Palestinian manpower continued.[14]

On 3 September the re-equipment programme of Eighth Army was given a considerable boost by the arrival of 300 Sherman tanks from the United States. Destined to become the standard Allied tank in the latter part of the war, the Sherman had a turret-mounted gun superior to any then in British service. By the time Montgomery was ready to open his offensive, Eighth Army's tank strength was over 1,300, of which 1,136 were deployed in the forward area. Artillery strengths were also increased: field artillery rose to 832 guns, medium to fifty-two, and anti-tank to 550 2-pounders and 850 6-pounders. The Desert Air Force was also reinforced and additional US Army Air Force units arrived.[15]

And, for the first time, Eighth Army's order of battle included a majority of British divisions: of Montgomery's eleven divisions when the offensive began, seven were British, 1st, 7th, 8th and 10th Armoured, and 44th, 50th (which was reconstituted) and 51st Infantry, alongside 2nd New Zealand Division, 9th Australian, 4th Indian and 1st South African, all desert veterans.

As with Auchinleck before, Montgomery came under pressure to mount an early offensive. Churchill had been confident that the new team of Alexander and Montgomery would act quickly, but he was informed by Alexander that Montgomery would not be ready until October, whereas Auchinleck had suggested September. Monty justified the further delay by the need to launch the offensive in a full-moon period:

> The minefield problem was such that the troops must be able to see what they were doing. A waning moon was not acceptable since I envisaged a real 'dog-fight' for at least a week before we finally broke

out; a waxing moon was essential. This limited the choice to one definite period each month. Owing to the delay caused to our preparations by Rommel's attack, we could not be ready for the September moon and be sure of success. There must be no more failures.[16]

Montgomery said that he would attack on the night of 23 October as the full moon would be on the 24th. Churchill signalled Alexander that the offensive had to be in September to co-ordinate with Soviet operations and with planned Allied landings on the north-west African coast in November.

Alexander came to see me to discuss the reply to be sent. I said that our preparations could not be completed in time for a September offensive, and an attack then would fail: if we waited until October, I guaranteed complete success. In my view it would be madness to attack in September. Was I to do so? Alexander backed me up whole-heartedly as he always did, and the reply was sent on the lines I wanted. I had told Alexander privately that, in view of my promise to the soldiers, I refused to attack before October; if a September attack was ordered by Whitehall, they would have to get someone else to do it. My stock was rather high after Alam Halfa! We heard no more about a September attack.[17]

First plans for the attack were drafted at the beginning of September as the echoes of the battle of Alam el Halfa faded. Montgomery intended to launch simultaneous assaults on both flanks with XXX Corps (Leese) making the main attack in the north and Horrocks' XIII Corps breaking into the enemy positions in the south. This latter was intended to draw the enemy armour in that direction easing the task of X Corps which was to pass through two corridors created by Leese's corps in the north to position itself astride the enemy's supply routes, forcing a counter-attack and an engagement which would lead to the destruction of the Axis armour.

As the training programme continued, Montgomery became concerned about 'whether the troops would be able to do what was being demanded'.[18] His plan, although simple, was ambitious and he began to feel that Eighth Army, having suffered 80,000 casualties since its formation, had not had enough time to train its replacements and reinforcements. Nor was he convinced that many of the commanders were good at training their men. So it was, on 6 October, that he revised his battle plan to place an emphasis on 'crumbling'.

By 'crumbling', Montgomery meant the detailed destruction of the opposing infantry divisions in their defensive locations by attacks from the flank and the rear. Such operations would entice the enemy armour into heavy counter-attack and to attack the British armour in position:

> I aimed to get my armour beyond the area of the 'crumbling' operations.
> I would then turn the enemy minefields to our advantage by using them
> to prevent the enemy armour from interfering with our operations; this
> would be done by closing the approaches through the minefields with
> our tanks, and we would then be able to proceed relentlessly with our
> plans.[19]

The plan hinged on XXX Corps successfully breaking in to the Axis lines
and creating corridors for X Corps' armour. So that the leading armoured
brigades would move through the corridors as quickly as possible, Monty
intended to push them into those corridors immediately behind XXX
Corps' leading infantry divisions. That mean committing the first
armoured formations before he knew whether the corridors were clear.
Should the corridors not be clear on the morning of 24 October, D+1, X
Corps' armour was to fight its way into the open beyond the western edge
of the minefields.

In the earlier battles at Alamein, Auchinleck had identified the Italian
formations as providing the weak links in the Axis chain. Montgomery
now revived Auchinleck's principle of breaking those links in his
'crumbling' operations. However, he attributed this idea to one of his
intelligence staff, Major Bill Williams, who pointed out to Monty that the

> German and Italian troops were . . . 'corsetted'; that is, Rommel had so
> deployed his German infantry and parachute troops that they were
> positioned between, and in some cases behind, his Italian troops all
> along the front, the latter being unreliable when it came to hard fighting.
> Bill Williams' idea was that if we could separate the two we would be
> very well placed, as we could smash through a purely Italian front
> without any great difficulty.[20]

Montgomery described this as 'very brilliant analysis' and wrote that, as
a major feature of his 'crumbling' plan, it was to pave the way to final
victory at El Alamein.

Another important feature of Montgomery's plan was deception which
was organised throughout Eighth Army's area to conceal the intention to
launch an offensive for as long as possible and, thereafter, to mislead
Rommel about the timing and location of the main thrust. Dumps for
supplies were camouflaged so well as to be invisible to aerial reconnaissance, while large numbers of dummy vehicles and guns gave false
impressions of the locations of formations preparing for the offensive. In
the northern sector, real intentions were concealed, while signs of con-

siderable activity and build-up in the southern area gave the impression that the main assault would be launched there. Among deception measures adopted in the south was the laying of a dummy pipeline over twenty miles from west of Ruweisat station to a point four miles east of Samaket Gaballa. Three dummy pump-houses were built along the pipeline's route with waterpoints and storage reservoirs at two pump-house locations. The rate of progress was also intended to indicate a November completion date for the work.[21]

False information was also planted to mislead enemy agents in the Delta; wireless frequencies and call-signs were changed often; only troops actually holding the front line would be allowed to patrol so that any taken prisoner would not have seen the build-up to the rear; those knowing the battle plan were not allowed to leave the Eighth Army area; and the plan was not passed down to officers below lieutenant-colonel level until 21 October and to the soldiers not until a day or two after that.[22]

On 14 September, Montgomery's plan, Operation LIGHTFOOT, was outlined in a 'Most Secret' document issued to corps and divisional commanders and senior staff officers. The paper opened with the object of the plan:

> To destroy the enemy forces now opposing Eighth Army.
> The operations will be designed to 'trap' the enemy in his present area and to destroy him there. Should small elements escape to the West, they will be pursued and dealt with later.[23]

Monty emphasised that success in this operation depended on high standards of training and close co-operation between arms. Divisional commanders were instructed to ensure that training was realistic; that tanks would train with the infantry alongside whom they would fight; and that individual soldiers should reach high degrees of skill with the weapons they would use in battle. Above all, morale and fitness were stressed:

> I am not convinced that our soldiery are really tough and hard. They are sunburnt and brown, and look very well; but they seldom move anywhere on foot and they have led a static life for many weeks.[24]

Officers and men were to be made really fit over the next month: in Monty's words 'they must be made tough and hard'; normal fitness would not suffice. Thus began a programme of training to reach high levels of physical fitness as well as battle skills. All the while the troops would also be carrying out specific training for their own part in the battle.

At this time the enemy forces in Egypt were not commanded by Rommel. The Desert Fox had gone to Austria to recover from illness;

General Georg Stumme assumed temporary command of the Panzer Armee. However, Montgomery's offensive would bring Rommel back to Africa on the third day of battle at El Alamein.

Montgomery was confident of winning. He had done his utmost to improve training and raise morale. His Army had the best possible equipment and enjoyed a significant numerical superiority over the enemy. On 23 October he issued a personal message to Eighth Army exhorting every officer and soldier to enter the battle determined to see it through, in which case Eighth Army would knock the enemy for 'six' out of North Africa. He called on 'the Lord mighty in battle' to give Eighth Army victory.

At 9.40pm on 23 October, under the light of a full moon, the guns of Eighth Army roared out in a counter-battery programme against enemy artillery positions. As the guns hammered at the German and Italian gunsites, Eighth Army's infantry moved to their start lines, ready for the order to advance. On XXX Corps' front of seven miles almost 500 field and medium guns engaged the known positions of the opposing artillery. The medium guns, of which there were forty-eight, fired 1,800 rounds in fifteen minutes; each enemy battery had ninety-six shells dropped on it in the space of two minutes. Then the guns fell silent for five minutes before opening fire again at 10pm, this time on the forward Axis infantry positions.

As the guns dealt death to the soldiers of Panzer Armee Afrika, XXX Corps' four attacking divisions began their advance, bayonets fixed, in the moonlight. The savage skirl of the pipes played the soldiers of 51st (Highland) Division into battle. Operation LIGHTFOOT, the final Battle of El Alamein, had begun.

NOTES

1. Montgomery of Alamein: *Memoirs*, p.94
2. PRO: WO169/4171,War Diary, 51st (H) Reconnaissance Regt
3. PRO: CAB44/99
4. ibid
5. Montgomery: op cit, p.92
6. PRO: WO201/423, Defensive Planning in Western Desert, 24 August to 6 November '42.
7. ibid
8. Lucas: *War in the Desert*, p.43
9. Carver: *El Alamein*, p.54
10. loc cit
11. Quoted in CAB44/99, p.135
12. Montgomery: op cit, pp.112-113
13. ibid, p.113
14. PRO: CAB44/99

15. ibid
16. Montgomery, op cit, p.117
17. loc cit
18. ibid, pp.119-120
19. ibid, p.120
20. loc cit
21. PRO: CAB44/99, passim
22. ibid
23. PRO: WO201/433
24. ibid

CHAPTER VII

Victory at El Alamein

He'll remember with advantages what feats he did that day.

As the artillery bombardment obscured everything in its area in a cloud of dust and smoke, the leading infantry companies advanced towards the edge of the first minefield at a steady pace of 100 yards in two minutes. Light anti-aircraft guns helped them keep their bearings by firing tracer shells along fixed lines, a task in which searchlights also assisted by projecting their beams straight into the sky at fixed points.

The advance to the first minefield was about a mile and a half for most of the infantry. Mineclearing was generally the task of the sappers although minefield task forces had been set up in some cases: in 7th Armoured Division the force was built around 44th Reconnaissance Regiment which had been re-roled and included all 44th Division's carriers as well as 4th Field Squadron, RE. However, in spite of the effort dedicated to mineclearing, there were delays: clearing anti-personnel and anti-tank mines took longer than anticipated with much work, both 'prodding' and lifting, having to be done by hand. Thus it was that, by dawn on the 24th, the attacking divisions were not in line with each other; progress had been variable:

> The corridors behind them, with lanes being cleared by the two armoured divisions of Lumsden's corps, were, similarly, in a state of confused and only partial achievement. Nowhere was the armour through the mined area and on to clean ground deployed for its main task. And behind the front, in and behind the corridors themselves, military police struggled to disentangle an appalling congestion of vehicles, support weapons for the infantry, minefield clearance parties of Lumsden's corps, commanders, signallers; all amid the sound and fury of battle and in thick, choking dust, smoke and sand, making darkness utterly impenetrable.[1]

The old axiom that no plan survives the first contact had once again been proved true. Montgomery's timings had gone out of kilter and progress had been slower than planned. By daylight the armour had not deployed nor had the infantry gained their objectives; it would take many more

95

hours' fighting before this had been achieved all along the front.

Some minor objectives had been attained: 1 Greek Brigade had launched a raid to provide a diversion from operations taking place elsewhere; to take prisoners and identify their formations; to distract the enemy; and to create alarm and despondency. The raid was

> carried out at 2200 on 23 October by 1 company plus 1 platoon of infantry and 1 section of engineers aided by artillery support. The Greeks claimed to have killed or wounded 50 of the enemy, but this figure is certainly excessive. The raiding party returned, however, with 18 Italian PWs belonging to 1st and 2nd Bns, 20 Infantry Regiment, Brescia Division. Greek casualties were 1 killed and 3 wounded. The enemy showed little fight during this raid.[2]

Apart from this operation 1 Greek Brigade maintained its position throughout the night and was not otherwise engaged.

Montgomery was angry at the delays in the attack for which he blamed the armoured commanders, all of whom he suggested in his *Memoirs*

> were pursuing a policy of inactivity. There was not that eagerness on the part of senior commanders to push on and there was a fear of tank casualties; every enemy gun was reported as an 88-mm . . . The 10th Corps Commander was not displaying the drive and determination so necessary when things begin to go wrong and there was a general lack of offensive eagerness in the armoured divisions of the corps. This was not the sort of battle they were used to.[3]

All through that day and night he kept pressure on Lumsden to force his armour through the minefields, even threatening to sack the divisional commanders. But, as David Fraser argues,

> at least part of the blame should have been directed inwards, at his [Monty's] own failure to comprehend what tanks can and cannot reasonably be made to do.[4]

A subsequent report on AFVs in operations between 23 and 29 October produced by 24 Armoured Brigade Group* (10th Armoured Division in X Corps) pointed out just how little scope there had been in the early stage of the battle to use the formations and tactics practised. Even within the limits set by the minefields, however, these proved effective:

---

* The Brigade Group included 41, 45 and 47 RTR; 11 KRRC; 5 RHA, B Bty/73 A/T Regt and 116 LAA Bty, RA; 1 Tp 6 Fd Sqn, RE; 332 and 334 Coys, RASC; and 6 Lt Fd Amb, RAMC.

Holding ridges hull-down we found effectively done with tanks 50 yards apart, 100-150 yards between troops, with 1 tank per troop observing till all were called up for fire action. This function also avoided casualties from spells of heavy artillery concentrations on the ridge. FOOs with forward squadrons secured quick and accurate support either from a battery or, using the artillery regimental FOO net, all the regiment.[5]

This brigade's experience exemplified the problems faced by the armour: along with the Royals, 24 Armoured had to try to disperse its tanks, prior to moving off, in the former no-man's land which was already congested with artillery and New Zealand and South African transport; in addition, the tail of 8 Armoured Brigade was just leaving the area.

Dispersion, as far as it was possible at all, was a hazardous business, as mines were by no means confined to regular fields and slit trenches abounded. The congestion was appalling and the confusion considerable. The whole area looked like a badly organised car park at an immense race meeting held in a dust bowl.[6]

When 24 Armoured Brigade finally moved off on the morning of the 25th, it was after considerable delay caused by difficulties with gap-clearing in the minefields. Brigadier Kenchington sent 47 RTR through the minefield first, followed by 41 RTR with 45 RTR in reserve on Miteiriya ridge.

In our first action as we moved through the minefield gaps, 47 RTR moved out to a threatened flank of 8 Armd Bde which was in process of deployment. With 3 RTR hulldown they successfully engaged and drove off a thrust by some 20 enemy tanks. This was normal work and the fire of the Sherman 75mm* hulldown knocked out 5 or 6 German tanks at 1,500 yards.[7]

In spite of the setbacks, Montgomery resolved to continue his crumbling operations against enemy infantry that had yet to be engaged. Such a task was being carried out by 2nd New Zealand and 1st South African Divisions at Miteiriya; farther south XIII Corps was also moving against enemy positions. By 6pm on the evening of the 24th, the lead brigade of 1st Armoured Division had debouched from the northern corridor through the minefields to be attacked by 15th Panzer Division. That attack, however, suited Montgomery's plan.

During the course of the fighting on the 24th, Stumme had gone

---

* There were 246 Shermans in Eighth Army when the battle opened, plus 204 Grants, from a total tank strength of 1,113.

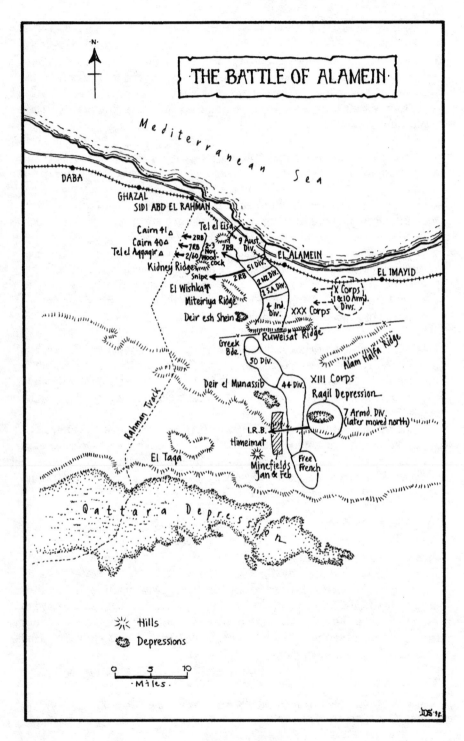

THE BATTLE OF ALAMEIN

·N·

Mediterranean Sea

DABA

GHAZAL
SIDI ABD EL RAHMAN

Cairn 41 △   Tel el Eisa
Cairn 40 △   ← 2 RB
Tel el Aqqaqir △ ← 7 RB   2-3   9 Aust
        ← 2/60 Nov.   7 RB Div.
Kidney Ridge   Wood-
        ← Snipe cock
              2 RB   51 Div.
El Wishka   2 NZ DIV.
Miteiriya Ridge   2 S.A.DIV.
Deir esh Shein   4 Ind.
                  Div.   XXX Corps

EL ALAMEIN
                    EL IMAYID
        X Corps
        1 & 10 Armd.
        Divs.

Ruweisat Ridge

Greek   Alam Halfa Ridge
Bde.
        50 Div.

Deir el Munassib   44 Div.   XIII Corps
                        Raqil Depression
                              7 Armd. Div.
                              (later moved north)
I.R.B.
Rahman Track
Himeimat
El Taqa   Minefields   Free
                    Jan & Feb   French

Qattara Depression

☼ Hills

🜲 Depressions

0   5   10
·Miles·

forward to find out at first hand what was happening. Initially planning to go only as far as 90th Light Division, he took neither escort vehicle nor wireless truck, being accompanied by Corporal Wolf, his driver, and Colonel Büchting. However, Stumme decided to go right to the front where his vehicle was fired on, probably by Australians. Büchting was mortally wounded, Wolf made a rapid turn and an even more rapid retreat but, as he turned, Stumme had been about to jump out and was, apparently, left hanging on the outside of the vehicle. There the general suffered a heart attack and fell to the ground. Not until he slowed down did Wolf realise that Stumme was missing; his body was not found for another twenty-four hours. The loss of its commander was hardly conducive to effective retaliatory action by Panzer Armee Afrika. That situation was to change with Rommel's return on 25 October.

By 8am on the 25th, all Montgomery's armour was in the open and in the positions he had hoped to have held exactly a day earlier. As the day progressed Monty decided to abandon the south-westerly move of 2nd New Zealand Division as 'it became clear that it . . . would be a very costly operation'[8] and instead moved the emphasis of the 'crumbling' operations to 9th Australian Division's area. Morshead's Australians had made good progress in the opening phase with their operations going almost as planned. Their new task was to switch through 180 degrees and thrust northwards for the coast which, it was hoped, would take the enemy unawares.

The Australians also gained two Victoria Crosses during this period. Both awards were posthumous as Private Percival Eric Gratwick and Sergeant William Henry Kibby were killed in action with their unit, 2/48th (South Australia) Battalion. Gratwick, just a week past his fortieth birthday, was in a platoon which suffered many casualties during the attack on Miteiriya Ridge on the night of 25/26 October. The platoon commander and sergeant were both hit and Private Gratwick

realizing the seriousness of the situation, charged on alone and with hand grenades killed the crew of an enemy machine-gun and an entire mortar crew. Under heavy machine-gun fire he then charged the second post with rifle and bayonet. In inflicting further casualties he was killed by machine-gun fire, but his brave and determined action enabled his company to capture the final objective.[9]

Sergeant Kibby, who had been born in County Durham, had first distinguished himself on the night of 23 October when he took command of his platoon after the officer had been killed:

On 23 October, he silenced an enemy machine-gun, killing three of the enemy and capturing 12 others. During the following days he moved among his men directing fire and cheering them on. Several times under intense fire he went and mended the platoon [telephone] line communications. On 30/31 October in order to achieve his company's objective, he went forward alone, throwing grenades to destroy the enemy only a few yards away. Just as success appeared certain, he was killed.[10]

Kibby was also a relatively old infantryman at 39 years. He and Gratwick are buried in El Alamein War Cemetery.

Rommel was most concerned about the possibility of a breakout by the British armour and thus ordered counter-attacks against the Australians' west flank and against Kidney Ridge. The latter feature, really a depression, was at the mouth of the northern minefield corridor where 1st Armoured Division's motor brigade had fought off attacks by Afrika Korps. Such operations were allowing Montgomery to achieve his object of both wearing down the German commander's armour and destroying his infantry. On the evening of the 26th, Rommel ordered 21st Panzer and Ariete Divisions to move up from the southern area, where XIII Corps had not pushed in to the hilt, to the northern sector where fighting was toughest. With virtually the entire Afrika Korps masking the northern corridor with tanks and anti-tank guns, it was going to be very difficult to effect a breakthrough there. Rommel had anticipated Montgomery's intentions and acted to prevent him carrying them out although Afrika Korps' armour was suffering steady attrition from 1st Armoured Division.

During the fighting at Kidney Ridge the third VC of the battle was won by the CO of 2nd Rifle Brigade. Victor Buller Turner, whose brother Alexander had won a posthumous VC during the Great War, led his depleted battalion, reinforced by eleven 6-pounders of 239 Anti-Tank Battery and sappers of 7th Field Squadron, on a 4,000-yard westward advance from Kidney Ridge to establish a firm base on a feature known as Snipe, which had been an enemy position. Having done that, he established defences to rebuff a fierce counter-attack by some ninety tanks. A number of the tanks were knocked out and Buller was to be found wherever the fire was heaviest, encouraging his men. By noon on the 27th he had thirteen anti-tank guns at his disposal, the enemy were still attacking and the battalion had no means of resupply. At 1pm an attack by eight tanks was engaged:

During the action, one of the 6-pounder guns was left with only one officer and a sergeant, so Colonel Buller joined them as loader, and between them they destroyed another five tanks. Not until the last tank had been repulsed did he consent to having a wound in his head attended to.[11]

Three of the attacking tanks had been destroyed at just 200 yards when the gun was down to its last four rounds. It was during this phase, when the position was being shelled heavily, that Turner received his head wound. In all, his battalion fought off six attacks and claimed the destruction or immobilisation of fifty tanks.*

Montgomery had reduced operations on XIII Corps' front to patrol activities and defensive duties, enabling him to widen divisional fronts and pull divisions into reserve to prepare for the final blow. This reserve was created under X Corps' command and, by 28 October, included 7th and 10th Armoured Divisions with the New Zealanders:

> Hard fighting had been going on for the previous three days and I began to realise from the casualty figures that I must be careful. I knew that the final blow must be put in on 30 Corps' front, but at the moment I was not clear exactly where. But I had to get ready for it.[12]

Eighth Army's casualties had been heavy but, like Auchinleck during CRUSADER, Montgomery appreciated that his enemy was in a worse state, being assailed relentlessly by ground and air forces. With strong enemy forces facing the northern corridor, he decided that that area should also become a defensive zone and pulled 1st Armoured Division into reserve, thus putting most of X Corps in reserve. The time for the final major effort that would unhinge completely the Axis defences had arrived and Monty planned to make that effort on 30 October in the coastal sector with the New Zealanders leading. Orders were issued for the intensification of operations towards the coast by 9th Australian Division as a prelude to a breakout on the axis of the coast road.

In spite of his ill health, the Desert Fox had lost none of his feel for battle: anticipating his rival's planned thrust he shifted his weight to his left by moving northwards as many reserves as possible. Aware of Rommel's return, and foiled in his original plan by the German's move, Montgomery demonstrated his own battle cunning by drawing up a new plan: Operation SUPERCHARGE.

> . . . we had now achieved what Bill Williams had recommended. The Germans had been pulled against our right and were no longer 'corsetting' the Italians. The Germans were in the north, the Italians together in the south; and the dividing line between them appeared to be just to the north of our original northern corridor.[13]

---

* A full account of the defence of Outpost Snipe will be found in *Last Stand!* by Bryan Perrett (pp.117-126).

SUPERCHARGE would thus be launched on the original XXX Corps' front, north of Kidney Ridge, and directed at the junction between the German and Italian troops with the major weight falling on the latter. Led by 2nd New Zealand Division, with two British infantry brigades under command, and 9 Armoured Brigade, the attack would thrust towards Tel el Aqqaqir, across the Rahman track, which ran north-south behind the Axis front, into open desert. Following the New Zealanders, 1st Armoured Division would advance to meet Rommel's armour which, Montgomery anticipated, would move to meet the new threat.

The Australians were also to continue thrusting northwards prior to the main attack, to distract the enemy while, in the south, XIII Corps would launch diversionary operations in its own sector. RAF operations, especially against 15th and 21st Panzer Divisions, would intensify as SUPERCHARGE was being prepared, culminating as the ground attack was launched on the night of 31 October/1 November. However, Monty reluctantly decided, after pressure from Freyberg and Leese, that the 'stage management problems' involved in the operation were such that a twenty-four hour delay was needed to ensure its success.

The Australian diversionary attack was launched on the night of 30 October but the leading battalions met stiff opposition. By dawn, the remnants of 26 Brigade were grouped in a small area about two miles north-east of the nearest elements of 20 Brigade and some three miles north of the remainder of the division. The enemy, who had been relieving 21st Panzer with Trieste, had been taken by surprise but had reacted quickly and vigorously. During the day the Australians came under intensive artillery bombardment and were subjected to dive-bombing and tank attacks. The British armour supporting them was heavily engaged; 40 RTR lost a high proportion of the crews involved, but RAF bombing, artillery fire and the efforts of the Rhodesian 289 Anti-Tank Battery, RA, combined with those of 40 RTR to break up the enemy attacks.

There were, however, German troops behind 20 and 26 Brigades: 125th Panzer Grenadier Regiment was still holding positions around Thompson's Post which 26 Brigade had attacked on the night of the 28th. Von Thoma and Bayerlein wanted to withdraw 125th from Thompson's Post rather than suffer heavy losses in efforts to maintain contact; both accepted that such a withdrawal would mean the loss of the regiment's heavy weapons but this, they felt, was preferable to the alternative. Rommel overruled them and ordered further attacks to be made next day. By so doing, he was helping Montgomery's battle plan, even though Afrika Korps did re-establish contact with Thompson's Post during the 1st before withdrawing their forces under cover of darkness.

Just after 1am on 2 November, Freyberg's leading battalions had left their start lines: 151 Brigade, with 28th Maori Battalion and 8 RTR, suffered considerable losses but were on their objectives by dawn. To their right, 8th Durham LI, although also losing heavily in the two leading companies, reached their final objective by 4am. The two battalions had captured over 400 enemy soldiers. To the left of 8th Durhams, their comrades of the 9th Battalion met little opposition and reached their objectives with light casualties. Following up the 8th Battalion, 6th Durhams filled in on the right flank between 8 DLI and the Maoris. Although engaged with elements of 15th Panzer and Littorio en route, 6 DLI had also sustained relatively light casualties. By dawn, 8 RTR's Valentines, which had been delayed by mines, had joined 151 Brigade's infantry on their objectives.

The left wing of the New Zealand attack was provided by 152 Brigade from 51st (Highland) Division with 5th Seaforth, on the right, and 5th Camerons, on the left, leading. The Highlanders used their own night-time recognition system: each soldier had on his back a white St Andrew's cross fashioned from strips of four-by-two rifle-cleaning fabric fixed to the braces of his webbing. Each battalion had different experiences: the Seaforth had little difficulty and were on their objectives by 3.45am; the Camerons had problems in maintaining direction and contact as well as having a tougher fight but they, too, took their objectives as planned. The Camerons were harassed by enemy tanks at dawn which could have caused problems as their own anti-tank guns had not joined them, but support from Valentines of 50 RTR took the pressure off the infantrymen and the appearance of the main body of the British armour gave the enemy tanks problems of their own.

With the infantry on their objectives 1st Armoured Division was to pass through and advance up to the Rahman track, a distance of about 2,000 yards. This move was delayed by thirty minutes due to difficulties experienced by the tanks in the move forward. Brigadier Currie's 9 Armoured Brigade, in the van of the armoured advance, engaged the enemy first, tackling those tanks which had moved against 5th Camerons. Currie's tanks then moved forward towards the Rahman track where it was soon engaged with enemy armour and anti-tank guns; 3rd Hussars was reduced to seven tanks by the time it reached the track; the Royal Wiltshire Yeomanry and the Warwickshire Yeomanry each met heavy opposition and were told to fight it out until 1st Armoured arrived. The German anti-tank gunners were formidable opponents and continued to be feared by the British tank crews:

> Most of the longer range tank casualties, in my opinion, were from 76.2mm guns on a MkII chassis (in one case on wheels), or 88s, chiefly the former. This gun appears a more dangerous enemy than the 88, being less conspicuous and very powerful. I wish we could acquire some.[14]

Both Currie and Freyberg expressed exasperation at the delay in the advance of Fisher's 2 Armoured Brigade from 1st Armoured Division. By the time 3rd Hussars from Currie's command had reached the Rahman track, the Bays of 2 Armoured Brigade, had caught up with them. Fisher's brigade finally passed through what remained of 9 Armoured Brigade at about 10.40am to face the enemy anti-tank screen. Currie had lost seventy tanks in his advance with the Wiltshires reduced to two runners, the Warwickshires to seven and 3rd Hussars to eight:

> Currie and Freyberg both said that a vigorous push would carry Fisher through the anti-tank screen beyond the track. But in fact the position was now much stronger than it had been four hours earlier when Currie had tried just that, failed and lost heavily in the process.[15]

With opposition to X Corps stiffening, Monty looked to the southern flank where two armoured-car squadrons of The Royals had passed through the enemy lines into open desert. Most Axis troops they met mistook them for 'friendly' troops, either German or Italian, depending on which positions they were driving through. At least one Italian officer did not find them particularly friendly:

> As the dawn broke, we passed a man in bed. From the mass of vehicles and equipment surrounding him, he was obviously an Italian quartermaster. We woke him up by tossing a Verey light into his blankets. He broke the record for the sitting high jump. Into one of his lorries we heaved a hand-grenade. The results . . . were most satisfactory, but it scared the second-in-command who, following in his armoured car, had failed to see us toss the grenade.[16]

Montgomery felt that the weakness thus revealed in the south could be exploited. Therefore, Custance's 8 Armoured Brigade was ordered south-westwards around Fisher's left flank rather than waiting to follow through. At the same time XXX Corps was to attack Point 38, codenamed Skinflint, a feature about a mile to the south-west of 2nd Seaforth on the right of 152 Brigade. Harding's 7th Armoured Division was also to move forward as quickly as possible; its probable role was to advance on Ghazal station, eight miles west of Sidi Abd el Rahman, having passed through the southern flank of the salient.

In the meantime battle raged furiously on the Rahman track. The clash between 2 Armoured Brigade and the enemy armour around Tel el Aqqaqir was both the toughest and longest tank engagement of the entire El Alamein battle. An Afrika Korps counter-attack, lasting from 11am until 1pm, was fought to a standstill by the British armour, which was virtually stationary throughout this engagement, ably supported by artillery and aircraft. The action was being directed by Rommel himself in what Correlli Barnett describes as 'one of the best actions of his career in order to gain time for the organisation of the retreat that must soon begin'.[17] Desperate to gain that, Rommel switched every available 88mm gun to the anti-tank role, even though this reduced his anti-aircraft protection. In all, twenty-four 88s were so deployed but their numbers soon began to be whittled down by the attentions of British gunners, armour and the Desert Air Force. The Italian tanks were also suffering heavily with the result that their commanders could no longer keep them in action.

Another attack was ordered by Rommel at 2pm; at the same time he moved most of Ariete north with the bulk of the artillery from the southern flank, leaving that flank with virtually no reserves. The Axis front in the coastal area was also to be shortened by pulling it back to Sidi Abd el Rahman.

Custance's flanking move to the south-west had been delayed until mid-day when his brigade's tanks were finally pulled out of action against 15th Panzer. However, 8 Armoured Brigade soon ran up against the enemy anti-tank screen which stopped any further movement that day. The brigade had lost six Crusaders for the claimed destruction of eleven panzers.

The attack on Point 38, in spite of some delays and confusion in the preparation, was carried through with little difficulty by 2nd Seaforth supported by 50 RTR. The Seaforth had no casualties; 50 RTR lost four Valentines and 100 Italian prisoners were taken from Trieste Division. So rattled were the Italians that they surrendered the Snipe strongpoint, with another 60 prisoners, before 5th Royal Sussex could launch a planned attack on it.

Von Thoma ordered yet another counter-attack for last light; it does not appear to have been carried out. By the end of this day's hard fighting, Afrika Korps was reduced to thirty-five runners while its ammunition stocks were sadly depleted. Rommel's total tank strength was fifty-five; his Italian infantry had been neutralised, either by being captured, cut off or killed; and his supply situation was hopeless. On the evening of 2 November he made the decision to pull back sixty miles to Fuka in order to save what he could of Panzer Armee Afrika. During the night, his troops in the southern sector were withdrawn to the former Qaret el Abd-Gebel Kalakh line while, in the north, Afrika Korps, XX Corps and 90th Light Division would withdraw slowly on the 3rd to a line running south from El Daba, some twenty miles in the rear. These formations would hold off Eighth Army while Axis infantry made good their escape on foot or on any vehicles that could be found.

The following day Hitler took a hand in the battle by ordering Rommel to fight to the end at Alamein: there was to be no retreat. Rommel cancelled his orders and his command waited to carry out Hitler's suicidal order. However, the Führer relented in face of the argument that withdrawal was the only way to save Panzer Armee Afrika and told Rommel that he could act as he saw fit. It was during this final phase of the battle, on 2 November, that Eighth Army finally succeeded in breaking through the enemy positions into open desert.

The Battle of El Alamein was over. As Rommel made good his escape, Eighth Army was unable to stop him, although 30,000 Axis prisoners were taken and the Ariete Division was wiped out for total British casualties of 13,500. The German armour had not been cut off, due to the failure of 1st Armoured Division to get behind its foe, but the bulk of it had been destroyed by the combined efforts of tankmen, artillery and anti-tank crews. Freyberg was frustrated that the armoured breakout envisaged in the SUPERCHARGE plan had not materialised. Monty, however, took a more phlegmatic view: he had believed that he could break out to the south-west thus by-passing Afrika Korps; the infantry and armour attack on Point 38 had been part of this plan and had been successful.

Although Eighth Army had not entirely eliminated its opponents, as envisaged in Montgomery's memorandum of 14 September, some measure of its success can be gauged by the fact that its next major battle would be fought on the western frontier of Libya, some 1,500 miles to the west of El Alamein. There was little doubt that the tide of the war in North Africa had turned for the last time. There would be no more Benghazi Stakes: Eighth Army had won one of the pivotal battles of the war.

Although Monty's plan had not developed as he had anticipated, Eighth Army's morale was high. There were still problems with co-operation between arms, especially between armour and infantry, but many of the lessons that Auchinleck had tried to inculcate were beginning to percolate down. The Auk would, no doubt, have used a more flexible divisional structure at El Alamein based on the brigade groups system which later became the battlegroup system. One arm that performed exceptionally well at Alamein was the artillery: one of the recommendations that the Auk had made was for greater concentration of artillery with a senior officer, the Divisional or Corps Commander, RA, controlling gunner assets so as to be able to bring the greatest concentration of firepower possible down on any target.[18] Experience in the subsequent battles had proved the wisdom of this observation, a lesson already learned in the Great War, and the artillery's contribution to the battle, with its fifty-two medium and 840 field pieces, was of battlewinning proportions. By the end of the war it would be true to say that the British arm most feared and respected by the Germans was artillery. In the Second World War the British artillery showed its true potential for the first time at Alamein.

The Gunners had so far been condemned to a difficult war – often starved of ammunition, the wise handling of artillery imperfectly mastered by commanders of other arms, and dispersion rather than concentration the rule. Now they came into their own. With ample time for preparation and supply, no restrictions had to be placed on ammunition expenditure, and during the battle over one million rounds were fired by the field artillery alone. [19]

In Britain, church bells rang out for the first time since 1939 to celebrate the victory of El Alamein, while Winston Churchill described Eighth Army's achievement as 'the end of the beginning'.

NOTES

1. Fraser: *And We Shall Shock Them*, p.242
2. PRO: CAB44/101, Battle of El Alamein
3. Montgomery: *Memoirs*, p.131
4. Fraser, op cit, pp.243-244
5. PRO: WO201/545, Notes on AFVs on Operations 23-29 Oct '42
6. Carver: *El Alamein*, pp.110-111
7. PRO: WO201/545, op cit
8. Montgomery: op cit, p.131
9. *Register of the Victoria Cross*, p.128
10. ibid, p.181
11. ibid, p.318
12. Montgomery: op cit, p.131
13. ibid, p.132
14. PRO: WO201/545, op cit
15. Carver: op cit, p.151
16. Quoted in ibid, p153
17. Barnett: *The Desert Generals*, p.285
18. PRO: WO201/452: Notes on main lessons of recent operations in the Western Desert, July 1942
19. Fraser: op cit, p.246

CHAPTER VIII
Pursuit to Tripoli:
November 1942 – January 1943

You have nightly pitched your moving tents a day's march nearer home.

The defeat of the Panzer Armee at El Alamein marked the beginning, for Eighth Army, of the long march that would take it to final victory and Vienna, over thirty months later. El Alamein marked not only the turning point in North Africa but also one of the turning points of the war itself. Coupled with the US Navy's victory some months earlier at Midway in the Pacific and the defeat of the German Sixth Army at Stalingrad, which occurred shortly after Alamein, it marked the period when defeat started to turn into victory for the Allies.

As the Axis forces withdrew there was a feeling of elation in Eighth Army especially among the soldiers of the armoured formations as they began their pursuit of the defeated enemy. Many stragglers were rounded up as Eighth Army's tanks rolled westwards. Some enemy soldiers found themselves surrendering more than once. Karl Eisenfeller, of the Ramcke Parachute Brigade, one of the formations left to fend for itself, was in a group of Fallschirmjäger who surrendered to a troop of British tanks. However, the tank crewmen had no facilities to deal with prisoners so, having disarmed the Germans, they gave them some water and told them to march eastwards until they could be dealt with by other troops. As soon as the tanks had disappeared the Germans turned to trek westwards in the hope of eluding Eighth Army units and eventually catching up with their own side. It was not to be. They were again taken prisoner by British tankmen, given water and told to make their own way to the PoW handling units in the rear. Once again they watched the tanks disappear into the distance before turning westwards. On the next occasion that they met British troops they were not so lucky. These were lorried troops who took the Germans on board their vehicles and then arranged for them to be transported to the PoW cages.[1]

The elation of the pursuit was short-lived in Eighth Army. Although elements of the Army had struck through into open desert on 2 November, it was not until the 5th that the full-scale pursuit was organised. And this was in spite of the fact that X Corps had been formed as a *corps de chasse*. But X Corps had been committed to the wearing-down battle and, like XXX Corps, had been fought to exhaustion. For the pursuit, a new *corps de chasse* was hastily created under X Corps Headquarters to include 7th Armoured Division and the New Zealand Division. The latter formation, with 4 and 9 Armoured Brigades, was directed towards Fuka on 3 November but became so badly entangled with supply columns that it ground to a standstill. After this false start the pursuit finally got under way on the 5th.

On 6 November the heavens opened. Torrential rain lasted into the following day giving Rommel a new and unexpected ally of which he made full use. Although Montgomery had attempted to entrap Rommel's forces by sending elements of X Corps on a short thrust to the coast, only Custance's 8 Armoured Brigade had any measurable success. Led by a squadron of 11th Hussars, the desert veteran Cherrypickers, the brigade reached Galal and established a block on the coast road and railway. Shortly after this an enemy column appeared which was engaged by 3 RTR. Then a substantial column of enemy transport, artillery and tanks came into sight which, clearly not expecting to meet British tanks or artillery, made no effort to deploy into battle formation. They drove, unsuspecting, into the massed fire of 8 Armoured Brigade resulting in a rout for the Axis units who lost over fifty German and Italian tanks, several artillery pieces, over 100 lorries and about 1,000 prisoners. In his book *El Alamein*, Field-Marshal Lord Carver suggests that the vanquished enemy column was probably the remnants of de Stefanis' Italian XX Mobile Corps.[2]

But Custance's success was not matched by similar successes elsewhere. Such was the congestion in the Eighth Army salient that it was difficult for units to strike into the desert; most had little, if any, experience of travelling through the desert by night. Thus Eighth Army's move was sluggish. Rommel was able to fall back on the single good road where, even though his retreating army's densely packed vehicles presented excellent targets, the Desert Air Force concentrated on tactical close support of the ground forces rather than attacking the large transport columns on their westward journey. The air commanders preferred to wait until ground troops had eliminated enemy landing grounds at Sidi Haneish and El Daba, thus reducing the risk of interception by enemy aircraft, before striking farther west.

Montgomery had dispersed his pursuit forces, thereby dissipating Eighth Army's efforts. Despite his commitment to use divisions as divisions and not to employ brigade-sized groups, he was doing just that. In the summer of 1944 Montgomery was to accuse Eisenhower of dispersing his pursuit forces after the battle for Normandy, arguing that a single axis of advance ought to have been used. But this was the very mistake that Monty himself made after Alamein. He thus denied Eighth Army the fruits of victory which, Clausewitz argued, are won in the pursuit.

Monty's short stabs to the coast went against the advice of the desert veterans who advised that the pursuit should strike deeply westwards through the desert, keeping parallel to Rommel's retreating forces, before swinging for the coast to cut the latter's line of retreat; this latter manoeuvre could be as far west as Tobruk. Persevering with his own tactics, Monty planned to spring his principal trap at Ma'aten Baggush, east of Mersa Matruh, on 6 November. The trap was sprung but no enemy forces were taken; they had gone. However, elements of 21st Panzer Division, halted by lack of fuel, were engaged by 22 Armoured Brigade. The Germans held the British armour off until nightfall, when supplies of fuel were received, after which the panzers slipped away.

Rommel's retreat was disciplined and orderly and, with the heavy rainfall on the night of 6 November, took him out of danger. With the soft desert sand south of Matruh transformed into a morass, X Corps was bogged down. Although Montgomery was to use the rains as his explanation for his failure to cut off Rommel's retreat, the fact remains that he had already struck towards the coast four times and, on each occasion, he had missed Rommel. Monty's dispersion of effort on these occasions had allowed the Desert Fox to increase the distance between himself and his pursuers. The rain hindered Rommel as much as it hindered Eighth Army: it did not fall solely on the British and it was not the reason for the failure to trap Rommel in spite of Monty's assertion.

> Twice Rommel's forces were saved from complete disaster by heavy rain. The first occasion was on the 6th and 7th November when we had three divisions 'bogged' in the desert, unable to move, and it was not possible even to get petrol to them; this setback saved Rommel's forces from complete encirclement at Mersa Matruh.[3]

Mersa Matruh was taken by 8 Armoured Brigade on 8 November and the port was soon opened up to assist Eighth Army's logistic support operations; Matruh was the first of a series of ports to fall over the next two months. All Egyptian territory had been cleared of Axis troops by the 11th and the leading elements of Montgomery's* command pushed forward into Libya, having advanced 270 miles from Alamein.

By now Rommel's tank strength was down to ten runners. Even that paltry figure exaggerated his strength as shortage of fuel frequently left the tanks immobile. And yet, in spite of his enemy's weakness,

---

* After Alamein Montgomery was promoted to General 'for distinguished services in the field' and appointed a KCB.

Montgomery continued to push forward with extreme caution. His argument was that he was not going to be pushed back into Egypt 'like the others' and corps and divisional commanders who suggested any form of rapid advance were refused permission to do so. Gatehouse, commanding 10th Armoured Division, the strongest such division under Monty's command, asked to be allowed to thrust hard and fast with his division towards Sollum and on to Tobruk with the aim of engaging and destroying Rommel's armour. But Montgomery would have none of it.[4]

Rommel expressed to Bayerlein his delight that Montgomery would not hurry: it enabled the Desert Fox to carry out his retreat almost at his own pace. Correlli Barnett suggests that Montgomery's behaviour at this stage shows 'a curious limit' to his confidence in his own ability and that that limit was created by Montgomery being overawed by Rommel's reputation.[5] There can be little in the way of alternative explanations as Montgomery was fully aware, through Ultra, of just how weak the Axis army really was. Instead of being the antidote to Rommel, Montgomery may well have been in thrall to the German

> and the Panzerarmee's shield during that epic retreat was its commander's reputation. And this interpretation is corroborated by a senior officer close to Montgomery at the time, who agrees that 'Rommel's reputation did make an impression on Monty's mind'.[6]

Whatever the feelings of senior commanders, the soldiers on the ground had their tails up. The 'big push', as it was known, had captured the imagination of the ordinary soldier of Eighth Army. He had every confidence in Monty; he believed that Monty had the measure of the Desert Fox; and he was certain that he and his comrades were moving westwards for the last time. Not for him any argument over strategy; his crusade to knock the enemy out of North Africa imbued him with a belief that permeated the entire Army: victory was within his grasp.

As Eighth Army made its way into Libya its first significant objective was the port of Tobruk. South African soldiers were first to enter the much fought over town on 12 November; the task of garrisoning the port devolved on the Sudan Defence Force. The capture of Tobruk not only provided another port to help reduce the dependence of the Army's logistic tail on the single road along the coast, it was also a boost to morale in view of the importance assigned to Tobruk earlier in the campaign. At Gazala, Rommel fought a brief delaying action before withdrawing; behind his army roads were blown, mines laid, trucks, buildings and palm trees were all booby-trapped. In the van of Eighth Army, sappers of the Royal Engineers dealt with all these obstacles.[7]

From Tobruk elements of Eighth Army were charged with the seizure of the landing grounds around Martuba which were considered vital to the provision of air cover for a convoy scheduled to sail for Malta from Alexandria on 15 November. On that morning a column from 4 Light Armoured Brigade reported the Martuba landing grounds free of enemy troops and in good condition.

Ahead of Montgomery's advancing Army lay another port, Benghazi, which fell on 20 November. Although the harbour itself was taken in usable condition, with berths in the inner harbour for three ships and an uninterrupted channel into that harbour for vessels of up to twenty-five feet draft, the retreating Axis forces had carried out considerable demolitions. Harbour installations and stores had been damaged or destroyed. Aerial bombardment had knocked out the town's power station, leaving Benghazi without electricity, running water or a working sewerage system.[8] In spite of all this, the town was selected by Monty to be the site for a time of Eighth Army's rear headquarters. Benghazi had fallen for the last time.

Eighth Army had changed considerably since El Alamein. The Australians, who had been so much a part of the desert war, had departed for home. Australia's prime minister, John Curtin, had asked Churchill for the early return of Major General Leslie Morshead's 9th Division only days before the battle of El Alamein. Curtin had been concerned that there were insufficient forces available to defend Australia against the Japanese threat. His request had been passed to Morshead who received it after the battle had begun and, as a result, 9th Australian Division was withdrawn from Eighth Army after the breakthrough and sent to Palestine whence it returned to its own shores. Alexander had expressed the view that the Australian division was the formation he least wanted to lose in the Middle East but the reality of Australia's strategic situation had to take priority over Alex's wishes.

Gone too was 1st South African Division which departed soon after the capture of Tobruk. This division was to be converted into an armoured formation in which guise it would rejoin Eighth Army in the Italian campaign. As well as the loss of the Australians and South Africans, the bulk of the Greek Brigade had been sent back to Egypt by Monty. Two British divisions had also gone from Eighth Army's order of battle. Alexander judged that the need for reinforcements for Eighth Army, coupled with the supply problems inherent in a lengthy advance on a single road, meant that two divisions could no longer be kept in being. The victims of this reduction were to be 8th Armoured Division and 44th (Home Counties) Division. Both were withdrawn to Egypt where they were disbanded on 1 January and 31 January 1943 respectively. However, 44th Division's Reconnaissance Regiment was reprieved and later assigned to 56th (London) Division which arrived in Egypt in March 1943.[9]

Although General Freyberg asked the officers of 2nd New Zealand Division whether they felt that their division should be repatriated when Egypt had been cleared of enemy forces, the overwhelming opinion was that the division should remain with Eighth Army. So it was that the New Zealanders marched all the way to Austria under the sign of the Crusader's Cross. Brigadier Kippenberger suggested that the taking of Tripoli would 'at the least' have been difficult without the New Zealand Division.[10] And they were to play an important role in the fighting in Tunisia.

The desert war had see-sawed between El Alamein in the east and El Agheila in the west. With Rommel on his way back to El Agheila the prospect of a battle on the El Agheila line loomed. By now Axis forces had received some reinforcements but Rommel's armour strength was still not much more than thirty tanks and his fuel situation continued to be precarious. On 24 November he halted his retreating army on the El Agheila line and deployed into battle positions. His retreat down the coast from Benghazi had not been interrupted by Montgomery in the manner O'Connor had executed at Beda Fomm almost two years before. Indeed Montgomery had refused to push a strong force through Msus across the chord of the Cyrenaican bulge in an effort to cut off Rommel.[11] He did agree to allow a light force to take that route while the main body of Eighth Army followed Rommel's rearguards. However, the light force became bogged down in rainsoaked terrain and its efforts came to naught.

Rommel's deployment along the slightly more than one hundred miles of the El Agheila line included two divisions of Afrika Korps, whose combined strength was just about that of a brigade; 90th Light Division, which was reduced to a battalion and a half; 164th Infantry Division with 3,000 men but no heavy weapons; a Fallschirmjäger battalion; the brigade-strength remnant of the Italian XX Corps; and eight artillery batteries. With thirty-five tanks, twenty armoured cars, forty 88mm guns and forty-six anti-tank guns, Rommel realistically could not have offered any serious obstacle to Eighth Army. He was engaged in a game of bluff. And he succeeded.

Eighth Army's spearhead at El Agheila was provided by 7th Armoured Division, with 120 tanks, and 51st (Highland) Division. Superiority rested with Montgomery and yet he hesitated. In his *Memoirs*, he explains this hesitation thus:

As we approached the Agheila position I sensed a feeling of anxiety in the ranks of the Eighth Army. Many had been there twice already; and twice Rommel had debouched when he was ready and had driven them back. I therefore decided that I must get possession of the Agheila position quickly; morale might decline if we hung about looking at it for too long. It was a difficult position to attack.[12]

Concerns about Rommel launching a counter-attack were understandable among the soldiers of Eighth Army and especially those who had been as far west as Agheila before, although it must be said that such men were few in number. It is less understandable from an army commander who had excellent intelligence on his enemy's strength. And Montgomery's worry about morale suffering 'if we hung about looking at it for too long' seems less convincing when it is remembered that he spent three weeks preparing for his attack on the Agheila position.

That attack was to be launched on 15 December, before which Monty took a period of leave to discuss further plans with Alexander; ' . . . get some more clothes, and generally get cleaned up after nearly four months in the desert'.[13] Montgomery's plan was for the New Zealanders to make a south-flanking move to hit Rommel's forces in the rear while 51st (Highland) and 7th Armoured Divisions would make a frontal assault.

On the night of 7/8 December, Rommel withdrew his Italians from Agheila with as much fuss as possible: lorry headlights were blazing and the maximum noise was created. Following this very obvious demonstration, Montgomery decided to bring his attack forward by two days to 13 December. Rommel had, meantime, planned his retirement for the night of 12/13 December. When Monty's attack went in, after an intensive air and artillery bombardment, it met thin air: Rommel had slipped away without losing a single soldier. All that awaited the British troops were mines and booby traps. And yet Monty claimed this as a great victory: 'Everything went well' was his assessment and he wrote that the 'enemy began to withdraw the moment our frontal attack developed'.[14]

What fighting did occur came about as a result of clashes as Eighth Army pursued the retreating Germans. Afrika Korps tanks, now up to fifty-four in number, had reached Mugta on the coast road when their pursuers of 7th Armoured Division made contact with them on 15 December. Major-General A F (John) Harding, the divisional commander, ordered an immediate attack with sixty Sherman tanks. Since the Germans were short of fuel, and the New Zealanders, with an armoured brigade under command, had reached the coast road at Merduma, on the enemy line of retreat, Montgomery had, at last, trapped Afrika Korps and his two hundred tanks could deal with his foe's immobile fifty-four. Furthermore, Rommel was not in command that day; General Fehn, fresh from the Russian front and with no desert experience, held the reins of Afrika Korps.

Someone at Division told me that Afrika Korps was 'in the bag': the rest had gone, but we had Afrika Korps, 15 and 21 Panzer Divisions, and 90th Light, the elite of the German Army.[15]

It looked as if a complete victory was in the bag. The BBC announced that Rommel was in a bottle in which Montgomery was about to place the cork.

The Desert Fox proved to be something of a genie. On the morning of the 16th, Afrika Korps, deployed in small battlegroups, fought its way through the New Zealand Division's positions, between 5 and 6 Brigades, and was off again to the west with light British forces in pursuit.

> It was profoundly disappointing, but it was nobody's fault. If 5 and 6 Brigades had been linked up, Afrika Korps would simply have slipped round our southern flank instead of between us, and our supply columns would have suffered.[16]

Rommel was pulling back to Buerat, where he was ordered by both Hitler and Mussolini to make a last stand. En route a rearguard was deployed at Nofilia which was engaged by the New Zealanders on 17 and 18 December; once again the enemy got away after a brisk battle, 'leaving a few dead but no prisoners or wounded'. Freyberg's losses were light and a number of artillery pieces were captured.[17]

The reinforcements and supplies necessary to make a stand at Buerat were not, however, forthcoming from either Berlin or Rome even though the port of Tripoli, Rommel's main supply port, was only some 250 miles away. Although Buerat provided an intrinsically strong position, it was not fortified adequately and the line of defences would be too long for Rommel's small force to hold. It would be a simple matter for Montgomery to outflank the position and entrap the Axis army.

On 29 December, Panzer Armee Afrika deployed at Buerat. Over the previous four days 15th Panzer and 90th Light Divisions had fought a rearguard action on the road from Sirte. Once again Monty began to prepare for a set-piece battle in order to destroy the enemy force. He calculated that he needed ten days' supply of fuel, ammunition and equipment for the battle and the subsequent advance to Tripoli. According to his staff, building up that supply would take until 14 January. D-Day for Eighth Army's attack at Buerat was therefore set for the 15th, with the aim of being in Tripoli within ten days.

The capture of Tripoli was vital to Eighth Army's logistical support as the port would remove much of the dependency on the long road from the Nile delta. Tobruk and Benghazi had been some help but fierce gales which began on 4 January 1943 virtually wiped out Benghazi as a base port; its daily capacity was reduced by storm damage from 3,000 tons to 400 by the 12th. Thus the need to take Tripoli before the Germans had destroyed the port's facilities became even more urgent.

Although the build-up programme had been disrupted by the storm damage at Benghazi, Montgomery decided to stick to his planned timings and diverted X Corps' transport to complete the supply dumping programme by 14 January. His principal concern was that if he did not take Tripoli within the planned timescale then he would be forced to retreat through lack of supplies.

On 12 January Monty issued one of his famous personal messages to Eighth Army which concluded with the exhortation

ON TO TRIPOLI! Our families and friends in the home country will be thrilled when they hear we have captured that place.[18]

Eighth Army's attack was launched as planned on 15 January preceded by the customary heavy air and artillery bombardment, after which 51st (Highland) Division, under Monty's direct command, struck forward along the axis of the coast road. The main blow was to come from 7th Armoured Division and 2nd New Zealand Division both of which thrust south to come around Rommel's desert flank. On that flank some 450 British tanks were opposed by about fifty German tanks; 15th Panzer Division fell back steadily towards Tarhuna in the face of the British advance, knocking out fifty-two of Montgomery's tanks as they did so and 'giving up one promising position after another'.[19]

4 Light Armoured Brigade, now under John Currie, and our [New Zealand] Divisional Cavalry, had a few brushes; on the Wadi Zem Zem there was a brisk artillery duel, and for a while indications of a serious affair, but nothing came of it.[20]

The remainder of Rommel's force withdrew in step with 15th Panzer; there were no Axis troops without transport as these had all been withdrawn earlier. On the coast road, Montgomery's advance made excellent progress; once again Monty had hit thin air as 90th Light had already withdrawn.

In spite of the need for 'tremendous drive and energy', Montgomery's advance was so slow that he lost all contact with the retreating foe even though Rommel was not making a hasty withdrawal. Four days later the forward elements of Eighth Army ran into opposition on the Homs-Tarhuna line. This was a rearguard action and, although Homs fell that day, Montgomery felt it necessary to deliver an 'imperial rocket' to 51st (Highland) Division's commander. He felt that the Highlanders had appeared 'to be getting weary, and generally displayed a lack of initiative and ginger'.[21]

In fact, 51st (Highland) Division had been in the forefront of Eighth Army's advance for over a month and it was small wonder that there were

A Noble Crusade

signs of weariness. Moreover, the Division, in common with all the leading troops, faced the problem of mining. A heavy anti-aircraft battery, 25 HAA Battery, had been placed under the Division's CRA and experienced the difficulties of movement in heavily-mined country.

> Only the main road and a track, known as Highland Division track, were cleared of mines and the advancing army had to take great care. Even so there were many casualties from the mines . . .. There were occasions when there were close shaves however. One . . . occurred when a gun and tractor of 25 Battery got into difficulty. One of the gunners jumped over the tapes, laid by the sappers, to mark the dangerous areas, to assist in the rescue operation and he returned the same way. Moments after the lorry and gun moved off a mine exploded where they had been stopped.[22]

With the capture of Homs, Eighth Army had only a short distance, about seventy-five miles, to travel to Tripoli. Although the port fell on 23 January, Montgomery had not succeeded in smashing what remained of Rommel's command. The latter was withdrawing in good order to Tunisia in French North-West Africa where substantial Axis reinforcements had been committed to meet Allied forces which had landed in Algeria in early-November 1942, as Eighth Army was fighting the final Battle of El Alamein. That landing, Operation TORCH, had brought another British army to North Africa: First Army under Lieutenant-General Kenneth Anderson. For a time it had appeared as if there might be a close-fought race for Tripoli between Eighth and First Armies but the latter soon became bogged down in a slogging match in Tunisia. And, after the fall of Tripoli, it was in Tunisia that the bulk of Eighth Army was next to see action.

There was one final action in Libya on 27 January when units of 7th Armoured Division, now under the temporary command of Brigadier Pip Roberts since John Harding had been severely wounded at Tarhuna, met elements of 90th Light holding rearguard positions at Zuara. After four days, 90th Light pulled back along the road to the Tunisian frontier. On 12 February 1943, two years after Rommel had arrived in North Africa, the final units of his Panzer Armee Afrika crossed into Tunisia. Thus ended the desert war, and the Italian empire.

At noon on 23 January, Montgomery entered Tripoli to accept the surrender of the city from the Vice-Governor of Tripolitania. However, the retreating enemy forces had carried out extensive demolitions in the harbour which was closed by eight sunken ships; the Spanish Quay had been badly damaged and the moles had all been partially demolished. Before the day was out, plans were being made to re-open the harbour, anti-aircraft defences were being deployed and a temporary military administration for the city had been established.[23]

Within days a number of landing craft were operating in the harbour and a salvage ship had arrived. By 3 February the first ship had entered the harbour. This was fortuitous as the prime minister visited the city on the 3rd and 4th. Churchill inspected parades representative of Eighth Army's formations and watched soldiers helping to unload cargo at the harbour. To those men he said 'You are unloading history' while to assembled officers and soldiers at Eighth Army HQ he made a memorable speech in which he commented that 'You have nightly pitched your moving tents a day's march nearer home'.

NOTES

1. Eisenfeller: interview with author, May 1990
2. Carver: *El Alamein*, p.167
3. Montgomery: *Memoirs*, p.142
4. Blaxland, *The Plain Cook and the Great Showman*, p.131
5. Barnett: *The Desert Generals*, p.291
6. ibid
7. PRO: WO201/430: RE Notes, Benghazi to Tripoli (the lessons are similar)
8. PRO: CAB44/108
9. PRO: WO169/4171, War Diary, 44 Recce Regt, 1942
10. Kippenberger: *Infantry Brigadier*, p.248
11. Hamilton: *Monty, Master of the Battlefield 1942-1944*, pp.57-60
12. Montgomery, op cit, p.146
13. ibid
14. ibid, p.147
15. Kippenberger: op cit, p.250
16. ibid, p.251
17. ibid, p.258
18. Montgomery: op cit, p.154
19. Kippenberger: op cit, p.261
20. ibid
21. Montgomery: op cit, p.154
22. Doherty: *Wall of Steel*, p.105
23. Howarth: *My God, Soldiers*, p.61

CHAPTER IX

The End in Africa: Eighth Army in Tunisia

I marched and fought with the Desert Army

Tripoli provided a firm base for Eighth Army as it prepared to advance into Tunisia. Morale was very high and the Army's daily sick rate, at one man per thousand, reflected that.[1] Health remained a major priority although the hazards posed by flies now reduced considerably and desert sores no longer made large numbers of men unfit for duty. At Tripoli the French element was strengthened by the arrival of General Leclerc's force of some 3,000 men, many of whom were Senegalese.

By late-February Tripoli harbour was working well with over 3,000 tons a day being discharged in spite of regular attempts by the Luftwaffe to bomb the harbour; the anti-aircraft defences ensured that these were ineffective.[2] With his supply situation resolved, Montgomery could now bring X Corps forward to the Tripoli area to join XXX Corps; XIII Corps had not been engaged since Alamein. Eighth Army's advance into Tunisia was led by 7th Armoured Division; on 18 February the village of Tatouine was captured followed by the village of Medenine two days later. Little opposition was experienced at this stage as Rommel had launched a major offensive against the US II Corps in the Kasserine area that threatened the Allied effort in Tunisia. The raw American troops had suffered heavily but they were to prove fast learners: Monty noted that they learned 'more quickly than we did'.[3]

The German attack at Kasserine led to Alexander assuming command of all Allied land forces in the theatre.* Alexander's new command was designated 18 Army Group and one of his first acts was to ask Montgomery if he could do anything to relieve the pressure on the Americans. Eighth Army was therefore tasked to exert pressure on the

---

* At the Casablanca conference in January, Eisenhower, the Allied Supreme Commander in the theatre, had been asked to accept General Alexander as his deputy and land forces commander. The timing of this appointment was left to Eisenhower who issued an official directive on 20 February, two days after Alexander assumed the command.

Germans in order to force Rommel to break off his attack at Kasserine and turn his attention to Eighth Army.

By the end of February Rommel's command was pulling back from attacks by both Allied armies. However, Monty expected the Desert Fox to turn his attention to Eighth Army: the New Zealand Division was ordered up from Tripoli to strengthen the front-line force. Ultra confirmed Rommel's intention to strike against Eighth Army, a move which Montgomery considered might 'upset the preparations for our own attack against the Mareth Line',[4] scheduled for 19 March. On 6 March, Rommel attacked Eighth Army at Medenine.

The attacking force included three panzer divisions, totalling 160 tanks, and four battlegroups, each at two-battalion strength, and some 200 guns, all under command of the Italian General Messe, a 'competent, conscientious, realistically pessimistic [commander], and not exactly a fighting general'.[5] Advancing under cover of fog, the panzers ran into devastating anti-tank gunfire as the sun burned through and were forced to withdraw. In spite of this the German tanks came on again, not once but three times before finally retreating from the battlefield. Most of the fighting had been done by anti-tank gunners, both Royal Artillery and infantry; only one squadron of British tanks, Shermans, had been engaged. The anti-tank guns which met the panzers were mainly 6-pounders but there were some of the new 17-pounders, a few 3.7-inch HAA guns and a troop of captured 88s, operating under New Zealand command.* Rommel lost over fifty tanks, all but seven to anti-tank guns, while Eighth Army lost no tanks. Montgomery chose not to pursue the retreating Germans, preferring to continue with his preparations for the attack on the Mareth Line.

The Line, built by the French to protect Tunisia against possible Italian aggression from Tripolitania, was based on a strong natural position which had been improved by the French and, more recently, by the Germans with concrete blockhouses, steel gun cupolas and many mines. Stretching some twelve miles from the coast roughly westward into the Matmata Hills, the line had a natural anti-tank ditch in front of it in the form of the Wadi Zigzaou. West of the Matmata Hills, Montgomery was informed by the French, was an impassable sand sea, apparently making

---

* This was Mac Troop, named after Brigadier H M J McIntyre, *Mad Mac*, who had long espoused the use of the British 3.7-inch HAA gun as an anti-tank weapon. After the fall of Tripoli, the CRA of the New Zealand Division, Brigadier Weir, and General Freyberg had been so impressed by a demonstration of 3.7s in a field role that they asked for HAA guns to be placed at their disposal in Tunisia. The result was the formation of Mac Troop, with captured 88s rather than 3.7s which, apparently, could not be spared, from 9th (Londonderry) and 51st HAA Regiments.

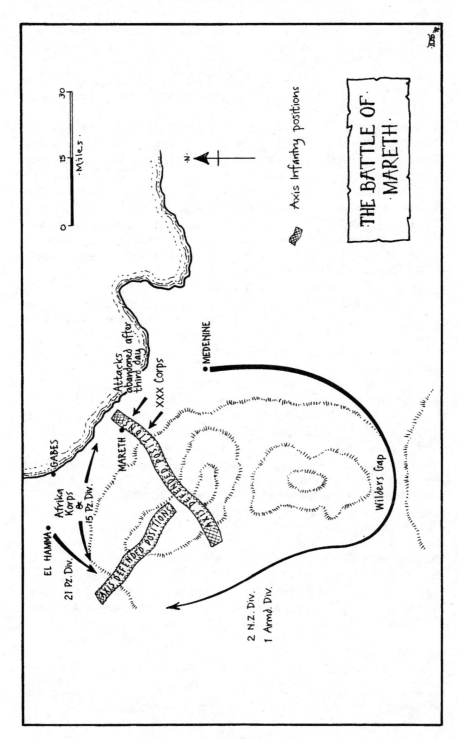

THE BATTLE OF MARETH

Axis Infantry positions

a left-flanking movement a non-starter.* But the main defences were so strong that Monty decided that an outflanking movement, coupled with a limited frontal assault, was necessary and there was insufficient space for such a move on the coastal flank. The Long Range Desert Group reconnoitred a suitable route and Monty's plan began to take positive shape.

By this stage Axis forces in North Africa had been reinforced considerably. The initial German build-up in Tunisia, following the TORCH landings, had been brought up to corps strength, as XC Corps, and then to army strength as Fifth Panzer Armee. The first commander, Walter Nehring, had been replaced by General Jürgen von Arnim. With Rommel's Panzer Armee Afrika revitalised, the Axis forces in Tunisia were a major obstacle to the Allies. On 20 February 1943, Axis forces were re-organised as Army Group Afrika with Rommel as its commander; Panzer Armee Afrika was restyled First Italian Army, under General Messe, and included Afrika Korps.

On 9 March, Rommel left Tunisia to try to persuade Hitler and Mussolini that the line should be shortened by a withdrawal to Wadi Akarit, some forty miles behind the Mareth Line which the German and Italian commanders realised could be outflanked. Rommel was never to return to Africa: he was ordered to take sick leave and von Arnim became Army Group Commander. But Rommel did persuade Hitler to agree to a partial withdrawal to Wadi Akarit with mobile troops being left at Mareth. However, although von Arnim issued orders to that effect, these were countermanded by the Italians on the authority of the Commando Supremo; this was still regarded as an Italian theatre. As a result the Mareth Line was strongly held with four Italian divisions and two German: from the coast were deployed the Young Fascist, Trieste, 90th Light and Spezia Divisions with Pistoia and 164th Light Divisions extending the line farther inland. Three panzer divisions were behind the line: 15th, though weak, was in immediate reserve; 21st was covering the Gabes Gap and 10th was in deep reserve behind Wadi Akarit.

As early as 26 February, Monty was issuing plans for Operation PUGILIST, the attack on the Mareth Line. Nothing was to be left to chance and once again X Corps was transformed temporarily into a carrying service; on this occasion its burden included the fresh tanks of 1st Armoured Division. As planning developed, the roles of Eighth Army's various

* In 1938 two French officers had studied the area and made a report which rejected the idea of impassability. Since that time the use of four-wheel drive had improved greatly the cross-country capabilities of vehicles and made possible the outflanking of the Mareth Line by skirting the Matmata Hills to the Tebaga Gap and then to El Hamma.

formations became known: XXX Corps, with 50th, 51st and 4th Indian Divisions plus 201 Guards Brigade, would break into the line at its northern end, nearest the sea, roll it up and then strike towards Gabes. Freyberg's New Zealanders, reinforced to corps strength by 8 Armoured Brigade, and Leclerc's L Force, and designated the New Zealand Corps,[6]* would flank left around the Matmata Hills to try to establish themselves on the Gabes-Matmata road to cut off the enemy. Behind XXX Corps the armour of X Corps, 1st and 7th Armoured Divisions, would be held ready to exploit success in the breakthrough battle; X Corps' objective was the port of Sfax. Such exploitation would be in line with 18 Army Group's strategic objective of taking Tunis by, first, passing Eighth Army through the Gabes Gap and, second, capturing enough airfields to strangle the Axis forces.

The defeat of the Axis attack at Medenine on 6 March increased morale in Eighth Army. There was no doubt in the minds of its soldiers that Monty would deliver victory. Another enemy spoiling attack on 10 March was repulsed by Leclerc's L Force at Ksar Rhilane; since this position was west of the Matmatas, it underlined the enemy's awareness of the possibility of a left hook around the mountain range.

Operation PUGILIST was planned for 20 March with the main attack being made in the coastal area by 50th (Northumbrian) Division. This formation, still at two-brigade strength, had not seen any action since Alamein where both brigades had been committed separately.[7] Prior to D-day, the divisional commander ordered the taking of an enemy outpost line along the Wadi Zeuss, three miles in front of Wadi Zigzaou. On the night of 16/17 March, 69 (Yorkshire) Brigade advanced on this line: 5th East Yorks and 6th Green Howards were assisted by 5/7th Gordons from 51st Division. By daylight the three battalions were established a mile beyond the wadi.

Farther to the left a feature known as the Horseshoe was attacked by 201 Guards Brigade with two battalions, the raw 6th Grenadiers and the veteran 3rd Coldstream. As both were motor battalions they deployed three, rather than four, companies. Attacking in bright moonlight under a creeping bombardment, the guardsmen made good progress until they ran into mines. Anti-personnel mines caused many casualties, while intensive enemy mortar fire created more and set off many anti-tank mines which added to the confusion. In spite of heavy casualties, both Grenadiers and Coldstreamers continued to their objectives but so few men were left that consolidation was virtually impossible, especially as carriers taking up ammunition were blown up on mines; a withdrawal

* The Corps also included British medium and field artillery regiments, 1st King's Dragoon Guards and the Greek Sacred Squadron.

was ordered. There were over 300 casualties: the Grenadiers lost 279 including fourteen officers killed, one of whom was the Commanding Officer, Lieutenant-Colonel Clive. The Horseshoe had been defended by 90th Light Division.

The casualties suffered in the Guards' attack were largely due to lack of reconnaissance; there had not been adequate close examination of the objective and its approaches by patrols and thus the work of the German engineers had been undetected until too late. However, there was to be no disruption to Montgomery's plan: the attack would still go in on the night of 20 March, even though heavy rain had added to Eighth Army's problems. Montgomery and Leese were content to leave the details of 50th Division's assault to Major-General Nichols, the divisional commander, although he had no experience in conducting a divisional attack.

> Like Wellington at the storming of Badajoz, they relied on the morale of the troops to reduce the fortifications, and in a pre-battle message to his men, bursting with confidence, Montgomery emphasised the effect on Rommel of his repulse at Medenine (without knowing that he had now retired hurt) . . .[8]

Monty told his soldiers that, if every man did his duty, nothing would stop Eighth Army. He finished his message with the exhortation, FORWARD TO TUNIS! DRIVE THE ENEMY INTO THE SEA![9] If such exhortations, and high morale, could win battles then Eighth Army would have had a relatively easy passage at Mareth. As it was, enemy resistance was determined, well organised and well led as the assaulting soldiers of 50th Division were soon to learn to their cost.

Fiftieth Division was to create the initial bridgehead, pushing inland for three miles, before 4th Indian Division passed through. In the van of 50th Division was 151 (Durham) Brigade, composed of battalions of Durham Light Infantry; this brigade was to form the bridgehead with 69 Brigade protecting its left flank by seizing the Bastion, a new position east of Wadi Zigzaou.

Massive artillery and air bombardment was carried out to soften up the enemy defences: thirteen field and three medium regiments provided the artillery programme while British and American aircraft bombed and strafed Axis positions. Fifty-one Valentine tanks of 50 RTR were allocated to support 151 Brigade while a squadron of Scorpion tanks was assigned to clear paths through the minefield in front of the wadi. The latter obstacle was to be crossed at two points, 1,200 yards apart, with infantry using ladders to get into and out of the wadi bed; sappers were to clear mines from the bed and collapse the wadi's banks to allow vehicles to cross. Fascines were carried by tanks to assist in crossing the wadi and an anti-tank ditch some distance beyond.

First into action were the special assault groups of 7th Green Howards from 69 Brigade. Rejoicing in the soubriquet 'Thugs', these groups tackled machine-gun posts that were putting down harassing fire on the paths cleared by sappers. In this tough and desperate fighting, the Green Howards' CO, Lieutenant-Colonel Derek Anthony 'Bunny' Seagrim played a vital part. When the left assaulting company's commander was wounded, Seagrim took personal command of the company:

> Realising the seriousness of the situation, . . . [he] pushed to the front and took personal charge of a team attempting to place a scaling ladder over the twelve-foot-wide anti-tank ditch. The first man across, he attacked two machine-gun posts with his pistol and grenades, killing or wounding ten or a dozen Germans. It was largely due to Seagrim's inspired courage that the 7th Battalion captured the 'Bastion' and held it throughout the following day against a succession of counter-attacks.[10]

His leadership and courage earned Seagrim the Victoria Cross but he was killed in action at Wadi Akarit before the award was announced.*

The two attacking battalions of Durhams had meanwhile made a shallow bridgehead over the wadi and the anti-tank ditch. They had come under heavy mortar and machine-gun fire as well as being held up by dust and breakdowns among their Scorpions. Opposition at Wadi Zigzaou and the anti-tank ditch was comparatively light and the assault companies were able to move on. The right company of 8th Durhams took a ridge while the left company struck left to take their objective, Ouerzi, from behind. The Young Fascists provided very tough opposition and the work of winkling them out of their positions cost many casualties. On Ksiba Ouest 9th Durhams had an equally tough and deadly task in mopping up after the objective had been gained.

As both leading battalions fought for their objectives, 50th Division's sappers worked to clear a route for the tanks, all the while enduring constant mortar fire and the attention of machine gunners in an enfilade position along the wadi. Their problems were compounded when some of the fascines being carried by tanks were ignited by hot exhausts. When a path across the wadi for tanks had been completed the sappers had the heartbreaking experience of seeing the first tank to cross become bogged down after stalling. A by-pass was constructed with fascines and four tanks crossed before another became stuck fast. With dawn approaching, Brigadier Beak, VC, DSO, MC and bar, commanding 151 Brigade, decided to

---

* Seagrim's family hold the distinction of having a VC and a GC winner. His brother, Major H P Seagrim, won a posthumous George Cross for gallantry in Burma in early-1944.

postpone operations until nightfall; no more tanks made the crossing and 6th Durhams, who were to have attacked through the brigade centre, were pulled back having endured a night of shelling in their assembly area.

Throughout the day that followed, 8th and 9th DLI continued with their mopping up. The area was full of underground passages and pits and the defenders were particularly stubborn, inflicting many casualties on the two Durham battalions; Lieutenant-Colonel Jackson, of the 8th, was among those killed.* On the 'Bastion', 7th Green Howards fought off a series of counter-attacks that day; they were later reinforced by 6th Green Howards who moved in on the evening of the 22nd.

After dark on the 21st Brigadier Beak pushed two more battalions, his own 6th DLI and 5th East Yorks from 69 Brigade, into the bridgehead. This reinforcement allowed progress to be made and a number of other positions were taken. The pressure of the fighting, coupled with the intensive artillery onslaught, had weakened Italian morale and they began to surrender in large numbers. The sappers continued their labours and succeeded in getting all 50 RTR's remaining Valentines across. However, heavy rain left the ground waterlogged which impeded the advance of other vehicles. Fortunately the engineers were able to work in daylight as the bridgehead had been extended; by noon on 22 March a route usable by light vehicles had been completed. Then came a rainstorm which demanded that the sappers redouble their efforts.

At much the same time, enemy artillery began a heavy bombardment of 50th Division's forward positions. The guns fired for about an hour, providing the prelude to an attack by some thirty tanks of 15th Panzer Division. Only the eight Valentines fitted with 6-pounder guns could provide any adequate defence against the German tanks; the other forty-three Valentines carried 2-pounders. The division's anti-tank artillery had not yet been brought forward since they had not been regarded as a priority. In spite of the best efforts of 50 RTR, whose CO, Lieutenant-Colonel Cairnes, was killed, the Durham Brigade was forced back to the line of the anti-tank ditch. They were

> desperately weary, short of ammunition, out of touch with their guns, and yet still with spirit enough to dig themselves fire steps in the side of the ditch and to defy any attempt to shift them from their precarious perch. Twenty-seven Valentines lay derelict ahead of them, and of the survivors eleven were poised to support the infantry from the narrow strip between ditch and wadi. The 5th East Yorks were in better trim on the extreme right of the line, not having been attacked, but they too had no room for manoeuvre and were vulnerable to ejection into the wadi.[11]

* The battalions of 151 Brigade were all under strength since their losses at Alamein had not yet been made good. Each was organised on a three-company basis rather than the normal four-company format.

While the Durhams were being forced back, Major-General Nichols had been preparing a counter-attack for which he planned to use 69 Brigade. To prepare for the attack, the two Green Howard battalions on the bastion were therefore relieved by units from 51st Division. In this operation 69 Brigade was to be supported by 5 RTR, from 7th Armoured Division, while 4th Indian Division provided two companies of Madras and Bengal Sappers and Miners to clear paths for the advance. As the Indian sappers toiled at their task the moon rose and they were subjected to heavy fire. Nonetheless they persevered; their Commander, Royal Engineers, John Blundell, had the peak of his cap torn off by a bullet. But such was the congestion as the two infantry battalions moved up to their start line that it became obvious that 69 Brigade could not attack before daylight. The corps commander therefore gave permission for the attack to be cancelled.

When it had become clear that Eighth Army's initial thrust against the Mareth Line had been repulsed, Monty's staff decided that the Army Commander would have to be woken from his sleep. This was done at 2am on the 23rd and, although Monty was at first taken aback, he was soon revising his plans to reinforce the left hook. He decided that 50th and 51st Divisions, supported by 7th Armoured, would remain near the coast to contain the enemy while Horrocks' X Corps, less 7th Armoured Division, would join the New Zealand Corps in its outflanking move. A request from Monty for the US II Corps, under General Patton, to assist Eighth Army by striking south-east to Wadi Akarit was rejected by Alexander as being too ambitious. Ironically, Monty had earlier demanded that the Americans, while assisting his attack, should be kept out of his way.

There had already been fighting on the left flank with Leclerc's French troops and 8 Armoured Brigade heavily involved at Wadi Medfid on 19 March. During the course of its actions 8 Armoured Brigade suffered the loss of its second-in-command, Colonel 'Flash' Kellet, killed by a direct hit on his tank. Freyberg's infantry had also been in action with 6 Brigade capturing a hill in the middle of the Tebaga Gap on the night of 21/22 March.

The first phase of the strengthened left hook was to be an attack by the New Zealand infantry to take Djebel Melab on the night of 25 March after which, on the following afternoon, 8 Armoured Brigade would attack through the Tebaga Gap, supported by Freyberg's infantry. Once 8 Armoured Brigade had secured their objectives, 1st Armoured Division would pass through and advance towards El Hamma during the night. (Montgomery was later to describe this deployment as reinforcing success.[12]) Horrocks, with HQ X Corps, was sent to take charge of the left hook.

Djebel Melab was taken by 21st NZ Battalion's night attack on the 25th while 8 Armoured Brigade prepared for its part in the operation. On the morning of the 26th, a fierce khamsin threatened the postponement of operations; aircraft of the Desert Air Force, which had provided excellent support for Eighth Army, were grounded although other planes, based farther from the front, were able to fly. Then, at about midday, the storm abated and by mid-afternoon air operations were in full swing with tactical bombers and fighter-bombers attacking enemy positions.

At 4pm the artillery opened their bombardment and 8 Armoured Brigade began its advance, moving behind the bombardment which was lifting forward by a hundred yards each minute. The Brigade was attacking with the sun behind it; the wind was also from behind, a combination which gave the attackers a distinct advantage: in the first mile there was virtually no delay as the tanks ground forward. The enemy, waiting for the usual British night attack, were taken by surprise.

The first serious opposition came from a peak, Point 209, to the right of the Sherwood Rangers who were on the Brigade's right flank. In fairly rapid succession, the Rangers lost three tanks to fire from Point 209. But the accompanying New Zealand infantry, men of 28th (Maori) Battalion, quickly launched an attack against stiff opposition which allowed the Rangers to gain their objective. The New Zealanders also proved invaluable when 3 RTR, on the left, ran into mines and camouflaged 88s: once again it was the infantrymen who shook the enemy out of their positions and allowed the advance to continue.

First Armoured Division was able to pass through on time, although as they cleared 8 Armoured Brigade's area, there was still much fighting going on, especially around Point 209; this was not to end until the next day and it brought another Victoria Cross to 2nd New Zealand Division. The Cross was awarded posthumously to Second-Lieutenant Moana-Nui-a-Kiwa Ngarimu, of 28th Battalion, who led his platoon straight up a hill against a strongly-held enemy position

> personally annihilating at least two enemy machine-gun posts. The enemy at once counter-attacked under an intense mortar barrage. But the New Zealanders stood fast and the attackers were mown down, 2nd Lieut Ngarimu personally killing several. He was twice wounded but refused to leave his men.[13]

Only two of his platoon remained uninjured by daybreak. Reinforcements arrived with the dawn but in the next enemy counter-attack Second-Lieutenant Ngarimu was killed. His was the first VC awarded to a Maori.

Meanwhile 1st Armoured Division was racing for El Hamma. With clouds of sand still blinding the opposing gunners, and guns and aircraft providing close support, the division was within fifteen miles of El

Hamma when darkness forced a halt. Losses were negligible. The divisional commander ordered the advance to continue shortly before midnight and tanks of the Bays and 9th Lancers probed forward, knocking out enemy guns and vehicles.

> The Germans were in fact on the move all round them, some ahead of them, some on their flanks, and some tacked on to the columns. Then an 88 opened up, scored a hit and was in turn destroyed. When about three miles from El Hamma, the leading regiments were ordered to close up and consolidate. It was the first intrusion of a note of caution.[14]

Dawn on 27 March saw the beginning of a confused battle near El Hamma. The motorised infantry with the Yorkshire Dragoons had found the enemy holding a wadi in front of Djebel Halouga which barred the way to El Hamma. Effective anti-tank gunfire forced the attacking Bays and 9th Lancers into hull-down positions and it soon became clear that elements of both 15th and 21st Panzer Divisions were engaged against the tail of 1st Armoured Division and 8 Armoured Brigade. That led to 76th Anti-Tank Regiment being rushed back to engage the panzers. The regiment had a mix of 6-pounder portees and towed 17-pounders and the latter weapon more than proved its worth against the German tanks which were forced to withdraw.

However, the day's events had left 1st Armoured on the defensive with high ground on either side and demanded another major effort co-ordinated with the New Zealanders and 8 Armoured Brigade, who regained contact with 1st Armoured after nightfall. The new plan was for 1st Armoured to contain the enemy at El Hamma while the New Zealanders thrust right for Gabes. Over very difficult terrain an advance of five miles was made by 8 Armoured Brigade on the 28th. At the same time 4th Indian Division reported enemy rearguards falling back from the Mareth Line; the Indians had taken up positions high in the Matmatas but were too far away to have any effect on the battle.

First Armoured Division found El Hamma abandoned on the morning of the 28th and, by midday, the King's Dragoon Guards had reached Gabes ahead of the New Zealanders. The Mareth battle was over and Montgomery had demonstrated his flexibility as a commander with the most daring use of British armour thus far in the war. Alan Moorehead described Monty's switch to the left using all available armour and aircraft in support of New Zealanders as 'possibly the boldest thing Montgomery ever did'.[15] Had the left hook been delivered earlier the Tunisian campaign might well have been shortened.

> The battle demonstrated Montgomery's excellent flexibility of mind. It also once again showed his strength and will-power – Freyberg had to

be pushed hard, for he needed to husband New Zealand manpower and he was disinclined to take risks. Its aftermath demonstrated, too, Montgomery's proneness to exaggerated claims for the nature of his successes, untouched by error or miscalculation. Most of all it demonstrated the excellence of British troops who, from the preliminary operations . . . through to 1st Armoured Division's rapid move . . . and dashing assault on 26th March, showed a skill and energy which gave its true lustre to the day.[16]

The enemy had withdrawn to Wadi Akarit where Eighth Army was to have its last great battle in North Africa. As Monty's army moved up the Gabes Gap, most of Afrika Korps was to their left, engaged in holding off Patton's II Corps along the northern shore of Chott el Fedjadi, an apparently impassable sea of soft sand, salt and water with the appearance of a scum deposit.

Montgomery decided to make a direct attack on the Wadi Akarit line with XXX Corps making the initial assault which would then be exploited by X Corps. The attack would be made before the full moon and, therefore, before the enemy expected it. D-Day was to be 6 April. The most easterly of the hills between the wadi and the German positions astride the Gafsa road was Djebel Roumana which, with the stretches of low ground on either side, was to be XXX Corps' objective.

In the van of XXX Corps' attack was 51st (Highland) Division, on the right, and 4th Indian Division; the Highlanders were to take the djebel itself, plus associated defensive works to its right, while the Indians' objectives were an anti-tank ditch to the left and Rass Zouai, a high feature among the complex of high points known as Fatnassa. Rass Zouai was to be the location of another VC-winning exploit.

Major-General Tuker considered that the rocky massif dominating the front before 4th Indian Division would be no real problem to his Indian soldiers. Tuker had a long fascination with mountain-fighting by night and was confident that the Gurkhas would be as at home on these Tunisian mountains even in darkness as a Cockney would be in blacked-out London.[17] He also felt that there was not an effective defence in the mountains as the Axis forces had insufficient strength for this; consequently the apparently strong mountain feature would be the weakest part of the enemy line. This thinking led Tuker to suggest to Leese that the two brigades of 4th Indian Division (it had still not been restored to full strength) should be directed solely against the high ground, under cover of darkness and without artillery support, so as to obtain maximum surprise. Leese and Montgomery agreed and 50th Division was drafted in to attack the anti-tank ditch in the gap between Roumana and Fatnassa. That attack, along with 51st Division's, would be launched at dawn with artillery support.

Tuker's own regiment, 2nd King Edward VII's Own Gurkha Rifles, provided the vanguard of 7 Indian Brigade's assault on the massif. As darkness deepened, 1/2nd Gurkhas began their climb towards the enemy positions.

Nothing was heard of their progress until a scream rent the air around midnight. This was followed by a terrifying cacophony of automatic fire, the bark and crumps of grenade and mortar-bomb, and many more screams, and on top of it came an eerie whimper, as if a pack of beagles were in full cry. It was the cry of the Gurkhas, surging forward with kukris drawn, and indeed one platoon commander, Subadar Lalbahadur Thapa, cut a lone trail as far as the ledge of the escarpment under which the other brigade was to pass. All his own men lay dead or wounded behind him, among such dead Italians as had refused or failed to join their comrades in flight.[18]

Lalbahadur Thapa was subsequently awarded the Victoria Cross. His platoon had first encountered the enemy at the foot of a pathway up a narrow cleft which was covered by machine-guns. The enemy outpost garrisons were dealt with by bayonet and kukri.

The next machine-gun posts were dealt with similarly, the Subadar personally killing two men with his kukri and two more with his revolver. This Gurkha officer continued to fight his way up to the crest where he killed another two men with his kukri and the two riflemen with him killed two more.[19]

Lalbahadur Thapa's men eventually secured the whole feature, charging for the crest through a storm of bullets. The citation for Thapa's VC states that his action made possible his division's advance. Tuker subsequently wrote that the Battle of Wadi Akarit was won 'single-handed' before the formal attack was even launched. Certainly the Indian brigades had done sterling work: 1st Royal Sussex had taken the heights of Djebel Meida, overlooking the anti-tank ditch while 4/6th Punjabis had secured a track through the mountains. Five Brigade had passed through 7 Brigade to carry the attack farther into the massif.

Eighth Army's guns opened fire at 4.15am on 6 April to support the attacks of five battalions from 50th and 51st Divisions. On Djebel Roumana, 152 Brigade's lead battalions, 5th Seaforth and 5th Camerons, found the Italian defenders dazed by the bombardment.

The 5th Seaforth's first encounter with the enemy was with half-dressed Italians, rubbing the sleep out of their eyes and very anxious to know their way to the prisoner-of-war cage.[20]

Shortly after 5th Seaforth had taken their objective, 2nd Seaforth who had moved up behind them before turning right along the ridge top, secured theirs. This was later lost to enemy counter-attack, thus exposing the flanks of 5th Seaforth and 7th Black Watch. Attempts to recapture the position were unsuccessful but the battalion held a defensive line farther down the slope for the rest of the day.

To the right, 154 Brigade's 7th Argyll and Sutherland Highlanders had to overcome three major obstacles, a minefield, a tributary of Wadi Akarit and an anti-tank ditch, to secure a bridgehead for the brigade attack. The greatest difficulty came with the latter obstacle where the leadership of the CO of 7th Argylls proved invaluable: Lieutenant-Colonel Lorne Campbell was inspiring; anti-tank guns were towed across by Valentine tanks and the passage of 7th Black Watch was secured despite heavy enemy fire.

Fiftieth Division's attack was made by 69 Brigade with 7th Green Howards and 5th East Yorks leading. Both battalions fell behind the artillery bombardment and both lost their COs killed; 7th Green Howards' was the redoubtable Seagrim who had won the VC at Mareth; he thus died before his award had been announced. The two battalions were forced to take cover from the fierce fire being directed at them from the anti-tank ditch. As the East Yorks suffered, their stretcher-bearers did their utmost to rescue wounded. One of those stretcher-bearers was Private Eric Anderson who

> went forward alone through heavy fire to rescue the wounded. Three times he brought in wounded comrades and was rendering first aid to a fourth when he was mortally wounded.[21]

Eric Anderson's outstanding courage was recognised with the award of a posthumous Victoria Cross.

In the meantime, 6th Green Howards, backed up by tanks from 4th County of London Yeomanry, made a right-flanking attack towards Roumana. This began to loosen the enemy's grip on the position and 4th Essex, from Tuker's division, broke into the left of the ditch below Djebel Meida. As battalions of 4th Indian Division moved rapidly through the mountains, rounding up hundreds of prisoners, Tuker was certain that the defences had been split apart. Horrocks then sought Montgomery's permission to unleash X Corps' armour at once but it was over four hours before 8 Armoured Brigade's tanks began moving through the breaches in the anti-tank ditch. This delay was largely due to the cumbersome command system resulting from Monty's insistence on having a *corps de chasse*, X Corps, with one command superimposed on another.

The armour ran into difficulties almost immediately: anti-tank guns and mines impeded their advance and it soon became clear that there would be no breakthrough that day. Then came the enemy counter-attack with infantry and armour against 7 Indian Brigade, who stood fast, and Roumana where 200th Panzer Grenadier Regiment with tanks of 15th Panzer Division and Italian infantry pushed back 2nd Seaforth who joined 5th Seaforth in a desperate struggle to hold the ridge with 1/7th Middlesex, the divisional machine-gun battalion, adding their contribution.

During this fighting, Lieutenant-Colonel Lorne Campbell won the Victoria Cross. His battalion and 7th Black Watch were counter-attacked by elements of 15th Panzer and 90th Light Divisions and several supporting Valentines were knocked out. Heavy fire fell on the infantry causing many casualties among the Argylls, including Colonel Campbell.

> . . . his position was subjected to heavy and continuous bombardment and in the late afternoon determined enemy counter-attacks started to develop, supported by tanks. It was chiefly owing to Lieut-Col. Campbell's inspiring leadership that these attacks were repulsed. Despite a painful wound in the neck he continued to direct the operations, which developed into a close-quarter struggle with the bayonet. But the Argylls stood fast.[22]

In the words of his subsequent VC citation, Campbell's 'presence dominated the battlefield'.

That night the enemy withdrew. Sixteen infantry battalions from three divisions of Eighth Army had put to flight an enemy force of six infantry divisions and three armoured in spite of the strength of the positions they had held. Appropriately, each attacking division had won a Victoria Cross. Eighth Army had taken over 5,000 prisoners for the loss of 1,289 dead or wounded, mostly from 51st (Highland) Division. Among the dead were two senior engineers: Brigadier Kisch, Chief Engineer, Eighth Army, had been killed by a mine while inspecting the battlefield; Lieutenant-Colonel Blundell, 4th Indian Division's CRE, fell to shellfire.

On the afternoon of 7 April elements of Eighth Army made contact with American troops of Patton's II Corps which had been disappointed that it had not managed to disrupt the enemy retreat from Wadi Akarit. With the Axis now in full retreat from the coastal plain the next phase of the fighting was to fall upon soldiers of First Army. Eighth Army was able to advance rapidly up the coast, taking Sfax on 10 April and Sousse, some sixty miles farther north, only two days later.

Alexander's strategy hinged on making his main attack from the west, breaking through to Tunis and splitting the enemy forces in two. The smaller element in the north could be mopped up by Allied forces in that area while the larger portion would be driven southwards against a line 'firmly held by the Eighth Army'. This strategy was also dictated by 18

Army Group's dispositions: of 156 infantry battalions under Alexander's command, fifty-three were in First Army, forty-three in Eighth Army, thirty-eight were French and twenty-two American. Eighth Army had 460 tanks from 18 Army Group's total of 1,193.[23] Opposing Alexander's forces were ninety German and Italian infantry battalions and 143 tanks.

Eighth Army's principal role was to keep constant pressure on the enemy thus drawing Axis forces off First Army. Montgomery's command was now up against a very strong defensive position that allowed an attacker little room for manoeuvre. This was the Zaghouan mountain, over 3,500 feet high, and its neighbouring hills and ridges which ran down to the sea on either side of Enfidaville and thus dominated the narrow coastal strip. Zaghouan was thirty-five miles south of Tunis and Monty still felt that he could break through with X Corps* to the Cape Bon peninsula.

Once again Eighth Army moved to battle. On the night of 19 April 4th Indian and 2nd New Zealand Divisions were launched against hills in the Zaghouan range. On the left 5 Indian Brigade gained half of Djebel Garci where 6th Rajputana Rifles and 9th Gurkhas fought with ferocious courage, using bayonet and kukri in bitter hand-to-hand fighting. In the course of this battle Company Havildar-Major Chhelu Ram of the Rajputs won a posthumous VC. When the brigade's advance had been checked by machine-gun and mortar fire, Chhelu Ram had charged forward

> with a tommy-gun and killed the occupants of a post and then went to the aid of his company commander who had become a casualty. While doing so he was himself wounded, but taking command of the company, he led them in hand-to-hand fighting. He was again wounded, but continued rallying his men until he died.[24]

To the right of the Indians the New Zealanders had attacked the small Takrouna feature. So tough was the fighting that Freyberg's men did not secure Takrouna until after three days' fighting. Once again there were numerous examples of tremendous courage as the New Zealanders fought to take their objective. Takrouna had been assigned to the Maori Battalion and Lieutenant-General Brian Horrocks later expressed wonder at how the Maoris had taken the feature which is capped by a flat space some thirty yards square, most of which is occupied by stone buildings and an Arab tomb. Below is a sheer drop of about thirty feet and, at some points, there is an overhang.

The platoon commander leading the attack on the night of 20/21 April was wounded in the early stages of the operation but his men carried on,

---

* X Corps was now minus 1st Armoured Division which had been transferred to IX Corps in First Army.

even though there were several more casualties. By dawn only nine men, including two sergeants, were left of the platoon. They persisted with the attack under the leadership of Sergeant Manahi and, against all the odds, they not only reached the top but took seventy German prisoners.

> Horrocks, who followed the assault and carefully inspected the ground afterwards, recommended Manahi for a VC. He was not pleased when the intrepid sergeant was merely awarded a DCM (Distinguished Conduct Medal).[25]

But Eighth Army's progress had been halted with a gain of only three miles. Some twenty-three battalions held the mountain feature and none of them looked as if they intended to be shifted. Although Montgomery wanted to continue with a thrust along the coastal strip, his subordinates felt this to be ill-considered; Horrocks told him that, if the plan went ahead, there would not be much left of Eighth Army. A frustrated Monty then agreed to Alexander's proposal to transfer more Eighth Army divisions to First Army whose advance had also been stalled. Crocker, IX Corps' commander in First Army, had been wounded and Monty suggested Horrocks to fill the vacancy. This was accepted and Horrocks took with him 4th Indian and 7th Armoured Divisions as well as 201 Guards Brigade from X Corps.

Horrocks' new command played a key role in the final battles in Tunisia. The first Allied troops to enter Tunis were men from the Derbyshire Yeomanry and 11th Hussars. Both regiments claimed the honour; but it was probably shared as there was more than one road into Tunis. Monty, however, attributed the honour to 'our own 7th Armoured Division',[26] i.e. 11th Hussars. In Monty's mind, Eighth Army was there at the finish.

The war in North Africa ended on 12 May with over 200,000 Axis soldiers, their equipment, stores and weapons falling into Allied hands. Eighth Army had fought its last battles in Africa; attention was now turning to its next operation, on which Montgomery was already spending much effort. This was to be Operation HUSKY, the invasion of Sicily.

NOTES

1. Brooks: *Montgomery and the Eighth Army*, p.131
2. Doherty: *Wall of Steel*, pp.107-116
3. Montgomery: *Memoirs*, p.158
4. ibid
5. Blaxland: *The Plain Cook and the Great Showman*, p.189
6. Kippenberger: *Infantry Brigadier*, p.276
7. Blaxland, op cit, p.193

8.   ibid, p.195
9.   Montgomery, op cit, p.161
10. Powell, G, *The History of The Green Howards*, p.198
11. Blaxland, op cit, p.199
12. Montgomery, op cit, p.162
13. Smyth: *The Story of the Victoria Cross*, p.379
14. Blaxland: op cit, p.207
15. Moorehead: *The Desert War*, p.219
16. Fraser: *And We Shall Shock Them*, p.256
17. Howarth: *My God, Soldiers*, p.81
18. Blaxland: op cit, p.213
19. Smyth: op cit, p.380
20. Salmond: *The History of the 51st Highland Division*, p.89
21. *Register of the Victoria Cross*, p.14
22. Smyth: op cit, p.380
23. PRO: CAB44/122
24. *Register of the Victoria Cross*, p.60
25. Warner: *Horrocks*, p.96
26. Montgomery: op cit, p.165

CHAPTER X

The Sicilian Campaign: July – August 1943

Give signal to the fight

Sicily, 'a land of heat and smelly socks' as one veteran described it,[1] was to be Eighth Army's next area of operations. Since the Casablanca conference of January 1943 planning had been going on apace for the invasion of Sicily under the codename HUSKY with the aim of securing Allied lines of communication through the Mediterranean; diverting German pressure from the Russian front; and intensifying pressure on Italy to quit the Axis.

The Americans were keen to launch an invasion of north-west Europe across the English channel in 1943 but Churchill had persuaded them of the wisdom of taking Sicily.* The practicalities of the plan included the fact that it would make use of the large numbers of troops already in the Mediterranean theatre, which made sense to the Americans, and it might also persuade Turkey to join the Allies. At Casablanca, Churchill and Roosevelt agreed that the invasion of Sicily would form the next element of Allied strategy once the campaign in North Africa had ended.

As planning for HUSKY progressed, the participating formations for the Sicilian campaign were identified. There would be both British and American forces, each eventually at army strength, under an army group command. Initially, General Eisenhower was the Supreme Commander, as he had been in North Africa, with Alexander commanding all land forces. The latter's command was at first referred to as Force 141; the subordinate commands were Force 545, or Eastern Task Force, under Montgomery, and Force 343, or Western Task Force, under Patton.[3]

The land elements of the Task Forces later took on army designations although Force 545's first such designation was, for a short period,

---

* The UK Chiefs of Staff had deliberated between Sardinia and Sicily with the latter becoming the preferred option since, in the view of the CIGS, Sir Alan Brooke, 'enemy reinforcement would be more laborious than in Sardinia'.[2] After careful consideration the US Chiefs agreed but made it clear that accepting an invasion of Sicily did not imply that they would approve a series of operations in the Mediterranean.

Twelfth Army: a file dated May 1943 and entitled *Twelfth Army Operations Folder No. 1* includes in its order of battle formations which had served under Eighth Army.[4] It would appear that there was an intention in some minds that Eighth Army was to be broken up, as happened to First Army. This is borne out in Nigel Hamilton's biography of Montgomery in which the author points out that

> whereas the operation was seen by the planners as an independent 'show', mounted by the anonymous Forces 141, 343 and 545, there was no question of Eighth Army being broken up merely at the whim of planners in London, Algiers or Cairo. Ever since Alexander had nominated him for the British part of 'Husky', Monty had insisted on casting the Eighth Army mantle over the British contribution, as he wrote on 16 February 1943 to Brooke, and he refused to go back on this. 'We must use the whole Eighth Army team, as we do now,' he wrote to Alexander – and informed his superiors that, when the fighting was over, he would take his Eighth Army HQ to Tripoli, midway between the two Corps selected for 'Husky': 30 Corps at Sfax/Sousse, 13 Corps in Egypt.[5]

It would appear, therefore, that Montgomery saved Eighth Army from disappearing to be replaced by Twelfth Army in the summer of 1943.* However, this was not the only aspect of the HUSKY planning about which he was unhappy. The overall strategy, involving two national commands and with his own Army dissipated in small brigade-size landings did not appeal to him at all,[6] even though he had earlier agreed to such a plan.† His opposition brought change, with the landings being consolidated so that each would be stronger. Monty also felt that one commander, himself, should conduct operations and that II (US) Corps should be under Eighth Army command. This was unacceptable to the Americans and brought about a change of plan by them: whereas the American Force 343 was to have been an augmented corps, it was now decided that, since the British element had transformed into Eighth Army, the US element would also be at army strength: this was Seventh Army. Alexander's Force 141 became 15 Army Group.

There were eventually to be twenty-six landing beaches, spread over 105

---

* The Twelfth Army title was later used as a phantom army to deceive the Axis into thinking that an invasion of Greece was being planned. In May 1945, the title was revived in Burma as a successor to Fourteenth Army.
† He was not in fact enthusiastic about the Mediterranean strategy at all, believing that the numbers of Allied troops in North Africa would keep large numbers of Axis forces pinned down in Italy while the main Allied effort went into the invasion of France.

miles of coast with D-Day for HUSKY being 10 July 1943; H-Hour for the first landings was set at 2.45am. Prior to those landings the Allied air forces had bombed heavily the defenders' communications, airfields and fixed defences. Elements of Eighth Army also landed on the islands of Pantellaria and Lampedusa; in each case they had little more to do than accept the surrender of the Italian garrisons which had been so heavily bombed that they were pleased to see the invaders. Pantellaria surrendered on 11 June and Lampedusa followed suit a day later.

Large naval forces were to transport and support the invading troops. Eighth Army's area of operations was on the eastern and south-eastern coast of Sicily with elements landing either side of the south-eastern tip of the island, the Pachino peninsula. For HUSKY Eighth Army included XIII and XXX Corps, commanded respectively by Lieutenant-Generals Miles Dempsey and Sir Oliver Leese, with four infantry divisions, 5th, 50th, 51st and 1st Canadian; one independent infantry and two armoured brigades; a Canadian army tank brigade; and a gliderborne brigade of 1st Airborne Division. The assault forces were augmented by No. 3 Commando, Nos 40 and 41 (RM) Commandos and 1st Special Raiding Squadron of 2nd Special Air Service Regiment. These latter units were to seize or destroy targets in advance of the main invasion: 1st SRS and No. 3 Commando to eliminate coastal artillery batteries at Cape Murro di Purco and Cassibile; Nos 40 and 41 Commandos to land in the Pachino peninsula, west of Ponta Castellazo to provide a firm left flank for Eighth Army. On the right flank, 1st Airlanding Brigade was to seize and hold the Ponte Grande over the Anapo river until relieved by 5th Division; the bridge was vital to the capture of Syracuse.

The Axis defence of Sicily was in the hands of Armed Forces Command Sicily, the principal constituent of which was Sixth Italian Army, under General Alfreda Guzzoni. Sixth Army's XII and XVI Corps deployed six coastal and five field divisions and Guzzoni also had two German divisions, Hermann Goering and 15th Panzer Grenadier, formerly Sicily Division.

Although many of the Italian troops, especially in the coastal divisions, were not of the highest quality, Montgomery believed that they would fight fiercely in defence of home territory. He had been especially impressed by the tenacity of Italian units in the final phase of the North African campaign. The defenders also had the advantage of the rugged nature of Sicily.

As is well known, the general topography of Sicily is very mountainous and movement off the roads and tracks is seldom possible. In the beach areas there was a narrow coastal plain, but behind this the mountains rose steeply and the road network was very indifferent. It was apparent that the campaign in Sicily was going to depend largely on the domination of main road and track centres and the story of the operations will show that these invariably became our main objectives.[7]

Convoys carrying the troops of the assaulting formations sailed from ports as far apart as Oran and Port Said in North Africa and the Clyde in Scotland, whence sailed 1st Canadian Division, to rendezvous south of Malta on 9 July. The normal Mediterranean summer weather broke that day and gales and high seas threatened the landings next morning. Eisenhower, faced with a situation that would be repeated in June 1944, decided to go ahead as planned. The invasion force headed for Sicily.

Many soldiers were seasick* but most of the landings were carried out with little alteration to the planned timescale. Although some battalions landed on the wrong beaches as a result of the conditions, the landings were

as far as fighting goes, rather an anti-climax. The enemy's coast defence troops made little effort to hold the beaches or the immediate hinterland, since the Italian tactical plan did not contemplate a pitched battle on this field.[9]

Although the British medical services had been geared to a possible 10,000 battle casualties in the first week, only 1,517 were received.[10] British casualties in the early fighting came to 800, of whom 500 were from 1st Airlanding Brigade, the one formation that had had a disastrous start to operations.

On the evening of 9 July, over 140 aircraft and gliders carrying the brigade took off from airfields in Tunisia. However, as they were approaching Malta, where they were to turn north-east for the final leg to Sicily, the weather worsened; the aircraft were flying into the centre of the gale and winds were blowing glider-tug combinations off course. Searchlights were probing the sky and anti-aircraft guns, some of them Allied, opened fire. Most gliders were being towed by USAAF Douglas C-47s, the pilots of which were mostly inexperienced, and many tugs cast off their gliders too far out to sea. The result was that many gliders came down in the sea, often with tragic consequences. Those that did make land were scattered over a wide area and, in the circumstances, it was almost miraculous that the operation to take Ponte Grande was carried out successfully.

In fact, only two of the eight gliders carrying the *coup de main* party of 2nd South Staffords made the landing zone. By dawn, however, they had been joined by others so that the force at the bridge numbered just over seventy with a single 2-inch mortar and two Brens. A heavy Italian

* One soldier of 51st (Highland) Division actually died of seasickness.[8]

counter-attack by a battalion of infantry was launched during the morning. The defenders fought off the Italians for several hours until, with most of their number dead or wounded and their ammunition exhausted, they were forced to surrender at about 4.30pm. The Italians did not retain the bridge for long as it was retaken by 2nd Royal Scots Fusiliers of 5th Division.

No. 3 Commando and the SRS, the latter commanded by Major Blair Mayne, had successfully neutralised the coastal batteries near Cassibile prior to 5th Division's landing on the beaches there. Farther south, near Avola, 50th Division's leading brigade, 151, had been scattered over several, wrong, beaches which prompted the divisional commander to note, in a subsequent report, that there might have been complete failure and heavy casualties had determined resistance been met on the beaches.

The Highland Division landed on the southern tip of the Pachino peninsula in spite of the entreaties of a naval landing officer that one of the Division's two assigned landing beaches be abandoned and all forces transferred to the other. As the day progressed, Eighth Army's build-up continued with more units coming ashore and both XIII and XXX Corps making steady inroads under strong air support and with naval bombardment to assist in the suppression of Italian resistance. By the end of the first day, Eighth Army, with four divisions, 231 Brigade, 1 Airlanding Brigade, the SRS and the Commandos, held the coastal strip from Pozzallo to Syracuse, including the latter's port which was already usable; Seventh Army held about forty miles of coast from Scoglitti to Licata.

Montgomery was pleased with this progress and determined to push ahead rapidly. Both Leese and Dempsey were urged to 'operate with great energy', the former towards Noto and Avola, the latter towards Syracuse and Augusta. When Monty landed in Sicily early on the 11th, he was delighted to learn that Syracuse had already fallen. Eighth Army's commander now displayed another side of his character, being 'almost indecently concerned with making haste rather than consolidating the bridgehead'.[11]

Indeed, the image of the careful, cautious Monty was thoroughly dispelled in the early days of Sicily only to return several days later after the savage battles on the plain of Catania led to an unexpected and controversial change of plan for Eighth Army.[12]

Three days after D-Day, Eighth Army had captured all south-eastern Sicily. To their right, Seventh Army had made equally good progress, in spite of having had more serious counter-attacks in the beachhead. In Eighth Army's sector, 5th Division had encountered Battlegroup

Schmalz* on 13 July near Priola on the road from Syracuse to Augusta, but the Germans provided only a minor hindrance to the British advance and Allied air superiority impeded greatly the movement of enemy formations.

On the evening of 12 July Monty had asked that Seventh Army should push out westwards creating a defensive front while Eighth Army dominated the roads system in the centre of Sicily, to prevent east-west movement by Axis forces, before striking north-west to the coast and cutting the island in two. Patton objected to what he perceived as two British generals assigning his army a defensive role. Although the matter was resolved and Alexander ordered both armies to advance northwards, Patton still believed he had been held back deliberately. Thus began an unnecessary rivalry between the two army commanders, largely due to a lack of co-ordination and the absence of a clear strategic directive for the campaign.

By 13 July the soldiers of 5th Division's 17 Brigade had marched as much as 100 miles in boots that had been saturated with salt water during the landing. The brigade entered Augusta that day, joining up with 1st Special Raiding Squadron which had captured the port, and 15 Brigade passed through en route to Villasmundo. Fiftieth Division's† 69 Brigade was advancing towards Lentini with 151 Brigade mopping up around Solarini. In XXX Corps' area, 51st (Highland) Division had made equally good progress with 23 Armoured Brigade, under 51st's command, reaching Vizzini on the evening of the 12th. The Canadians had reached the hill village of Giarratana; 2 Canadian Brigade was north of Ragusa.

On the night of 13/14 July there was a further airborne operation in Eighth Army's area when 1 Parachute Brigade was dropped to capture the Primosole bridge over the Simeto river. The bridge was vital to Monty's planned thrust to Catania. Although many men were dropped wide of the bridge and there were heavy casualties, those who landed on their objectives‡ carried out their task effectively and the bridge was seized. The battle continued for several days before the arrival of 4 Armoured Brigade and elements of 50th Division.

The advance might have moved faster had there been more transport available. However, Eighth Army had only assault scales of vehicles; the

---

* Battlegroup Schmalz included a battalion and two batteries of Hermann Goering Division plus 115th Panzer Grenadier Regiment from 15th Panzer Grenadier Division.
† The Division had been restored to three-brigade strength for HUSKY by the loan of 168 Brigade from 56th (London) Division.
‡ Calculated at sixteen per cent of the 1,856 men who set out from North Africa. Over one-third were not dropped at all. Subsequently any further operations by 1st Airborne Division were suspended until further training could be carried out and better inter-service co-operation achieved.

bulk of the transport had been left to the follow-up convoys and so the infantrymen had to march with all their impedimenta. In the heat of a Sicilian July the men were tiring. All sorts of improvisations were made for transport: 51st (Highland) Division soldiers had even commandeered perambulators to carry mortar bombs, Brens and ammunition; bicycles were also used.[13] The enemy was falling back as even Battlegroup Schmalz, the most effective Axis force on Eighth Army's front, could offer little more than token opposition. But that was soon to change: on 15 July the German forces were upgraded to corps strength with HQ XIV Panzer Corps under General Hube arriving in Sicily. The addition of 1st Parachute Division and most of 29th Panzer Grenadier Division to the existing divisions created an effective corps.

Although the Germans were reinforcing the island, their strategic intention was to evacuate it. Hitler had ordered the establishment of a defensive line, covering Sicily's north-east corner and the straits of Messina which would be the escape route for the German forces. Hube's task was to take over command of operations on the island, shorten the defensive line and carry out a fighting withdrawal. His first priority was to form a line from south of Catania, on the east coast, to San Stefano, on the north coast.

On 18 July Montgomery and Patton were being encouraged to advance northwards. Eighth Army was to take Catania before advancing north-east to push the enemy into the Messina peninsula while Seventh Army struck north to 'split the island' in two. The latter move was too late to trap any significant number of German forces while Hube's plan to anchor his left flank on Catania meant that Eighth Army would be pushing against a very strong position. From now on the Army's advance was to be tough, painful and costly in casualties.

The topography of Sicily dictated the possible thrust lines and gave the advantage to the defender. Eighth Army HQ made the serious mistake of declaring that no pack transport would be needed in Sicily, whereas the countryside demanded the use of pack animals to provide tactical mobility. In the weeks ahead

> Fighting was often bitter – harder, their Commander said, than any Eighth Army had yet experienced. The fact that the Germans were withdrawing did not mean an easy advance. This was close-quarter infantry work with little scope for manoeuvre, on ground where every village was a fortress, every rockstrewn, terraced hill a natural defensive position, and greater numbers not always or easily decisive.[14]

The strength of the enemy positions opposite XIII Corps about Catania prompted Montgomery to plan an attack with XXX Corps at the centre of the Allied line: this was to be what Alexander described as 'a main thrust towards Randazzo' and it was to be made in strength. However, much of Hermann Goering Division with reinforcements from 1st Fallschirmjäger Division was now in the Catania plain and two German fortress battalions had also joined the defences. With all his divisions in Sicily committed, Montgomery ordered 78th Division to be brought over from Tunisia to reinforce XXX Corps' effort. The other reserve division, 46th, remained in North Africa as did X Corps.

Since a direct attack through the Catania plain would result in heavy casualties an alternative approach was decided upon by Monty: XXX Corps would move round the north of Mount Etna and hit the enemy from behind. The left flank of Leese's corps was to be Eighth Army's main thrust with the full-scale attack planned for 1 August by which time 78th Division would be ready for action. Meanwhile, XIII Corps and 51st (Highland) Division were to go on the defensive while the remainder of XXX Corps continued to advance on the axes Leonforte-Agira-Regalbuto and Catenanuova-Centuripe. These operations were designed to place XXX Corps within striking distance of Adrano which Monty reckoned was the key to the Etna position.[15]

Montgomery had also realised that he and Patton should devise a common strategy since Alexander seemed content to let both army commanders go their separate ways. The two generals met at Monty's headquarters on 25 July, by which time Seventh Army had taken Palermo, and Patton was surprised when Montgomery suggested that Seventh Army should take Messina. In fact, Montgomery was being entirely pragmatic: strong American pressure against the northern flank of the Etna line would reduce XXX Corps' vulnerability to a counter-attack from the left flank as it hooked around Etna.[16]

For some time 1st Canadian Division had been advancing along the Leonforte-Agira-Regalbuto axis. The Division's 2 Brigade took Leonforte on 22 July after a hard two days' battle, including house-to-house fighting, with the help of tanks from the Three Rivers Regiment. The nearby village of Assoro was taken by 1 Brigade following an equally difficult struggle: 1 Brigade lost almost 100 casualties; 2 Brigade suffered 175. The enemy resistance at this stage marked the beginning of over two weeks' hard fighting.

By the evening of 21 July Montgomery considered that he had won practically the whole of the Catania plain although the enemy line was contracting as planned. The Canadians continued to play a major part in Eighth Army's operations over the next few days with 1 Brigade moving against the hilltop town of Agira in a pincer movement co-ordinated with 231 Brigade which was placed under Major-General Simonds' command. Once again there was tough fighting as German troops from 15th Panzer Grenadier Division arrived on two heights, Points 462 and 532, on either side of the road three miles from Agira. Simonds ordered 231 Brigade to take Points 462 and 532 and then advance to within half a mile of the town; this was the limit of the range of the divisional artillery.

On 23 July, 231 Brigade took its objectives but 1 Canadian Brigade's advance was delayed until the next day when it was ordered to take Agira by nightfall while 231 Brigade was ordered to take a height about a mile east of the town to 'shut Agira's back door on the Germans'.[17] Two companies of 1st Hampshires accordingly took the height but the 1 Brigade attack was held up east of Nissoria on a ridge that crosses and commands the road to Agira.

> The Royal Canadian Regiment and a squadron of Shermans of the Three Rivers Regiment attacked this in the late afternoon (4.30p.m.) of the 24th with the support of five field and two medium regiments of artillery. But the infantry could not keep up the pace set in the fire-plan and lost its help, while ten of the road-bound tanks fell to anti-tank guns. In the end a German battle-group, based on 2nd Battalion, 104th Panzer Grenadier Regiment, maintained its position. At midnight 24th/25th July the Hastings and Prince Edward Regiment renewed the attack without success in the face of hot machine-gun and mortar fire.[18]

The brigade's other battalion, 48th Highlanders of Canada, was repulsed on the evening of the 25th; the two Hampshire companies were withdrawn from their eminence overlooking Agira that evening.

Next evening the attack was renewed: Princess Patricia's Canadian Light Infantry went forward under a bombardment from eighty guns at 139 rounds per weapon while fighter-bombers added their support. The Patricias' attack was successful and was followed on the 27th by the other two battalions of 2 Brigade, Seaforth Highlanders of Canada and the Edmontons, fighting their way eastward while aircraft struck at Agira and German positions west of the town. Although a battalion of Panzer Grenadiers had arrived to reinforce the defenders, the Edmontons scaled Monte Fronte on the 27th, capturing it by the next morning while the Seaforth took Monte Crappuzza. Since both heights overlooked Agira the enemy withdrew from the town. Although the Hampshires and Dorsets of 231 Brigade attacked on the 28th they were unable to intercept the retreating Germans.

In the meantime, 3 Canadian Brigade, which had been halted at Libertina in the Dittaino valley, had advanced towards Catenanuova on the 26th. Monte S. Maria and Monte Scalpello were taken by the Royal 22e Regiment. These two mountains, 800 feet and almost 2,000 feet high respectively, dominate the Dittaino valley and the western and southern approaches to Catenanuova. Although the enemy regained Monte S. Maria on the 27th, they subsequently abandoned the position and retreated towards Catenanuova next day. On 29 July 3 Canadian Brigade came under 78th Division's command for the attack on Catenanuova while the rest of the Division, with 231 Brigade in the van, headed east along Highway 121 for Regalbuto.

The Canadians had performed splendidly, adapting quickly and well to the heat and dust of Sicily and had become very much a part of the Eighth Army family. Montgomery was delighted with their prowess and singled their commander out for high praise.

The emphasis now turned to 78th Division, known as the Battleaxe Division from its emblem of a golden battleaxe. Originally part of First Army, the division had acquitted itself well in Tunisia and many of its soldiers had resented becoming part of Eighth Army when their own army was allowed to fade into obscurity. Indeed some of 78th Division's vehicles had even been emblazoned with legends suggesting that the division had no connection with Eighth Army.

For its first operation with Eighth Army, 78th Division was charged with the capture of the mountaintop town of Centuripe, or 'Cherry Ripe' as the soldiers knew it. During the preparation period the Division's sappers laboured in intense heat and under heavy shellfire to build a track to allow the Division to move up from Judica to Catenanuova. With that task accomplished 3 Canadian Brigade crossed the Dittaino river on the night of 29/30 July and moved on Catenanuova; 11 Brigade then moved forward to secure and enlarge the bridgehead over the river. During the next night 51st (Highland) Division crossed the Dittaino to protect 78th's right flank and 152 and 154 Brigades attacked the Iazzovecchio ridge beyond the river. A German counter-attack was beaten off and the Highlanders were able to push forward when the enemy abandoned the area. Over the next few days the Division was to advance towards the Carcaci-Paterno road.

The seizure of Catenanuova had been assisted by 'a rare case of mass cowardice'[19] in the German forces when Fortress Battalion 923 simply abandoned their positions. However, there was other opposition, including two Luftwaffe air strikes, but the way was ready for the next phase of 78th Division's operations: the attack on Centuripe by 36 Brigade after which the Irish Brigade was to force the crossings of the Salso and Simeto rivers. During the fighting around Catenanuova, Lance-Corporal Chadwick of 1st East Surreys brought in, under fire, a wounded officer from the Hermann Goering Division who was found to have marked maps and plans in his briefcase. Chadwick was subsequently awarded the Military Medal. The German officer's briefcase held the complete plans for their operations in Sicily. Centuripe was to be the pivot of the German front and was to be held at all costs. Since the overriding German intention was the evacuation of the island the plans included the warning that no German soldier would be evacuated unless he had his weapons.

Between Catenanuova and Mount Etna, Sicily is 'a tumult of ridges and hills, each seeming higher than the last, separated from each other by rocky gorges'[20] with Centuripe, key to the road to Adrano and Etna, perched atop this nightmarish scene. The town sits on a hill that resembles a letter E on its side with the arms of the letter being the approach slopes and the downstroke the actual ridge, razor-sharp and worse than anything 78th Division had encountered in Tunisia. So bad was the ground in this region of Sicily that it was possible to wear out a pair of army boots in a day[21] and the clammy heat and dust conspired to make conditions even worse.

There was the dry dust of a landscape toasted by the Mediterranean sun and there was volcanic dust from Etna, still active as the glow from its cone proved in the night hours. Before long men were coated with dust which combined with their sweat to form a layer of cloying goo. The volcanic dust even penetrated the makeshift facemasks which many used: there was simply no escape from the dust of Sicily.[22]

Centuripe was held by men of the Hermann Goering Division and 3rd Fallschirmjäger Regiment who had an ideal defensive position dominating the main approach road to the town which was also the only road to the west of Etna. That road corkscrewed up to Centuripe and had been mined and cratered. There were also three rough mule tracks but otherwise steep slopes, over forty-five degrees, would have to be negotiated while, close to the town, terracing with six-feet 'steps' had been cut into the slopes for cultivation.

Since the first element of the divisional plan had worked so smoothly, Major-General Evelegh, commanding 78th Division, brought forward the next phase by twenty-four hours, to reduce the possibility of Centuripe being reinforced. Thirty-six Brigade advanced to its forming-up positions in darkness and under shellfire but as 5th Buffs, one of 36 Brigade's lead battalions, moved up to their start line they were attacked by German paras who had been hiding in caves between Catenanuova and Centuripe and who were now behind 11 Brigade who were covering 36 Brigade. The intervention of the Fallschirmjäger meant that the Buffs did not reach their start line before daybreak. As a result the brigade's reserve battalion, 8th Argylls, was ordered to make a frontal attack on Centuripe while the Buffs, 6th Royal West Kents, 1st East Surreys and 5th Northamptons, the latter two battalions from 11 Brigade, were all committed to the assault.

However, the attack was stopped by the ferocity of the German defence and, by the afternoon of 2 August, the five attacking battalions were all pinned down. Evelegh decided that the attack had failed, although it had gained several points which were essential for a further attack by fresh troops. Thus 38 (Irish) Brigade was now to be committed.

The Irish battalions were to be supported by the entire divisional artillery which would put down a heavy concentration of fire on Centuripe. The brigade commander, Brigadier Nelson Russell, decided on a silent night approach in two phases with the first phase being a recce in force by two battalions, 6th Inniskillings and 1st Royal Irish Fusiliers, which would place those battalions within attacking distance of the town.

Both battalions moved up that night: the Inniskillings moved up by the mule tracks in single file with a fifteen-foot gap between each man. All equipment, as well as weapons and ammunition, had to be carried by the Skins themselves for almost four miles during which they climbed over 2,000 feet. The Irish Fusiliers, the Faughs, were held up by machine-gun fire, and by daybreak the two battalions were in close contact with the enemy. It was clear that a frontal attack up the final steep slopes 'would be a hazardous operation in daylight'.[23] Thus a new plan was developed which called for all three Irish battalions to attack in the evening when some daylight was left for the opening of the assault. The third battalion, 2nd London Irish Rifles, was to secure nearby features that threatened the two fusilier battalions.

By now the battle had dissolved into a kaleidoscope of company, platoon and even section actions. The two leading battalions endured heat, lack of water and the attention of German machine-gunners and mortarmen throughout most of the day. Then, at 4.30pm, the Inniskillings, who appeared unaware of the brigade plan for a later attack, launched their own attack. Their CO, Lieutenant-Colonel Neville Grazebrook, had decided to enter Centuripe 'by the front door'. That involved C Company scaling a hundred-foot high cliff to gain a lodgement in the town. Artillery support covered the move but the follow-up company, A, did not have that luxury and were fired on from both flanks as they climbed. Nonetheless, they made it and their company commander, Major Hobo Crocker, quickly re-organised his men and led them through C Company into the town against stiff resistance. There was much house-to-house fighting and a Panzer MkIII appeared at one stage. Although wounded, Crocker continued to lead his men until they were established in the town square.

With the Inniskillings' action unlocking the German defensive position the other battalions of the Irish Brigade were able to move forward and with elements of 36 Brigade in support the town soon fell.

Nelson Russell subsequently wrote of the battle:

> . . . the Bde made its attack on Centuripe and the Skins were fortunate enough to capture the town, though it must be admitted that the Boche were going anyway that night. The success brought the Bde . . . a good deal of praise, both local from the Div Comd, less local from Monty, and worldwide from a Churchillian speech in the House of Commons. Monty, when he came to view the scene, is alleged to have said that no

other div in his army could have taken it on, and when he was shown the place where A and C Coys scaled the cliffs he is reported to have said 'impossible'.[24]

As 78th Division fought for Centuripe, 1st Canadian Division, with 231 Brigade, had advanced towards Regalbuto and 231 Brigade attacked Regalbuto ridge on the night of 30/31 July. There was fierce fighting for the ridge which was taken by the Devons who were then hit by a strong counter-attack. However, the Devons' reserve company counter-attacked in turn and pushed the attackers off. Over the next two days the division probed into Regalbuto against determined opposition before, on the afternoon of the 2nd, a patrol of 48th Highlanders found the town abandoned. The division then sent patrols out into the Salso valley as a prelude to a divisional advance towards Aderno.

After the fall of Centuripe the Irish Brigade advanced across the Salso river with the Faughs and Irish Rifles in the lead; both battalions were on the river's south bank on the afternoon of 3 August. The crossing of the Salso was carried out next afternoon under heavy artillery support, including the guns of 51st (Highland) Division and Corps medium artillery, and against opposition that was mostly machine-guns and snipers.

The brigade then moved on to cross the Simeto river which was more heavily defended by Fallschirmjäger. Once again there was massive artillery support, including four batteries of medium guns, while 4.2-inch mortars from the divisional support battalion, 1st Kensingtons, also played their part. A tough battle saw a bridgehead secured by 9pm with the erstwhile defenders pulling back under cover of darkness.

Having advanced twenty-five miles and fought three battles in five days, the Irish Brigade was allowed to rest until 11 August. In the meantime, 11 and 36 Brigades forged ahead to take Aderno and Bronte. To 78th Division's left, Seventh Army was fighting its bloodiest battle of the campaign at Troina while XIII Corps had taken the port of Catania, an operation made possible by the capture of Centuripe.

Although the Germans were falling back to carry out their planned evacuation they were determined to delay the Allies as much as possible en route. At Aderno such delaying tactics were clearly in evidence. Scout cars of 56th Reconnaissance Regiment were the first elements of 78th Division to reach the town. The regiment lost four cars to mines or shellfire while two more were surrounded by enemy infantry; casualties were high and the patrols were ordered to withdraw. That night Aderno was subjected to heavy shelling and bombing and when the East Surreys of 11 Brigade probed forward in the morning, the enemy had abandoned the town.

Bronte was a tougher proposition and it was there that 78th Division first made the acquaintance of the German *nebelwerfer*, a multi-barrelled mortar with a fiercesome whine. Once again the defence made much use of mines, machine-guns and mortars but the topography of the area also created problems for the attackers. There was only one road and cross-country movement was impossible.

> . . . the four field regiments, 17, 132, 138 and 57, and detachments of 64 Anti-Tank Regiment, broke gaps in the stone walls and deployed from the road as best they could, in country that was virtually one vast slag-heap – except for the few and equally impassable terraced vineyards and olive groves. At times guns could come into action nowhere but on the road itself: it was remarkable in these circumstances that the artillery support was always so prompt and efficient and that positions were always found or made, somehow, so that the fire of the whole divisional artillery was available all through the advance.[25]

On the evening of 7 August the East Surreys were just south of Bronte 'slithering and scrambling over the glassy rocks and the lava beds'.[26] Although overlooked from nearby high ground they hung on through that night and the next morning before, on the afternoon of the 8th, attacking with 2nd Lancashire Fusiliers to take the heights on either side of Bronte while 5th Northamptons moved along the road into the town itself. Shortly afterwards, 36 Brigade arrived to be ready to move off towards Randazzo in the morning.

As the Germans were falling back on another defensive line there was much skilful and stubborn delaying action employed over the nine miles from Bronte to Randazzo. Thirty-six Brigade encountered fierce fighting on Monte Rivoglia before capturing the height on 10 August. On the next day patrols from 2nd Lancashire Fusiliers and 56 Recce made contact with US troops on the left flank. The Allied grip was tightening in north-east Sicily with US forces and 78th Division moving in from the west while XIII Corps pushed northwards from Catania. On that flank the Germans had also been effective in delaying Monty's advance: 50th Division took a week to advance the sixteen miles from Catania to Riposta.

The Battleaxe Division fought its way to Randazzo through a series of sharp, bitter battles around Monte Macherone, Maletto and La Nave before reaching the Randazzo area.

> . . . the Argylls moved into Maletto in the darkness of the night August 12-13, and the Royal Irish Fusiliers pounded down off the road to chivy the enemy into and beyond Randazzo. There was a running fight in the darkness, there was some American shelling from the left that came uncomfortably close, there were mines and more mines. But there was

little actual resistance now, and at 9.30 on August 13 the Royal Irish Fusiliers and the Americans made contact short of Randazzo itself.[27]

The shattered town of Randazzo had been abandoned by the Germans. At this stage XXX Corps' part in the Sicilian campaign effectively came to an end as 78th Division was pulled into reserve and US forces continued the drive for Messina. Both 51st (Highland) and 1st Canadian Divisions had also played significant roles. These divisions had secured 78th Division's flanks and had made notable advances in doing so: the Highlanders' 152 Brigade had taken Biancavilla on 6 August after which the division passed into reserve before passing to XIII Corps command a week later; the Canadians were also relieved that day, having taken Monte Seggio on 78th Division's left flank. On the east coast XIII Corps had pushed northwards with 50th Division advancing via Fiumefreddo and Calatabiano on the coast road while 5th Division moved inland through Linguaglossa and Castiglione. On 10 August the corps was disengaged with control of operations moving to XXX Corps but two days later Montgomery decided that 78th Division should stand fast at Randazzo allowing Seventh Army to press on to Messina while elements of XIII Corps moved up on the coast; 50th Division therefore continued along the coast road, Highway 114.

In those closing days Eighth Army launched an amphibious operation using Lieutenant-Colonel 'Mad Jack' Churchill's No.2 Commando and a force of tanks, artillery and sappers; all were commanded by Brigadier J C Currie of 4 Armoured Brigade. The force sailed from Augusta and Catania to cut Highway 114 at Scaletta, some ten miles south of Messina. Making an unopposed landing at 4.30am on 16 August the British force found itself on the wrong beach.

> . . . the day passed in brushes with isolated lorryloads of the enemy and with demolition parties. Towards evening Currie was ordered to push on to Messina, and told off a mobile force of two troops of Commandos, a half-squadron of tanks, and some self-propelled guns and a party of engineers.[28]

A patrol of 7th Infantry Regiment from 3rd US Division reached Messina just after dark on the 16th. Early next morning further elements of 7th Infantry arrived to be followed by Colonel Churchill, complete with bagpipes at about 9am. General Patton arrived soon after. Meanwhile 50th Division's painful slog up the coast ended at Taormina where the Italian garrison surrendered to an Eighth Army staff officer.

The Sicilian campaign was over. Most of the German troops had been evacuated in an efficient and successful operation after fighting a doughty and skilful series of rearguard actions on the way to Messina. For their part, Eighth Army had fought well in a totally different environment to that in which it had previously been engaged. But the hard battles of Sicily, the tough grain of the country, the pushing against a series of strong positions, held by determined defenders, all presaged the harrowing campaign that was to follow in Italy.

NOTES

1. R.Baxter, 2 LIR, interview with author
2. Fraser: *Alanbrooke*, p.311
3. Molony et al: *The Mediterranean and Middle East, vol v*, p.7
4. PRO: WO201/1812
5. Hamilton: *Monty, Master of the Battlefield*, p.246
6. ibid, p.268
7. Montgomery: *Alamein to the Sangro*, p.120
8. Salmond: *The History of the 51st Highland Division*, p.105
9. Molony at al, op cit, p.52
10. ibid
11. Hamilton: op cit, p.298
12. D'Este, *Bitter Victory*, p.281
13. Salmond: op cit, p.108
14. Fraser: *And We Shall Shock Them*, p.266
15. PRO: CAB44/127
16. Hamilton: op cit, p.325
17. Malony at al: op cit, p.155
18. ibid
19. D'Este, op cit, p.437
20. Ray: *Algiers to Austria*, p.63
21. R Baxter: 2 LIR, interview with author
22. Doherty: *Clear the Way!*, p.67
23. Russell: *Account of the Irish Brigade*
24. ibid
25. Ray: op cit, p.73
26. ibid: p.72
27. ibid: p.76
28. Malony et al: op cit, pp.181-182

CHAPTER XI

Italy: Advance to the Sangro,
September – November 1943

Of our labours thou shalt reap the gain

While 15 Army Group had been fighting its way through Sicily, the Italian dictator, Mussolini, had fallen from power and the new Italian government had begun negotiating an armistice with the Allies. The Italian mainland was the next objective for the Allied forces in the Mediterranean although, once again, it was not an objective about which Britain and the USA were in complete harmony.

At the Trident Conference in Washington in May 1943, Churchill had pushed for an invasion of Italy after the conquest of Sicily and argued against American proposals to invade Sardinia. He felt that such a limited strategy was politically and militarily wrong because of the pressure on the Russians and was appalled at the possibility of keeping more than a million and a half troops, with their naval and air support, idle for almost a year until they could be employed in operations in north-west Europe.[1] Unable to persuade the Americans to his view, he did manage to obtain Roosevelt's permission for General George Marshall, head of the US Army, to accompany him (Churchill) to Algiers to meet Eisenhower and the commanders there for discussions on post-HUSKY policy.

Those discussions were inconclusive as the Americans, still wishing to concentrate on the invasion of France, were reluctant to make a choice between Italy and Sardinia until after HUSKY. US thinking was that if progress was good in Sicily then they would agree to invade Italy itself. As a result American approval was not obtained for an Italian campaign until late-July. The British planners had meanwhile come up with a scheme for a two-pronged invasion of Italy. Landings on the 'toe' would be followed by an amphibious assault part-way up the west coast.* The limited range of supporting fighter aircraft meant that this latter operation could be no farther north than Naples; thus the Gulf of Salerno was selected for Operation AVALANCHE, to be carried out by the US Fifth Army, under

---

* A third landing, at Gioia, had been planned but was cancelled on 16 August because of insufficient landing-craft.[2]

General Mark Clark. In Fifth Army's order of battle was the British X Corps, commanded by Major-General McCreery, thus reducing Eighth Army to two corps.

Eighth Army's part in the invasion of Italy was twofold: 5th British and 1st Canadian Divisions would cross the straits from Messina to land at Reggio Calabria in Operation BAYTOWN on 3 September; six days later 1st Airborne Division would land, by sea, at Taranto in Operation SLAPSTICK. The latter operation would take place on the same day as the Salerno landings.

Montgomery was told by Alexander that his objectives in BAYTOWN were 'to secure a bridgehead on the toe of Italy, to enable our naval forces to operate through the Straits of Messina' and, if enemy forces withdrew from the area

> to follow him up with such force as you can make available . . . the greater extent to which you can engage enemy forces in the Southern tip of Italy, the more assistance will you be giving to Avalanche.[3]

The first troops of Eighth Army to land in mainland Italy did so at 4.30am on 3 September under cover of an artillery bombardment across the Straits of Messina and air strikes by Allied aircraft. Reggio's zoo suffered damage from shellfire and a number of animals escaped, among them a puma and a monkey which later attacked men of HQ 3 Canadian Brigade.*[4] The Canadians spearheaded XIII Corps' effort in Italy and 3 Brigade had secured Reggio by 11.45am on the first day. The other assaulting Canadian brigade, 1 Brigade, was ordered by General Simonds to advance up the Aspromonte plateau to Straorino which it reached at 2am next day. At the same time, 5th Division's brigades were also pushing ahead with 15 Brigade directed on Scilla by the west coast road on the 4th.

On the day that Eighth Army first stepped on Italian mainland soil the new government of Italy concluded an armistice with the Allies which was to be kept secret for several more days. The effect of that armistice was to break the Berlin-Rome Axis by taking Italy out of the war, an achievement that was very much due to the efforts of Eighth Army and its predecessors in North Africa since Italy had first entered the war in June 1940.†

---

* The Canadians opened fire on the two animals. The puma got away and it was believed that the monkey was wounded although it, too, escaped in the confusion.
† Italy did not remain out of the war for long as it formally declared war on Germany at 4pm on 16 October. This decision was communicated to the German ambassador in Madrid by the Italian minister there. Italy thus became a co-belligerent partner of the Allies.[5]

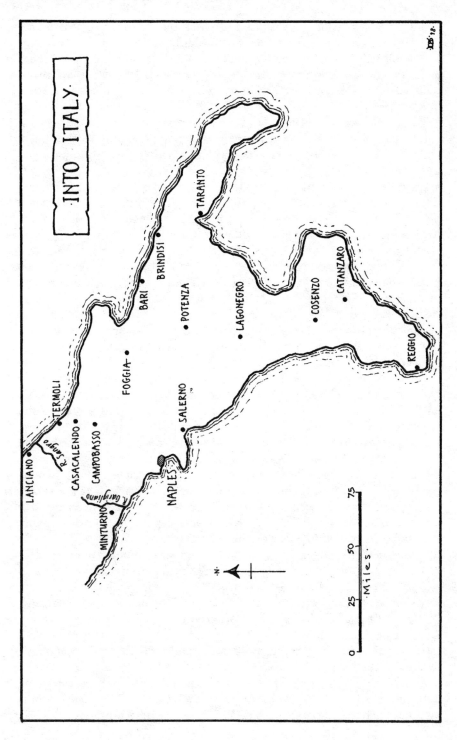

INTO ITALY

TARANTO

BRINDISI

BARI

POTENZA

LAGONEGRO

COSENZO

CATANZARO

REGGIO

FOGGIA

TERMOLI

CASACALENDO

CAMPOBASSO

LANCIANO

R. Sangro

MINTURNO

R. Garigliano

NAPLES

SALERNO

Miles
0   25   50   75

N

Behind the men of the first assault wave the build-up of stores and equipment went on at such a pace that, as darkness fell on the second day, it was already thirty-six hours ahead of the planners' timetable. This achievement was aided by the air cover provided by the Allied air forces which drove off those German aircraft which attempted to interfere with operations.[6]

The landings in Calabria had not been contested seriously; the Germans had already decided to revoke a previous plan to defend the 'toe' of Italy. Only a small force of enemy troops remained in the area south of Catanzaro: 3/15th Panzer Grenadier Regiment withdrew from the Reggio area on the afternoon of 3 September to Bagnara which it was ordered to hold until the 6th. Behind them was a battlegroup of 71st Panzer Grenadier Regiment which was to hold the line Nicotera-Laureana until further orders. Thus it was that neither 1st Canadian nor 5th Division met much opposition to their advances other than demolitions and booby-traps. Since the rugged countryside usually made by-passing obstacles an impossibility, the speed of any advance depended very much on the skill of the Royal Engineers; they were rarely found wanting as they toiled to clear obstructions, often bringing forward bulky bridging equipment along difficult roads. The fact that such difficulties had been foreseen was the reason why the Canadian advance was directed across the Aspromonte plateau.

On 4 September, 1st Special Raiding Squadron landed in Bagnara in the early hours and forced the Panzer Grenadier battalion out after a sharp battle. Later that day 15 Brigade linked up with the SRS in Bagnara and 5th Division continued its advance, leapfrogging its brigades and sometimes ferrying troops forward in landing-craft. There was a brisk skirmish with elements of the German rearguard at the Mesima river on the 7th and, next evening, 5th Division's forward troops met 231 Brigade near Pizzo where that brigade had landed in a seaborne operation and fought a spirited engagement with a force from 26th Panzer Division, coming from the north, and Battlegroup Krüger, which was approaching from the south having been ordered to abandon the Nicotera-Laureana line.

When a patrol from the Calgary Regiment found Highway 106 relatively clear the Canadians were ordered down from the mountains to use that road as their divisional axis. By 10 September, 1st Canadian Division was at Catanzaro Marina; 5th Division was approaching Nicastro; thus XIII Corps had reached the Catanzaro 'neck' having advanced some 100 miles since landing in Italy. By now Fifth Army had landed at Salerno in Operation AVALANCHE and 1st Airborne Division had arrived at Taranto in Operation SLAPSTICK.

The leading troops of 1st Airborne landed without opposition at Taranto on 9 September but, next day, the cruiser HMS *Abdiel*, while swinging to her anchor, struck a mine and sank within minutes. With her went forty-eight naval personnel as well as 120 soldiers of 6th Parachute Battalion and much equipment; another 120 soldiers were wounded. However, the division had taken control of Taranto and sent patrols out east and north. An encounter at Castellanata on the 11th, involving 10th Parachute Battalion, saw the divisional commander, General Hopkinson, mortally wounded; he was succeeded by Major-General E E Down. That same day Bari and Brindisi were entered. Having taken Bari, the divisional Reconnaissance Squadron began to probe towards the Foggia plain. Eighth Army was now carrying out a two-pronged advance: XIII Corps was moving to ease the pressure on Fifth Army at Salerno while V Corps, newly arrived at Taranto, was pushing towards the Foggia plain and the east coast of Italy.*

By this stage Fifth Army's situation at Salerno was critical. Hitler, anticipating Italy's capitulation, had issued orders for German forces to take over the defence of Italy. Initially the intention had been to defend only the north of Italy and Rommel had been appointed to command Army Group B, formed for that purpose; in the event of an Italian surrender the army group was to seize all important military installations as well as lines of communications in the north while Kesselring's army in the south made a fighting retreat. However, Kesselring believed that the Allies could be held south of Rome and Hitler agreed to a change in strategy. Thus, as Fifth Army came ashore at Salerno, General von Vietinghoff's Tenth Army was deployed to resist the Allied force.

Although resistance was light when the first Allied units landed at Salerno this was because Vietinghoff was holding back until he was certain that Salerno was the Allied point of maximum effort rather than a diversion. He then concentrated two Panzer and two Panzer Grenadier divisions against the Allied troops in the beachhead and attempted to exploit the inexperienced US 36th Division. Because of this pressure Alexander urged Montgomery to

> maintain pressure upon the Germans so that they cannot remove forces from your front and concentrate them against Avalanche.[7]

Although Montgomery was now suffering supply difficulties with his divisions so strung out and wanted to give his formations two days' rest, he had to accede to Alexander's pressure; he had no choice but to advance to Fifth Army's assistance. Continuing to concentrate XIII Corps in the

---

* Strictly speaking V Corps was not, at this stage, part of Eighth Army but was operating under 15 Army Group command. However, Alexander had told Montgomery that V Corps would come under his command when Eighth Army arrived within supporting distance of it.

Nicastro-Catanzaro area, he began pushing light forces as far north as possible. On 11 September elements of 5th Division, including its Reconnaissance Regiment, began moving towards Castrovillari and Belvedere, which was reached on the 12th while Canadian patrols entered Crotone. Meanwhile 26th Panzer Division was pulling back northwards with a detachment moving to Lagonegro to counter a rumoured Allied landing near Sapri.

Montgomery began his general advance on the 14th with 5th Division pushing towards Sapri, which was reached two days later, and the Canadians towards Spezzano. Patrols from the two divisions met at Castrovillari while Canadian and 1st Airborne Division patrols also met up.

On the 16th also, a squadron of 5th Reconnaissance Regiment met up with elements of the German rearguard at Lagonegro where the squadron was forced to halt. After a sharp battle the Germans abandoned the town that night and the recce men were able to move on. Next day men of 5 Recce made Eighth Army's first contact with Fifth Army when 8 Troop met a reconnaissance party from 36th (US) Division.[8]

The balance at Salerno had tipped in favour of the Allies on the 14th and 15th; on 16 September Vietinghoff decided to begin a withdrawal of his forces. He had failed in his aim to drive Fifth Army into the sea although, as Wellington might have put it, it had been a close-run thing: Mark Clark had, at one point, considered beginning an evacuation of his command. Although Eighth Army did not influence the tactical situation at Salerno, it did pose a threat and the Official History suggests that its approach

> to the German southern flank undoubtedly contributed to this outcome, for the threat forced the Germans at Salerno to use up their resources in hurried and unco-ordinated attempts to force a decision quickly. And so on the 16th it could be said that the Allied armies were at least in touch across the land of Italy from the Tyrrhenian coast to the Adriatic.[9]

In spite of their withdrawal from the Salerno area the Germans were to hold the Allies in southern Italy throughout the following winter and well into the spring of 1944. It would be June 1944 before Allied troops entered Rome whereas Montgomery had believed that possible before the end of 1943. For most of that time, Eighth Army's efforts were to be concentrated on the east coast, recalling its situation in North Africa with its right flank on the sea.

Working their way northwards elements of 1st Canadian Division reached Potenza on the night of 19/20 September. There was some German resistance but 1st Fallschirmjäger Division was too lightly spread along the Potenza-Altamura line, with detachments elsewhere, to offer serious resistance and Potenza fell to the Canadians. It was only the second sizeable town the Canadians had thus far seen in Italy and its sports stadium was soon being put to good use as a divisional recreational facility. Meanwhile 5th Division reached Auletta on 21 September. General Dempsey then ordered XIII Corps to halt on the line Altamura-Potenza-Auletta until 1 October, during which time the corps was to re-organise administratively before advancing to Foggia with the Canadians moving on that objective on Highways 97 and 16.

However, that plan became redundant when General Herr decided not to allow 1st Fallschirmjäger Division to be outflanked; the German paras took up fresh positions west and north of Foggia. In turn that allowed a rapid advance by elements of V Corps, now firmly under Eighth Army command, and on 27 September A Force, drawn from units of 4 Armoured Brigade with a squadron of 56th Reconnaissance Regiment, took Foggia. Here, also, was the last scene of operations in Italy for 1st Airborne Division. Soon after taking part in operations against the Foggia airfields the division was withdrawn from Italy, eventually to return to the UK for operations in north-west Europe. Canadian troops from XIII Corps had patrolled beyond Melfi as far as the Ofanto river.

On 29 September General Alexander issued instructions for the next phase of 15 Army Group's operations which included the capture of Rome and its airfields and an overall advance by both armies to a line stretching across Italy from San Benedetto on the east coast through Visso, Terni and hence to Civitavecchia on the west coast above Rome.[10] Alexander's strategy committed Eighth Army to operations on the eastern side of the spine of Italy with the boundary between it and Fifth Army being drawn, roughly, along that spine. Eighth Army's next move forward was to be to the line Termoli-Isernia, along the Biferno river. With Clark confident that his situation around Salerno was secure, Montgomery had been able, on 25 September, to begin regrouping Eighth Army for its next advance.

Eighth Army had by now been reinforced by the arrival of 78th Division from Sicily while 8th Indian Division, the first Indian division to land in Europe, had begun to arrive from Egypt.* Monty's regrouping for the advance to Foggia had placed 78th Division alongside the Canadians in XIII Corps with which 5th Division had remained. However, a new order of battle was to take effect from 3 October with 5th Division, 8th Indian and 1st Airborne in V Corps and 1st Canadian† and 78th Divisions, with 4 Armoured Brigade, in XIII Corps.

* The Special Service Brigade, including 3 Commando, 41 (RM) Commando and 1st SRS, would also arrive from 28 September.
† Also included in 1st Canadian Division was 1st Canadian Armoured Brigade, which had been styled an Army Tank Brigade until 26 August. This Brigade included The Ontario Regiment, Three Rivers Regiment and The Calgary Regiment.

On 1 October XIII Corps began an advance to establish itself on the line of the Termoli-Vinchiaturo road which would secure the entire area of the Foggia plain. Thereafter Montgomery's orders were to 'continue the advance as quickly as possible to secure the lateral road Pescara-Popili-Avezzano, in order to outflank Rome'.[11] It was to prove much too optimistic an objective.

The advance to the Termoli line was to be conducted by XIII Corps on a two-divisional front with 78th Division on the axis of the main coast road while 1st Canadian Division pushed into the mountains to Vinchiaturo from where it would be able to operate westwards towards Naples with Fifth Army, if by then the city had not been captured. As XIII Corps advanced, V Corps was to move up behind to protect its left flank and rear, a sensible precaution as contact between Fifth and Eighth Armies would be difficult to maintain in a mountainous region.

While the Canadians advanced on Vinchiaturo and Campobassa along Highway 17, the Special Service Brigade, now under XIII Corps' command, was to take Termoli by seaborne assault and would be followed by 36 and 38 (Irish) Brigades of 78th Division, also seaborne. At the same time, 56 Recce, 11 Brigade and 4 Armoured Brigade* would approach Termoli through Serracapriola. The landward advance began on 1 October and 1 S S Brigade sailed on 2 October. Bad weather over the previous week had reduced air operations supporting XIII Corps.

To reach Serracapriola the land force had to cross the Fortore river but the bridge had been blown necessitating a detour on a route where a strong German presence was reported. The advance elements, from 56 Recce, The Royals and 3 CLY, with support from 1st Kensingtons, crossed the river under shellfire on the morning of the 1st and Serracapriola was taken after a fierce scrap. The road forward from the town had been subjected to many demolitions and booby-traps by the enemy and the resources of the sappers were in constant demand. Off the main road, tracks were so bad that a 56 Recce patrol abandoned vehicles and continued on foot. Bridges had been blown and heavy rain made the going even more difficult. The next major obstacle before Termoli was the Biferno river which B Squadron and Battle HQ of 56 Recce reached on 3 October 'by many and devious detours' although no contact was made with the retreating enemy, save for their demolitions. At the Biferno the reconnoitrers had to wait until a pontoon bridge had been erected, during which time there was a Luftwaffe bombing raid. At 11pm, the first troops crossed the river to harbour two miles south of Termoli in pouring rain. Next day they recce'd beyond Vasto before returning to Termoli.

Before dawn on 3 October the Special Service Brigade landed near

* At this stage deploying only 3rd County of London Yeomanry.

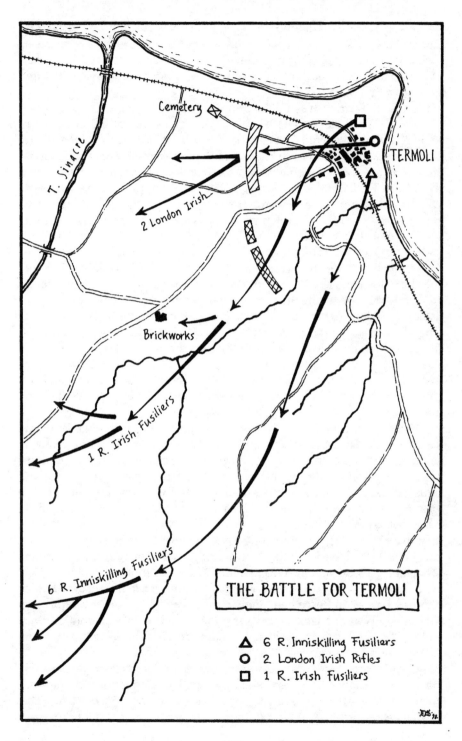

Cemetery

T. Sinacre

TERMOLI

2 London Irish

Brickworks

1 R. Irish Fusiliers

6 R. Inniskilling Fusiliers

THE BATTLE FOR TERMOLI

△ 6 R. Inniskilling Fusiliers
○ 2 London Irish Rifles
□ 1 R. Irish Fusiliers

Termoli, saw off a German battle group and, reporting the town clear of enemy troops, secured the port and moved to secure the approaches, including the Biferno crossings. During the next night, 36 Brigade landed at Termoli to take over the town's southern defences and move on to high ground at first light.

However, Termoli was not to be taken quite so easily. On 4 October patrols of 56 Recce encountered enemy troops along the coast road although it was believed that German forces in the area were restricted to Fallschirmjäger with some artillery and limited armour. That belief had to change when a 56 Recce patrol captured a German motorcyclist on the road from Petacciato who turned out to be from 16th Panzer Division which, according to intelligence reports, was on the west coast. The prisoner revealed that 16th Panzer had been travelling towards Termoli for the past two nights; his information was soon confirmed by the sighting of German tanks.

Before noon a German counter-attack had been launched on Termoli but the British tanks, and most of the anti-tank guns, were still on the far side of the Biferno where the sappers were working on a Bailey bridge and a tank crossing. An attack towards San Giacomo by 8th Argylls, of 36 Brigade, was stopped. Lieutenant-Colonel Kendal Chavasse, DSO, CO of 56 Recce, was given command of a force including his own RHQ and B Squadron, 3 Commando, a troop of SRS and an anti-tank battery with orders to position his men on the high ground overlooking the Simarca river from the sea to west of the Valentino brickworks and give right flank and rear protection to the Argylls.

Colonel Chavasse's force was soon deployed and Brigadier Howlett, commanding 36 Brigade, ordered the Argylls to resume their attack towards San Giacomo that night. He also requested urgent armour support and, next morning, six Shermans of 3 CLY crossed the Biferno but churned the tank crossing into a morass thus preventing any other tanks crossing. Enemy attacks on the Termoli perimeter had pushed it in at some points; the Argylls were forced to fall back. The Shermans had been sent to help the Argylls; four were knocked out before the survivors and the infantry fell back to the brickworks about an hour before noon. Attacking panzers managed to turn the Argylls' right flank and their CO, with two 56 Recce soldiers, manned an anti-tank gun in the ensuing battle. Trooper Ives of 56 Recce had single-handedly manned an anti-tank gun, taking on several panzers before his gun received a direct hit and he was killed. The brickworks was also under artillery bombardment from German and British guns.

As the enemy advance continued that afternoon many anti-tank positions became untenable. Pressure on 3 Commando and the SRS increased as three tanks with supporting infantry approached. The Argylls were ordered to fall back from the brickworks where they had suffered over 160 casualties, including Major J T McK Anderson who had won the VC at Longstop Hill in Tunisia. RHQ and B Squadron, 56 Recce were being shelled heavily, the SRS were being overrun, and a farm overlooking B Squadron's line on the left flank had been occupied by the Germans; B Squadron was out of touch with RHQ as its rear-link wireless vehicle had been destroyed. Colonel Chavasse ordered the evacuation of all vehicles except the wireless recce cars and B Squadron was ordered to fall back by the Argylls' CO. With the Germans attempting to encircle his RHQ, and only 3 Commando still holding the line, Kendal Chavasse informed his men that they now had 'an all round shoot'.

It was getting dark and the voices of enemy infantry could be heard through the shelling. The order to withdraw came to me from Division. I remember walking through the olive grove, with bullets whistling, to contact the C.O. of the Commando to tell him to withdraw. Then came the problem of getting our vehicles out. I got on to Division and asked for as much noise as possible so that the enemy would not hear the engines starting up. I remember the gunner saying he had never been asked for 'noise' before! Anyway, they gave it, and plenty of it too, and we slipped away unnoticed to behind the firmer line that had been established behind us.[12]

That firmer line had been established by 2nd Lancashire Fusiliers. Withdrawal was complete by 2.45 on the morning of the 6th by which time the Irish Brigade was making its landing at Termoli. In the course of the morning the Irish, supported by Canadian armour, prepared a counter-attack which went in at 11.30am with only fifteen tanks as the remainder of The Three Rivers Regiment's tanks had been held up by obstructions. By 1pm the brickworks had been taken by A Company of the Irish Fusiliers and the attack on the right half of San Giacomo ridge jumped off from there; the Inniskillings were directed on the left half of the ridge. By 5pm the ridge was in Irish, and Canadian, hands. The Three Rivers' tanks had knocked out four panzers in rapid succession. Their attitude was summed up in their motto, 'Have a Go, Joe', while Bala Bredin, second-in-command of the Faughs, felt that 'they hadn't got too careful' as this was virtually their first time in action.[13]

With the San Giacomo ridge secure, 2nd London Irish took over the brigade advance and pushed the Germans back beyond the Simarca river by nightfall. A battalion of 36 Brigade then took Guglionesi. As the Termoli battle raged, the East Surreys, of 11 Brigade, had been directed on Larino, fifteen miles from Termoli on the lateral road. Supported by 322 Battery of 132 Field Regiment and two platoons of Kensingtons, the battalion was soon in control of the ridge before the town. Then they came under heavy fire and were forced to dig in. On 5 October the corps commander ordered that the position be held but that no further advance be attempted and told the CO, Lieutenant-Colonel H B L Smith, MC, that the Surreys, by containing the enemy troops in Larino, were making an invaluable contribution to the battle for Termoli which was then in the balance:

> For four days the Battalion held on to its positions under continuous artillery, mortar and machine-gun fire until the afternoon of October 8th when they entered Larino to be joyfully received by the Italians as the last of the Germans left on the other side of the town.[14]

The Surreys had suffered seventy-one casualties during this action; two of their stretcher-bearers, Lance-Corporal S C Kemp and Private F A W Ramsay, were each awarded the Military Medal for bringing in casualties under fire.

Following the Termoli battle operations were limited in scale as Eighth Army prepared to move up to the Trigno river which was covered by positions held by the much-weakened 16th Panzer with elements from 26th Panzer and 1st Fallschirmjäger Divisions. However, Montgomery did not launch an immediate attack on the Trigno as

> my forces were regrouping and once again major operations awaited the administrative adjustments which were being made in the rear area.[15]

Maintenance difficulties over the long haul from Reggio had plagued Eighth Army, delaying its advance. Although additional ports had become available the Army's supply and administration had not been able to keep pace with operational planning and this, in Montgomery's words, 'was now to have serious consequences'.[16] It was 21 October before he felt able to begin strong efforts to get into close contact with the German positions. Operations on the coastal sector were now the responsibility of V Corps, including 78th Division, 8th Indian Division, 4 Armoured Brigade and 1st Army Group, Royal Artillery. The Battleaxe Division had already begun its move to the Trigno with the Buffs taking Guglionesi; the West Kents and 56 Recce Montecilfone; and 56 Recce Montenero. Then, on the night of 19/20 October, the London Irish, supported by 46 RTR, took the Petacciato ridge as a jumping-off position for the Trigno crossing.

A London Irish patrol found a bridge across the Trigno intact but as 1st Royal Irish Fusiliers approached, early on 23 October, it was blown. The Faughs waded across, for the river, although wide, was only ankle-deep and there was little opposition as they set up their bridgehead. Only mines and some shellfire gave testimony to the proximity of the enemy. On the

Irish Fusiliers' right, the Lancashire Fusiliers established another bridge-head by wading across, probed towards the town of San Salvo and skirmished with German patrols before falling back to the bridgehead.

From the bridgehead, on the night of 27/28 October, the Irish Brigade attacked San Salvo. Their commander had asked for a postponement, due to very heavy rain, but this was refused and the London Irish and the Irish Fusiliers went forward over rain-sodden terrain with artillery support. But several German machine-gun posts were overshot by the guns and caused many casualties, as did enemy shell and mortar-fire. Before long the Irish Fusiliers were pinned down; their two leading company commanders and all the platoon commanders of one company were dead: then the CO, Lieutenant-Colonel Beauchamp Butler, was killed by a machine-gun bullet in the head as he rallied his Faughs for another attack.

The London Irish had also suffered: the attacking company commanders became casualties and one platoon commander, 2nd Lieutenant Marmorschtein, was killed with most of his men as he led an attack on a machine-gun post. The attack had failed and the order was given to withdraw to the bridgehead where the Rifles' second-in-command, Major Kevin O'Connor, was killed by shellfire the following morning.

The obstacle of San Salvo remained and its capture became part of a larger 78th Division plan involving 36 Brigade, reinforced by 6th Inniskillings and supported by 46 RTR and a much larger artillery programme.* Objectives for this fresh attack, to be launched on 3 November, were San Salvo and the Buonanotte canal north of the town. In addition to 36 Brigade's effort, 11 Brigade was to attack San Salvo railway station, on the coast some four miles from San Salvo, while two destroyers and some light craft were to simulate a landing by bombarding Vasto and other targets. This latter diversion was to ensure that coast defence guns and mobile troops of 3/2nd Panzer Regiment were kept engaged and away from the main battle.

As 78th Division prepared to renew its attack, 8th Indian Division was committed on its left, some ten miles upstream on the Trigno, to cross the river on the night of 1/2 November with artillery support from four field and one medium regiments. Nineteen Brigade was to take the hills at Tufillo and Monte Farano; 21 Brigade was directed on Celenza and Torrebruna; the aim was to cut the lateral road from Vasto to Isernia. Early on 2 November 19 Brigade hit Tufillo which was held by 3rd Fallschirmjäger Regiment. The German paras were not prepared to give ground easily and a savage battle ensued. Throughout that day the Frontier Force Rifles made attempt after attempt to work their way up a wooded spur and break into Tufillo. Three times the Germans counter-

* The divisional artillery of 78th Division was reinforced with three additional field regiments and three medium regiments.

167

attacked and, with 5th Essex also stalled on the left after some initial success, the day ended in stalemate.

In the small hours of 3 November 3/8th Punjab Regiment began to cross to support the Frontier Force Rifles but suffered intensive enemy mortarfire. The brigade commander, Brigadier Dobree, now planned a night attack for 3/4 November which led to a series of further vicious battles. Although the Indians did not gain much ground, the Germans were thinning out and the Indian battalions were able to occupy Monte Farano and Tufillo on the 5th. The enemy had withdrawn as part of a redeployment of 1st Fallschirmjäger Division. By contrast, 21 Brigade reached Celenza without meeting serious opposition.

Back in 78th Division's area, 36 Brigade's attack went in at 4.30am on 3 November. The attacking battalions, 5th Buffs and 6th Inniskillings, with two squadrons from 46 RTR were soon climbing the hill towards San Salvo. The attack penetrated the junction between two German battalions and, with Allied aircraft strafing the area and enemy communications disrupted, 36 Brigade had seized San Salvo and the canal by noon. Although 11 Brigade met tough opposition at the railway station, and endured a counter-attack which was seen off by 46 RTR and the artillery, the Germans finally abandoned their positions that evening.

That was not the end of the battle, however, as the German commander intended to keep the British from Vasto as long as possible. He therefore organised a fighting withdrawal in which 78th Division had to fight hard for every gain between San Salvo and Vasto: in 36 Brigade's advance the West Kents were checked by a doughty rearguard group while, to their right, the Argylls drove back that same group in a very confused engagement.

It was clear at first light on 4 November that the enemy were withdrawing and General Evelegh ordered a general advance by 78th Division. By 9 November the Division was along the Sangro river between Paglieta and Monte Calvo while 8th Indian Division had 19 Brigade southwest of Atessa, 17 Brigade, which had advanced on 78th Division's left flank, at Gissi and 21 Brigade covering the left flank at Torrebruna-Castiglione.

XIII Corps had been carrying out diversionary operations during this phase. Montgomery had decided that the front had become too broad for a single corps and thus, after his re-organisation, had directed XIII Corps to attack on the Vinchiaturo-Isernia axis to draw the enemy's attentions inland while V Corps prepared for operations on the right flank.

Operations by XIII Corps' divisions, 1st Canadian and 5th, were delayed by weather conditions and demolitions. The Canadian 2 Brigade had cleared Colle d'Anchise and Boiano by 24 October; 1 Brigade had cleared the high ground between Molise and Torella by the 27th; 5th Division then passed through 2 Brigade on 28 October on its way to Isernia.

With a brigade either side of the Isernia road, 5th Division finally entered Isernia on 4 November after a two-day battle for a height overlooking the town. First into Isernia was a party of 2nd Inniskillings armed with paint, brushes and a large stencil of the battalion's castle capbadge.* Subsequent arrivals found every available wall adorned with the handiwork of the Skins' painting party.

All these gains were brought by feats of minor mountaineering, and toilsome slogging up long ridges, to dislodge an enemy who fought resolutely. The engineers were always at work clearing road-blocks, bridging craters, and shoring up hillsides to enable the hard-worked administrative units to perform their never-ending tasks.[17]

Eighth Army now prepared to take the Sangro positions. The objective of reaching the Rome line, from Pescara, through Avezzano to the Italian capital, before the end of the year was becoming increasingly remote. Allied to the onset of winter weather was the topography of Italy. Alexander's 15 Army Group was fighting against the grain of the country which favoured the defender for almost all its length. From Italy's mountainous spine, rivers run through valleys to either coast. Each river valley offered another opportunity for defensive operations: bridges could be demolished to hold up an advance; ridges and mountains gave good cover, good observation and good fields of fire. In trying to take Italy from the south the Allies were like someone climbing a ladder with an opponent stamping on his hands at every rung. Eighth Army was one of those hands and Albert Kesselring, master of the defensive battle, was doing the stamping.

Although it had initially been the German intention only to delay the Allied advance south of Rome, Kesselring's efforts had so impressed Hitler that large-scale defensive works south of Rome were approved.

Kesselring ordered a special construction staff under General Bessel to build a fortified position. It was to follow the general line Garigliano-Mignano-course of the Volturno-Maijella massif-Sangro, being strongest below the Cassino valley, in the Garigliano, at the southern spurs of the Maijella range and on the Adriatic plain. It was not to be a

---

* The two regular battalions of the Royal Inniskilling Fusiliers had different capbadges; that of the 1st Battalion was a fusilier grenade with the castle on the ball while the 2nd Battalion used only the castle.

single line, but a system of positions organised in depth which would allow possible enemy penetrations to be sealed off.[18]

Fifth and Eighth Armies were now knocking against the outposts of that German defensive system which was being dubbed the 'winter line'. Having already experienced the defensive skills of the German soldier in their advance to the Sangro, Eighth Army was to get further definite proof of those skills in the battle for the Sangro.

NOTES

1. Churchill: *The Second World War, Book viii*, p.356
2. Molony et al: *The Mediterranean and the Middle East, vol v*, p.231
3. Montgomery: *Memoirs*, p.192
4. Hamilton: *Monty, Master of the Battlefield*, p.396
5. PRO: CAB44/135, p.4
6. Molony et al: op cit, p.238
7. ibid, p.244
8. Doherty: *Only the Enemy in Front*, p.72
9. Molony et al: op cit, p.246
10. ibid: p.380
11. Montgomery: *Alamein to the Sangro*, p.169
12. K G F Chavasse: *Some Memories of 56 Reconnaissance Regt*
13. H E N Bredin: interview with author
14. Squire and Hill: *The Surreys in Italy*, p.15
15. Montgomery: op cit, p.171
16. ibid
17. Molony et al: op cit, p.458
18. PRO: CAB44/135, p.1

CHAPTER XII

Winter Warfare: November – December 1943

They come like sacrifices in their trim

The Official History suggests that 'It seems doubtful whether anyone in high places fully understood what a winter campaign in Italy implied'.[1] The Chiefs of Staff believed that Rome could be taken before Christmas without an amphibious operation; if, however, such an amphibious operation became necessary then Rome might not fall until January.

Alexander's strategy was for operations in three phases: Eighth Army would get astride the Pescara-Popoli road, then advance through Avezzano, threatening the lines of communication of German forces facing Fifth Army; in turn Fifth Army would attack up the Liri and Sacco valleys to Frosinone, the best route for an armoured thrust on the Italian capital; once Frosinone had been reached, a seaborne landing, directed against the Alban Hills, would be made south of Rome. The reasoning behind this strategy was simple: a clearly exhausted Fifth Army was facing either mountainous or muddy country against an enemy that matched it division for division. To drive the Germans from their positions would, therefore, require the co-ordinated efforts of both Allied armies. Eighth Army striking first and threatening enemy communications would assist Fifth Army's attack and give Clark time to re-organise.[2]

From the Sangro to the Pescara-Popoli road, along the Pescara river valley, is but twenty-two miles in a direct line, a small bound in the light of Eighth Army's 400-mile advance from Calabria. However, those twenty-two miles were to be covered in wet, wintry conditions with mud and floods on low ground, snow on the higher ground, weather-damaged roads and tracks and, above all, against a determined enemy in well-sited defensive positions. Those positions constituted the German Winter Line, some nine miles in depth, with the Bernhardt Line on the eastern side of Italy's spine; forward of the Bernhardt, north-west of the Sangro and in front of Eighth Army, was the advanced Sangro Line.

By now, Hitler's thinking had changed: Kesselring had been appointed CinC Southwest and CinC Army Group C with orders to defend central

Italy on the line Gaeta-Ortona; to protect the Tyrrhenian, Ligurian and Adriatic sea coasts; pacify those areas of northern Italy still 'in revolt'; and plan an attack on Apulia if it became clear that the Allies were preparing to invade the Balkans from southern Italy.* The Gaeta-Ortona line became the principal element in the German defensive system south of Rome and had been built up while the Allies fought through the various delaying lines farther down the leg of Italy: these included the Viktor Line, from the mouth of the Volturno to near Termoli; the Barbara Line, from Mondragone on the west coast to near San Salvo with the advanced Sangro Line as the final obstacle before the Bernhardt Line itself. The extension of the latter across the central mountains and down to the Gulf of Gaeta lay forward of the Gustav Line which was anchored on Monte Cassino. Along the Garigliano valley both Bernhardt and Gustav lines coincided. Allied troops had already heard of the vaunted Winter Line from German prisoners who expressed the confident opinion that the Allied armies would be smashed thereon. In addition to these defensive works a new German army, Fourteenth, was being formed under General von Mackensen in northern Italy and would come into formal existence on 21 November.

Montgomery was concerned that Eighth Army did not have enough manpower to carry out an advance as far as Pescara:

> At the beginning of November Eighth Army still had many of its units in Africa and it was becoming clear that we should not reach the Pescara Line with four infantry divisions only: I required at least one more. My troops were getting very tired and my formations had suffered considerable casualties since the landings at Reggio. In particular the officer situation in the infantry had become acute.[3]

There were also problems with the supply of ammunition that was to lead to shortages and the rationing of field and medium artillery rounds. Reinforcements were already a problem which would worsen as the campaign progressed. As Eighth Army made ready to force the Sangro defences it had been strengthened to some extent, the New Zealand Division having arrived in Italy. Freyberg's division now had an integral armoured arm, 4 New Zealand Armoured Brigade, in addition to two infantry brigades and was temporarily reinforced by 19 Brigade from 8th

---

* For some time the Germans were convinced that Allied operations in Italy were only a prelude to invading the Balkans where, in co-operation with the partisans, the Allies could deprive Germany of valuable mineral and oil resources; threaten Austria from Balkan airfields; and promote the collapse of the pro-German regimes in Bulgaria and Hungary.

Indian Division. The Army's artillery strength stood at twenty-two field regiments and seven medium regiments, deploying 690 guns, while its tank state was 186 Sherman IIIs and Vs with another thirty-seven tanks undergoing repair.

For the next phase of operations, Montgomery planned to gain a jumping-off area on the Sangro's north bank for the main attack by V Corps, while deceiving the enemy into thinking that XIII Corps would make the main attack on the direct route to Avezzano. The latter corps therefore began advancing towards the upper Sangro early. It was also to

> make ostentatious troop movements, and to plant bogus dumps in its maintenance area to simulate far-reaching administrative support. A wireless deception scheme was contrived to make the enemy think that Army Tactical Headquarters and 8th Indian Division would arrive in 13th Corps' sector. Operations by 19th Indian Infantry Brigade were to screen 8th Indian Division's actual eastward side-step to Paglieta and the New Zealand Division's arrival near Scerni. Wireless silence, patrolling of unimportant ground, dummies and camouflage all played their parts. A naval demonstration towards Pescara was arranged to foment the enemy's known fears for his sea flank.[4]

By 18 November XIII Corps was making for Castel di Sangro and Alfedena along roads on which the Germans had carried out many demolitions and in weather conditions belying the popular image of sunny Italy; continuous rain turned the earth into deep mud. Having established a base at Carovilli, 3 Canadian Brigade then reached Caprocotta and San Pietro and sent patrols across the Sangro. The brigade attacked Castel di Sangro on 24 November but this attack was called off by a change in Monty's plans. At the same time 5th Division had taken Monte Civitalta overlooking Alfedena which it attacked on 22 November; this attack, too, was called off.

Eighth Indian Division, less 19 Brigade, made its side-step to Paglieta between 14 and 18 November. The New Zealanders' first action took place on the 17th when 19th NZ Armoured Regiment, with 3/8th Punjab Regiment of 19 Indian Brigade, took Perano. Next day 19 Brigade took Archi and prepared to capture the high ground between the Sangro and Aventino rivers prior to the New Zealand Division's crossings. On the night of 22/23 November, 3/8th Punjab and 1/5th Essex waded across the swollen Sangro and began attacks on San Angelo and Altino. Many wounded died of exposure because they could not be brought back across the river.

Since 7 November elements of 78th Division and 4 Armoured Brigade had been on the Sangro and, from the 10th, patrols had been crossing the river almost every night. With those patrols 78th Division dominated the far side of the Sangro, a low-lying plain leading to an escarpment. Sappers and tankmen had also crossed to lift mines and reconnoitre suitable ground for armour with virtually no reaction from the Germans on the escarpment. Unfortunately very heavy rain from the 15th stopped the patrolling across the river for several days as the Sangro broadened from a narrow stream a hundred feet wide to fill the entire channel of some 400 feet while its depth increased to five feet and the flow became so fast that crossing was impossible. The Germans used this period to sow new minefields on the plain and strengthen their defences. Thus, when the river was once again passable, the sappers had to clear new paths through fresh minefields.

V Corps' battle plan was for 8th Indian Division to secure the left flank by taking the high ground around Mozzagrogna to allow 78th Division, with 4 Armoured Brigade, to pass through, turn right towards the sea, roll up the German defensive lines and then swing left along the coast road to the north. To establish a bridgehead, 36 Brigade sent companies from each battalion across the river on the night of 19/20 November but they were forced to return. The Germans had regained their aggression and, with it, control of the plain. Eleven Brigade was then sent to reinforce 36 Brigade as was 4 Armoured Brigade's infantry battalion, 2nd King's Royal Rifle Corps.

The sappers of 78th Division built two bridges across the Sangro, one of them the longest on V Corps' front. They laboured in appalling conditions, under shellfire and in torrential rain that saw a Bailey bridge submerged, washed away and then rebuilt. The rain also forced changes to the assault plan which was delayed and revised: 8th Indian Division was now to break the enemy line at Mozzagrogna; the Irish Brigade and 4 Armoured would exploit that break and clear the high ground between Mozzagrogna and the coast. However, the Germans had not been fooled by the deception measures and expected Eighth Army's main attack to come on the front held by 65th Infantry Division, rated as a low-quality division by Montgomery's HQ,[5] which was exactly where the attack fell.

Between 23 and 26 November Eighth Army regained control of the Sangro plain and two bridges were restored to use; a third was completed on the 26th. Early the next day 1/12th Frontier Force Regiment of 17 Indian Brigade seized a jumping-off place below Mozzagrogna and the Irish Brigade also crossed the river. That evening 1/5th Royal Gurkha Rifles, supported by over 200 guns, took Mozzagrogna where they were joined by some 1st Royal Fusiliers. There followed a close-quarter battle through houses and other buildings in which German soldiers were winkled out; grenades, bullets, bayonets and kukris were all used by the attackers. Although 65th Infantry Division's troops had been shaken and its communications destroyed, elements of 26th Panzer Division, amounting to a company of tanks and a reconnaissance squadron, which had only arrived at Mozzagrogna on the morning of the 28th, a fine, dry day, launched a counter-attack. Seventeen Indian Brigade's commander, assessing this as a strong counter-attack, withdrew his troops to re-organise to meet it. In fact the Germans deployed but five Mark IV tanks, five flame-throwers, the first time this frightening weapon had been used in Italy, and six Italian SPGs. Brigadier Wyndham's decision to withdraw yielded the hard-won ground to the enemy and it had to be retaken by 1/12th Frontier Force that night.

Another result of the withdrawal was that confidence in 8th Indian Division at Corps HQ was seriously eroded for a time. Brigadiers Nelson Russell, of the Irish Brigade, and John Currie, of 4 Armoured, argued for a joint plan of attack in which both brigades would take the Li Colli ridge and San Maria to secure their own base for the main attack. This was accepted by Evelegh, 78th Division's commander.

According to Nelson Russell the chief argument in favour of this plan was the fact that 'when we took a place we knew we had it'. He lacked confidence in the troops of the Indian Division who had only recently joined Eighth Army and had not as yet found their feet. Against this the men of Currie's and Russell's Brigades had been practising tactics together, the companies knew their supporting squadrons and vice-versa, and there was an overall air of confidence.[6]

Thus it was that, at 6.30am on 29 November, B and D Companies of 6th Inniskillings, supported by two squadrons of 44 RTR, attacked the ridge. Against heavy fire, and with the tanks temporarily stopped by mines, the Inniskillings worked their way forward and methodically fought from strongpoint to strongpoint. When the tanks rejoined, the pace of the advance quickened, and by 3pm the ridge was in 78th Division's hands; two hours later San Maria had also been taken. Elsewhere 5 and 6 New Zealand Brigades had taken the high ground north of the Sangro and were attacking towards Castelfrentano. German counter-attacks were smacked aside by artillery fire and air strikes. Eighth Army had broken into the enemy's line and was not going to be dislodged.

In the next phase of operations, on the night of 29/30 November, 17 Indian Brigade took high ground north-west of Mozzagrogna overlooking the road to San Maria and Fossacesia which allowed that road to be used by tanks. By noon on the 30th, 3 CLY, 44 RTR and 2nd London Irish rolled down the ridge into Fossacesia to be followed by the tanks and Irish Fusiliers advancing to the sea. On 1 December the Irish Brigade took Rocca while the New Zealanders were overlooking Castelfrentano.

Although German reinforcements were being brought forward the commander of LXXVI Panzer Corps, General Herr, decided that the situation could not be retrieved and prepared to delay Eighth Army on the line San Vito-Lanciano-Castelfrentano while new positions were made ready on the line of the road from Ortona to Guardiagrele via Orsogna and Melone.

On 1 December two companies from the Irish Brigade took the town of San Vito but were quickly counter-attacked. Although driven out they remained close to the town and held off further attacks until 3 CLY and 6th Inniskillings took and secured San Vito.

The new German line was north of the Moro river and forcing that river became Eighth Army's next task. While 8th Indian Division was to hold Li Colli ridge as a firm base, and secure Lanciano, which it did on 3 December, 78th Division was to push light forces forward towards Ortona, a task performed by the Irish Brigade. While the Inniskillings secured the flank, the London Irish and Faughs advanced to the Feltrino and thence to the Moro. After meeting and seeing off a number of counter-attacks, patrols were reconnoitring the Moro's banks on the night of 4/5 December. However, the Irish were not to attack across the river as 78th Division was to be relieved by the Canadians from XIII Corps. Mont-gomery considered that 78th needed a rest and that XIII Corps now only had a holding role which needed but a single division in the line.[7] After its relief 78th Division went into XIII Corps' reserve and then, when Montgomery ordered XIII Corps HQ with 5th Division to move to the coastal sector, it took over the mountain sector and came directly under Army command.

The next phase of Eighth Army's operations was to be undertaken by Canadians, New Zealanders and Indians. Divisional objectives were Orsogna for the New Zealanders; Ortona for the Canadians; and Villa Grande for the Indians. However, Eighth Army's pause at the beginning of December gave the Germans sufficient respite to re-organise and concentrate their forces ready for a determined defence of the line Melone-Orsogna-Arielli-Villa Grande-Ortona. Stubborn defence was a charac-teristic of the German soldier which he was to show in full measure in the days ahead.

The New Zealand Division had already been pushing towards Orsogna; that push continued but without success. Orsogna was important since it could provide

> the starting-point of an attempt to roll up the German line by a stroke eastwards down the road to Ortona. It would form moreover a necessary guard for the right flank of any force which might advance northwards, aiming at Chieti via Guardiagrele and S. Martino.[8]

1: A troop of 25-pounders of an unidentified field regiment open up on enemy positions in March 1942. The 25-pounder was the standard field gun of the Royal Artillery and was an excellent weapon.

2: British tanks move up towards Knightsbridge during the battles of June 1942.

3: Far from being the golden sands portrayed so often on celluloid the desert varied in terrain. This is the Knightsbridge area, scene of the Cauldron battles of May/June 1942. The land is hard and stony with many small rocks making the going difficult for any vehicle but especially so for ambulances carrying wounded. The thin black line in the distance is a Bedouin with his flock of goats.

4: The desert could also be barren land with thorny scrub, as in this photograph at Tamar. The ground is covered with loose pebbles and there are tank tracks in the foreground.

5: Not all tanks damaged in battle were lost. Both sides went to great lengths to recover tanks that had been knocked out. Here a tank recovery team loads a Crusader onto a transporter under enemy fire during the Knightsbridge/Gazala battles.

6: The courage and tenacity of the French Foreign Legion at Bir Hakeim in June 1942 became legendary. Here Colonel Amilakvari, commanding 13th Regiment, FFL, is seen in conference with battalion commander Puchois and other officers at Bir Hakeim.

7: One of the greatest scourges of the desert soldier was the fly. This photograph shows how a 'brew-up' by a Bofors 40 mm LAA gun crew became the centre of attention for a swarm of flies. Even more could be expected when food was present and they brought with them the risk of serious infection.

8: Another scourge for the desert soldier was the khamsin or sandstorm which could last for two days. The heat was unbearable, the breath seemed to be sucked out of an individual and sand got everywhere.

9: General Sir Claude Auchinleck, C-in-C Middle East and Commander Eighth Army, visits troops along the Alamein line in July 1942. He is driven in a 'peep' by his ADC, Captain Cunningham.

10: In August 1942 the Auk was sacked by Churchill. The new GOC Eighth Army was Lieutenant-General Bernard L Montgomery, seen here talking to a group of officers in the El Alamein area. The Australian bush hat was Monty's first effort at creating a distinctive and easily recognisable appearance.

11: Among the many tasks in the preparation for the battle of El Alamein was the marking of paths through minefields. These had to be illuminated for a night attack which was done by oil lamps placed inside petrol tins which showed a faint light towards the advancing troops. Here Military Policemen of 10th Armoured Division Provost Company service some of the thousands of lamps that were used for this purpose.

12: Eighth Army's advance after the Alamein breakthrough was hampered by heavy rain. Here a Grant tank makes its way along a muddy stretch of road that has proved much more difficult for the wheeled vehicles in the background.

13: In the midst of war the Army's chaplains ministered to soldiers in all conditions. In this photograph a padre celebrates Divine Service for a group of gunners as Eighth Army advances through Cyrenaica in December 1942.

14: Some of the most vital members of Eighth Army were the sappers of the Royal Engineers. Their tasks were many and varied, and often extremely dangerous. In Italy they were often called upon to erect Bailey bridges to allow armour and supply vehicles to move forward. This picture shows one of their earliest efforts in Italy. The photographer has chosen an angled shot to emphasise the impressive nature of the sappers' work.

15: Among the fiercest actions in the early phase of the Italian campaign was the battle for the town of Ortona which involved Canadian troops of Eighth Army in intense house-to-house fighting. Here men of the Loyal Edmonton Regiment, supported by Sherman tanks, advance along a street in Ortona.

16: Farewell to Monty. A guard of honour was mounted at Eighth Army HQ to mark the departure of General Montgomery who had been appointed to command an army group in Britain. The guard was found by 2nd London Irish Rifles.

17: Soldiers of D Company, 5/5th Mahrattas support 5th Royal West Kents during the battle for Cassino in May 1944.

18: During the fighting around Aquino on 25 May 1944, Fusilier Jefferson of C Company, 2nd Lancashire Fusiliers won the Victoria Cross when he knocked out a Mark IV tank with his PIAT. The tank was one of two which broke through C Company's positions; the second tank turned and fled.

19: During the attack on the Gothic Line in September 1944, there was fierce fighting around Croce. These knocked-out Shermans are evidence of the price paid by Eighth Army in Operation OLIVE.

20: The Germans also paid a heavy price in the Gothic Line battles. This self-propelled gun was one of the victims of Eighth Army's tanks or artillery.

21: Vickers machine guns firing on German positions at Monte Gemmano in the Gothic Line defences.

22: The crew of *Mohawk*, a Sherman of 4 Troop, A Squadron Warwickshire Yeomanry, rest beside their tank in the Apennines in September 1944. The Troop had just spent a night trapped on an Apennine hillside when the track along which they had passed fell away behind them. They had been supported by Indian troops of the Frontier Force Rifles and by an elderly Italian, Angelo Rossi.

23: Tank regiment in strength. A photograph of a tank park of the Warwickshire Yeomanry in Italy. The regiment was equipped with M4 Shermans.

24: In the final operations in Italy Eighth Army was faced with many water obstacles. Here a Churchill tank crosses the river Senio using a Churchill AVRE bridging tank of the Royal Engineers on 10 April 1945.

25: One of the largest water obstacles in northern Italy was Lake Comacchio. The Germans extended the lake by blowing a hole in the dyke on its south-west side, thereby flooding a wide area of countryside. To overcome the problem presented by this Eighth Army used American 'Fantails' to carry infantry across the flooded areas. Here men of 2/5th Queen's cross the flooded landscape in American-manned 'Fantails'.

26: First into Austria. Soldiers of 6 Troop, 56th Reconnaissance Regiment in their M8 Greyhound armoured cars were the first members of Eighth Army to cross the frontier into Austria. The customs' barrier on the Plockau Pass has been lifted for the cars.

Orsogna, perched on a 1,300-foot high ridge, is the western strongpoint of a natural defensive wall formed by two other ridges, Pascuccio and Sfasciata, which run into each other and stretch for over four miles. North of the wall formed by these ridges is a length of the road from Orsogna to Ortona. This stretch of highway became the prize in the struggle between New Zealanders and Germans as it was one of only two practicable approaches close to Orsogna, the other being the Brecciarola ridge which is 'steep, narrow-crested, and dotted with olive-trees, vineyards, and farm buildings'.[9]

To take Orsogna the attackers needed to capture the ridges and the road; without Orsogna an attacker could not hope to be secure on the ridges once they had been captured. Freyberg was faced with the task of taking Orsogna, the ridges and the road with a division of two infantry brigades and an armoured brigade* supported not only by the division's own three field regiments but also by 6th AGRA (Army Group, Royal Artillery) with two medium and two field regiments; considerable air support was also available.

On 2 December 6 New Zealand Brigade found a gap which had developed between 26th Panzer and 65th Divisions in the area of Colle Chiamato. That morning the brigade had entered Castelfrentano while 24th New Zealand Battalion reached Brecciarola ridge during the afternoon and patrols from 25th Battalion reached Colle Chiamato where a machine-gun battle broke out. Not knowing that the enemy positions could be rushed the New Zealanders halted.

As the Germans hastened to plug the gap, Freyberg concluded that the enemy before him needed but a shove to remove them. He ordered 6 Brigade to take Orsogna while 4 Armoured Brigade thrust straight for San Martino via Guardiagrele; 5 Brigade was to remain at Castelfrentano. The respective brigadiers ordered 25th Battalion to take Orsogna at dawn on 3 December, as a stepping stone in an advance towards San Martino, and 22nd Motor Battalion to clear a route for the Shermans.

Success almost crowned 6 Brigade's efforts. On a cloudy, misty morning 25th Battalion surprised the Germans by passing two companies along Brecciarola ridge and into the eastern edge of Orsogna where one dug in while the second charged into the main street. The enemy reaction was furious: beginning with a single armoured car, it developed to include infantry and other AFVs. Although the New Zealanders had no pre-arranged artillery support they did have a gunner FOO and should have been able to call down accurate fire on the enemy positions. However, the

---

* The New Zealand Division had been restructured after the heavy losses suffered by 4 Brigade at Alamein and now deployed 4 NZ Armoured Brigade, with 18th, 19th and 20th NZ Armoured Regiments equipped with Shermans, and 22nd NZ Motor Battalion, alongside 5 and 6 NZ Brigades, each of three infantry battalions.

FOO's jeep, with its wireless sets, took a direct hit and no fire support was called down. Such was the ferocity of the counter-attack that 25th Battalion was forced to withdraw, having suffered eighty-three casualties, before any follow-up could be organised by 6 Brigade. The advance of 22nd Motor Battalion had also come to grief with the battalion held up three miles south-west at Melone.

Supplemented by 2 Independent Parachute Brigade and an airborne artillery regiment, Freyberg made another effort on the afternoon of 7 December. The timing was to allow the infantry to consolidate on their objectives before dark while denying the Germans all but a few hours' daylight in which to counter-attack. This time 5 Brigade was to take and hold points on Sfasciata ridge and on Pascuccio with 23rd and 28th (Maori) Battalions respectively; 24th Battalion from 6 Brigade was to attack Orsogna from Brecciarola; and 18th NZ Armoured Battalion was to support the infantry. The third battalion of 5 Brigade and two 6 Brigade battalions were carrying out holding roles while 2 Parachute Brigade guarded the divisional flank.

The plan went awry even before the infantry moved off. Thirteen squadrons of fighter-bombers were to attack over a two-and-a-half hour period but this massive air support was almost completely ruined by low cloud and only a few strikes were made towards the end of the day. However, the artillery programme went ahead. Both 23rd and 28th Battalions took their objectives, the former with relative ease while the Maoris had some hard fighting. German counter-attacks were launched, including tanks, and persisted until past midnight. Brigadier Kippenberger then withdrew 28th (Maori) Battalion to its earlier forming-up place as the position it had taken on Pascuccio would be untenable in daylight; the battalion was in 'a kind of a saucer'.

In the meantime 24th Battalion, with artillery support, entered Orsogna and a period of house-to-house fighting followed. A squadron of tanks advancing to the battalion's support was delayed by mines, demolitions and the inevitable anti-tank fire. Once again the objective proved too much: Freyberg ordered tanks and infantry back. For the loss of 163 casualties and two tanks the New Zealand Division had gained one firm lodgement on Sfasciata. The failure to achieve more was attributed to German local superiority in tanks, a factor aggravated by the inability to manhandle 6-pounder anti-tank guns up the steep ridges. And, of course, there had been too few infantry for the task assigned to them.

It was just over a week later that the New Zealanders made yet another attempt to crack the enemy line with the added aim of assisting V Corps' operations. Patrols had shown no softening of the German positions and foul weather reduced the number of air strikes possible between the 8th and 14th, the day prior to the next attack. On this occasion 5 Brigade had the main infantry role with 21st Battalion striking north-west from

Sfasciata to seize a dominating ridge while 23rd gained control of a stretch of the Orsogna-Ortona road. Once this had been achieved an armour and infantry thrust would be made

> along a strip of fair going north of the road. The idea was to by-pass Orsogna and sweep down to Melone, where a renewed attempt to penetrate would be made by part of 4th N.Z. Armoured Brigade. If all this succeeded, Orsogna – isolated – might fall.[10]

The armour was to include up to two regiments, if sufficient space was available for their operation, while the infantry would be provided by 6 Brigade.

In icy rain and sharp cold, the attack began at 1am on 15 December. There was initial success for 5 Brigade on its right flank but on Pascuccio hard fighting cost 23rd Battalion two-fifths of its attacking infantry in casualties. And this was a successful attack. However, the opposing German unit, 2nd/9th Panzer Grenadier Regiment also suffered heavily. The inevitable counter-attacks were repulsed. That afternoon, 18th and, later, 20th Armoured Regiments moved off towards Orsogna but were stopped by intensive anti-tank fire. Advancing on a narrow front, the tanks could not outflank the enemy anti-tank gunners and twenty-five New Zealand tanks were out of action when daylight faded. In spite of this setback the Division was ready to move again on the 16th.

At 3am on 16 December a strong German counter-attack, with tank support, was beaten off and, four hours later, nineteen Shermans of 20th Armoured Regiment with 28th (Maori) Battalion made another thrust towards Orsogna. This attack was brought up short by doughty resistance. Although the New Zealanders held the ground which they had gained, the situation was stalemated. Freyberg still thought of attacking from his right flank but the Germans were resisting so strongly that any forward movement could only be made at a cost that the New Zealanders were not prepared to pay.

While the New Zealanders had been struggling against Orsogna their Canadian cousins had arrived in the coastal sector and relieved 78th Division in V Corps. On 5 December 1st Canadian Division was deployed with 1 Brigade near San Vito, 2 Brigade near San Apollinare and 3 Brigade trying to cross the Sangro which was in flood. Facing them was 90th Panzer Grenadier Division which had relieved 65th Infantry Division. On the previous day V Corps' commander, Allfrey, had told Major-General Vokes, the Canadian commander, that his division should cross the Moro as soon as possible: a rapid thrust forward was more important, in the light of the New Zealanders' difficulties than waiting for flood-proof crossings of the Sangro. Vokes accordingly set his objective as Cider

Cross-Roads,* the junction of Route 16 with the Ortona-Orsogna road, four miles away in a straight line but almost twice as far by road with four 500-foot high ridges en route.

The Canadians crossed the Moro, which was fordable everywhere, at San Leonardo, Villa Rogatti and near the coast, east of San Leonardo, on the night of 5/6 December. At Villa Rogatti, Princess Patricia's Canadian Light Infantry (PPCLI) took the Germans by surprise while the Seaforth Highlanders of Canada gained a two-company lodgement at San Leonardo after five hours of fighting. To the right of the Seaforth, The Hastings and Prince Edward Regiment, the *Hasty Pees*, of 1 Brigade won a small bridgehead on the far side of the river. Then, in the early hours of the 6th, the Germans mounted furious counter-attacks against the Canadian intruders: both the PPCLI and the Seaforth were eventually dislodged and forced to return to their own bank but the Hastings tenaciously hung on to their gains.

Vokes lost no time in putting in another attack: on the 7th he ordered a further two-brigade operation with 1 Brigade effecting a crossing at San Leonardo and 2 Brigade, with tanks from 1 Armoured Brigade, passing through en route to the final objective. San Leonardo was to be attacked on the afternoon of 8 December with The Royal Canadian Regiment passing through the Hastings' bridgehead before right-hooking to San Leonardo while the 48th Highlanders of Canada would make a frontal assault on San Leonardo and La Torre. Heavy air and artillery support was to be provided with fighter-bombers and light bombers as well as six field and two medium artillery regiments. The guns were supplemented by some of 8th Indian Division's artillery and, in total, the gunners fired almost 45,000 rounds on 8 and 9 December.

Zero hour for the attack was 4.30pm on the 8th. For an hour before that time, V Corps' artillery thundered out across the lines; then the infantry moved off. As the leading Royal Canadian company pushed forward from the Hastings' positions, the Germans launched an attack on the bridgehead. For two hours Canadians and Germans fought a slugging match as shells flew in both directions. The other Royal Canadian companies were able to advance steadily and by 10pm the battalion was midway to San Leonardo, at which point it was hit by a counter-attack. However, the German effort was broken when the Canadian CO, Colonel Spry, called down defensive fire almost on top of his own battalion. The Germans pulled back and the Royal Canadians were able to re-organise.

The 48th Highlanders, on the left flank, had taken the La Torre spur with comparative ease, providing a start line for a Seaforth company and

* This name was applied to the objective after the plans for its capture were drawn up.[11]

a squadron of 14th Armoured Regiment (The Calgary Regiment) to take over the fight for San Leonardo. That battle continued throughout the 9th with the entire Seaforth and Calgary Regiments being drawn into the struggle. By 6pm San Leonardo was in Canadian hands although the Calgarys had lost twenty-seven of their fifty-one tanks. In spite of all their efforts the Germans had failed to smash the Royal Canadians and, harassed by heavy artillery fire, drew back as darkness fell.

To the Canadians' left 21 Brigade of 8th Indian Division had taken over Rogatti on the 8th and had pushed forward to create a small bridgehead. This lodgement was noteworthy for the building of a Bailey bridge by 69th Field Company, Bengal Sappers and Miners. Dubbed the 'Impossible Bridge' this structure was actually built backwards: since space on their own bank was so restricted as to defy the assembly and launching of a Bailey, the engineers opted to manhandle their equipment to the enemy bank and erect the bridge from there, showing both ingenuity and courage.[12] Their action was typical of the many occasions on which the Sappers of Eighth Army performed incredible tasks almost as a matter of routine.

The Canadian advance continued against strong opposition and the grain of the country. On the morning of 10 December the Loyal Edmonton Regiment and a squadron of Calgarys reached the position known as the Gully, where a ravine and ridge crossed Route 16. Here the Germans were determined to stop the Allied advance and the defence was in the hands of Fallschirmjäger, always tough and redoubtable opponents. As the Edmontons and Calgarys reached the Gully that morning their CO signalled 'We are now proceeding on final objective'.[13] But the Germans thought otherwise and the Canadian advance came to a stop in the face of a hail of mortar bombs and machine-gun bullets.

The battle for the Gully was to last until the 19th when both that location and Cider Cross-Roads finally passed into Canadian hands. In the intervening period, 1st Canadian Division launched a series of eight main attacks on the enemy defences, delivered in what was already a hallmark of the Canadian Division: small attacks on narrow fronts with strong artillery and tank support as had been demonstrated right through from Sicily. On this occasion the front on which the division was operating was little more than a mile, and Vokes appears to have made an early decision to push straight for his objective in the hope that a quick blow would take the attackers through the crust of the enemy defences. Furthermore, such an approach would have seemed reasonable in view of the fact that cross-country movement was hampered by rain-sodden ground.

In each attack, whether by one or two battalions, armour support was provided but every attack save the last, which was made by three battalions, failed for much the same reasons:

The enemy's fire, much of it cross-fire, was very heavy and his counter-attacks were frequent, determined, and well-timed. The Canadian infantry often 'lost' their artillery support because of the ordinary mischances of battle and because the artillery was fighting at a disadvantage. This was because the succession of attacks was so quick that often two or three fire plans were being prepared at once, largely from not altogether accurate maps. The resulting fire plans were often faulty, and frequent calls for heavy Defensive Fire to meet counter-attacks sent them further astray.[14]

On 13 December the first crack began to appear in the German defences although it might not have appeared that way to the attacking soldiers of the Carleton and York Regiment, who made a frontal attack towards Cider Cross-Roads, and the PPCLI and West Nova Scotia Regiment who made flanking attacks on either side. All three were repulsed by the defenders but, while they were heavily engaged, two reconnaissance patrols found a chink in the German armour. B Squadron, Ontario Regiment (11th Armoured) with a platoon of West Nova Scotias and a second patrol of four tanks from C Squadron, Ontarios with A Company, Seaforth followed a very basic track from San Leonardo to the Ortona road about a mile west of Casa Berardi. Operating independently along the track both groups probed weaknesses in the German right flank, eliminated some enemy detachments and pushed forward almost to Casa Berardi.

With the main battle in full sway there could be no immediate exploitation of the approach discovered by the recce groups, but Vokes seized the opportunity so presented as soon as he could: on 14 December he ordered The Royal 22^e Regiment with C Squadron, Ontario Regiment to advance by the track while the PPCLI made a frontal attack. Although the Germans were now guarding their right flank the Canadians hit them with such fury and determination that a lodgement was gained in Casa Berardi by Captain Paul Triquet's C Company, Royal 22^e and the Ontarios' tanks. Such was the tenacity of the German resistance that Triquet's company was reduced to two sergeants and fifteen men by the time they entered Casa Berardi; only four supporting tanks were left. Nonetheless, they held out against fierce counter-attacks with Triquet inspiring his men with the call 'Ils ne passeront pas', General Pétain's stirring order from Verdun in 1916. And, as at Verdun, the Germans did not pass for Triquet's little force

held out against attacks from overwhelming numbers until the remainder of the battalion relieved them next day.[15]

By 3am on 15 December, the Royal 22e's CO, Lt-Colonel Bernatchez, had brought up a larger force to consolidate Triquet's gain. Paul Triquet was subsequently awarded the Victoria Cross for his courage and inspiring leadership. Throughout the action

> [his] utter disregard for danger and his cheerful encouragement were an inspiration to his men.[16]

The next phase of operations was designed to take advantage of the threat offered to the German flank by Casa Berardi. Vokes ordered another tank squadron forward to Casa Berardi while the Carleton and York Regiment launched a frontal attack. Contrary to Vokes's expectations, the German defence did not collapse and the Canadian attack was repulsed. However, the German commanders, Heilmann of the Fallschirmjäger and Baade of 90th Panzer Grenadier Division, were concerned that they had no immediate reserves following the fighting of the 13th and 14th and a two-day respite following the failed Canadian attack of the 15th was a boon to them. Then, on 18 December, Vokes attacked again in a carefully staged three-phase operation from west of Casa Berardi. Supported by fighter-bombers, 48th Highlanders, the Royal Canadians and the Hastings, with tanks from the Three Rivers Regiment, smashed into the German positions. The attack was 'admirably executed' and, although bitterly opposed, met with success. A German withdrawal began and the Canadians had finally achieved their objective of the Cider Cross-Roads.

As the Canadians and New Zealanders had battered against the Gully and the Orsogna ridge-wall, 8th Indian and 5th Divisions were advancing between them. On 14 December the Indians had taken Villa Caldari, north of the Moro, followed by Villa Jubatti two days later, on the same day that 5th Division entered Poggiofiorito. These gains were made as a result of a determined, slugging advance

> in which very often two out of three battalions of each brigade in succession drove home limited attacks, and broke the almost invariable counter-attacks.[17]

Villa Grande village, taken by 19 Indian Brigade after heavy fighting between 22 and 27 December, provides a clear example of just how vicious was the fighting on 8th Indian Division's front. Nineteen Brigade's battalions, but principally 1/5th Essex Regiment and 3/8th Punjab Regiment, fought the Germans almost toe-to-toe for six days. At times the Indian battalions would storm part of the village, perhaps only a house or two, and seize it, only to be forced back by the Fallschirmjäger; at other times the Germans would attack in like manner and suffer repulse. It was fighting that took place, literally, from house to house and it was grinding down both sides. The Essex suffered 285 casualties and were thus no longer an effective battalion, being withdrawn from action to re-form. General Russell was beginning to feed in 21 Indian Brigade during the morning of the 28th when it was realised that the enemy were withdrawing, not defeated but in accordance with their army commander's orders to pull back to a new line. Rather than drawing back along the entire line, however, 1st Fallschirmjäger and 90th Panzer Divisions withdrew to positions along the little Tesoro river from Torre Mucchia on the coast to a point west of Villa Grande. From near Crecchio to Orsogna there was to be no change in the defended line.

As the Indian brigades slugged it out with the Fallschirmjäger, the Canadians to their right were engaged in battle of a similar nature in Ortona. This was Villa Grande writ large; in the words of the Official History 'The fighting in Ortona was the first example in the Mediterranean war of a large pitched battle in a town'.[18] Although of neither strategic nor tactical significance the Germans were determined to defend the town and assigned the task to three Fallschirmjäger battalions.* Arguably the finest of German soldiers, the Fallschirmjäger appear to have decided that Ortona would be defended as if it were Sparta of old while the British, according to Kesselring, were attributing to Ortona an importance on a par with Rome.

The battle for Ortona was one in which company, platoon and even section actions dominated. Once again it was house-to-house and toe-to-toe fighting almost from the moment, on 21 December, that the Edmontons with some tanks of the Three Rivers Regiment entered the town. That first incursion was on a narrow front of 500 yards along the line of the central streets, but it soon became clear that this was too broad a front for a single battalion; thus 2 Brigade's commander, Brigadier Hoffmeister, sent in a company of the Seaforth, committing the entire battalion on the 23rd.

> Thereafter the Edmontons on the right, and the Seaforth on the left, with tanks, and detachments of anti-tank guns, fought house by house until on the 28th December they emerged victorious at the town's northern end, leaving behind them mounds of rubble.[19]

Ortona was hard won with the Canadians suffering 650 casualties. The layout of the town was skilfully adapted by the Germans in their defence. Narrow side streets, too narrow to allow Sherman tanks to pass, funnelled the main fighting on to the wider south-north streets where the Germans created killing grounds by demolishing houses, or used the piazzas for

---

* The defence of Ortona was built around 2nd/3rd, 3rd/3rd and 2nd/4th Fallschirmjäger Regiments.

that purpose. Furthermore, groups of houses were turned into small fortresses dominating streets while the fronts of the houses facing them had been demolished to deny cover to the attackers. It was cruel, brutal, slow infantry fighting with every scrap of cover put to best advantage by the Fallschirmjäger. Every type of weapon and booby-trap was used; anti-tank and tank guns demolished buildings after which the infantry fought their way through. Alternatively the attackers used 'mouse-holing' from one house to the next: pioneers set 'bee-hive' explosive charges against top-storey dividing walls after which infantry storming parties charged through before the dust had settled and fought their way down from floor to floor, clearing each room with grenades and bullets.

Elsewhere 1 Brigade attacked on 23 December and fought through thick mud to San Nicola and San Tomassa which had both been taken by the 31st by which time 3 Brigade had joined in the fray. The latter brigade reached Torre Mucchia by 4 January 1944. While the Canadians and Indians were moving slowly forward Freyberg's New Zealanders attempted to make a breach on the Fontegrande plateau for armoured exploitation. On Christmas Eve 5 Brigade attacked but the Germans held firm; by the afternoon of Christmas Day it was clear that there could be no further advance for the time being. Indeed Freyberg remarked that it was more a question of holding on to what the division had rather than moving forward.

As the Canadians entered Ortona on 23 December, 5th Division, pushing forward from Poggiofiorito, took the little town of Arielli. This effort had been co-ordinated with the New Zealand attack on the Fontegrande plateau with the aim of isolating Orsogna but the German garrison there continued to hold out.

At the end of December Eighth Army's advance had taken it forward fourteen miles in a direct line since 28 November and it was now some eight miles from Pescara; and a long way from Rome. The average rate of advance was down to a half mile per day whereas from Termoli to San Vito it had been marginally better than a mile per day. German resistance, in the form of Herr's LXXVI Panzer Corps, was toughening and the weather had broken. In front of Eighth Army lay country no better than that over which it had so recently fought and thus there could be no immediate prospect of bringing to bear the British superiority in armour. The burden of the struggle would continue to fall on the infantry and the infantry were being worn down. During December Eighth Army had suffered 6,453 casualties:* from the Sangro the three divisions most

* LXXVI Panzer Corps sustained 2,051 casualties in the first ten days of December while the German Fourteenth Army had 13,362 casualties during the month

heavily engaged had suffered almost 7,000 casualties with the largest proportion, 3,400, in 8th Indian Division while the Canadians had 2,339 and the New Zealanders 1,200.[20]

Faced with continuing stiff resistance, the lack of opportunities to use armour in any strength, the weather, the nature of the country, and the losses sustained by his infantry, Montgomery decided that Eighth Army's offensive operations should halt temporarily.[21] In this decision he was supported by his superiors. Monty's decision to halt Eighth Army was virtually his last on its behalf for, on 30 December 1943, he handed over command to General Sir Oliver Leese, an Eighth Army old hand who had commanded XXX Corps before the final El Alamein battle.

Monty left Eighth Army to take command of the invasion forces for Operation OVERLORD, an appointment for which his handling of Eighth Army since August 1942 had indicated his suitability. He left an indelible mark on Eighth Army which would be forever associated with his name. During his tenure of command he had established a belief almost of invincibility within the ranks of the Army. In his farewell message to his troops he wrote:

> In all the battles we have fought together we have not had one single failure; we have been successful in everything we have undertaken. . . . this has been due to the devotion to duty and whole-hearted co-operation of every officer and man, rather than to anything I may have been able to do myself. But the result has been a mutual confidence between you and me, and mutual confidence between a Commander and his troops is a pearl of very great price. . . . You have made this Army what it is. YOU have made its name a household word all over the world. YOU must uphold its good name and its traditions.[22]

NOTES

1. Molony et al: *The Mediterranean and the Middle East, vol v*, p.473
2. ibid: pp.473-474
3. Montgomery: *Alamein to the Sangro*, p.175
4. Molony at al: op cit, p.485
5. Montgomery: op cit, p.182
6. Doherty: *Clear The Way!*, p.98
7. Montgomery: op cit, p.183
8. Molony et al: op cit, p.495
9. ibid
10. ibid, p.499
11. ibid, p.501
12. ibid, p.502
13. ibid, p.503
14. ibid, p.504
15. *Register of the Victoria Cross*, p.316

16. ibid
17. Molony et al: op cit, p.505-506
18. ibid, p.507
19. ibid
20. ibid
21. Graham and Bidwell: *Tug of War*, p.119
22. Montgomery: op cit, pp.195-196

CHAPTER XIII
Cassino Looms: January – May 1944
Our soldiers stand full fairly for the day

As the new year of 1944 dawned, Eighth Army had broken into the German Winter Line but had not penetrated that line in order to advance to Pescara. General Alexander wrote in his despatch on the campaign that the difficult country of the Molise mountains

> offered few chances of a decisive success to an army attacking as Eighth Army had always done, across the grain of the country. The further north we pushed our advance the more numerous and close together were the river lines.[1]

German reinforcements had been fed into Italy on Hitler's orders and the arrival of these additional formations had ensured that the Allies would not break through to Rome before the end of 1943.

> The impetus of the Allied attacks had been blunted and held at the point where the coastal strip between the impassable Maiella and the sea is narrowest. To make the positions even stronger, Kesselring exchanged the battered 65th Division for the 334th, which was at Genoa. With this, and with the help of the prevailing bad weather, the northern flank was saved till spring.[2]

The weather had also deteriorated even more with heavy snowfalls adding to the misery of soldiers who had previously regarded Italy as a land of sunshine. Men suffered from exposure and frostbite and some even succumbed to the cold. Units were cut off in the mountains: 56 Recce and 6th Inniskillings of 78th Division were re-supplied by airdrops, although both were managing well in their mountain fastnesses. In 5th Division the main dressing station was cut off by deep snow at the turn of the year while 2nd New Zealand Division reported that it took at least six stretcher-bearers to carry a casualty in the mountains in snow or driving rain. On low ground the problem was one of sleet and rain, rather than snow, which soon turned the ground into a morass of mud and slush through which men and vehicles struggled to make progress.

189

Although Eighth Army was not involved in major offensive operations there was still considerable action, much of it at company and platoon level. German troops were particularly active in patrolling and in mounting smallscale raids, both of which meant that a high level of preparedness was demanded at all times. In the mountainous central area, where 78th Division had returned to the line, a blizzard which blew up on New Year's Eve led to snow that drifted up to ten feet in depth in 56th Reconnaissance Regiment's sector. The CO, Kendal Chavasse, withdrew some outposts and issued orders to watch for enemy ski patrols; the Regiment also instituted its own ski patrols with Captain Tony Michelle, MC, an expert skier, providing the necessary instructional expertise.[3] During its time in this sector 56 Recce had two encounters with the enemy; one was an attack on Pescopennataro about which 56 Recce was alerted by local civilians and which was fought off successfully with the aid of heavy artillery support; the second was an incursion by a small ski patrol which was sent packing by a shower of mortars and grenades.[4]

Another German ski attack proved more successful when a company of 2nd London Irish was hit by a surprise assault on the morning of 19 January. The attack occurred at breakfast time, just after stand-to, and resulted in most of 7 Platoon being captured; five men were killed and fifteen wounded. A counter-attack was quickly organised by the company commander, Major Mervyn Davies, and cleared the area of Germans in spite of well-laid enemy machine-gun fire sweeping the company's area; six Germans were killed, one was captured and 7 Platoon's commander, Nicholas Mosley, escaped with four of his riflemen.[5]

There were rumours of enemy intruders with one village priest reporting the presence of 'ghostly hooded figures in his home' while an American unit on 78th Division's left flank 'reported the loss of a perfectly good sentry not far away'; 'strangely coloured parachutes' were also reported falling near the Sangro river.[6] The state of mind induced by such reports could also lead to tragedy: on 4 January a patrol of strange soldiers was seen 'acting suspiciously' in the area held by 1st Royal Irish Fusiliers; the patrol was fired upon and one man was killed while another was wounded. Only then was it discovered that the 'intruders' were members of the Belgian Troop of 10 Commando.*[7]

Infantry patrols by night were to become one of the most important elements of the Italian campaign and, with the great strain that they presented on those taking part, would provide one of the most vivid lasting memories for survivors:

* No. 10 Commando was an inter-allied unit raised mainly from soldiers from the occupied countries of Europe. It included Troops from France, Belgium, Norway, The Netherlands, Poland and Yugoslavia as well as a miscellaneous Troop which included British soldiers.

Subject to all those fears and grotesque imaginings that patrols suffer from, I did my share of these excursions and like all the rest lay rigid, biting my hand and totally convinced beyond all doubt that waiting Germans were watching us. There were good patrol leaders . . . but I was not one of them, although I never pulled the old trick of getting out of sight and holing up for the night before coming back with a pack of lies. But I hated it; I hated the cold and the dark; above all I hated the loneliness. The men hated it too, as they knew too well that anyone hurt during these visits to no-man's land was nearly always left behind in the fracas to die or, if lucky, to be picked up later. To myself I admitted also that whereas an attack was infinitely more dangerous, there was a feeling of all being together and of someone, in our case the major, giving orders: too much imagination or the mentality of a born follower I suppose. The use of patrols will be argued for as long as they are sent out but they call for a peculiar brand of courage which I for one did not have.[8]

Nonetheless patrols remained an essential tactic as the opposing armies sought to garner information and gain the initiative, even if only locally and temporarily. Being able to identify formations was important to Allies and Germans alike and this could be done by bringing back prisoners. For the Germans such information might bring clues about an Allied offensive; Eighth Army sought clues about possible German withdrawals, especially towards the Fifth Army front. Without a doubt such patrols called for individual skill, much courage and good leadership on the part of the junior officers and NCOs who so often commanded the patrols. They also gave to the campaign in Italy a hint of the Great War which was heightened by the conditions so often encountered and in the way that, in so many instances, the emphasis on the battlefield lay in minor tactics rather than on manoeuvre. It was, in every sense, an infantryman's war.

Everywhere along the line skirmishing took place between the opposing formations with fighting between patrols an almost nightly occurrence. In a period of four days and nights, 2 Parachute Brigade made seven small attacks on their opponents near Poggiofiorito in which eleven prisoners were taken. Harassing fire from artillery and mortars was also a regular feature of the front, although the level of fire was reduced by constraints on the levels of ammunition available to Eighth Army.

As 1944 came to cold life the face of Eighth Army was changing considerably. Not only did Montgomery depart for England but a number of major formations also left Italy for the United Kingdom and the forthcoming invasion of France. These included 7th Armoured Division, which had fought briefly in Italy with X Corps in Fifth Army, 1st Airborne Division, 50th Division and 51st (Highland) Division. Montgomery had also wanted to take 2nd New Zealand Division with him but was overruled by Brooke, the CIGS. He was allowed to take some corps and divisional commanders, thus Horrocks and Simonds left for Britain, but the man he most wanted, Oliver Leese, remained in Italy as his successor rather than Monty's own nominee, Sir Richard O'Connor, the first desert victor and recently escaped from an Italian PoW camp. Nor were those the only departures: 5th Division moved across the peninsula to join X Corps in Fifth Army while the recently arrived 1st Infantry Division came under Army Group command before joining the US VI Corps on 1 January 1944.

However, additional Canadian troops had arrived in the Mediterranean to create a Canadian Corps which would include, in addition to 1st Canadian Division, 5th Canadian Armoured Division* and 1st Army Group Royal Canadian Artillery[†] with the necessary supporting corps troops. Both Eisenhower and Alexander were surprised by the decision to deploy 1st Canadian Corps in the Mediterranean theatre; Eisenhower was concerned that there might be political pressure for an early commitment to battle of the newly arrived Canadians while Alexander considered that he had enough armour for the conditions under which 15 Army Group was operating. Neither man had been consulted about the Canadian deployment and Alexander, in an uncharacteristically tetchy comment to Brooke, asked that he be consulted in future before such matters were agreed upon since such decisions could upset his order of battle and therefore his battle plans. By the end of January 1st Canadian Corps, under Lieutenant-General H D G Crerar, had joined Eighth Army's order of battle while Freyberg's New Zealand Division had passed to Army Group command.

The Canadians were not the only new corps to join Eighth Army. On 10 February 1944, Lieutenant-General Wladyslaw Anders, commanding II Polish Corps, reported to General Sir Oliver Leese at Eighth Army HQ at Vasto. Anders had been badly wounded in 1939 during the German invasion of Poland and was later transported to the Soviet Union when the Red Army invaded from the east. After a spell in the Lubianka prison in Moscow he was freed, as a result of an agreement between Stalin and General Sikorski, prime minister of the Polish government in exile, to command a Polish army to be formed in Russia to fight the Germans who

---

* The division included 5 Armoured Brigade and 11 Infantry Brigade. Within 5 Armoured Brigade were: 3rd Armd Recce Regt, The Governor-General's Horse Guards; 2nd Armd Regt, Lord Strathcona's Horse (Royal Canadians); 5th Armd Regt, 8th Princess Louise's (New Brunswick) Hussars; and 9th Armd Regiment, The British Columbia Dragoons. Comprising 11 Brigade were: The Perth Regiment; The Irish Regiment of Canada; and The Cape Breton Highlanders.
[†] The Group included 1st, 2nd and 5th Medium Regiments, RCA, as well as 11th Field Regiment, RCA.

had invaded the USSR. Anders later suggested to Stalin that this army should be moved to the Middle East to train. Surprisingly, Stalin agreed and over 100,000 Poles, including women and children, crossed the border into Persia. They then moved to Iraq where the Polish Carpathian Brigade, which had fought in the desert campaign, joined them.* Although effectively commanding a corps, Anders was nominally an army commander and was regarded as the CinC of an Allied contingent. When it joined Eighth Army II Polish Corps was both well trained and well disciplined and enjoyed exceptionally high morale.

> There was also a deep seriousness in its attitude to war, derived largely from a knowledge of what the Germans were doing in their country. Harold Macmillan wrote of the Polish Second Corps: 'It was more than a military formation. It was a crusade.'[9]

The arrival of the Canadian and Polish corps and their inclusion in Eighth Army's order of battle meant that by the end of January 1944 only one British formation, 78th Division, was left in the Army. The Army's line was held by 1st Canadian Corps on the right, deploying 1st Canadian Division and 8th Indian Division, and by XIII Corps on the left, deploying 78th Division, 4th Indian Division (recently arrived from the Middle East) with part of 5th Canadian Armoured Division, 3rd Carpathian Division and HQ 5th Canadian Armoured Division.

Eighth Army now held a static front and was to do so until it moved to the Liri valley in March and April. The only exception to this was a planned Canadian attack to take high ground north of Ortona, overlooking the Arielli, after which part of XIII Corps would turn against Orsogna, Guardiagrele and San Martino while V Corps prepared to continue the advance towards Pescara. Although 11 Canadian Brigade began operations on 17 January, the attack was soon called off to avoid unnecessary loss of life.

The static situation was brought about by Alexander's new plan which gave Fifth Army the main burden of the Allied offensive while Eighth Army maintained pressure on LXXVI Panzer Corps to prevent the latter sending reinforcements to the formations facing Fifth Army. Leese believed that minor operations by Eighth Army would not assist Fifth Army and that Eighth Army was not giving the Germans the impression

---

* The Corps included 3rd Carpathian Division (1 and 2 Carpathian Rifle Brigades); 5th Kresowa Division (5 Wilenski and 6 Lwowska Infantry Brigades); and 2 Polish Armoured Brigade, with divisional and corps troops including field, anti-tank, HAA and LAA artillery, reconnaissance and support regiments, and engineers; the total strength was over 56,000 men.

of an impending major thrust along the Adriatic coast and so proposed to intervene in the second half of February when his new formations had settled down. Alexander agreed to this in principle on 23 January but warned Leese that he should be ready to make a major effort at short notice from 26 January. Leese disagreed, maintaining that success was more likely to accrue from an Eighth Army attack in force in mid-February to coincide with Fifth Army operations. However, Alexander had made a definite decision to reinforce Fifth Army which could be done only at the expense of Eighth Army: on 30 January Leese was ordered to send 4th Indian Division to Fifth Army while 78th Division was to be held ready to follow from 7 February.

On the German side 90th Panzer Grenadier Division had left the line in early January while 26th Panzer Division had been moved to Avezzano later in the month. Eighth Army's main task, that of containing LXXVI Panzer Corps, remained; to that end 1 Canadian Brigade was ordered to take part of the road from Villa Grande to Tollo on 30 January. However, German opposition was determined and the attack was called off since it could only result in unnecessary casualties. Following this Eighth Army passed firmly to the defensive.

It had now become clear that Eighth Army's part in 15 Army Group's plan to reach Rome had become redundant. On the Adriatic side of Italy the coastal plain stretched for about a hundred miles to the port of Ancona while, on Eighth Army's left flank, the bony spine of Italy, the Apennine mountains, was blanketed in snow and formed an impassable obstruction to any large force. The advance to Pescara and operations from there to support Fifth Army could not happen while General Winter held control; hence Alexander's decision to reinforce Fifth Army.

Mark Clark's command had already been pushing hard against the enemy defences on the western side of the Apennines. In the December battles Fifth Army had sustained heavy casualties but had made some gains. However, the fighting for Monte Camino and San Pietro in the area of the Mignano Gap had been fierce and costly with advances measured at times in yards. In mid-December 2nd Moroccan Division of the French Expeditionary Corps took Pantano and the northern slopes of Monte Casale while the US 45th Division took Monte Cavallo, catching the Germans in the course of the relief of 305th Division by 5th Mountain Division. The general aim was to reach the Liri valley through which ran Highway 6, the main road to Rome. In early January Fifth Army succeeded in pushing forward to the Gustav Line with Monte Trocchio being taken, unopposed, by the US 34th Division on 15 January. The Germans had abandoned Monte Trocchio on which a garrison might have been isolated in favour of pulling back into the main Gustav Line positions. That line was anchored on the Monte Cassino position and it was to be several long months before Allied troops took Cassino.

On 22 January the US VI Corps, including 3rd US Division and 1st British Division, landed at Anzio, south of Rome, in Operation SHINGLE, an amphibious left hook designed to assist and accelerate the break-through to Rome. On 10 January Clark had issued orders for Fifth Army to continue its offensive with three main aims: to pin down German troops in the Gustav positions thus preventing their transfer to meet the threat from Anzio; to draw in German reserves to the Gustav Line; and to break through that line, advance quickly up the Liri valley and then link up with VI Corps breaking out of the Anzio beachhead.[10] Bold in concept, the plan was flawed in its execution: VI Corps' commander, Major-General John P Lucas, proved too timorous and, although his command landed without resistance, he spent much time in preparing to meet enemy counter-attacks. In the end the operation lost its momentum and VI Corps was doomed to a lingering purgatory in the beachhead until the end of May.

Fifth Army's attacks on the Gustav Line met with no further success: an attempt by 36th Division, of II Corps, to cross the Rapido river and create a bridgehead for Combat Command B of 1st Armoured Division to strike into the Liri valley was twice repulsed with heavy casualties: 143 were killed, 663 wounded and 875 were missing. An operation by the British 46th Division of X Corps to cross the Garigliano river to protect II Corps' flank also failed although both 5th and 56th Divisions had crossed the river in their respective sectors to form a bridgehead: casualty levels, however, militated against further extensive operations with the three British divisions receiving only 219 reinforcements in January against their total requirement of 4,686. Only the French Expeditionary Corps completely achieved its objectives with Moroccan, Tunisian and Algerian soldiers showing special skill in mountain fighting and a relish for battle that often unsettled their opponents.

Attention now turned to Monte Cassino with its Benedictine monastery, first established by St Benedict himself in the sixth century. Below the monastery lies the town of Cassino through which passes Highway 6. What has been termed the first battle of Cassino began on 1 February and was fought principally by II US Corps supported by the French Expeditionary Corps. Those operations failed to unlock the Cassino position and a further attack, the second battle of Cassino, was planned. This assault was to be made by a reconstituted New Zealand Corps, under Freyberg, which included 78th Division and 4th Indian Division as well as 2nd New Zealand Division. All three divisions had passed from Eighth Army to Army Group command and were now to be committed as part of Fifth Army.

The second battle of Cassino began on 15 February with 4th Indian Division storming Monastery Hill at night while the New Zealanders attacked the town of Cassino. After taking the mountain Tuker's* men were to swing into Cassino from the west but their attack ground to a halt and was a complete failure as the assaulting soldiers were cut down systematically by intensive fire from the defenders. The New Zealanders fared little better: they gained a lodgement in the town but were evicted after a few hours by the Germans. The battle continued until the 18th and Freyberg likened it to Passchendaele in the Great War, such was the devastation in the area.

In retrospect it can be seen that the preparations for this attack actually strengthened the German positions. The assault had been preceded by the bombing of the abbey itself which Tuker had demanded in the belief that it was being used by the Germans. In fact this had not been the case but General Ira Eaker, commanding the Allied air forces, had concurred with this flawed conclusion after flying over Monte Cassino. In destroying the monastery the bombing provided good cover for German defenders.

Plans for a renewed offensive by the New Zealand Corps were drawn up with the intention of mounting a fresh attack towards the end of February. Alexander laid down two conditions for this assault: it was only to take place after three successive fine days so that the ground would be dry enough for tanks to operate; and visibility had to be good on the day of the attack so that bombers could support the ground troops. But the weather broke on 23 February and foul conditions, rain, sleet and snow, persisted until 15 March by which time 1st Fallschirmjäger Division had relieved 90th Panzer Grenadier Division in the Cassino sector.

The third battle of Cassino was another New Zealand Corps operation. Launched after heavy bombing of Cassino town and the unleashing of almost 200,000 artillery rounds into the town, it nevertheless faltered in the face of stubborn German resistance and renewed rainfall. Although the New Zealanders did not succeed in their overall objectives they had some success with the capture of much of the town and Castle Mountain; the Gurkhas of 5 Indian Brigade then took Hangman's Hill. Alexander proposed to use these gains in the major offensive which he had already been planning and which was to be the fourth and final battle of Cassino.[†]

On 21 March Alexander met with Leese and Clark to discuss future operations. Freyberg was also present to outline the most recent Cassino attack. Alexander made clear that there were two options: to continue

---

* Tuker was in hospital at this time and Brigadier Dimoline, the divisional CRA, had taken command of 4th Indian Division.
† The postwar Battles Nomenclature Committee defined only two Cassino battles: Cassino I, from 20 January to 17 March; and Cassino II, from 11 to 16 May. However, the official history uses the more precise breakdown into four battles which is adopted in this narrative.

with the Cassino operation in the hope of taking the monastery within days; or abandoning the operation.[11] The decision was taken that a further assault would be made on Monte Cassino. This new operation would be undertaken by Eighth Army which would move across from the Adriatic sector. In turn that sector would be held by V Corps under Army Group command. Eighth Army Headquarters began its move from Vasto on 11 March and settled near Venafro two days later. On 26 March the New Zealand Corps was disbanded and XIII Corps took over the Cassino sector with 78th Division moving into many of the gains made by the New Zealanders.

Alexander also undertook a re-organisation of his command, regrouping his armies on a, loosely, national basis: thus all British and Commonwealth divisions, save for 1st and 5th in the Anzio beachhead, passed from Fifth Army to Eighth Army which also, of course, held II Polish Corps. Fifth Army was to include American and French formations. Eighth Army was to be further reinforced by the return of South African troops, now in the form of 6th South African Armoured Division which had arrived in Italy and was under Army Group command.* The departure of major formations for Operation ANVIL, the invasion of southern France planned to coincide with OVERLORD was also delayed at Alexander's request, to ensure an Allied superiority in manpower.[†]

The Allied Armies' next operation was intended to break into the Liri valley with an assault on a twenty-mile front, stretching from the coast to the heights overlooking Cassino. The attacking force's strength, at double any previously committed, would give the Allies the three-to-one superiority needed to succeed. On Eighth Army would fall the major burden of the attack: Leese's force was to smash through the Gustav and Hitler lines to allow his armour to charge through the Liri valley and advance on the general axis of Highway 6 to the area east of Rome; the tanks would be greatly aided by the effects of the spring sun drying out the ground. Eighth Army would then 'pursue the enemy on the general axis Terni-Perugia' and 'thereafter advance on Ancona and Florence, the main objective at that stage to be decided later'.[13] Fifth Army was to make a supporting attack through the Aurunci mountains with six divisions while VI Corps was to break out from Anzio at a time considered

---

* Alexander's command was designated Allied Armies Italy on 11 January 1944. It became Allied Central Mediterranean Force on 18 January but reverted to Allied Armies Italy on 10 March.[12] It would later revert to the title 15 Army Group.
† As well as 6th (SA) Armoured Division, Eighth Army received the balance of 6th (British) Armoured Division, two armoured brigades and an infantry brigade while Fifth Army was reinforced by two US infantry divisions and additional French elements. A proposal to transfer the British 2nd Division to Italy from India did not go ahead

appropriate by Alexander. That attack was to be directed northwards in order to cut off the retreat of the German armies. The strategic objective of the forthcoming operation, codenamed DIADEM, was the destruction of the German armies rather than the seizure of any geographical objective, thus forcing the Germans to pour more reinforcements into Italy at the expense of other theatres:

> To destroy the right wing of the German Tenth Army; to drive what remains of it and the German Fourteenth Army north of Rome; and to pursue the enemy to the Rimini-Pisa line inflicting the maximum losses to him in the process.[14]

As preparations were being made for DIADEM, Eighth Army's soldiers held positions fraught with all the tension of trench warfare. Fred Majdalany, a company commander in 2nd Lancashire Fusiliers, described the conditions on Hangman's Hill for 1st/9th Gurkhas as 'one of the genuine epics of the war'.

> One of the most touching sights on these corpse-littered mountains was a Gurkha cemetery. The graves seemed too short for a man, and the boots at the end of each one, too small. (There was always a steel helmet at one end of the grave, boots at the other.) The rows of little boots always gave the impression that this was a burial ground of children.[15]

Colin Gunner, a platoon commander in 1st Royal Irish Fusiliers, described the conditions endured by his battalion in the valley from Cairo village up towards Monte Cairo.

> Sangar life engulfed us now. No digging down six feet into the sandy soil of Capua – laborious piling of rock with a pathetic little roof took place on those adamantine slopes. Where were you now Corporal Boyce with your tales of the Waziris and Khyber from those long ago marches in the Algerian heat? There were no Pathans or Afridis facing us here. This enemy dealt not in the single brain-splashing shot of the rifle, but in generalised and wholesale death. No need to view Dead Mule corner for proof; by day and night the stench was eloquent testimony to their efficiency. Many alarms there were during that three weeks when we crouched and lay in those shelters; no excursions save for the odd, in every sense, one, of the battle patrol. We were many times better off than the battalion directly facing the Monastery, where throwing the contents of his lavatory tin out the back of his sangar earned for many a man a hail of mortar bombs.[16]

Supplying troops in such positions created an administrative nightmare.

Food, ammunition and all the other necessities had to be brought up under cover of darkness along a route every yard of which had been registered by enemy artillery. Wheeled transport made the first part of the journey before handing over to mules, some of whose drivers were Cypriots, which made the final trek forward to those units whose positions were otherwise inaccessible. Many mules were killed by mortars or fell to their deaths from the mountain tracks and, since the rocky ground prevented burial, the stench of their decomposing bodies was added to Cassino's horrors.[17]

In such manner did the soldiers of 78th Division spend much of April before being relieved by Polish troops. No one was sorry to hand over to the Poles and say goodbye to the positions around Cassino. Fred Majdalany summed up the handover in his book, *The Monastery*:

As we marched along the track and began the slow, twisting, weary climb on the far side of the valley, the happenings of the past thirty days and nights passed in review through the tired mind like a dream in the half-conscious moments of waking. . . . [The Fusiliers] marched back from the battle in the way of the Infantry, their feet scarcely leaving the ground, their bodies rocking mechanically from side to side as if that was the only way they could lift their legs. You could see that it required the last ounce of their mental and physical energy to move their legs at all. Yet they looked as if they could keep on moving like that for ever.

Their clothes were torn and ragged. They carried their weapons every conceivable way they could be carried. Every few minutes they would change shoulders or change positions. The heavier burdens, like the Brens and the mortars, were passed along from one to another. Every man took his turn.

Their bearded faces were black with honourable dirt, and their eyes stared to their front and appeared to see nothing. No one sang or whistled, and hardly anyone spoke unless it was to utter a curse when his rifle slipped off his shoulder.[18]

Their division would soon be back in action around Cassino as part of Operation DIADEM.

It was necessary to gain as much surprise for DIADEM as possible. The Germans knew that there would be further attacks on the Gustav Line. What they did not know was where or when those attacks would fall and in what strength, nor by what troops they would be undertaken. In order to keep the Germans guessing as long as possible an elaborate deception plan, Operation DUNTON, was put into effect.

DUNTON was the work of Alexander's brilliant Chief of Staff, General John Harding (later Field Marshal Lord Harding of Pemberton) and it involved sidestepping Eighth Army from east to west of the Apennines without the Germans realising what was happening. In order to prevent the concentration of defending forces in the area of the planned attack, deception exercises were carried out to keep Kesselring and his staff thinking that there might be further amphibious operations. Thus the US 36th Division, allegedly part of 1st Canadian Corps, undertook seaborne exercises in the Naples and Salerno area which was also liberally marked with the maple-leaf signs of the Canadians who had moved back to the front in unmarked transport. Reconnaissance aircraft flew many missions over the beaches around Civitavecchia to create the impression that a landing would be made there.

The deception plan also fooled the Germans about the move of the Polish Corps into the Cassino sector by the simple expedient of having English signallers in the Corps so that any communications monitored by the Germans would be in English rather than Polish. Kesselring's staff also 'lost' the French Corps after its withdrawal from the area north of Cassino; this was a matter of particular concern to Kesselring.

To guard against all possibilities German reserves were held back to respond to a variety of threats. Hermann Goering and 92nd Infantry Divisions were deployed to react to a landing near Civitavecchia; 26th and 29th Panzer Divisions were near Anzio in case of further landings there, while 90th Panzer Grenadier Division waited for a possible airborne attack near Frosinone.

But it was in timing that Alexander's planners scored their greatest success. Kesselring began a regrouping which he intended to complete by mid-May before, by his assessment, the Allied offensive. General von Senger und Etterlin, commanding XIV Panzer Corps which, with LI Mountain Corps, held the front on which the attack would fall, went back to Germany on leave until late May, certain that no attack would be launched before his return. But, at 11pm on 11 May, one of the quietest nights in months was shattered as over 1,600 guns began an intensive bombardment of the enemy positions. For forty minutes the artillery hammered the known positions of every German gun battery on the front before switching to the first objectives of the assaulting infantry. The storm of artillery fire lit up the night sky and shook the earth for miles around: Operation DIADEM had begun.

NOTES

1. *London Gazette*, 6 June 1950 (Alexander's Despatch (ii) 2905)
2. PRO: CAB44/135, p.17
3. K G F Chavasse: *Some Memories of 56 Reconnaissance Regiment*
4. Doherty: *Only the Enemy in Front*, p.120
5. A D Woods: *A personal account of his service with 2 LIR in Italy*
6. PRO: WO170/605, War diary, 1944, 38 Bde

7. Russell: *Account of the Irish Brigade*
8. Gunner: *Front of the Line*, p.121
9. Howarth: *My God, Soldiers*, p.108
10. Molony et al: *The Mediterranean and the Middle East, vol v*, p.602
11. ibid, p.799
12. PRO: CAB44/135, p.77
13. Molony et al: *The Mediterranean and the Middle East, vol vi, Pt I*, p.58
14. ibid, p.57 (Allied Armies Italy, Op Inst No. 5, 5 May 1944)
15. Majdalany: *Cassino*, p.200
16. Gunner: op cit, p.81
17. Scott: *Account of the Irish Brigade*
18. Majdalany: *The Monastery*, pp.75-76

CHAPTER XIV

From Cassino to Rome

Let each man do his best

Eighth Army's part in the offensive was codenamed Operation HONKER, the plan of battle for which was to involve all four corps: II Polish Corps was to

I 1 Isolate the area Monastery Hill-Cassino from the north and north-west and dominate Highway 6 until a junction is effected with XIII Corps;
  2 Attack and capture Monastery Hill
II 1 Gain contact with the Adolf Hitler Line North of Highway 6 and develop operations with a view to turning it from the North.[1]

XIII Corps was to push 4th British and 8th Indian Divisions across the Rapido while X Corps, with only the New Zealand Division under command, protected the north flank. Once 4th and 8th Divisions had formed a bridgehead across the Rapido both 6th Armoured and 78th Divisions were to reinforce and expand that bridgehead; they would then break out of the bridgehead and crack open the Gustav Line south of Cassino. When the line had been broken I Canadian Corps would take over and exploit through the Liri valley towards Valmontone.

The attacking Fifth and Eighth Armies were opposed by von Vietinghoff's Tenth Army in the Gustav Line while von Mackensen's Fourteenth Army faced VI Corps in the Anzio beachhead as well as covering the approach to Rome. In total the two German armies disposed eleven divisions, of which Tenth Army had six, although Kesselring held a further three divisions, including a panzer division, in general reserve. Thus the Germans were outnumbered in overall terms but especially in the area of attack. Against this they had the advantage of excellent defensive positions which they had had time to prepare and improve and the German forces did not suffer the political and national sensitivities that marked the Allied armies.

Prior to the attack General Anders had issued an order of the day to his troops in which he told them that the moment for battle had arrived and with it the time for 'revenge and retribution' on Poland's hereditary foe.

> Shoulder to shoulder with us will fight British, American, Canadian and
> New Zealand divisions, together with French, Italian and Indian troops.
> The task assigned to us will cover with glory the name of the Polish
> soldier all over the world. At this moment the thoughts and hearts of
> our whole nation will be with us. Trusting in the Justice of Divine
> Providence we go forward with the sacred slogan in our hearts: God,
> Honour, Country.[2]

Anders' infantry attacked at 1am on 12 May meeting a storm of enemy
artillery and mortar fire to which was soon added machine-gun fire and
small-arms fire as they closed up on their objectives. Hill 593 was taken by
1 Carpathian Rifle Brigade which then fought for Hill 569. After climbing
Phantom Ridge the men of 5 Vilno Infantry Brigade engaged the
defenders in bitter hand-to-hand fighting which continued through the
morning into the afternoon, although elements of the brigade moved on
to penetrate the slopes of the next objective.

As the day wore on it became clear to Anders that taking some
objectives was easier than holding them. Since consolidation could not
easily be carried out by the attacking units, and fresh forces could not be
inserted quickly because of traffic problems on the approach roads and
tracks, Anders ordered his attacking brigades to return to their start lines
for relief by other formations which would continue the attack.

> Our detachments accordingly withdrew in the evening of May 12, but
> some remained in their positions until May 13. One lesson learned was
> that our artillery fire, intense though it was, was unable effectively to
> silence the enemy batteries or to destroy the enemy infantry in their
> battle stations, which ... were mostly laid on the opposite hill slopes, in
> places inaccessible to our supporting fire.[3]

After Anders had ordered his attacking brigades to regroup, Leese arrived
at the Polish headquarters and expressed himself satisfied that Anders'
men had played a valuable role thus far in the battle. The Polish attack had
kept the Germans bottled up in Cassino, had drawn German artillery fire
from other sectors of the front and had prevented the use of German
reserves, especially in the area where XIII Corps was operating. By
reducing the possible enemy reaction to XIII Corps' crossing of the
Rapido, II Polish Corps had been 'of great assistance' to the British corps.
On Leese's orders further attacks by the Poles would depend on the
progress made by XIII Corps; Leese had no wish to see the Polish Corps
fight an isolated battle.

*

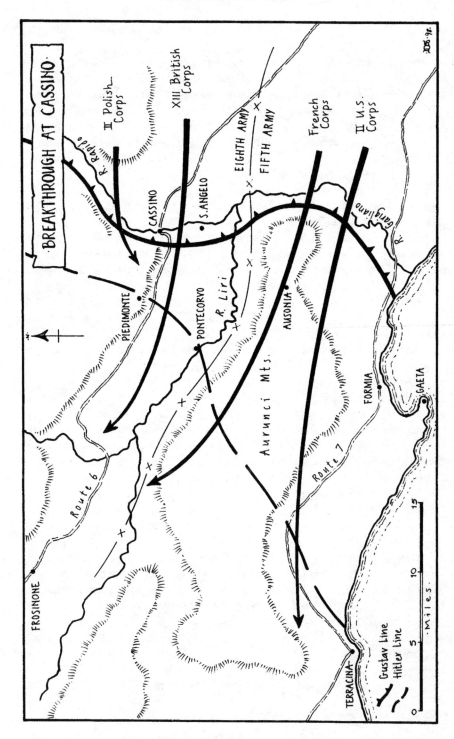

BREAKTHROUGH AT CASSINO.

II Polish Corps

XIII British Corps

French Corps

II U.S. Corps

EIGHTH ARMY
FIFTH ARMY

R. Rapido

CASSINO

S.ANGELO

R. Garigliano

PIEDIMONTE

PONTECORVO

R. Liri

AUSONIA

Aurunci Mts.

FORMIA

GAETA

FROSINONE

Route 6

Route 7

TERRACINA

Gustav Line
Hitler Line

0   5   10   15
Miles

However, XIII Corps' attack had been far from straightforward:

> The first phase of the attack . . . was as confused and bloody as the first
> night of Alamein. The river crossing was greatly impeded by mist and
> by the strength of the current. Getting assault boats across was, in most
> cases, impossible. Small parties that did achieve the far bank were cut
> off and destroyed. Bridging was consequently often impracticable. Men
> approaching the bank or the bridging places were cut down by German
> machine guns firing on fixed lines or by German field guns and mortars
> firing pre-arranged tasks.[4]

In spite of such well organised and determined opposition, a shallow
bridgehead had been created in XIII Corps' area by the morning of 12 May
and two bridges had been constructed by the sappers. The Engineers had
performed superbly: although working on river banks that they had been
unable to reconnoitre, under heavy shellfire and in darkness, they had
brought forward all their bridging equipment behind what was but a thin
line of infantry. By so doing the sappers had allowed DIADEM truly to
enter its opening phase. But building the bridges was far from the total of
the Engineers' work; ahead of them lay heavily sown minefields and
strong enemy fortifications, the elimination of which called for the
sappers' skills.

On XIII Corps' right flank 4th Division had the task of establishing a
bridgehead to a depth of 1,000 yards (Brown Line), followed by a further
advance of almost a mile to secure the low ridges overlooking the river
(Blue Line), after which the division would push on to the Cassino-
Pignataro road north of the Piopetto river (Red Line) before finally
swinging right to cut Highway 6 and make contact with the Poles who
should, by then, have cleared the high ground. Although the division was
to be on Blue Line by dawn on 12 May its commander, Lieutenant-General
Dudley Ward, would give no predictions about progress thereafter.

Fourth Division's attack was made at the northern end of the Liri valley
with 10 Brigade on the right and 28 Brigade to the left. Although the
former managed to get most of all three of its battalions* over the river,
none reached the Blue Line and only some companies pushed forward to
the Brown Line. As dawn broke the brigade was dug in around its
perimeter ready to repel the inevitable counter-attacks, some of which
were supported by single tanks. General Ward 'ordered only minor
advances and consolidation until each Brigade had four [anti-tank] guns
on the west bank'.[5]

On the division's left flank, however, 28 Brigade was unable to move
forward at all. Its assaulting battalions, 2nd King's (Liverpool) and 2nd

---

* 2nd Beds and Herts; 2nd Duke of Cornwall's LI; 1/6th Surreys.

Somerset LI, were both hit hard by the Germans. The King's arrived thirty minutes late at the two crossing points by which time the counter-battery artillery programme was drawing to an end, and by the time their boats were launched heavy enemy fire was being brought down on them. Many boats were lost and although three companies crossed these were disorganised and had already suffered heavy casualties. B Company's advance was stopped by a minefield; D Company was reduced to ten men and an officer, while C Company incurred severe losses while passing through a minefield under fire from the defenders.

The Somersets were to follow the King's, passing through them to advance to Blue Line. In the confusion that had ensued from the King's efforts to cross, the Somersets became badly disorganised and a company even withdrew to the boat assembly position in the mistaken belief that an order to do so had been issued. The brigade attack had failed and both battalions, as well as Brigade HQ, seem to have been lacking in effective leadership. Certainly 28 Brigade was withdrawn for re-organisation on 14 May and its third battalion, 2/4th Hampshires, was put under command of 12 Brigade. Not until 20 May did 28 Brigade rejoin 4th Division.

On the left of XIII Corps, 8th Indian Division also had difficulties crossing the Rapido with many of the assault boats, cumbersome and without keels, being swept downstream before they managed to reach the far bank. When soldiers did get across they found thick mist that obscured even the tracer bursts from Bofors LAA guns that were intended to help them in direction finding. But the mist also helped conceal the attackers from the German artillery observers and mortarmen; it was not a completely negative aspect.

Divisional objectives for the first twenty-four hours of DIADEM included the establishment of a bridgehead; pushing out that bridgehead to a depth of about 2,000 yards; mopping up in Sant'Angelo village; and consolidating positions on the ridge beyond. Following that, either 78th Division or 1st Canadian Corps would pass through to advance to and through the Hitler Line.

Eighth Indian Division's advance fell behind the timetable: the schedule called for 100 yards every six minutes but, although the guns kept to this programme, the infantry could not keep up. The Royal Fusiliers' regimental historian noted how

by 04.00 the Commanding Officer signalled the leading companies to halt and later to reorganize on the river bank. . . . The Commanding Officer went boldly forward into the mist to locate the line of advance and, encountering wire, made the complete circuit of an enemy strongpoint. But no attack could be launched in such conditions [and the battalion] proceeded to dig in and wait for the mist to clear. It cleared all right the following morning and the sun came out at 09.00 hours. But with it came . . . enemy fire . . . and the slightest movement brought down [that] fire.[6]

First Royal Fusiliers were serving in 17 Indian Brigade whose other assaulting battalion was 1/12th Frontier Force Regiment. They too had a difficult time: before their crossing began there was a hint of farce when the Beachmaster could not find the river; the battalion adjutant, far from pleased at this development, curtly informed him where he might find the Rapido.

In trying to extend the bridgehead 1/12th Frontier Force attacked to the left of Sant'Angelo but ran into a barrier of wire and mines. Working their way around the obstacle they came under fire, platoons became dispersed and the leading companies lost contact. Flares proved useless in the mist but the shouting of regimental warcries soon allowed locations to be pinpointed. Flanking attacks by the Frontier Force and the Fusiliers on Sant'Angelo were brought to a halt by enemy fire and 17 Brigade's reserve battalion, 1/5th Gurkhas, was brought forward for a frontal attack. Unfortunately only one company of Gurkhas was used initially, and two platoons lost their way crossing the Rapido and moving to the start line. Thus the assault was mounted with a single platoon, which had already lost several soldiers, and was easily rebuffed.

Pignataro was 19 Brigade's principal objective and the attack was led by 3/8th Punjabis. This battalion got almost all its men across the river, after most of the boats had been sunk, by an improvised shuttle service on the remaining boats. As a result they fell badly behind time and did not move off until early next morning. A Company ran into a minefield and lost many dead to mines and small-arms fire; only fifteen men were left standing but six more were lost before the survivors reached the road that paralleled the river. Although they tried to make further progress they were forced to take cover after only a few yards. This little group then fought off several counter-attacks during the day but, by the morning of 13 May, only three remained able to fight. They were forced to surrender when their ammunition ran out. Theirs was not the only example of outstanding courage to be shown by the *jawans* of 3/8th Punjabis for the battalion had gained Eighth Army's first Victoria Cross of the Cassino battle. Sepoy Kamal Ram had silenced three enemy machine-gun posts when

his company advance was held up by heavy machine-gun fire from four posts on the front and flanks. The capture of the position was essential and Sepoy Kamal Ram volunteered to get round the rear of the right post and silence it. He attacked the first two posts single-handed, killing or taking prisoner the occupants and together with a havildar he then went on and completed the destruction of a third. His outstanding bravery undoubtedly saved a difficult situation at a critical period of the battle.[7]

Nineteen-years-old Kamal Ram, who had never been in action before, thus became the youngest soldier to be awarded the VC during the Second World War.

B Company were fortunate not to meet any strong enemy positions and, by noon, they were close to Point 63, the capture of which was assigned to D Company which moved up to within yards of the objective before charging in line abreast. Several machine guns and barbed wire stopped the charge. The officer who led was killed as was a complete platoon which had almost reached the German positions. A further attack took the ridge by which time only thirty men of D Company were still on their feet.

With both attacking divisions so far behind schedule, and the bridgehead still so shallow, there was little possibility of moving reserve divisions forward into the bridgehead. The sappers had constructed two bridges in 8th Indian Division's area in the face of great difficulties. Both were in use by 9.15am on the 12th although one, codenamed Plymouth, was damaged by enemy artillery and its use thereafter was restricted to light vehicles. The other bridge remained intact; four squadrons of Canadian tanks passed over it into the bridgehead and by dusk had helped 8th Indian Division to push forward, clear part of Sant'Angelo and advance towards Panccioni.

Fourth Division still had no bridge in its area, although three had been planned. On the evening of 12 May orders were issued for the completion of one bridge. Artillery cover was provided for the sappers as well as a smokescreen and the men of 7 and 225 Field Squadrons worked throughout the night to accomplish their task which was complete at 4am on the 13th. But the bridge, codenamed Amazon, had cost the two squadrons eighty-three of the 200 men involved in its building.

The pace of advance now began to increase: on the 13th the Indians took Sant'Angelo, cleared most of the horseshoe ridge and moved on to clear up the Liri Appendix the next day; elements of the division were also probing towards the Cassino-Pignataro road. In 4th Division's area 12 Brigade advanced more than a mile westwards on the 13th; at several points the Blue Line was reached. During these operations Eighth Army's second Victoria Cross at Cassino was won by Captain Richard Wakeford of 2/4th Hampshires which had been attached to 12 Brigade from 28 Brigade.

On 13 May Captain Wakeford, armed only with a revolver, and accompanied only by his orderly

went forward and killed several of the enemy and took 20 prisoners.

When attacking a hill feature the following day his company came under heavy fire, but although wounded in the face and both arms, Captain Wakeford pressed home the attack. He was wounded again, but reached the objective and consolidated the position.[8]

On the 13th and 14th, 10 Brigade moved northwards towards Highway 6.

Some German defenders had begun to show a less than enthusiastic attitude towards the defensive tasks. The men defending Platform Knoll, a strongpoint just north of Sant'Angelo had seen that village fall to the Gurkhas with support from Canadian tanks and had immediately hung out white flags to surrender, thus saving 1st Royal Fusiliers the trouble of forming up and attacking their position. Although there were some other similar incidents, these were isolated: in general opposition was more akin to that met by 6/13th Frontier Force who attacked a position held by an ad hoc group of mountain warfare students who

> fought fanatically as the Pathans swarmed in amongst them. After the position had been overrun little groups which had fled in the face of the onslaught returned to dig in and to die in last stands. Prisoners emerged with their hands above their heads, holding grenades which they hurled as their captors went forward to secure them.[9]

Although progress was now being made it was not always smooth: the inevitable muddle created by the fog of war, and the real fog that descended on the battlefield, led to confusion and difficulties in deployment. At times, however, mist could prove a blessing, as it did for 2nd Royal Fusiliers of 12 Brigade who were shrouded in the mist, and thereby hidden from German eyes, as they crossed the Rapido on the 13th to move to the start line for an attack. Next day 12 Brigade launched an attack towards the Cassino-Pignataro roads using 6th Black Watch supported by tanks of the Lothians and Border Horse. With heavy mist closing on them the CO of the Black Watch, Lieutenant-Colonel Madden, formed his men into a hollow square around the tanks and moved off in that fashion. The attackers were able to overrun a strong German position from which an anti-tank gun had been unable to fire as the crew could not see the tanks through the mist.

When the mist cleared, however, 6th Black Watch who were well ahead of the flanking battalions suffered a series of counter-attacks which they repulsed, holding out until 1st Royal West Kents, and some tanks, relieved them that evening. The tanks were having a difficult time: not only was the mist creating problems but the ground had not yet dried out to its summer hardness and many became totally bogged down. Since the terrain also favoured the defender, the German anti-tank guns, hidden in sunken lanes, behind walls or hedges, could often engage at point-blank range with devastating effect. One armoured regiment, 17th/21st Lancers, lost fifty-seven killed or wounded in the first six days of action.

To date XIII Corps had achieved much of the first part of their initial objective: to capture and secure a bridgehead over the Rapido between Cassino and the Liri river. The second part of that objective required the Corps to isolate Cassino from the west, cut Highway 6 and effect a junction with the Polish Corps. However, the Poles had regrouped on the 12th and Leese had ordered Anders not to renew his attack until XIII Corps had made sufficient progress. It was now clear to Leese that the Poles could only successfully renew their attack when 1st Fallschirmjäger Division's retreat was threatened by the cutting of Highway 6. Since 4th Division, who could move against Highway 6, needed protection for their already exposed left flank, Leese chose to order 78th Division into 4th Division's bridgehead rather than into 8th Indian's which had been his other option.

Led by the Irish Brigade 78th Division moved forward into the bridgehead but it was not a straightforward move. The dearth of bridges, and the fact that both 4th and 8th Divisions were still using the existing bridges, meant that 78th Division had to take its turn with other traffic; the result was that the Battleaxe Division fell behind schedule.

The Irish Brigade moved into the bridgehead on the afternoon of 14 May to face a German position that was held strongly in depth with mines, dug-in machine guns, concrete emplacements and skilful and courageous defenders. Lieutenant Jim Trousdell, 1st Royal Irish Fusiliers, later noted the quality of the German defences:

> I remember crossing the Rapido by a Bailey Bridge which was subject to sporadic shelling and being led to what had been the German trenches covering the Rapido part of the Gustav Line. They had been very well dug and camouflaged, all the spoil removed and until you were right up to them they were practically invisible – also safe from anything but a direct hit, they were so deep.[10]

As the forward battalions of the Irish Brigade advanced to their start line, codenamed Grafton, they found the Germans still in possession of large chunks of it; these enemy rearguards had to be evicted before the attack proper could begin. The Inniskillings were ordered to take Grafton by dawn and the CO, Lieutenant-Colonel Bala Bredin, ordered his battalion to move off at 3am on the 15th. The initial advance went well with the two leading companies on their objectives without opposition by 4am but, at 4.45, the advance was brought to a standstill by heavy machine-gun fire. Dawn found the leading companies some seventy yards from the enemy positions and German tanks entering the fray. Fortunately there was again heavy mist and the tanks were virtually blind, milling around without causing any harm although one Inniskillings' platoon commander was almost run over.

However, 78th Division's sappers had just completed a bridge over the Piopetto river, a tributary of the Rapido, and at 8am a squadron of 16th/5th Lancers crossed to be led forward over marshy ground by Inniskillings' soldiers. With the tanks tackling the panzers and an artillery concentration coming down in support, the Inniskillings were soon on their objective; by 12.10pm all objectives had been taken with considerable loss to the Germans. The Inniskillings had lost eleven dead and under sixty wounded. The next phase of the Irish Brigade advance was to be undertaken by 2nd London Irish Rifles.

While the Inniskillings consolidated their newly won positions, 11 Brigade had also crossed the Rapido and were moving up on the Irish Brigade's right flank. Leading 11 Brigade towards Grafton, 5th Northamptons, also without tank support, met stiff opposition from machine-gun, mortar and shell fire. Although the battalion was moving up to a start line there were still many enemy troops about: two men, Lance-Corporal Allkin and Private McGill, put paid to an SPG with a PIAT while Lieutenant Hillian earned an immediate MC when he launched a one-man attack, firing a Bren from the hip, on a German patrol which he had spotted moving towards his platoon; he drove off the Germans, killing or wounding five of them.

The next phase of the operation was due to be an attack at 3pm that day by 2nd London Irish with 2nd Lancashire Fusiliers, of 11 Brigade, moving up on their right. However, as the Rifles' CO, Ion Goff, and the CO of the supporting armoured regiment, 16th/5th Lancers, John Loveday, held an O Group preparatory to the attack, enemy shellfire came down on the area with one shell falling among those in the O Group. Both Goff and Loveday were fatally injured; several others were badly wounded including one of the company commanders. The brigade commander, Brigadier Pat Scott, was soon on the spot and Major John Horsfall took command of the Rifles. But the attack was delayed, first to 7.30pm, and then to 9am next day; the second delay came as a result of an order from the divisional commander, Major-General Charles Keightley, to allow 2nd Lancashire Fusiliers to prepare their part as they only reached their start line at nightfall.

In spite of the delay, the attack was successful: three companies of London Irish reached their objectives although they had to endure intensive enemy shellfire. H Company under Major Desmond Woods, MC, in the centre, was to take the hamlet of Sinagoga. The advance was held up by shelling, to which two platoon commanders fell victim, but the riflemen pressed on and reached Sinagoga. There, however, their supporting tanks began to suffer from accurate anti-tank fire with several being knocked out as soon as they reached the village. Most damage was being done by an 88 until Corporal Jimmy Barnes led his section against the gun's position:

> . . . one by one the men were cut down by machine-gun fire on their left flank until Corporal Barnes remained alone. He went on by himself and then he fell dead, cut by a machine-gun, but by then the crew of the 88 had baled out and the tanks were able to get forward once again.[11]

Barnes had lobbed a grenade at the gun, killing at least one of its crew. Although Major Woods recommended him for a posthumous Victoria Cross this was never awarded. Desmond Woods' own bravery and leadership was, however, recognised by a Bar to his MC; H Company had finished the assault with only about a dozen survivors standing: the company commander, a sergeant, a few corporals and a handful of riflemen.

The Lancashire Fusiliers had advanced with two companies forward, also supported by 16th/5th Lancers, against stubborn opposition. C Company was counter-attacked by enemy tanks and a tank deadlock soon developed with opposing tanks on either side of a rise in the ground and a sunken lane preventing an outflanking move. That deadlock was broken by Fusilier Francis Jefferson who, as he saw tanks advance on his company's partially dug trenches, seized a PIAT and ran forward under heavy fire to take up a position behind a hedge but

> as he could not see properly he came into the open, and standing up under a hail of bullets, fired at the leading tank which was now only twenty yards away. It burst into flames and all the crew were killed. [He] then reloaded the P.I.A.T. and proceeded towards the second tank, which withdrew before he could get within range. By this time our own tanks had arrived and the enemy counter-attack was smashed with heavy casualties.

> Fusilier Jefferson's gallant act not merely saved the lives of his company and caused many casualties to the Germans, but also broke up the enemy counter-attack and had a decisive effect on the subsequent operation. His supreme gallantry and disregard of personal risk contributed very largely to the success of the action.[12]

The Lancashires were able to resume their advance and took their objectives although C Company had lost about half its number either killed or wounded. By nightfall 2nd London Irish were on the Colle

Monache ridge beyond the objective and had beaten off a counter-attack.

On the 17th it was the turn of 1st Royal Irish Fusiliers to take up the Irish Brigade's advance. The Faughs attacked with two companies, C and D, up and support from a squadron of 16th/5th Lancers. Heavy fire from mortars, artillery and machine guns met the attackers and C Company's commander, Laurie Franklyn-Vaile, was killed as was the squadron leader of the supporting tanks, Robert Gill. Nonetheless the Faughs took their objectives and, after dark, sent a patrol out to disrupt traffic on Highway 6.

The Gustav Line had been pierced and was about to fall. To Eighth Army's left the French Expeditionary Corps had carved a way through the Aurunci mountains and that sector of the line was crumbling quickly as the Germans withdrew. With 4th and 78th Divisions menacing Highway 6, Leese had ordered the Poles to make another attempt to capture Monastery Hill. This effort was preceded by a reconnaissance in force by the 16th Battalion of 5th Kresowa Division which succeeded in taking the northern sector of Phantom Ridge during the night of the 16th; by sunrise on 17 May the 15th Battalion had also captured the southern part of the ridge.

At 7am on the 17th the Polish Corps went in to the attack strengthened by extemporised infantry battalions composed of men from the 'Anti-Tank Regiment, M.T. drivers, workshop personnel and so forth'.[13] Colle Sant'Angelo and Monte Calvario (Point 593) were principal objectives and were fought for bitterly. At one stage a German counter-attack pushed the Poles back, but Anders' men persevered in spite of heavy casualties and some gains were made. Point 593 fell into Polish hands and the east side of the Snake's Head ridge, which the Carpathians had scaled using ropes, had been wrested from the Germans. Enemy resistance was still fierce however: a 4th Division attack on Cassino town had also been repulsed for a time.

But the French success in driving through the Aurunci mountains, and the fact that Highway 6 was now dominated by XIII Corps, stripped Monastery Hill and Cassino of all importance. Kesselring ordered the Fallschirmjäger to withdraw; towards midnight the paratroopers slipped out of their positions to fall back to the Hitler Line, now renamed the Senger Line since the Führer's name could not be associated with defeat. Patrols from 3rd Carpathian Rifle Division reported that night that the Germans appeared to have abandoned Monastery Hill as well. That report was proved true when a patrol from 12th Podolski Lancers, under Lieutenant Gurbiel, reached the Monastery Hill and found it deserted save for some wounded men, two medical orderlies and a junior officer. A regimental 'pennant hastily cobbled together from parts of a Red Cross flag and a blue handkerchief',[14] was hoisted on a makeshift flagpole on the ruined walls. The Poles had taken Cassino. The brutal battle for Monte Cassino was over.

Although the fighting around Cassino had finished there were more battles to be fought. As the Germans withdrew they prepared to delay their pursuers as much as possible through vicious rearguard actions. The first of these was on the 17th at Piumerola where the situation was initially confused due to misleading reports that the Lothians and Border Horse had taken the town and had advanced beyond it. They had, in fact, been held up short of Piumerola by Fallschirmjäger with anti-tank guns, SPGs and a Mark IV tank.

The taking of Piumerola was assigned to the Irish Brigade with armour support from both the Lothians and 16th/5th Lancers. Early in the battle the Inniskillings lost their CO, Bala Bredin, who had been wounded in both legs. Although suffering from loss of blood, Bredin refused to leave his men and had himself strapped to the bonnet of a jeep. He left the battlefield only after he had passed out from loss of blood. It took the efforts of the entire brigade to clear Piumerola but this marked the final crumbling of the Gustav Line.

The next defensive line was the Senger Line which was, in several respects, even more impressive than the Gustav. In the Liri valley the line contained twenty-feet deep steel shelters as well as concrete strongpoints that could house anti-tank or machine guns while allowing 360 degrees of traverse:

> ... mobile steel cylindrical cells that were nicknamed crabs ... could be inserted in pits above which their steel domes rose to a height of only 30 inches; and the turrets of new Panther tanks, eighteen in all, mounting 75mm guns with all-round traverse, which also made barely visible intrusions above their concrete emplacements. All were sited and camouflaged with great skill, and since installation they had received an extra layer of covering from the great sproutings of spring ... [15]

Eighth Army's first attack on the Senger Line was entrusted to 78th Division, reinforced by units of 6th Armoured Division, and it was the latter's reconnaissance regiment, the Derbyshire Yeomanry, which, with 10th Rifle Brigade, was first to tackle the line on 18 May. Although a troop of the Derbys penetrated Aquino, the Rifles were held up and the tanks were withdrawn. Next day 5th Buffs and 8th Argylls of 36 Brigade, supported by two squadrons of the Ontario Regiment, made a further effort. At first fog helped the advance but its sudden dissolution led to the tanks falling victim to very effective anti-tank gunfire; every Sherman was hit and thirteen were lost. Without tank support the infantry were repelled by sustained machine-gun fire and the attack was called off after noon. Both Buffs and Argylls lost their COs, Lieutenant Colonels G M de B Monk, MC and J Taylor, MC; the former was killed, the latter wounded.

The following morning the Poles entered the battle for the Senger Line, having finally taken the summit of Sant'Angelo. A battlegroup built around two battalions from II Polish Corps closed on Piedimonte, one of the critical points of the line, and was hurled against the defences on the 20th. The Poles broke into the German lines but their advance soon came unstuck and Heidrich's paratroopers pinned them down. In an effort to pinch out the Fallschirmjäger by pressure from the flanks, 8th Indian Division came back into the battle to the left of the Poles, astride Highway 6. Matters were complicated further by the presence of two brigades of the Canadian Corps which meant that Leese now had the undesirable situation of three corps operating over a restricted frontage of about six miles.

The Canadians had been passed through the Indians on the night of 15/16 May directed on Pontecorvo but the leading Canadian infantry brigade ran into the newly arrived 361 Panzer Grenadier Regiment of 90th Panzer Grenadier Division who constrained the Canadian advance. Support for the Canadian infantry was pushed forward in the shape of 25 Army Tank Brigade, committed to battle with their Churchills for the first time since Tunisia, who found the Liri valley made excellent country for ambushes with anti-tank guns and *panzerfausten*, the German equivalent of the bazooka. Having suffered such ambushes the tank crews became less enthusiastic about pressing forward into the cornfields and vineyards where the enemy infantry waited. Not until 19 May did the Canadians, with the tanks, close up on the Senger Line; they had advanced only five miles beyond Pignataro which the Indians had taken.

On 20 May Leese issued orders for the assault on the Senger Line with the main effort coming from the Canadian Corps during the night of the 21st/22nd while XIII Corps maintained pressure against Aquino and the Poles continued to press against Piedimonte. However, preparation for the Canadian attack did not run smoothly: traffic congestion delayed the deployment of the artillery to support the attack; and Leese criticised the Canadian plan, Operation CHESTERFIELD, which imposed more pressure on an already loaded wireless network. The end result was that CHESTERFIELD was delayed until 6am on 23 May. On the 22nd Major-General Vokes, 1st Canadian Division's commander, launched an attack on Pontecorvo in the belief that the rapid French advance through the mountains to the west might make it easier to shake the German defenders out of that town. All that the attack proved was that resistance was firm and determined. In fact the stretch of the Senger Line against which the Canadians were to be pitted, the six miles between Pontecorvo and Piedimonte, was arguably the strongest sector of the line; it was certainly held by formations under two of the best German commanders: Baade of 90th Panzer Grenadiers, on the German right, and Heidrich of 1st Fallschirmjäger.

At 6am on 23 May the Canadians moved off under cover of a storm of artillery fire,* half an hour before General Truscott's VI Corps began the breakout from Anzio. Three battalions led the Canadian assault which was made partway between Pontecorvo and Aquino: in the centre were the Seaforth of Canada of 2 Brigade, supported by the North Irish Horse, as were the PPCLI, also of 2 Brigade, on the right; on the left 51st Royal Tanks supported 3 Brigade's Carleton and York Regiment.

The might of the artillery support did not suppress entirely the German resistance, as the Patricias especially found out to their cost. A and C Companies led the battalion's advance with B Company following up.

Immediately, the enemy opened a devastating defensive fire from concealed pill-boxes and from Aquino on the flank. Col Ware received a report that A Company had reached the wire. Then nothing more was heard. All attempts to communicate by liaison officers and runner failed and supporting arms could not get forward through the intense enemy fire. The North Irish Horse attempting to help the Regiment forward were restricted in their movement by the Forme D'Aquino on the right and by deep laid mines which had defied detection. They were caught in a trap of concealed self-propelled guns and twenty-five of their tanks were destroyed that day.[16]

The Princess Pats suffered heavily with companies and platoons broken up. Their attack dissolved into little bounds with small groups sallying from cover to cover. A Company's commander, Major W de N Watson, saw his entire HQ become casualties; he carried on alone in the hope of finding his platoons on the objective. It was not to be and by the time he made the objective he had been wounded twice. Taking shelter in a shell hole he evaded capture and was eventually found there next morning by a fellow officer, suffering from an arm wound, a head wound 'and a tremendous appetite'.[17]

Although the Seaforth reached their objective, the assaulting companies were wiped out and their supporting North Irish tanks also suffered heavily, especially from the Panther turrets. However, eleven Irish tanks,

---

* For the previous eighty-four hours the artillery, over 800 guns, had been firing at the rate of 1,000 rounds per hour which increased to 810 a minute as the attack began.

using a different axis of advance, breached the Senger Line to reach the road linking Pontecorvo and Highway 6, the Phase II line. Bereft of infantry support there, they were forced to withdraw.

The Loyal Edmontons, 2 Brigade's reserve battalion, who had moved up in support of the PPCLI, were also unable to make progress in the face of what was described as murderous machine-gun, mortar and artillery fire. Although the enemy wire was reached, and penetrated in two places, the attacking companies had lost contact with battalion HQ and the attack fizzled out. Eventually the Edmontons were withdrawn. However, 3 Brigade's attack met with more success. Reconnaissance patrols of the Carleton and Yorks had, the previous day, identified routes through the barbed wire and minefields; these were used in the attack. Following close behind the artillery curtain the battalion pushed forward to their objective although the tanks of 51 RTR suffered many casualties from the fixed defences and SPGs as they followed the Canadian infantrymen.

At about 10am, the tanks linked up with the infantry on the Pontecorvo-Aquino road and the brigade's supporting battalion, the West Nova Scotias, moved up ready to take over the running for the next phase of the attack. Vokes delayed their jumping-off as he waited for some positive news from 2 Brigade but, when such was not forthcoming, he decided to push 3 Brigade ahead alone. Accordingly the Royal 22^e Regiment were sent forward as a brigade reserve and tanks from the Three Rivers Regiment arrived to support the West Novas. At 4.40pm the infantry and tanks moved off.

The Canadians advanced quickly and had the good fortune to catch the German reserves off balance. The latter were preparing for a counter-attack when they were caught in a heavy artillery bombardment and thus only a few local counter-attacks were made which did not deter the West Novas; by 6.15pm they were on the Phase II line. The Royal 22^e were brought forward to expand the gap in the enemy defences and seized objectives in front of the Seaforth. Their task had been achieved by 9.15pm and the battalion was consolidated on high ground less than a mile north of the West Novas.

The Germans were now beginning to fall back: the Senger (formerly Hitler) Line had been breached and its destruction had been aided when 1 Brigade was able to expand its bridgehead on the southern flank near Pontecorvo, scene of the abortive attack just prior to CHESTERFIELD. The efforts of the 48th Highlanders and the Hastings and Prince Edwards were such that the Germans had begun to fall back there by early evening and, on the 24th, the Royal Canadian Regiment made a virtually unopposed entry into Pontecorvo.

By the evening of the 23rd the German line had been breached, although the Canadian 2 Brigade had suffered the highest casualties for a single day of any brigade in the Italian campaign. The day had also seen another record set, by Eighth Army's artillery: when Brigadier Ziegler, CRA of 1st Canadian Division, called for a 'William Target'* he brought all Eighth Army's artillery into operation. Little more than thirty minutes after Ziegler's call, more than 600 guns opened fire together and, in a period of two minutes, 3,500 shells were dropped on the enemy positions.[18]

Now the armour could be unleashed: 5th Canadian Armoured Division deployed for their first operation in their true role. Tanks moved forward northwards through the Royal 22^e's bridgehead at 8am on the 24th as Pontecorvo fell to the Royal Canadians of 1 Brigade. During the morning Canadian tanks clashed with German armour, including several of the new Panthers; four Shermans were knocked out while the Germans lost three Panthers. By midday the leading tanks had reached Mancici, north-west of Aquino, while others pushed on to create a bridgehead over the Melfa river. At first the Canadians had the enemy off balance but the situation changed in the afternoon when resistance stiffened and Lord Strathcona's Horse lost seventeen Shermans.

While the Canadian tanks were advancing, XIII Corps' front remained static but next morning, 25 May, soldiers from 78th Division found that Aquino had been abandoned by the Germans. Likewise the Poles found that the Fallschirmjäger had slipped away from Piedimonte under cover of darkness. Over a period of two weeks' fighting the German paratroopers, II Polish Corps had sustained 3,784 casualties, of whom 860 had been killed.

Along the sides of the Liri valley 8th Indian Division, supported by the New Zealand Armoured Brigade, pursued the Germans; Freyberg's infantry probed north of Cassino and then struck out in pursuit around Monte Cairo. Also in the pursuit were the soldiers of 78th Division supported by 9 Armoured Brigade, in action for the first time since El Alamein.

A further formation assigned to the pursuit was 6th Armoured Division whose 26 Armoured Brigade was ordered to break out through the Canadian sector. However, this exacerbated congestion in the valley and not until late afternoon did the Derbyshire Yeomanry reach the Melfa. Although some tanks made the crossing they had no infantry support; the crews were later ordered to abandon their vehicles and recross the river which they did with twenty-one prisoners.

The Derbyshires had run into enemy infantry and anti-tank guns. Once

---

* Fire task definitions were: Mike Target – a quick concentration of fire by all guns of an artillery regiment (usually twenty-four in a field regiment); Uncle Target – quick concentration by all guns of a division (usually three field regiments); Victor Target – quick concentration by all guns of a corps; William Target – quick concentration by all guns of an army.

again German resistance had stiffened, as the Canadians had already discovered before the Derbys' arrival. Fierce counter-attacks had threatened to force the Canadians back from their bridgehead but, thanks to the courage and initiative of Major John Keefer Mahony of the motorised Westminster Regiment, each counter-attack was beaten off:

> Major Mahony and his company were ordered to establish the initial bridgehead over the river [Melfa]. This was accomplished and for five hours the company maintained its position in the face of enemy fire and attack until the remaining companies and supporting weapons were able to reinforce them. Early in the action Major Mahony was wounded in the head and twice in the leg, but he refused medical aid and continued to direct the defence of the bridgehead. The enemy saw that this officer was the soul of the defence and consequently made him their particular target.[19]

For his actions, which saved the bridgehead, Mahony was subsequently awarded the Victoria Cross. While he was conducting the defence of the Westminsters' bridgehead, 11 Canadian Lorried Infantry Brigade made an assault crossing and pushed a thousand yards beyond the Melfa. That night the Germans again withdrew and the Canadians were able to make a further advance.

To the left the French were advancing through the mountains although General Juin was highly critical of Eighth Army's failure to keep pace with his corps. However, Eighth Army had five divisions pushing through the Liri valley and the resultant congestion played a significant part in slowing the pace of advance; the toughest of the German divisions were also matched against Eighth Army. With the heavy commitment of armour in the Liri valley, Eighth Army was also dependent on roads and bridges, the demolition of which obstructed the advance. The Royal Engineers once again played a major role in ensuring that the best possible pace was maintained. On the Melfa, Major Donald Booth's 577th Field Company erected a bridge in twenty-four hours even though the Germans were constantly shelling the site; 577th went on to erect a bridge at Arce in the record time of five hours.

Advancing to Arce the Canadians and 78th Division were once again operating close together. As the Irish Brigade met up with the Canadians about five miles from Ceprano, 1st Royal Irish Fusiliers relieved the Irish Regiment of Canada, an occasion on which one Canadian soldier, giving directions, was heard to shout 'Canadian Irish this way, English Irish that way', a remark that caused considerable mirth.

Many actions were being fought at battalion and brigade level as Eighth Army pushed hard against the retreating German forces: 6th Armoured

Division's infantry, 1 Guards Brigade,* suffered heavy casualties in fighting for hills flanking Highway 6; nearby 17 Indian Brigade also assaulted mountains against doughty resistance; at Rocca d'Arce 1/5th Gurkhas fought a tough battle against Fallschirmjäger to take the village on the morning of 29 May. On that day also 3rd Grenadier Guards found that the Germans had abandoned Monte Grande and the Welsh Guards entered Arce on the Lothians' tanks. Once again the Germans were giving up ground at their own pace. In the six days following the breaching of the Senger Line XIII Corps had advanced only eleven miles.

Although the Canadians had made better progress they still lagged behind the French Expeditionary Corps. By 30 May the Canadians were moving along the Sacco valley while 8th Indian Division was pursuing the Germans through the mountains in a north-westerly direction:

> The jagged terrain was ideally suited to delaying tactics, by gun, mine, and demolition, and 8th Indian had a long, gruelling, and daunting task in an advance towards Terni, for ever trying to maul nightly shifting rearguards of skilled Para or Mountain troops; they persevered and had occasional successes which sustained their enthusiasm.[20]

The New Zealand armour had been supporting the Indians while the New Zealand infantry had been trying to cut Route 82 at Sora and block Feuerstein's Mountain Corps; the Maoris entered Sora on the afternoon of 31 May and there linked up with the Armoured Brigade. For its part 78th Division was leading XIII Corps against Frosinone during which the Buffs, of 36 Brigade, evicted the Germans from Ripi on the 30th while the Canadians were cutting Route 6 on the way to Frosinone which the Edmontons captured from armour and infantry of 26th Panzer Division on the 31st.

In front of the Canadian Corps there now stretched a plain across which the going was good for tanks. On 1 June the Churchills of 25 Army Tank Brigade advanced with Canadian infantry on Ferentino; next day the Royal Canadian Regiment entered Anagni which was occupied by Italian partisans. Then, on the 3rd, the first junction was made with Truscott's US VI Corps, breaking out of the Anzio beachhead: that junction was effected by a US Army sergeant on a motorcycle and soldiers of 1 Canadian Infantry Brigade. The sergeant had travelled down Route 6. On the same road, but in the opposite direction, 6th South African Armoured Division was trying to make its entry into the war, fighting traffic congestion to pass through the Canadians and continue the advance.

The breakout from Anzio had also made contact with the main body of

* 3rd Grenadier; 2nd Coldstream; and 3rd Welsh Guards.

Fifth Army but the strategic aim of the operations since 11 May was now to be thrown away on the whim of Mark Clark. The Allied Armies were presented with the opportunity of inflicting such a crushing defeat on the retreating Germans that the war in Italy might be brought to a conclusion in 1944. Winston Churchill had summed up the essence of the battles south of Rome when he noted that the glory of the battle would not be measured either by the capture of Rome or the link-up with the Anzio bridgehead but with the number of German divisions cut off and captured.

Clark saw instead the glory of entering Rome as a hero, the liberator of the first European capital to fall to the Allies. Instead of co-ordinating Fifth Army's operations with Eighth Army in order to cut off the retreating enemy forces, he ordered VI Corps to switch its main thrust of advance from the axis Anzio-Valmontone, as Alexander had ordered, to strike towards Rome. In so doing he allowed large elements of Kesselring's command to escape north of the Eternal City. General Mark Clark made a personal entrance into Rome on 5 June with an entourage that included cameramen. Although he had to hammer on the doors of the City Hall to gain entry he was cheered by large crowds and noted that he was the first conqueror of Rome from the south since Belisarius in AD 536. After the war Clark told an American journalist that he had ordered his troops to open fire on any Eighth Army formations that attempted to beat Fifth Army in the race for Rome. Although that statement was undoubtedly a piece of hyperbole it does illustrate Clark's single-minded attitude to the capture of Rome.

Fifth Army's failure to cut off the retreating German Tenth Army compounded the situation caused by Eighth Army's slow advance which had allowed the enemy to retreat almost at their own pace. In turn that slow rate of advance was caused, at least partially, by the deployment of three separate corps in the Liri valley. By throwing so many troops at the enemy line, Alexander was operating like a man trying to swing a sledgehammer in an area where he had virtually no elbow room. However, unlike a man with a sledgehammer, Alexander was acutely aware of the national sensitivities within his command: a homogenous army could have been handled more firmly and pushed harder, with fewer troops being committed in the Liri valley. And he could have allowed the French Expeditionary Corps to swing in from the left, cut Highway 6 well ahead of Eighth Army and thus force the enemy to lose a substantial part of their cohesion.

However, the Allied offensive had caused the Germans to reinforce the Italian theatre and, in this respect, Alexander had achieved the strategic objective of drawing German troops in from other theatres. The Germans remained convinced that a large Allied force remained uncommitted in

North Africa and this swayed Hitler's Operations and Intelligence staffs
to move divisions to Italy from the Eastern Front, Hungary and Croatia.[21]

National rivalries and pride had denied the Allies the opportunity of
removing a large proportion of Tenth Army from Kesselring's order of
battle. That failure was to lead to another long winter in the mountains of
Italy and to many more casualties in Eighth Army which had, between 11
May and the fall of Rome, suffered 13,756 casualties.

NOTES

1. Molony at al: *The Mediterranean and the Middle East, vol vi, Pt I*, p.59
2. Anders: *An Army in Exile*, p.174
3. ibid, p.177
4. Fraser: *And We Shall Shock Them*, pp.288-289
5. PRO: WO170/407, War diary, 4th Division
6. Parkinson: *Always a Fusilier*, pp.186-187
7. *Register of the Victoria Cross*, p.173
8. ibid, p.322
9. Anon: *The Tiger Triumphs*, p.78
10. P J C Trousdell, letter to author
11. Woods, *A Personal Account of his service with 2LIR in Italy*
12. Ray: *Algiers to Austria*, p.130
13. Anders: op cit, p.178
14. Piekalkiewitcz: *Cassino, Anatomy of the battle*, p.181
15. Blaxland: *Alexander's Generals*, p.103
16. Williams: *Princess Patricia's Canadian Light Infantry*, p.56
17. ibid, p.57
18. Mead: *Gunners at War*, p.90
19. *Register of the Victoria Cross*, p.213
20. Blaxland: op cit, p.125
21. Molony et al: op cit, p.128

CHAPTER XV

To the Gothic Line:
June – August 1944

Now sits Expectation in the air

The fall of Rome was a milestone in the Italian campaign: but it was not the end of that campaign. Within two days of the Allied capture of the Italian capital, another Allied force landed on the beaches of Normandy in Operation OVERLORD. Public interest swung away from Italy to north-west Europe; so too did the attention of the strategic planners. That attention had long since been diverted from the Mediterranean theatre as formations had been moved out of Italy to the United Kingdom for OVERLORD.

Even as Alexander prepared for Operation DIADEM he had had to fight to keep all the troops necessary for that operation in Italy. The overall strategy for the invasion of France had envisaged two simultaneous invasions: OVERLORD in Normandy and ANVIL on the southern coast of France. Alexander succeeded in retaining in Italy forces designated for ANVIL for use in DIADEM and thus brought about the postponement of the former operation. But, although Churchill and the British Chiefs of Staff believed ANVIL to have been cancelled, the operation was to be revived under the new codename DRAGOON and was to be launched on 15 August.[1] The revival of the operation led to the withdrawal of forces from Alexander's command, including several experienced American divisions (Lucian Truscott's VI Corps) and the French Expeditionary Corps which would form a reborn Seventh US Army under General Alexander M Patch.*

Morale was high in the Allied Armies in Italy in early-June: there was a distinct feeling among soldiers that they were winning and Alexander was aware of that high level of morale when he proposed to Maitland-Wilson, Supreme Commander in the Mediterranean, that Fifth and Eighth Armies should now race for the Gothic Line. Fifth Army was to be

---

* The French Expeditionary Corps was later augmented to army strength as First French Army and, with Seventh US Army, formed 6 Army Group.

directed on Pisa and Eighth on Florence which, on Alexander's assessment, could be in Allied hands by mid-July. An attack on the Gothic Line, 170 miles away, could be opened by mid-August with the main effort being made in the centre of the line, in the highest mountains, indicating that Juin's lessons had not been lost on Alexander. Once through the Gothic Line, which he was certain would be no real obstacle to his troops, Alexander's forces would be in the Po valley whence they could strike either west into France or north-east into Austria through the Ljubljana gap. All this Alexander considered possible provided that no reductions were made in either his ground or air forces.

There had, of course, been no real break in the fighting. Rather there had been a change to a more fluid style of battle as German forces were pursued north of Rome. In this phase of operations more use could be made of armour, and 6th South African Armoured took their first prize with the capture of Civita Castellana on the Via Flaminia (Route 3) on 6 June. But the shape of the armoured divisions had changed considerably with additional lorried infantry being added to their orders of battle. Thus 6th Armoured Division which had included 26 Armoured Brigade and 1 Guards Brigade as well as 1st Derbyshire Yeomanry, as reconnaissance regiment, was now strengthened with the addition of 61 Brigade; 6th South African Armoured had 24 Guards Brigade added to 12 South African Motorised Brigade.

Even as this modification of the armoured divisions was taking place, Eighth Army was facing the beginning of an infantry manpower crisis. The build-up for OVERLORD meant that no replacements or reinforcements for infantry battalions were being sent out from Britain, a policy laid down in February 1944; the last infantry reinforcements for Italy sailed from the UK in May. Eighth Army had now to find the manpower to replace battle and other casualties from within the Mediterranean theatre. This was achieved by re-roling soldiers from other tasks. Fortunately, the huge reduction in Luftwaffe strength in the Mediterranean meant that the need for anti-aircraft defences was much reduced; thus AA gunners found themselves converted to infantry as did redundant RAF personnel, including aircrew, and some naval personnel. In time this expedient was to cause morale problems. A training programme for these men had to be created whereas infantry reinforcements from Britain would have been trained as such before arriving in Italy. The creation of a training battalion at the Infantry Reinforcement Training Depot in Italy also absorbed manpower and the training syllabus was reduced from three months to two because of the manpower crisis.[2]

In early June, however, Eighth Army's tail was high; its formations surged forward in pursuit of an enemy which it was believed 'could be hustled to defeat'. Alexander had ordered both Army commanders to take 'extreme risks' in the parallel pursuit of Kesselring's forces. Sixth South African Armoured Division advanced at a rate of ten miles each day which made the division the spearhead of the Allied Armies: moving through broken countryside with the Tiber on their right and Lake Bolsena on their left, the Springboks outstripped their flanking formations. However, such a pace could not be maintained indefinitely and a time had to come when the Germans attempted to check the Allied advance. That happened on 11 June, a day that dawned wet and misty, near the village of Bagnoregio when 5th Grenadier Guards reported that the enemy were holding the line of a ravine in strength. The defenders were from 356th Division, newly arrived and inserted by Kesselring into a favourable blocking position. Kesselring now deployed nineteen divisions, of varying strength and quality, against the nine which Alexander could deploy in the field.* Initially the German aim was to disrupt the advance of the Allies on the routes around Lake Trasimene before falling back to the Gothic Line, the final major defensive position before the Po valley, via a series of forward lines of which the first was the Albert Line, stretching from near Orvieto via the Tiber and Lake Trasimene to Gubbio, where St Francis had once tamed a wolf that had terrorised the residents. After the Albert Line the advancing Allies would meet the Arno Line, from Ribbiena to Pisa with its famous tower, and the Arezzo Line, both designed to permit rearguard actions, the latter at gaps in the Tuscan mountains south of Arezzo.

The marvel was that Kesselring could form a cohesive defence at all in the light of the hammering his forces were taking. Allied airpower was particularly effective at this stage, with the longest days of the year allowing more sorties against enemy positions and transport:

One gratifying sight on all the main roads going North from Rome was mile after mile of burnt out German vehicles, varying from Tigers and seventy ton Ferdinands down to volkswagens. One seldom went more than a quarter of a mile without seeing one of these edifying spectacles. Some of it had been caused by the advancing armies, but most of it had been done by the Air Force[s]. It was a most impressive, visible tribute to their excellent work. The Boche slit trenches, dug every four or five hundred yards along the road as funk holes from air strafing, were a tribute to the air activity that must have gone on for a longish period along those roads to Rome.[3]

Although Kesselring had had serious problems, particularly with a

---

* Alexander had a total of twenty-six divisions when he launched his pursuit from the Tiber, at which time Kesselring had only fourteen. The demands of DRAGOON took four French and three American divisions away from Allied Armies Italy; others were re-organising after the Cassino battles.

change of command in Fourteenth Army where Mackensen had resigned – before he was pushed – to be replaced by Lemelsen, he had also received reinforcements, including the troops facing the South Africans at Bagnoregio.

On the afternoon of 11 June the mist cleared around Bagnoregio to show a village of solid dwellings set on a ridge and presenting a formidable challenge to the attackers. But before the village could be tackled the soldiers of 356th Division had to be cleared from the ravine which 5th Grenadiers did during the night of 11/12 June and through most of the 12th. With that obstacle out of the way, a plan was developed for an assault on Bagnoregio. Early on the 13th the Grenadiers and the Royal Natal Carabineers put in a two-pronged attack which pinched the Germans out of the village. Grenadiers and Carabineers

> met inside this apparently impregnable village of Bagnoregio, having forced the enemy into retreat. The steadiness and discipline of the Guards blended surprisingly well with the stealth and informality of the Afrikaners – or Springboks as they preferred to be called – forming a firm fellowship.[4]

On 14 June the South Africans took Orvieto. In the ten days since Rome had fallen 6th South African Armoured had advanced seventy-five miles beyond the capital. But the battle at Bagnoregio had shown that Kesselring had restored his forces' equilibrium and the Allied advance was now to be subjected to further checks, many consisting of minor rather than major skirmishes.

Leese had deployed his two armoured divisions with one on either side of the Tiber. Thus 6th British Armoured Division was transferred to McCreery's X Corps to operate with 8th Indian towards Perugia, an ancient and historic city set on a hill about ten miles east of Lake Trasimene. Eighth Indian Division had already been engaged against a constant series of rearguards, and its sappers had had to overcome many demolitions on the road to Terni which they entered on the 14th.

On its drive for Perugia 6th Armoured Division was faced with a major natural obstacle at Narni, about fifty miles south of Perugia, where the river Nera flows through a gorge and passage was impossible without a bridge. Once again the sappers were called upon; in twenty-four hours they erected a Bailey bridge strong enough to bear the weight of the division's tanks. Fortunately there was very little opposition at this stage, a situation that continued after the crossing, early on the 15th, and allowed 6th Armoured to make good progress with 1 Guards Brigade striking along the direct road to Perugia while 26 Armoured Brigade moved out to their left flank to swing around the city.

Although the advancing brigades crossed the Tiber with few problems, they were soon into more difficult terrain approaching Perugia where the country becomes closer and hillier. On 18 June, as they moved into this area, rain began to fall.

In spite of brilliant summer weather with stifling heat and billowing dust for two thirds of the time, sudden storms and longer periods of rain occurred which were so heavy that they turned Sapper built diversions into impassable quagmires and prevented the supply vehicles from reaching the forward troops with essential fuel, ammunition and food.[5]

With the rain fell German shells. That night 61 Brigade made the first attack on the enemy defences of Perugia: 10th Rifle Brigade took Monte Lacugnano to the west of the city, by-passing several German positions in their daring strike. The following night 7th Rifle Brigade moved through inky darkness and heavy rain to seize Monte Malbo, north-west of Lacugnano.

The Guards met stern resistance on the main road to Perugia with every movement forward being followed by a counter-attack. Every yard of road had to be fought for by the Grenadiers whose casualties included the King's nephew, Lieutenant Lord Lascelles, who strayed into the enemy lines, was wounded and captured. As the Grenadiers battled their way forward, 2nd Coldstream attacked round their left flank to take their objective, the railway below Perugia, early on the 20th.

As dawn's light crept across the countryside the Grenadiers discovered that their opposition had melted away in the night: the road to Perugia was open and the Germans had abandoned the city. When the nearby city of Assisi, home of St Francis, Italy's patron saint, was entered by 12th Lancers on the 17th, it was already held by Italian partisans. North-east of Perugia, 1 Guards Brigade cleared the heights overlooking the city and thus allowed the King's Dragoon Guards to move forward. But now Intelligence reported that 15th Panzer Grenadier Division had deployed to block any further advance on the eastern shore of Lake Trasimene and Leese accordingly switched 6th Armoured Division back to XIII Corps on the other side of the lake. The division was relieved by 10th Indian from the Adriatic sector on 27 June; the Indians had themselves been relieved by the Poles.

As 10th Indian Division moved to X Corps, 8th Indian moved out but not until after they had advanced some miles beyond Assisi and Perugia:

They had their stiffest fight on June 18-19, when the 1st Royal Fusiliers and 1/5th Gurkhas suffered 300 casualties in gaining the Ripa ridge. They themselves inflicted such loss on the 44th Division that they could not withstand the Shermans of the 3rd Hussars, who on June 23 made a rare and brilliant dash across four miles of mountainous terrain to seize the village of Biccione and capture 200 Germans and eleven guns. It was a fitting parting gesture by Pasha Russell's men.[6]

Eighth Army HQ had switched 3rd Hussars, of 9 Armoured Brigade, from supporting 78th Division to supporting Russell's Indians. During this phase of operations the Army's HQ staff were excellent in their reading of the tactical picture and units were moved from corps to corps as the situation demanded. As 3rd Hussars moved to Ripa the other regiments of 9 Armoured Brigade, Royal Wiltshire Yeomanry and Warwickshire Yeomanry, remained with 78th Division which had been covering XIII Corps' right flank.

After a brief rest period the Battleaxe Division had returned to operations on 8 June and moved rapidly to Orvieto, passing through towns and villages that had already been taken by the South Africans or the Americans although 2nd London Irish had a brief skirmish at Pianicciale. Perhaps the most spectacular aspect of 78th Division's operations was the swift advance made by Chavasseforce, a battlegroup commanded by Lieutenant-Colonel Kendal Chavasse of 56th Reconnaissance Regiment. As well as his own Regiment, Colonel Chavasse commanded a squadron of Warwickshire Yeomanry; A Company 1st Royal Irish Fusiliers,* later augmented to the entire battalion; two troops of 315/105 Anti-Tank Battery; a battery of 17th Field Regiment; and a detachment from 237 Field Company, Royal Engineers.

Chavasseforce enjoyed a most successful run towards Lake Trasimene:

As the Recce boys advanced and probed during the day they usually met something that needed to be dealt with by infantry and the Faughs then came into the picture. From Orvieto to Lake Trasimene [Chavasseforce] captured or destroyed twenty-six enemy guns of more than 26mm, fifty-five machine-guns and almost forty vehicles. A total of one hundred and twenty-one prisoners were taken while a further one hundred and forty-five Germans lay dead on the route. In one sharp, savage encounter a Faugh company, supported by mortars, defeated a small German force leaving twenty-five of the Germans dead. One of the vehicles captured . . . was found to be a German 'NAAFI' truck loaded with French brandy and sweets. . . . The run ended with the capture of Castello di Montelara, taken by D Company on June 21st.[7]

*

* Colonel Chavasse's parent regiment was The Royal Irish Fusiliers (Princess Victoria's) so that the inclusion of the Faughs in Chavasseforce was a happy coincidence.

By then 78th Division's main body had pushed forward until the leading troops were half-way between Rome and Florence. Alexander's classic pursuit was going as planned but it was just about to come unstuck. On 15 June 11 Brigade crossed the Paglia river and, next day, 5th Northamptons attacked Monte Gabbione, midway between Orvieto and Lake Trasimene. Supported by artillery, Wiltshire Yeomanry tanks and mortars from 1st Kensingtons, the Northamptons met stiff opposition. They persevered with the attack and, in the words of the divisional historian, 'the capture of this little town proved to be one of the best actions ever fought by the battalion'.[8]

The attack was led by A Company which ran into heavy rifle fire. Leaving 7 Platoon behind as fire platoon both 8 and 9 Platoons went forward, the former to take the school and the latter to seize a large building to the right. Both were successful and Company HQ joined the platoons which were then subjected to several hours of rifle and machine-gun fire from nearby buildings. Meanwhile C Company had also fought their way into the town and S Company's commander was able to direct fire from the Wiltshires' Shermans on to buildings still occupied by Germans. Contrary to expectations no counter-attack materialised and C Company was able to move unopposed into the centre of the town on the morning of the 17th; the Germans had slipped away during the night.

That afternoon 1st East Surreys, operating under command of 9 Armoured Brigade, became heavily engaged at Città della Pieve, a hillside town some 2,000 feet above sea level, where 1st Fallschirmjäger Division was covering the retreat of 334th Division's battlegroups on their left. Also under 9 Armoured Brigade's command as lorried infantry was a platoon of Irish Fusiliers, under Lieutenant Len Manson. Having taken Montelione, Manson's men made for Città della Pieve but, about a mile before the town, ran into heavy resistance from Fallschirmjäger. However, thanks to the courage and initiative of Corporal Patton and Fusilier Bell, MM, the resistance was broken and thirty paratroopers were captured; several more were killed or wounded. Manson's men, with a troop of tanks, then advanced into the centre of Città where they began consolidating. Inexplicably, they then received an order to withdraw and the Germans rapidly repossessed the town and strengthened their positions. The order appears to have been issued by the Faughs' CO, James Dunnill,* a man in such a state of fatigue that he ought not to have been commanding a battalion at all.

The failure to hold Città meant that a brigade attack had to be made by

---

* Dunnill's Adjutant, the late Brian Clark, told the author that Dunnill had already lost his nerve when he took command after the death in action of the previous CO. John Horsfall, who commanded the Battalion after Dunnill was captured, confirmed Brian Clark's assessment.

36 Brigade who by-passed the town and were north of it by nightfall on 18 June. A wireless message giving the Paras' time of withdrawal was later intercepted, and at the appointed time, plus two minutes, 78th Division's artillery plastered all exits from Città. Next morning the outskirts were littered with the bodies of dead Germans. Survivors subjected the attackers to what the divisional commander, General Keightley, later described as 'the deadliest sniping he had seen in the war'.[9] His opinion may have been coloured slightly by the fact that a sniper's bullet shattered his field-glasses. Opposition was finally overcome by 5th Buffs and 6th Royal West Kents who advanced through the town to the higher ground beyond.

That time lost at Città della Pieve was to have serious consequences for 78th Division which was approaching Lake Trasimene on the axis of Route 71 and making better progress than 6th South African. Moving over difficult countryside the South Africans were delayed by soft ground due to heavy rainfall and then by a fierce defence of the town of Chiusi. At Vaiano, on 20 June, 8th Argylls, of 36 Brigade, were forced to withdraw by a strong counter-attack; a further attack by 5th Buffs on the 21st was also repulsed. Following this setback, 36 Brigade was relieved by 28 Brigade from 4th Division which had been ordered forward by Kirkman, XIII Corps' commander; 78th Division turned its attention to San Fatucchio which was held by a strong German garrison.

That garrison's strength was amply demonstrated to 2nd Lancashire Fusiliers of 11 Brigade on 20 June. Advancing towards Lake Trasimene with 5th Northamptons to their right and 1st East Surreys to the left and Warwickshire Yeomanry tanks in support

> the Lancashire Fusiliers . . . became wedged against the village . . . and their brigaded colleagues could make no progress either on the left or across the flat approach to the seven-mile expanse of water, of which view was obtainable only from the hills behind.[10]

Shortly before midnight a strong Lancashires' fighting patrol trying to force its way into the village was forced to withdraw under a storm of artillery, mortar and machine-gun fire. Coupled with the rebuff of 36 Brigade, this demonstrated that the German line was hardening in the area where Hannibal had trounced Flaminius and his Romans two thousand years earlier. The Carthaginian had enjoyed the valuable advantage of surprise, having moved south from the Alps much faster than his enemies had expected. In June 1944 Alexander's armies were expected by Kesselring, the master of the defensive battle, who was determined to ensure that the Allies would not debouch into the plain of Lombardy in 1944.

The renewal of 78th Division's assault on San Fatucchio was entrusted to the Irish Brigade with the London Irish leading the assault. At first the Rifles' CO, John Horsfall, was amazed to hear from Brigadier Pat Scott that

> the general had had an inspiration. The following day, or rather night, he proposed to sail the 2nd Rifles in 'ducks' [DUKWs] down the ten-mile length of Lake Trasimene and land us behind all this vexatious opposition.[11]

Fortunately Scott soon disabused Keightley of this idea and a more conventional plan was developed for the attack for which the London Irish had the support of a squadron of Shermans from 11th Canadian Armoured Regiment (The Ontarios).

Artillery support presented a problem for 17th Field Regiment: with Lancashire Fusiliers pinned down close to the village it was impossible for the gunners to put down an initial concentration for fear of causing casualties among them. However, smoke was put down, since the Germans overlooked all lines of approach, and one troop of 17th Field did 'some delicate shooting'. Colonel Horsfall had decided to deploy his men in a flanking movement through folds in the land to the west and thus approach the village from behind. The Lancashire Fusiliers could be relied on to support the attacking riflemen while further support would come from Vickers-gun teams of 1st Kensingtons and the anti-tank platoon's guns, both of whom were making a direct approach from the front. The 6-pounders were intended to keep enemy positions on the Pucciarelli ridge occupied in the initial phase of the attack; they could also engage buildings in the village and act as support weapons throughout the battle.

Two companies attacked and, as soon as forward movement was spotted, the Germans opened fire with artillery and machine guns. Most of the latter, fortunately, was aimed at the Canadian tanks. Good progress was made against what one company commander described as an enemy 'possessed and fighting like maniacs';[12] the defenders were from 334th Division. The tanks worked their way on to the Pucciarelli ridge and, by 10.30am, E Company, closely supported by tanks

> blasted their way into the first block of buildings. The defenders were tenacious and prepared to fight to the death. Before the position was taken many of E Company's men had been killed or wounded: most of the defenders died from the fire of the tanks; of those taken prisoner hardly one was uninjured.[13]

The other attacking company, F, also had a bloody struggle through cornfields while E Company fought its way in from the north from house to house supported by the anti-tank guns which poured armour-piercing shells in from the south. At 1pm resistance collapsed and Colonel Horsfall ordered E and F Companies, with the mortar platoon and the Kensingtons' Vickers, to consolidate the defence of San Fatucchio which was soon under heavy German shellfire.

H Company now moved forward for its phase of the operation which was to be continued until the Rifles had been 'finally and physically stopped by the enemy',[14] after which the Inniskillings would take over the running. H Company fought their way forward to the San Felice cemetery with G Company moving up behind. Once again there was tank support and once again German resistance was fierce and determined.

During this attack H Company lost their company commander, Major Desmond Woods, MC and Bar, wounded in the leg. His successor was wounded soon after and then the second-in-command took over. The attack continued, however, in spite of camouflaged 88s knocking out all but one of the supporting tanks. Fighting took place in the cemetery with heavy mortar fire, over a hundred bombs in a few minutes, being dropped on the Germans. With the cemetery firm at 4pm, E and F Companies moved forward again, the former to gain a foothold on the Pucciarelli ridge, the latter to take a crossroads to the north. Only seven tanks remained from the supporting Ontarios' squadron.

By evening the objectives had been taken but a determined enemy counter-attack had to be broken up by artillery and mortarfire; E Company, reduced to forty men, shared the ridge with Germans throughout the night. The London Irish had shot their bolt and the Inniskillings moved forward next morning, supported by another squadron of 11th Canadian Armoured.

The Inniskilling attack was successful and Pucciarelli village was taken although there were still some Germans on the ridge between the two Irish battalions. A German counter-attack next morning was beaten off although, for a time, the Kensingtons found themselves the centre of a close-quarter battle. Two German strongpoints remained between the Rifles and Inniskillings but these were nipped out in fierce fighting throughout the day with close co-operation between infantry, tanks and artillery. As the Irish Brigade worked its way forward, taking the farm at Casa Montemara by 6pm, the Germans counter-attacked. This was broken up by the tenacity of F Company and the effectiveness of its artillery support with Captain Alan Parsons, the FOO with the company, calling down fire from single guns all around the farm. John Horsfall described this shooting as 'masterly', for friend and foe were so close together that Alan Parsons' job called for the greatest skill and judgement.

Parsons was wounded next day during a German attack on Casa Montemara, one of a series of localised battles that raged throughout the day. On the 24th 1st Royal Irish Fusiliers captured the villages of Pescia and Ranciano, close to the shore of Trasimene, as part of a broader XIII Corps' attack in which 4th Division, which had taken over 78th's left sector, also participated with 2nd Somersets of 28 Brigade attacking Vaiano.

An attack across the Pescia river by 5th Buffs on the evening of the 24th left them isolated because of bridging difficulties, but the fact that they were not forced back by the enemy showed that the German cohesion had been broken. Although heavy rain caused its usual problems the advance began to pick up impetus with 4th Division moving forward along the hills between the main roads; 6th South Africans found Chiusi abandoned and raced forward and 56 Recce, of 78th Division, probed around the north shore of Lake Trasimene to contact the King's Dragoon Guards, moving from the other side. The Albert Line had been broken and the enemy were now pulling back to their next defensive positions.

But should there ever have been a battle at Lake Trasimene? Lieutenant-Colonel John Horsfall believed that if the Irish Fusiliers' platoon had not been ordered out of Città della Pieve, that town would not have been retaken by the Germans. In turn

> 78th Division would have piled in to the enemy at Trasimene three days earlier – before they were ready-and probably rolled the whole lot up in the process.[15]

Città della Pieve was the key to the Albert Line. Had Eighth Army been able to 'bounce' the latter, the war in Italy might have followed a very different course thereafter.

Although XIII Corps had broken the Albert Line in their sector, the French Expeditionary Corps had encountered strong resistance on the left flank. This was finally broken through the efforts of XIII Corps and VI US Corps whose 1st Armored Division's untiring efforts wore down the opposition. Thus Fifth Army was able to move on Siena which they took on 3 July. Two days later Alexander was told that the French corps, together with Truscott's VI Corps, would soon be withdrawn for Operation DRAGOON, now renamed ANVIL, which was intended, inter alia, to secure Marseilles, thus providing a port of entry in southern France for convoys from the United States. That would reduce Alexander's strength to twenty divisions against Kesselring's twenty-six, although the German front-line strength was little more than half that of the Allies. Nonetheless this did not diminish Kesselring's capacity in defensive operations.

Eighth Army was now directed on the Arezzo Line with the aim of taking the communications centre of Arezzo with its access to the Arno valley some twenty miles north of Trasimene. Already 78th Division was over a third of the way there, having advanced to Cortona where, on 4 July, it was relieved by 6th Armoured Division. Thereafter the Battleaxe Division was withdrawn to Egypt for a period of rest and training; it was not to return to Italy until the autumn.

Led by 16th/5th Lancers, 6th Armoured moved off along the Chiana valley but soon ran into stiff opposition from 15th Panzer Grenadier Division. The infantry of 61 Brigade were stopped in their tracks by determined counter-attacks; 26 Armoured Brigade was blocked in the valley and a flanking movement by 9 Armoured Brigade soon ran out of steam. The divisional commander, Evelegh, had to ask for support which Eighth Army HQ provided in the form of 2nd New Zealand Division who had dropped from the great pursuit at Avezzano, and whom Leese had intended to keep fresh for the attack on the Gothic Line.

It took seven days for Freyberg's brigades to reach the battle zone which they entered on 14 July. An hour after midnight that night 25th NZ Battalion and 3rd Grenadiers assaulted the heights of Monte Lignano. Although delayed by a counter-attack the attackers pressed on and by dawn on the 16th the high ground dominating the road to Arezzo had been secured allowing 16th/5th Lancers to race into the town. At Ponti Burriano the Lothians, also of 26 Armoured Brigade, seized a bridge over the Arno.

On the Adriatic sector Anders' Poles had been advancing towards Ancona, the only decent port on that coast north of Bari. After relieving 4th Indian Division on 13 June the Polish Corps, with the Italian Corps of Liberation under command, had begun its advance and was within ten miles of the port by 5 July. En route the Poles had inflicted severe losses on 278th Division. Anders then paused in his advance and deployed his divisions to create the impression that 3rd Carpathian would attack along the coast road. Instead, he shifted to his left foot and launched 5th Kresowa Division on an encircling sweep inland which would bring them parallel to the coast north of Ancona. This strike involved all Anders' armour, including 7th Hussars, and so unbalanced the Germans that Ancona was swiftly evacuated on 18 July: over 2,500 were captured. The first British convoy to unload there arrived five days later. With Fifth Army's capture of Livorno on 19 July almost all the preliminaries for an attack on the Gothic Line had been achieved. It remained only for XIII Corps to take the city of Florence.

The approach to Florence was made along the Arno valley with 6th Armoured Division working its way down the valley as its Guards Brigade secured the Pragmato foothills, clearing them of the German defenders. On the Arno's west bank 61 Brigade confronted Fallschirm-jäger while, to their left, 4th Division fought from hill to village, hill to village, pushing back 715th Division and deflecting the inevitable counter-attacks.

The key to progress lay in the Chianti hills, along which the Shermans of [11] South African Armoured Brigade gave valuable support to the infantry and achieved some remarkable feats of mountaineering up the rocks and dense scrub that surmount the vineyards, unnerving the tired men of 356th Division. On July 20 the Scots Guards stormed the king of the range, Monte San Michele, 892 metres high. It gave them an excellent view of the enemy's defences to right and left and a distant one of Florence, 15 miles away.[16]

Kirkman could now expand XIII Corps' frontage leftward, broadening out to a thirty-mile front on which he deployed five divisions. On the left flank he put 2nd New Zealand and 8th Indian Divisions which relieved, respectively, 2nd and 4th Moroccan Divisions. (The relief of the Moroccans on 22 July marked the end of the involvement of the French Expeditionary Corps in Italy.) Under command of 8th Indian Division was 1 Canadian Armoured Brigade, to add to the eclectic nature of Kirkman's command.

As XIII Corps pushed forward relentlessly, II Polish Corps continued to advance along the Adriatic coast while McCreery's X Corps, with 4th and 10th Indian Divisions and 9 Armoured Brigade, fought eastwards from Arezzo, widening Eighth Army's approach to the Gothic Line. Tenth Indian Division had earned another posthumous VC for Eighth Army on 10 July during the advance on Città di Castello. The division was engaged against 114th Jäger Division when, on the 10th

a rifle section [of 3/5th Mahratta Light Infantry] commanded by Naik Yeshwant Ghadge came under heavy machine-gun fire at close range which killed or wounded all members of the section except the commander. Without hesitation Naik Yeshwant Ghadge rushed the machine-gun position, first throwing a grenade which knocked out the machine-gun and then he shot two of the gun crew. Finally, having no time to change his magazine, he clubbed to death the two remaining members of the crew. He fell mortally wounded, shot by an enemy sniper.[17]

Città di Castello fell to 10th Indian Division on 22 July after an attack into the mountains on its west side led by 1st Durham LI and 2/4th Gurkhas. In the wake of the infantry 3rd Hussars charged forward, forded the Soara river on the far side of the Tiber, and shook up the enemy defences.

The other Indian formation in X Corps had taken the heights of Alpi di Poi in its advance across the mountains to the east of Arezzo. By the end of July both 4th and 10th Divisions stood ready to drive north-westwards around the east side of Pratomagna towards Florence. The New Zealanders were also ready to attack and did so as dawn broke on the

22nd. Two New Zealand battalions made good progress that day which was accelerated next day when the South Africans and their Guards Brigade forced 356th Division off the Chianti ridge. By 27 July the New Zealanders had taken San Casciano and were within striking distance of Florence.

As 4th Division's 3/12th Royal Frontier Force Rifles attacked the hamlet of Campriano, north of Arezzo, on the evening of the 24th they were being watched by none other than their King-Emperor. George VI, travelling under the pseudonym of General Collingwood, was in Italy to visit his troops from all over the Empire and the Commonwealth. A formal inspection of Eighth Army took place in which representative detachments of every division paraded before the King who decorated many of his soldiers and dubbed the accolade of knighthood on Generals Richard McCreery and John Harding.

An attack on Florence was launched by the New Zealanders on the night of 1/2 August. Only partially successful, it was followed by a further attack the next night to dislodge the enemy from the Pian dei Cerri hills dominating the route to the city. During the 3rd Freyberg's men fought a series of small but vicious actions against German groups that included infantry, 88s and heavy tanks.

With the New Zealanders thus engaged it fell to the Imperial Light Horse/Kimberley Regiment* of 6th South African Division to make Eighth Army's entry into Florence on the morning of 4 August. As they did so they were being shelled heavily; not until nightfall did South African infantry push into the city as far as the Arno to find all bridges blown except the Ponte Vecchio which was blocked by demolitions at either end and was, in any case, incapable of supporting tanks. Although Florence had been declared an open city, the commander of 1st Fallschirmjäger Corps, Schlemm, actively disobeyed Kesselring by defending along the Arno within the city.

Both New Zealanders and South Africans were relieved at Florence by 1st Canadian Infantry Division who were quickly joined by 1st British Infantry Division, in action for the first time since Rome. On 8 August the Canadian front was taken over by 17 Indian Brigade. There was a stand-off across the Arno until 11 August when it was discovered that the enemy had finally gone. Three platoons of 1st Buffs from 18 Brigade then crossed the river to occupy the city centre. In a further act of defiance German shells fell on some of the buildings which the Buffs occupied.

Alexander could now prepare for his attack on the Gothic Line: Operation OLIVE. Since both German flanks rested on the sea, Alexander's options were limited and he

---

* A number of South African units were made up from elements of two regiments and bore the titles of both. The Imperial Light Horse/Kimberley Regiment was but one example: the Witwatersrand Rifles/Regiment de la Rey was another.

could only hope to achieve decisive results by concentrating force at a chosen point, while being prepared to shift his weight to another point if the battle demanded, and to do so with greater agility than his opponent. No great manoeuvres were possible – indeed they seldom were in Italy.[18]

Since Kesselring had the advantage of well-prepared defensive positions, the Allies had to devise a plan that, to a very large extent, depended on making the German commander misjudge where the main attack would hit. Alexander's initial plan was for Eighth Army to force the centre of the Gothic Line through Lemelsen's Tenth Army and then pin von Vietinghoff's Fourteenth Army between the Adriatic and the River Po. Eighth Army had already begun to move formations in readiness for the attack in the central sector of the Gothic Line.

However, Leese disagreed: he wanted the main effort to be made on the Adriatic coast where, he believed, he could deploy all of Eighth Army and make best use of the 1,000 guns available for the assault. Kirkman, commanding XIII Corps, had also persuaded Leese that the coastal area provided the finest opportunity for armoured operations. In addition

Leese, for emotional and personal reasons, had resolved never to fight shoulder to shoulder with Clark again if he could avoid it, and Kirkman now supplied him with a persuasive tactical argument.[19]

There was also the topography of the area to consider:

In the region of the upper Tiber, the Apennines . . . turn north-west to join the Maritime Alps in Liguria, and thereby isolate central Italy from the Po Valley. In the west the narrow coastal plain north of Pisa does not give access to the Po Valley, the mountains still bar the way. In the east, however, there is direct access to the north along the coastal belt south-east of Rimini. This is the easiest route to Northern Italy but nonetheless it has disadvantages: the Apennine foothills extend in difficult ridges to within not many miles of the coast, there are a series of water obstacles at right angles to movement north-west, there is only one first class road for an access . . . , the route gives access only to the most extreme north-east corner of the Po Valley, the Romagna, itself dissected by another series of parallel water obstacles, and, finally, this eastern approach is separated from Western Central Italy by the central Apennines across which lateral communications are long, few and difficult.[20]

The outcome of a meeting at Orvieto airfield between Alexander, Harding and Leese on 4 August was that Leese's view prevailed. Although Clark accepted the revised plan, he did not want to see Fifth Army reduced to a supporting role and argued for a major role for his army. This was agreed and Fifth Army was to be strengthened by the addition of Kirkman's XIII Corps, thus depriving Leese of a reserve for Eighth Army.

Under the revised plan, as Eighth Army struck the Germans with a right hook, Fifth Army was to jab hard, straight through the central Apennines to bring about the final collapse of the enemy; the timing for this move would be decided by Alexander. Although OLIVE was originally planned to coincide with DRAGOON it was eventually delayed until 25 August. Surprise was certainly achieved as was shown by the absence, on leave, of von Vietinghoff and Heidrich when the attack was launched.

For Operation OLIVE Eighth Army, stronger than at any time in its history, disposed four corps with a total of eleven divisions: I Canadian Corps; II Polish Corps; V Corps and X Corps. Of these, V Corps was by far the strongest including 1st Armoured Division,* returned to Eighth Army's order of battle for the first time since North Africa and the only British Alamein veteran division to rejoin the Army in Italy, 4th, 4th Indian, 46th and 56th Divisions. The movement of both V Corps and I Canadian Corps from concentration areas near Foligno across the Apennines to the Adriatic demanded a massive logistic effort and the construction of sixteen Bailey bridges. Since the move had to be carried out in secret all movement was by night over a ten-night period with vehicles being hidden by day. Complete success was achieved in the operation.[21]

Just before midnight on 25 August the assaulting brigades of 5th Kresowa, 1st Canadian and 46th Divisions crossed the Metauro river, which was not held by the enemy. Only as the troops began their crossing did the artillery open fire along their seven-mile front. Some eight miles to the left 4th Indian Division, tasked with left-flank protection, moved forward through mountainous territory. Leese's assault on the Gothic Line, which he had presented as a march on Vienna,† had begun.

---

* Eighth Army now had only one armoured division: 6th Armoured, and 6th South African Armoured, were in XIII Corps which Alexander had transferred to Fifth Army on 10 August, to Leese's chagrin. The South Africans later moved to the US IV Corps
† James Lucas, then serving in 2/7th Queen's, recalled Leese addressing his battalion and telling them that in two days they would be in Bologna, in four days Venice and in seven days Vienna.[22]

NOTES

1. Churchill: *The Second World War, book xi*, pp.50-62
2. Molony et al: *The Mediterranean and the Middle East, vol vi, Pt I*, pp.447-450
3. Scott: *Account of the Irish Brigade*
4. Blaxland: *Alexander's Generals*, p.144
5. Molony et al: *vol vi, Pt II*, p.25
6. Blaxland: op cit, p.148
7. Doherty: *Clear the Way!*, p.163
8. Ray: *Algiers to Austria*, p.144
9. ibid, p.145
10. Blaxland: op cit, p.149
11. Horsfall: *Fling Our Banner to the Wind*, p.143
12. ibid, p.151
13. Doherty: op cit, p.167
14. Horsfall: op cit, p.148
15. ibid, p.137
16. Blaxland: op cit, p.155
17. *Register of the Victoria Cross*, p.342
18. Fraser: *And We Shall Shock Them*, p.353
19. Bidwell and Graham: *Tug of War*, p.348
20. PRO: CAB44/145, p.7
21. Molony et al: op cit, pp.129-134
22. James Lucas: interview with author, December 1996

CHAPTER XVI

Operation OLIVE: Assault on the Gothic Line, August – October 1944

The foe vaunts in the field

Operation OLIVE met with initial success and engendered enthusiasm in Allied Headquarters. Against little opposition the assaulting brigades had moved forward some two miles by dawn on 26 August. Canadian troops were amazed to see a jeep driven by General Alexander arrive in their bridgehead and even more amazed when they realised that Alex's passenger was Winston Churchill.[1] The premier had watched American troops land on the south coast of France ten days earlier before returning to Italy and a flying visit to his own regiment, 4th Hussars, whose Colonel he was, prior to travelling on to Leese's tactical HQ.

During the 26th Leese and his staff were concerned that Kesselring might have anticipated Eighth Army's offensive and pulled his forces back to stronger defences on the Foglia river, about eleven miles to the German rear. However, it transpired that the withdrawal was only local and that 4th Fallschirmjäger Regiment had been hit hard by Eighth Army's artillery while pulling back. Interrogation of prisoners elicited the further, and pleasing, information that von Vietinghoff, commanding Tenth Army, and Heidrich, of 1st Fallschirmjäger Division, were both on leave. The deception plans prior to OLIVE had worked: the night-time movements of men, equipment and vehicles had gone undetected. For the third time that year Alexander had gained the advantage of surprise over Kesselring who believed that this offensive was but a continuation of the Polish advance with reinforcements from other formations.

The attacking troops of 1st Canadian, 46th and 5th Kresowa Divisions made steady progress during the first two days. By that stage the Canadians, having already overcome considerable opposition, were eight miles beyond the Metauro and preparing to attack the hilltop town of Monteciccardo. Around 1 o'clock in the morning of 28 August the Edmontons moved into the town but were soon engaged against some German troops who had also entered and were forced to withdraw. Monteciccardo was regained by the Edmontons after a day of skirmish and heat; the nearby monastery also fell to them. To their right 1 Canadian

Brigade had attacked a ridge defended by Fallschirmjäger who fought stoutly and even set fire to haystacks to illuminate the battleground. In the light of day the Canadians were able to see the Foglia, the far bank of which had been turned into a killing ground with every tree or building removed so that the defenders should have clear fields of fire from steel and concrete strongpoints above the river.

During the 29th the attacking brigades of 46th Division also reached the Foglia with 139 Brigade to the left of 128 Hampshire Brigade; both had fought hard over the ground from the Metauro. By evening 5th Kresowa Division had pushed forward to conform with the Canadian line, although Pesaro had been by-passed; it could be dealt with later. Anders' men had been engaged against Fallschirmjäger who had suffered more casualties from the Poles than at Cassino.

Throughout the morning of the 30th, Allied aircraft carried out bombing raids intended to destroy enemy minefields and thus ease the passage of the attacking troops in the next phase of operations. OLIVE had fallen behind schedule but Leese still hoped to be able to bounce the Gothic Line rather than having to mount a major setpiece battle to breach it. Corps commanders were ordered to probe forward to make such gains as were possible.

The Canadians advanced again that afternoon with a revised order of battle: 11 Infantry Brigade, from 5th Armoured Division, took the place of 2 Brigade and 3 Brigade relieved 1 Brigade. On the left 11 Brigade's Cape Breton Highlanders suffered much as they crossed open ground strewn with mines and obstructed with wire while enemy machine guns and mortars carried out the Grim Reaper's work amongst them. A similar fate befell 3 Brigade's West Novas on the right but, in the centre, 11 Brigade's Perth Regiment made much better progress as did the PPCLI of 3 Brigade; both battalions crossed the Foglia and forced the defenders out of their positions during the night. By dawn most of the German positions were in Canadian hands.

It was now 5th Canadian Armoured Division's turn to strike but their advance was met by stiff opposition; thirty British Columbia Dragoon Shermans were knocked out in half a mile with the regiment's CO among the dead. But the Canadians continued to advance and inflict loss on the enemy. On 1 September 1st Canadian Division thrust northwards to the coast, cutting across the front of the Poles in an advance that saw Monte Luro taken by the Edmontons supported by Churchills of 12 RTR, while Monte Peloso was captured by the Princess Louise's Dragoon Guards, a cavalry regiment converted to infantry.* By 3 September the Carpathian

---

* In July 1944 5th Canadian Armoured Division was re-organised with two infantry brigades. To achieve this 4th Princess Louise's Dragoon Guards (4th Reconnaissance Regiment) was re-roled as infantry and brigaded with the Lanark and Renfrew Scottish Regiment and the Westminster Regiment to form 12 Infantry Brigade.

Lancers and the Household Cavalry Regiment had cleared up the opposition in Pesaro.

On that same day the Canadians were within sight of Rimini, having bumped 1st Fallschirmjäger Division out of that segment of the Gothic Line and back across the Conca river. Forty-sixth Division had made a similar advance from the Foglia with 128 Hampshire and 139 Brigades still leading. On the night of 30 August 1/4th Hampshires and the North Irish Horse had begun scaling Monte Gridolfo from which the defenders had been driven by dawn on 1 September. During this battle Lieutenant Gerard Ross Norton, MM, a South African attached to the Hampshires had won the Victoria Cross* when his

> platoon was pinned down by heavy fire. On his own initiative and with complete disregard for his own safety, he advanced alone and attacked the first machine-gun emplacement, killing the crew of three. He then went on to the second position containing two machine-guns and 15 riflemen, and wiped out both machine-gun nests, killing or taking prisoner the remainder of the enemy. Throughout these attacks he was continuously under fire from a self-propelled gun, nevertheless he calmly went on to lead his platoon against the remaining enemy positions.[2]

Battalions of 139 Brigade had also taken hilltop or hillside villages: 5th Sherwood Foresters secured a village on Monte Vecchio through which 2/5th Leicesters passed to take Mondaino in a night attack. It was discovered that grenadiers from 26th Panzer Division had reinforced 71st Division in spite of which the defenders were briskly evicted from apparently impregnable positions.

Fourth Indian Division, operating on the left flank, had advanced twenty miles over high ground on a two-brigade front in order to hit the Gothic Line. En route they had liberated Urbino, where Raphael was born, on 28 August and were into the enemy line two days later. Supported by fighter-bombers, 3/10th Baluchs took the strongpoint of Monte Calvo, having been twice beaten back. The Indians then made for Tavoleto where opposition was stronger.

At this stage Keightley committed 56th (London) Division to the battle, using them to fill the gap between 4th Indian and 46th Divisions. The Black Cats made good progress: on 1 September Monte Capello was taken against 'terrific spandau fire' and, despite heavy casualties.[3] In spite of some strong counter-attacking from 98th Division, recently arrived from

* Norton had won the Military Medal as a sergeant after escaping from Tobruk. He had subsequently been commissioned into the Kaffrarian Rifles.

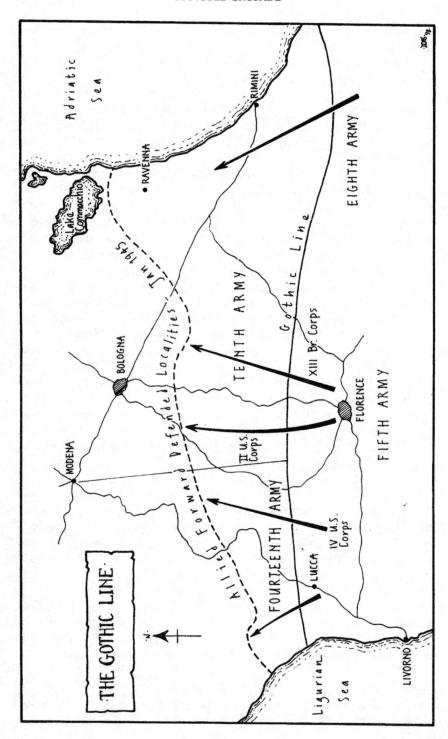

THE GOTHIC LINE

the Russian front and whose sign was also a Black Cat, 169 Queen's Brigade were patrolling beyond the Ventana river, two miles from Mondaino on the 3rd. That night an enemy air raid, a rare occurrence at this stage of the war in Italy, caused more than a hundred casualties in the Queen's Brigade.

With the Canadians already over the Conca, 46th Division did likewise during the night of 2/3 September with 6th York and Lancaster in the lead. The bridge at Morciano was seized by 2/4th King's Own Yorkshire LI after which 138 Brigade moved on to take San Clemente, a village on a small hillock two miles beyond the Conca. Thus 46th Division's advance was roughly level with that of the Canadians whose 1 Brigade was also fighting two miles beyond the Conca. But Leese had failed to have 1st Armoured Division close enough to the front to take advantage of the opportunities presented by the Canadians.

Leese had been surprised by the speed of the Canadian penetration. . . . he had deliberately kept 1st Armoured well back to avoid blocking the roads forward. Had he been prepared to commit it to the Canadian Corps that would not have been a problem, for there was plenty of room immediately behind them. Third, Leese's mind worked at infantry pace. At Alamein he had commanded [XXX] Corps which had done most of the infantry work to crack the line, for the armour had at first refused to fight its way through the German positions, insisting that its task was to go through 'the gap' and 'pursue' the enemy. The 1st Armoured Division still held that outdated notion – shared, apparently, by Leese. It was looking for a gap.[4]

Meanwhile, the Canadians, believing that the road to Rimini was open, prepared to motor down that road. That their belief was but an illusion was brought home two miles beyond the Conca when they ran into German resistance and were forced to take to their feet and try to break through the enemy positions. Determined resistance also faced 46th Division which opened the way for the New Brunswick Hussars to attack Coriano. The Hussars were beaten back and heavy shellfire prevented 5th Hampshires moving forward from their start-line. German resistance was stiffening with more reinforcements arriving to bolster the front. Although the Gothic Line had been pierced there was no easy road to Rimini, or Bologna, never mind Vienna for Eighth Army whose way forward lay, as ever in Italy, across the folds and ripples of ridges and river valleys. Several operations mounted by 46th and 1st Armoured Divisions were brought up short against the Coriano ridge. Although some local gains were made the overall picture was one of stalemate:

At Coriano, ten miles south-east of Rimini, the last ridge before open

247

country, V Corps was halted and failed to 'take it on the bounce'. Instead German reinforcements, tanks and anti-tank guns were hurried to the sector and by 5th September Vietinghoff had six divisions, including one Panzer and one Panzer Grenadier, facing Eighth Army and defending the Coriano Ridge. To break through now would demand more strength, more preparation, a mass of artillery and time. Every day that passed brought nearer the possibility of a break in the summer weather and the sort of rains which had so often before, notably on the Sangro, reduced fighting on the Adriatic Front to near-Flanders conditions.[5]

To move forward Eighth Army had to eject the Germans from the Coriano ridge. With fire support from offshore naval vessels, aerial bombardment and its own artillery, V Corps launched a major attack on 12 September which drove Vietinghoff's men from the ridge but the cost was high in casualties.

The attack had been preceded by some preliminary operations to gain the heights flanking the Coriano ridge. Fourth Indian attacked and took Piandicastello and the neighbouring ridge after a protracted and bitter struggle while 169 Queen's Brigade of 56th resumed its thwarted divisional attack on Gemmano. The latter operation was successful in that Gemmano itself was taken, but the nearby ridge remained in German hands giving them a view of the Conca valley and I Canadian and V Corps' support zones. Another Black Cat brigade, 168, was also fully engaged in and around Croce and suffered greatly from enfilading fire.

Eighth Army's renewed offensive was preceded by Fifth Army's attack, launched on 10 September. In ordering Clark's army to join in the offensive Alexander was hoping to knock Kesselring off balance by hitting him with alternating attacks. Thus did Alexander expect to break the German defences and allow his armies through the Gothic Line. Rather than throw his left jab at this juncture Alexander would have done better to reinforce Eighth Army's efforts to accelerate the crumbling of the German defences on that front.

Leese had planned that Eighth Army would leap forward from the Coriano ridge with Ravenna, thirty-five miles beyond, as the objective for the attack's third phase. But Eighth Army could not leap: it could only heave against the ridge. The German defences were well-sited and manned with skill and determination; anti-tank guns wrought terrible losses among the attacking armour as did German tanks; Tigers and Panthers were better-armed and better-armoured than Shermans and Churchills which proved highly vulnerable to enemy fire. The Sherman, in particular, had gained the reputation among its crews, and among German anti-tank gunners and tankmen, of igniting rapidly when hit, so much so that it became known as the 'Tommy cooker' to the Germans and the 'Ronson'* to its crews.

The first infantry committed to the attack on 12 September were 18 Infantry and 43 Gurkha Brigades of 1st Armoured Division; the latter deployed 2/8th and 2/10th Gurkhas. Although both Gurkha battalions were making their first assault, the Germans, dazed by the intensity of the bombardment, put up little resistance. With the Yorkshire Dragoons leading them, 18 Brigade also enjoyed a successful attack and took San Savino after house-to-house fighting through the village. The Canadians had entered the fray shortly after 1st Armoured with 11 Infantry Brigade from 5th Armoured Division pushing its attacking battalions, the Perth Regiment and Cape Breton Highlanders, forward either side of Coriano by dawn. The brigade's third battalion, the Irish Regiment of Canada, then began mopping-up operations in the town which proved no easy task. In all some 1,000 prisoners were taken by the infantry of the two armoured divisions. But swift exploitation had not proved possible: 9th Lancers, due to exploit forward from San Savino, were held up by a deep ditch and well concealed Panther tanks.

On 13 September 56th Division began its part in the attack. Almost immediately 169 Queen's Brigade lost its commander, Brigadier Smith-Dorrien, to enemy shellfire. However, a squadron of 7 RTR raced round the Fabbri spur from Croce under cover of mist and was later joined by 2/7th Queen's; 300 men of 98th Division were taken prisoner. West of Croce the Germans remained resolute and inflicted severe loss on their attackers.

The Gemmano ridge's defenders were also obstinate; 46th Division gained the summit only to be pushed off by 5th Mountain Division. Fourth Indian Division was then ordered to make a further assault and thus became the third division entrusted with the task. On the night of the 14th a storm of gunfire, put down by 260 artillery pieces, covered the approach of 2nd Cameron Highlanders of 11 Indian Brigade. This attack proved to be the limit for 5th Mountain Division who had held the ridge so stolidly. The Camerons' attack achieved success and by dawn's early light

> they could survey the tangle of corpses and tree trunks on its summit, having taken twenty-four survivors of its garrison. Round the base of the great black crucifix at the top were the arms of a dead soldier of the 6th Lincolns.[6]

---

* From the eponymous cigarette-lighter manufacturer's advertising claim that its lighters lit first time, every time. John Gorman, a Sherman troop commander, who served in the Irish Guards, described the tank to the author as having the 'softest armour known to man'.

Meanwhile 46th and 56th Divisions had pressed ahead, trusting that 4th Indian would remove the danger from Gemmano on their flank. Both divisions pushed beyond Croce through difficult countryside and by early evening of 14 September 2/5th Leicesters of 139 Brigade had reached Monte Colombo which fell with some two-score prisoners.

The advance continued not as the leap that Leese had hoped for but as a series of probes and pushes. Against the coast 1st Canadian Infantry Division was grappling with Fallschirmjäger. Although he might have preferred not to do so, Leese placed 4th British Division under command of 1st Canadian Corps. The British 12 Brigade moved up through the Canadian 11 Brigade on the 14th, a day on which the Canadians ejected the last German defenders from Coriano, and advanced to the Marano river which 1st Royal West Kents forded that day before establishing themselves in Ospedaletto by dawn of the 15th. Thus an objective set ten days earlier for 128 Hampshire Brigade had finally been reached.

The tanks of 1st Armoured Division were beset with a number of problems: well camouflaged enemy guns were a major delaying factor; so too were deep, muddy ditches which posed difficulties in crossing. On the evening of the 15th, however, 43 Gurkha Brigade crossed the Marano in a successful attack that revealed disorder in the German defences. Heavy rain made the going even more difficult and 1st Armoured was ordered to re-organise for its next move forward while 4th Division's 28 Brigade attacked across their front to seize Cerasola ridge on the night of the 16th/17th. At 6am on the 17th the Hampshire Brigade took Point 475 against strong resistance from soldiers of 5th Mountain Division. By this time 167 Brigade of 56th Division had also crossed the Marano, captured Mulazzano ridge and allowed 168 Brigade to pass through in an advance intended to conform with 4th Division. Stiff opposition met them and they suffered heavy fire from their left flank.

The Ausa river, shallow but fast flowing, now lay before 4th Division's leading troops with, beyond it, the last range of hills before the plain. Those hills ran down from the heights of the tiny republic of San Marino to San Fortunato which guarded the approach to Rimini. To 4th Division's right the Canadians were still enmeshed with Fallschirmjäger on a ridge overlooking the coastal plain, on either end of which were the villages of San Martino, closer to Rimini, and San Lorenzo. The latter had been taken by the Canadians but they had been rebuffed in their efforts to take the former. On the coastal plain, 3 Greek Mountain Brigade were engaged, marking the return of Greek troops to Eighth Army's order of battle.

The Canadian Corps commander, General Burns, ordered his 1st Infantry Division to maintain pressure at San Martino while preparing an attack across the Ausa in concert with 4th Division. This attack was intended to throw the Germans out of positions overlooking the Ausa before reserves were able to settle into newly created switchline positions. Burns planned to attack on the night of 17/18 September after the enemy positions had been pounded by aerial bombing; 486 sorties a day were flown to achieve this and to immobilise German reserves. The usual artillery support would be supplemented by the guns of the New Zealand Division which was still in Army reserve. And there would be an innovation to assist assembly of the attacking troops: artificial moonlight created by searchlights.[7]

Fourth Division led off with 12 Brigade's West Kents crossing the Ausa and reaching San Antimo where they lay low throughout the 18th as they were under enemy observation from the next ridge. To their right 2nd Beds and Herts of 10 Brigade made another small lodgement which they were unable to enlarge. Dire as the situation was for those battalions it was as nothing compared to the fate of the Canadians who

had met disaster and spent the 18th writhing amid ditches and vineyards on the flats below San Fortunato, with shells pelting upon them, together with bombs from Allied aircraft, and with black smoke billowing from Churchills of the hard-fought 21st Tank Brigade.[8]

Keightley's V Corps had also renewed the attack. In spite of the demands already made on the troops, which one veteran* described as 'more persistent' than had been made on any British division in the Liri valley battles, Keightley's men responded enthusiastically to his call for a major effort to smash through to the plain. Once again 4th Indian Division led: 3/10th Baluchs of 5 Brigade crossed the Marano during the night of 17/18 September to gain a lodgement within San Marino at Faetano, an important enemy observation post, through which 1/9th Gurkhas passed to continue the advance.

The Gurkhas were hit almost immediately by a sharp counter-attack, aimed at regaining Faetano, which knocked them off balance but the day was saved by the actions of one man, Rifleman Sherbahadur Thapa.

Rifleman Sherbahadur Thapa and his section commander, who was afterwards badly wounded, charged and silenced an enemy machine-gun. The rifleman then went on alone to the exposed part of a ridge where, ignoring a hail of bullets, he silenced more machine-guns, covered a withdrawal and rescued two wounded men before he was killed.[9]

---

* Gregory Blaxland, of the Buffs, in his book, *Alexander's Generals: The Italian Campaign, 1944-45*, p197.

Sherbahadur Thapa's courage, typical of that so often associated with the Gurkhas, had saved the Faetano bridgehead and was recognised by the posthumous award of the Victoria Cross.

Throughout the 17th the battalions of 168 Brigade, 1st London Irish, 1st Welch and 1st London Scottish, had struggled to cross the Ausa against 356th Division. As the London Scottish appeared to be making best progress they were reinforced by London Irish companies and the group thus created managed to push beyond the riverline, seize Point 140 and hold it against the usual determined counter-attacks. The latter phase lasted throughout the night, the third night of intense activity for the soldiers and 'men made prisoners in one action were released in the other'.[10] Although they held off all attacks, the London Scottish were reduced to less than a hundred men by noon of 19 September.

During the night of the 18th/19th the Yorkshire Dragoons had taken the Monte Arboreta feature but had lost the most important part of it to an armour-supported counter-attack. Subsequently 8 RTR attacked the Ceriano ridge, to the left of Monte Arboreta, but met fierce opposition. Reinforcements were called for: 2 RTR found it impossible to make the ridge in the face of enemy fire but two weak companies of Ox and Bucks LI and some Queensmen eventually reached the top and relieved two much weakened Royal Tanks' squadrons.

The intention was that 1st Armoured should break out from this sector, striking for Point 153, a mile north-east of 7 Armoured Brigade's foremost position. But this plan came unstuck even before it began: the Bays, spearheading the advance, had been unable to attack due to the very difficult going on the approach. However, the Yorkshire Dragoons did regain the lost part of Monte Arboreta that night while 2/6th Queen's attacked Ceriano but ran into heavy fire partway up the ridge and were then counter-attacked.

Another effort by the Bays on 20 September turned into tragedy for the regiment which came under fire while assembling for the attack. A troop of Shermans was sent to deal with the harassing machine-gun fire but all three were knocked out by 88s. The brigade commander tried to have the attack cancelled or postponed but was told that the Bays were to press ahead at 10.05am to assist the Canadians on their right. When they did so they ran into such opposition that, within an hour, all but three tanks from two squadrons had been knocked out. A total of twenty-four Shermans were lost with six officers and fifteen men killed.

On the Canadian front Burns' men, including 4th British Division, had pushed to considerable effect. Supported by 21 and 25 Army Tank Brigades' Churchills plus Wolverine tank-destroyers* from the anti-tank regiments, 10 Brigade exploited the success of an attack made on the night of 18/19 September with 2nd Duke of Cornwall's LI penetrating beyond

San Aquilina. Ten Brigade thus secured the left flank for the Canadians to renew their attacks on San Fortunato ridge the following night. The presence of the slow Churchill I-tanks, rather than the nimbler Shermans, epitomised how Leese's vaunted leap had become a heave.

With well co-ordinated artillery support the Royal 22^e made a series of stabbing attacks that took them to their objective while, on their right flank, the Edmontons did likewise. By daybreak the Canadians were secure on the ridge and had taken a mixed bag of prisoners that indicated the haste with which von Vietinghoff had reinforced his front line: there were Fallschirmjäger, Panzer Grenadiers and Panzer troops, men from a Turcoman division (162nd) and a Luftwaffe ground division (20th).

There was no further purpose to be served by continuing to hold Rimini and during the night of the 20th/21st the Germans withdrew. In the morning the first Eighth Army troops to enter this ancient town were those of 3 Greek Mountain Brigade. In spite of a series of explosions heard the previous evening the Greeks found the Ponte di Tiberio intact.

On Eighth Army's left flank 4th Indian Division had also scored success. The Germans had made a stand on every suitable piece of high ground in neutral San Marino and the Camerons spent all day on the 20th winkling out soldiers of 278th Division from their many posts. By dusk they had finished their task and were able to enter the town of Borgo Maggiore, capital of San Marino, perched like a fairytale invention overlooking the peaks and ridges and the coastal plain.

Rain was now coming down heavily and continued to fall torrentially throughout 21 September thus stopping V Corps' advance to Bologna, intended to cut off and destroy the retreating enemy forces. The rain eased and stopped and on the 22nd movement began: the advance on to the plain bore the codename CAVALCADE. In the lead was 2nd New Zealand Division, under command of 1st Canadian Corps, which set off on the coast road for Ravenna with 5th Canadian Armoured on its left. But it was an advance that never accelerated beyond the pace of a heavily burdened infantryman. Boggy land, much of it reclaimed marsh, was scored with streams, ditches and small rivers that made most effective tank obstacles. Added to the nature of the ground itself was the abundance of vineyards which, in full leaf, provided superb cover for ambush parties as well as denying movement to tanks. And, as if those problems were not enough, the many solidly built farms and barns could be quickly turned into strongpoints. More rain came down and the infantry had to push their

(See previous page)
* Wolverine was the name given to the M10 tank-destroyer in British service and was a self-propelled 3-inch anti-tank gun mounted on a modified Sherman chassis. The turret was open-topped. British M10s were later fitted with 17-pounder anti-tank guns and were then renamed Achilles.

weary way forward through what had appeared to be an area where fast movement by armour could be expected.

As if to emphasise that the advance could not accelerate as planned, 43 Gurkha Brigade did not achieve sufficient penetration over the Marecchia river to cut the Bologna road, Route 9, until 24 September. This was to be the start-line for V Corps' dash on to the plain, led by 1st Armoured Division but, instead, came news that the division was to be broken up although 2 Armoured Brigade was to remain as an independent support brigade. The Gurkhas of 43 Brigade were transferred to 56th Division to replace 168 Brigade which was amalgamated with 167 Brigade: 8th Royal Fusiliers and 7th Ox and Bucks LI were disbanded and 1st Welch Regiment was reduced to cadre.[11] However, the other infantry brigade of 1st Armoured, 18 Brigade, was not to be retained: its battalions were used to restore 46th Division to strength; 14th Sherwood Foresters and the Yorkshire Dragoons were disbanded while 1st Buffs were reduced.

For 18 Brigade this was a bitter end to its wartime service: of Eighth Army's British infantry brigades it had the greatest proportion of desert veterans and there were more Africa Star ribbons with the distinctive figure '8' in its ranks than in any other. Not for nothing did 46th Division's commander, Major-General Hawkesworth, make a point of greeting 18 Brigade's veterans as they arrived for posting to his battalions

> . . . propped on his long ashplant stick, he told them that they should regard themselves as footballers transferred from one team to another and that in his division the infantry were regarded as the elite, always to be allotted the best billets when out of the line, always to be provided with every possible ounce of fire support when making an attack. Certainly the men needed every possible ounce of encouragement to keep them going.[12]

Eighth Army's offensive was bogging down in the mud of the Romagna plain which sucked at the wheels and tracks of its vehicles and the boots of its infantrymen as surely as had the mud of Flanders frustrated an earlier generation of British soldiers. And the infantrymen of Eighth Army were now exhausted: the Army had suffered more than 14,000 casualties since Operation OLIVE began with most of those in the infantry; half those casualties had been inflicted on British infantry units while II Polish Corps had sustained over 3,500 casualties.[13] Since no further reinforcements were available from the UK, Eighth Army's infantry battalions had had to depend since July, when the last reinforcements from Britain had been posted to battalions, on anti-aircraft gunners from disbanded regiments who had undergone infantry training. Some 9,000 of these men had joined infantry battalions before the offensive, having undergone a two-month long infantry training course.

The disbandment of further AA regiments had released another 5,000 men for conversion to infantry but these had only begun training in August and so would not be available for some time. Hence the disbandment of 18 and 168 Brigades and the reduction of most infantry battalions to three rifle companies; those that still deployed four rifle companies would be reduced to three by attrition during the coming months. This manpower crisis in Italy reflected the overall manpower crisis felt by the Army generally in the last eighteen months of the war. With commitments in north-west Europe, in Italy and the Far East, as well as the defensive duties of garrisons elsewhere, the British Army was stretched as it had never been before. Only the availability of Dominion and Imperial forces allowed the deployment of field armies in various theatres; in Italy much use was to be made of Italian formations in Eighth Army in the final phase of the war. It was perhaps the ultimate paradox that Eighth Army, which had done most to defeat Italy and bring about its surrender, should now find its former foes contributing to its order of battle.

Another major change for Eighth Army came with the departure of Sir Oliver Leese to command 11 Army Group in the Far East. Leese left Eighth Army on 1 October and many of his soldiers associated his departure with the collapse of the offensive, believing that Leese was being relieved because of the failure to reach the plain of Lombardy. In fact the Army Commander was being promoted, a recognition of his success in smashing the Gustav, Senger/Hitler and Gothic Lines. Had he not promised so much with his final offensive, history might have accorded him greater status.

As with Montgomery before him, Leese took many of Eighth Army's best staff with him including the man who had played such an important, but often unrecognised role in the Italian campaign, Brigadier Ray, Eighth Army's Chief Engineer.

Appointed to succeed Leese was Sir Richard McCreery who was to command the Army until disbandment. McCreery's was a totally different style of command: whereas Leese had continued the Montgomery model of being seen as much as possible by his troops and of operating from a forward HQ, McCreery was to remain with his staff at Eighth Army Main HQ. He was, nonetheless, a frequent visitor to the forward area but his purpose in so doing was to assess problems rather than indulge in public relations work with the troops. Nor did he effect any eccentricities in dress, wearing regulation uniform and headgear at all times. It may be noted that he had never enjoyed friendly relations with Montgomery.

Commissioned into the 12th Lancers as a 17-year-old in 1915 McCreery was the only cavalryman to command Eighth Army; with the exception of Cunningham, a Gunner, the other commanders had been infantrymen.

But he was Alexander's obvious choice to succeed Leese. He had been in action as a corps commander ever since the start of the Italian campaign before which he had been an outstanding chief of staff to Alexander in North Africa. During the final Alamein battle he had visited Montgomery's HQ in company with Alexander and Casey, the resident minister in Cairo, where he advised on where to launch Operation SUPERCHARGE suggesting to Monty that the attack should be launched farther south than planned, against the junction between a German and an Italian division. This, in many eyes, including Alexander's, had been the decision that won the battle.[14]

McCreery took over Eighth Army at a depressing time. Leese's great offensive had foundered in the mud of the Romagna plain; there could be no sweeping strike to cut off a retreating enemy. Instead Eighth Army seemed doomed to a war of attrition, keeping up the offensive against the enemy as part of a two-handed pummelling with Fifth Army. The role which McCreery's army now had was one of containment, as it had been in southern Italy, while Mark Clark's made a fresh, and more direct, effort to reach Bologna. That role was underlined by the commitment of 78th Division, on its return from Egypt, to XIII Corps in Fifth Army. The Battleaxe Division had been in Eighth Army reserve at Fano, south-east of Rimini, ready to join V Corps but, twenty-four hours before 78th Division was due to leave Fano, orders were changed to send it to XIII Corps on Fifth Army's right wing.

Morale in Eighth Army was undoubtedly affected by this depressing situation but, in spite of this, the Army continued to jab at the enemy throughout the winter months, continuing the steady push that had taken the place of Leese's leap. By 1 October Eighth Army units were some ten miles past Rimini on Route 16, the coast road, and much the same distance along Route 9, the Via Emilia, towards Bologna. Small rivers that had been but streams in September were now in full flood; seven of these obstacles had been crossed. The burden on the Royal Engineers, especially in terms of bridging equipment, had been at least doubled and tremendous effort in men and equipment was needed simply to keep the Army's lines of communication open.

There were two further rivers in front of Eighth Army, whose leading troops were now across the Uso river: these were the Fiumicino, well covered by daunting fortifications, and the Pisciatello. In ancient times one of the three had been the Rubicon by crossing which Julius Caesar had declared open rebellion on the Roman Senate.* There was no certainty as to which river was the Rubicon but some unit war diaries nevertheless note the crossing of the famous river:[15] whether the possible crossing of a

---

* Caesar said, on crossing the Rubicon, 'Iacta alea est' – *the die is cast.*

river significant in classical history had any effect on the morale of ordinary soldiers is purely a matter for conjecture. What was certain was that more rivers faced Eighth Army's men.

On the coastal sector the Canadian Corps had 3 Greek Mountain Brigade by the sea with the New Zealand and 5th Canadian Armoured Divisions continuing the front inland to the junction with V Corps. The right flank of the latter was held by 56th Division whose advance was directed along Route 9; 167 Brigade had crossed the Uso on 25 September before handing over to 169 Queen's Brigade which had taken Savignano and the ridge overlooking it, but two London Scottish companies had been savagely mauled after crossing the Fiumicino on the last night of the month. Also along that river was 46th Division, while 4th Indian had been repulsed at Sogliano, before reaching the Fiumicino.

McCreery had previously commanded X Corps as a result of which he had valuable experience of mountain fighting which he brought to bear in his handling of Eighth Army. Before his departure Leese had ordered II Polish Corps to move forward so that he could revitalise his attack with the same trio of corps with which he had initiated his great offensive in August. On his second day of command McCreery changed the orders: Anders was now to take his men in a leftward sweep through the mountains, where X Corps' line had been, before advancing down the valleys into the plain behind the German lines. McCreery's intention was to work with, not against, the grain of the country. HQ X Corps was no longer operational, its sole division, 10th Indian, having been transferred to V Corps to relieve 4th Indian: the corps sector was taken over by a scratch force under command of HQ 1st Armoured Division which force included the Lovat Scouts and the Nabha Akal Infantry.*

McCreery intended to use V Corps to eject the Germans from the line of the Fiumicino with 10th Indian Division leading. The Indians used their skill in outflanking tactics to drive the enemy from their positions: 1/2nd Punjab with 2/3rd Gurkhas had taken Sogliano by dawn on 5 October after which 3/5th Mahratta crossed the Fiumicino in gale-force conditions and moved on, in spite of the most adverse weather conditions, to take Monte Farneto during the night of the 6th/7th. The importance to the German defences of this dominant feature was indicated by the fierce counter-attack which was launched in a vain effort to regain it.

Forty-sixth division now sent the Hampshire Brigade across the Fiumicino to conform with 10th Indian. This attack could have proved disastrous for the Hampshire battalions. Two officers on a reconnaissance patrol with marked maps had been captured by the Germans. It had to be assumed that the maps, and therefore details of the attack, were in enemy

---

* A State Forces unit raised in 1757 and which was redesignated 14th (Nabha) Bn The Punjab Regiment in 1954.[16]

hands: the plan was therefore changed. This proved a sensible precaution: as the Hampshires attacked on the night of the 7th German artillery pounded the intended lines of approach. But rain began to fall heavily from midnight, bringing its own problems, especially with bridging; some pack mules drowned in the flood conditions. It took until dawn on 9 October for the Hampshire Brigade to secure its objectives after which 138 and 139 Brigades passed through to continue the advance.

Major-General Denys Reid, of 10th Indian Division, was using three brigades in his attack: 25 Brigade on the right, 10 Brigade in the centre and 43 Gurkha, attached to 10th Indian, on the left. The infantry moved quickly and with stealth and, in several cases, took enemy troops completely off guard.

> But tenacity was the quality needed most of all, in gaining objectives, in beating off counterattacks that were invariably made under heavy artillery fire, and in lugging forward supplies both for the infantry and the indefatigably manned Churchills of 25th Tank Brigade. The rain caused awful suffering. So deep and liquid was the mud that the muleteers, Indian and Italian, often sank in it up to their waists, and their wretched beasts collapsed, enforcing the abandonment of their loads. One of them drowned, not in water but in mud.[17]

A main crossing of the Fiumicino was postponed several times before becoming unnecessary as the advance through the mountains forced an enemy withdrawal. The Canadian Corps, with elements of 56th Division, crossed the Fiumicino on the night of 10/11 October and followed the retreating Germans to the Pisciatello; 56th Division was squeezed out by the Canadians in this pursuit. But it was the Indians who most harried the Germans: 2/6th Gurkhas wrested Monte Chicco from the Germans between dusk on 13 October and dawn on the 15th. During this battle artillery and fighter-bombers played a vital role and even the presence of some of the best German troops, men of 90th Panzer Grenadiers, could only delay the decision.

The main effort now switched to 5th Kresowa Division which attacked out of the mountains some ten miles to the Indians' left. Their attack, directed on the Ronca valley, took the Germans completely off balance and four days of sustained and hard fighting culminated in Monte Grosso's fall. Continuing the advance, with support from the Italian Maiella Group, they took Mussolini's native town, Predappio, on the 27th. Progress had been slower for 46th Division but 138 Brigade had gained the Carpinetta ridge and forced the Germans back to the Savio river. In that retreat heavy loss was inflicted on the enemy by artillery fire which was intended to support a Canadian attack. On 20 October 16th Durham LI of 139 Brigade entered the town of Cesena, the first town of any size to have been liberated by 46th Division. The fall of Cesena marked the end of two months' continuous fighting for the division and there was pleasure at the news of a relief by 4th Division for a brief spell out of the line.

Fourth Division maintained the impetus of the advance, clearing a ridge overlooking the Savio of Germans on the night of 19/20 October. Then 2nd Royal Fusiliers waded the Savio, in spite of its wide fast-flowing waters, and fell upon unsuspecting Germans on the far bank; a bridgehead was quickly established around a village. The Germans recovered their equilibrium quickly and put in counter-attacks with tank support but the Fusiliers held firm, although they had only PIATs with which to fight off the armour; artillery fire was also brought down on the enemy by FOOs on the ridge behind the Fusiliers. The other battalions of 12 Brigade, 6th Black Watch and 1st Royal West Kents, soon strengthened the lodgement while the sappers, under heavy shelling, had a bridge across the Savio by the morning of the 24th.

Meanwhile the Canadians had also established a bridgehead over the Savio following an attack on the night of the 20th/21st. Counter-attacks were soon underway, in the course of which Private Ernest Alvia ('Smoky') Smith of the Seaforth Highlanders of Canada displayed outstanding bravery.

> With a P.I.A.T. gun he put an enemy tank out of action at a range of 30 feet, and while protecting a wounded comrade, he destroyed another tank and two self-propelled guns, as well as routing a number of the enemy infantry.[18]

Smith saw off the infantry with a Tommy gun; his actions subsequently earned him the Victoria Cross. The German counter-attacks lasted for three days after which pressure from the flanks caused an enemy withdrawal, allowing a resumption of the Canadian advance. The city of Ravenna now beckoned.

In the first phase of operations under McCreery's command Eighth Army had made steady, if unspectacular, progress. The new Army Commander's experience in the mountains had paid dividends and had demonstrated that success could be gained by working with the topography of the country rather than against it. However, the terrain on which Eighth Army was now operating was little better in terms of mobile operations than the mountains. Much of the flat land is reclaimed marsh and nature appeared to be trying to restore it to that condition with October's heavy rains transforming the area into a muddy nightmare. Since it is reclaimed land there is a system of drainage ditches as well as many small streams and canals, many of which have high flood banks as protection for the neighbouring land. Such waterways, mostly running west to east, hindered tank movement.

Although Eighth Army had breached the Gothic Line, the German defences had been constructed in depth and so the breakthrough to Bologna, and beyond, had not happened. Like a battered and splintered door, the Gothic Line now hung precariously on its hinges: McCreery had to plan the final heave that would bring that door crashing down.

NOTES

1. Blaxland: *Alexander's Generals*, p.173
2. *Register of the Victoria Cross*, p.241
3. Williams: *The Black Cats at War*, p.101
4. Graham and Bidwell: *Tug of War*, p.359
5. Fraser: *And We Shall Shock Them*, p.355
6. Blaxland: op cit, p.196
7. PRO: CAB44/145, p.47
8. Blaxland: op cit, p.197
9. *Register of the Victoria Cross*, p.292
10. *The London Irish at War*, p.180
11. Williams, op cit, p.105
12. Blaxland, op cit, p.203
13. PRO: CAB44/145
14. Nicolson: *Alex*, p.168; Blaxland, op cit, p.204; but *see* Carver, *El Alamein*, p.141
15. PRO: WO170/474-475, 46 Recce
16. Gaylor: *Sons of John Company*, p.266
17. Blaxland: op cit, p.210
18. *Register of the Victoria Cross*, p.297

CHAPTER XVII

Another Italian Winter: Rain, Mud and Cold

That winter lion

It was now clear that a renewed offensive was not feasible until spring 1945 thus presenting the troops in Italy with the prospect of another Italian winter. However, Alexander, who as far back as 2 October had indicated that his forces might not be quite strong enough to smash the Germans in Italy before winter set in, briefed McCreery and Clark on further offensive operations, to take place only if weather conditions were favourable. Such operations would be suspended by 15 December. Eighth Army was to take Ravenna and push on to the Santerno river, while Fifth Army was to take Bologna and then meet up with Eighth in a pincer movement.[1]

With these orders Alexander was satisfying a strategic imperative that lay outside Italy: Eisenhower planned to attack into Germany in December and wanted pressure maintained in Italy so that German troops could not be diverted from that theatre to the fatherland. Alexander still saw strategic possibilities in Italy: should Bologna fall then the enemy would fall back beyond the Po to the line of the Adige river which Eighth Army could outflank by an amphibious operation on the other side of the Adriatic. Thereafter, in conjunction with Tito's Yugoslav forces, Eighth Army could advance northwards on Vienna.[2]

This was not to be. Although the Americans, constantly suspicious of British intentions in the Mediterranean which they construed as being to defend British imperial interests, had indicated, without enthusiasm, that landing craft would be made available, Tito withdrew his consent, presumably believing that Eighth Army on his side of the Adriatic would reduce his opportunities to acquire new territory. And so soldiers in Italy, of whatever nationality, were to continue in what was effectively a war of attrition.

It is not easy to demand sacrifices, including men's lives, when the object of a campaign had become demonstrably subordinate to the claims of other theatres, and where attrition rather than victory appears the only aim. Hitherto, Alexander had been able to hold before his troops the vision of a great adventure into and across the North Italian Plain. . . . Without such stimulus, however, the Allied Armies in Italy had a hard and depressing winter ahead of them, it being clear that no further major offensive could be contemplated for several months; and even then it appeared to the soldiers doubtful whether the authorities cared if the armies in Italy advanced or not.[3]

Moreover, Eighth Army had been weakened by Operation MANNA, the withdrawal of formations to be sent to Greece which the Germans had evacuated and where there were threats of both a communist takeover and civil war. Britain had agreed to send a military force to Greece to prevent either threat becoming reality and to maintain order until elections could be held. Eighth Army was the major source for formations for this force: in mid-October, as the Germans were pulling out, 2 Parachute and 23 Armoured Brigades had arrived in Greece. These were followed by 4th Indian Division, on relief by 10th Indian, and by 3 Greek Mountain Brigade; both 4th and 46th British Divisions were also to be despatched to Greece.

There was another problem which was not peculiar to Eighth Army: a shortage of artillery shells. This affected all Allied armies in Europe and led to a rationing of shells. Since artillery support had always been of primary importance in Italy as a 'means of conserving, guiding, and sustaining the heavily used infantry'[4] the shortage would be felt acutely within Eighth Army's infantry units since they could no longer enjoy the levels of artillery support to which they had become accustomed.[5]

For Eighth Army McCreery decided to make Forlì the first objective since by doing so he could divert attention from the true objective, Ravenna, and also ease his supply problems by opening Route 67, the road from Florence to Forlì. In reality an advance on Forlì had been underway since Cesena fell on 20 October with Eighth Army's cutting edge being provided by 10th Indian Division. On the 23rd that division's 20 Brigade had captured Monte Cavallo in an attack by 3/5th Mahratta and 2/3rd Gurkhas. There followed an enemy withdrawal from the Savio back to the Ronco river which, on its seaward journey, passes less than two miles from Forlì.

On the night of 25 October 1st KRRC, from 2 Armoured Brigade but now attached to 4th Division, and 2nd Duke of Cornwall's LI crossed the Ronco by a ford that appeared suitable for tanks; two companies of each made the crossing and established a small bridgehead. Unfortunately heavy rain raised the river level, a tank broke down on the ford, blocking it, and all four companies were stranded. German infantry from 278th Division, supported by tanks, repeatedly attacked the riflemen and light infantry; slowly but surely the four companies were ground down.

That setback was countered by Indian and Polish operations. Men of 43 Gurkha Brigade and the Nabha Akal Infantry, now attached to 20 Brigade of 10th Indian Division, crossed the Ronco, advanced into the hills beyond Meldola and attacked troops of 356th Division who were already under attack by the Poles. This two-pronged effort loosened the enemy defences and allowed 1st King's Own, of 25 Indian Brigade, to take the advance as far as Grisignano which they reached on 2 November. That put the leading elements of Eighth Army two miles north of Forli. Meanwhile 4th Division's sappers were reinstating bridges as far back as the Savio, many of which had been washed away by the recent flooding, as well as bringing forward folding-boat equipment and spans of Bailey bridging to consolidate another bridgehead over the Ronco. With weather conditions improving on the 4th, aircraft were able to attack the defences of Forli; the planes deployed included rocket-firing Typhoons, newly arrived in Italy. Aerial attacks were carried out over the next three days with particular attention being paid to the defences around the airfield south of the main road.

On the night of 7/8 November V Corps' attack on Forli opened with an assault by 6th East Surreys across the airfield. This followed a silent approach in which the attacking soldiers had to negotiate a thirteen-foot-deep ditch in inky darkness before the moon rose. That accomplished, the Surreys charged across the runway towards the enemy positions around the control buildings. The element of surprise allowed about half the battalion to reach those positions before the Germans realised what was happening; this was one instance where the absence of artillery support was no real problem. Although resistance continued throughout much of the night, the arrival of Churchill tanks from 51 RTR before dawn soon brought it to an end.

On the corps' left flank 46th Division, which had relieved 10th Indian, attacked from Grisignano with 128 Hampshire Brigade leading and making considerable progress. The division had a new commander in Major-General Charles Weir, who had temporarily commanded 2nd New Zealand Division during Freyberg's absence. Weir had earlier been the New Zealand Division's BRA, having been commissioned into the New Zealand Artillery from 'The Shop', the Royal Military Academy at Woolwich.

A third element in the corps' plan came with 28 Brigade of 4th Division making an early-morning attack through the gap between Grisignano and the airfield. By now the Germans had decided that Forli should be abandoned and began withdrawing. Tiger tanks assisted in the rearguard action; although these caused some damage, the Germans suffered considerable harassment and loss from the Vickers MMGs of 4th Division's machine-gun battalion, 2nd Royal Northumberland Fusiliers.

With Forli now in British hands, 46th Division pushed ahead. That night 2/4th KOYLI, of 138 Brigade, put a platoon across the Montone river, just beyond the town. It suffered in the same manner as the four companies of KRRs and DCLIs more than a fortnight earlier: a sudden downpour brought the water level up cutting off the platoon and leaving them to the enemy's mercy. Farther along the Montone 4th Division was pushing the enemy back gradually from Forli. The area between the town and the river was liberally sprinkled with solidly built houses, factories and ditches, all offering cover for rearguard delaying actions. Against such opposition both 4th and 46th Divisions pushed gradually to the Montone which was eventually crossed where it loops around Forli.

Fourth Division's final action in Italy occurred in the advance from Forli. After the Montone the next river obstacle was the Cosina, a tributary of the former, which, aided by a feint attack by 4th Reconnaissance Regiment, 10 Brigade attempted to cross on 21 November; the attack was beaten off. A further effort, by 28 Brigade assisted by 139 Brigade, established a bridgehead the following night. This was expanded with the help of tanks of 142nd Regiment RAC, a detachment of 1st Assault Regiment RAC/RE and sappers of 7th Field Company allowing the brigade to renew its efforts.

> The second phase of 28th Brigade's attack was to begin at [3.30pm on 23 November]. The enemy's stubborn resistance on the division's left flank, however, had prevented 46th Division from advancing far enough to secure 28th Brigade's left flank. Brigadier Preston therefore proposed to send in 'B' Squadron, 142nd RAC, on the left, to take a house half a mile beyond the river and in 46th Division's sector. The army commander, who was visiting Brigadier Preston's headquarters at the time, approved the plan, and the tanks moved off. They were soon in difficulties in the soft ground, but their appearance was enough for the German garrison, which surrendered shortly afterwards to the Somersets.[6]

On the night of the 23rd/24th the Germans blew up the bridge across the Lamone river outside Faenza. It was at the Lamone the next night that 4th Division ended its time in Italy. Due to be withdrawn to Palestine to rest, refit and relieve 5th Division, they were instead sent to Greece for further, but different, active service.

> In its last five weeks of fighting against the Germans, the division had taken six hundred and five prisoners, completed the wreck of the German 114th Light Infantry Division, helped to damage the 256th Infantry and the 26th Armoured Divisions, and destroyed the greater part of 278th Division. The force of 4th Division's attacks during this

period drained the Germans of man-power at a time when they greatly needed every man . . .[7]

The Poles had been advancing steadily all this time, their progress less spectacular than that of V Corps because of the need to ascend the hills between the valleys as they pursued the retreating Germans. However, their efforts assisted V Corps while shortening XIII Corps' front in Fifth Army. The latter was on the defensive save for 17 Brigade of 8th Indian Division which nipped in to the Polish sector on 15 November, two days after 1/5th Gurkhas had taken Monte San Bartolo.* Seventeen Brigade went on to take the town of Modigliana, ahead of 3rd Carpathian Division.

With Forli taken McCreery's first objective for Eighth Army had been achieved. The second was the capture of Ravenna, assigned to 1st Canadian Corps, now under Lieutenant-General Charles Foulkes who had arrived from 1st Canadian Army in north-west Europe. The Canadians had been out of the line since 28 October, having been relieved by dismounted cavalry regiments. A number of armoured regiments had been ordered to leave their tanks or armoured cars and assume an infantry role. Among those relieving the Canadians were the men of 12th Lancers, the Army Commander's own regiment, as well as 27th Lancers, a wartime regiment which had been created around a cadre from 12th Lancers. Under command of Lieutenant-Colonel Horsburgh Porter, of 27th Lancers, these two cavalry regiments formed Porterforce which, in addition, included a miscellany of British and Canadian units. Also included in Porterforce was Popski's Private Army, a raiding unit which had been the Desert Raiding Squadron but which was better known by its commander's, Vladimir Peniakoff, soubriquet. This was the first occasion on which Popski's Private Army had been charged with defensive tasks and while doing so they maintained close contact with the Italian communist partisans of the Garibaldi Brigade. The latter were waiting to take part in the liberation of Ravenna but, meanwhile, assisted Peniakoff's men in staging several ambushes.[8]

While Porterforce carried out its defensive role, 10th Indian Division passed through the line held by 12th Lancers and crossed the Montone north of Route 9 to widen V Corps' frontage as it drove for Faenza. This involved 10 and 20 Indian Brigades in several days of bitter fighting against the armour-supported 356th Division. The Germans had breached many floodbanks to inundate the surrounding countryside while they made strongholds of groups of farm buildings. The Indians' task of ejecting the Germans from these positions was achieved by 2 December

---

* Before the attack Rifleman Thaman Gurung of 1/5th Gurkhas won a posthumous VC for his gallantry while acting as a scout to a fighting patrol.

when the division reached the line of the Lamone, alongside 4th Division's gains, where they were relieved by the New Zealanders.

McCreery now planned to co-ordinate the capture of Ravenna with two other attacks, involving all three corps of Eighth Army. Thus, while the Canadians struck through 10th Indian's gains towards the Senio and Santerno rivers to the north-west and Ravenna to the north-east, V Corps would make for Faenza, enveloping the city, and II Polish Corps would flank through the hills on V Corps' left wing.

The Canadians returned to the line on 25 November, ready for the attack which opened on the morning of 2 December. Two brigades led, with 3 Brigade from 1st Division on the left and 12 Brigade of 5th Armoured on the right. Good progress was made northwards and 3 Brigade captured the town of Russi that night. Next day Russi's liberators swung left to push the Germans over the Lamone. By nightfall on 3 December 12 Brigade was on the road to Ravenna at Godo having assailed several drainage ditches with their high floodbanks en route. On the 4th, Princess Louise's Dragoon Guards, accompanied by Shermans of the British Columbia Dragoons, raced the four miles to Ravenna. The former entered the city that afternoon. As the Princess Louise's men entered Garibaldi Square they were joined by Porterforce, then by partisans of the Garibaldi Brigade and, finally, by Popski's Private Army. The latter had carried out some daring raids in their advance on Ravenna and the partisans, under Arrigo Boldrini – codenamed Bulow – had so harassed the Germans in Ravenna, disrupting their communications, that they were probably glad to quit the city. Boldrini, who struck up a long-lasting friendship with Peniakoff, was wounded in the fighting before Ravenna fell. The partisan leader, a former officer in the Italian army,* was later decorated with the Italian Gold Medal for Valour which was presented to him by McCreery at a parade of partisan forces in Ravenna. Boldrini's partisan brigade subsequently became part of the Cremona Group, one of several Italian formations to join Eighth Army in early 1945.

Although an attack by 1 Brigade's Royal Canadians and Hastings across the Lamone that night was beaten back with heavy losses, the capture of Ravenna boosted Eighth Army morale. An historic city of some substance and considerable beauty, it was a tangible sign that the Army was making progress, albeit much behind schedule. Such signs are more easily

---

* According to Peniakoff, it was this military experience that brought Boldrini to the attention of Longo, the Italian resistance leader. Boldrini was asked to command the Garibaldi Brigade but that actually meant raising and training the brigade since it did not exist when the command was given to him. He proved to be an outstanding guerrilla commander although this surprised some of his countrymen who thought that, because he was no great speaker, he could not have leadership qualities.

appreciated and understood by soldiers than obscure strategic objectives of 'maintaining pressure' in a war of attrition so that progress might be made on another front in another country.

As the Canadians advanced on Ravenna the Poles continued their relentless push through the Apennine foothills south of Route 9 and, in so doing, assisted V Corps' move on Faenza:

> II Polish Corps made good progress in its difficult sector against stubborn resistance. Monte Fortino was captured by 5 Kresowa Division on 16 November but was lost to a counter-attack on the following night and did not return to our hands until 21 November when it was recaptured by 3 Carpathian Division which had relieved 5 Kresowa Division three days before. An Italian detachment and the Lovat Scouts sent patrols to the Lamone river on 24 November.[9]

The Italians of the Maiella Group, still under Polish command, had taken Brisighella by 29 November after which the Carpathian Division crossed the Lamone, by-passing the town, and made for the heights of San Rinaldo, Cassette and Besdone, south-west of Faenza and south of the Senio river. For 3rd Carpathian Division's soldiers it was their third assault on such an objective. Tough though they were, the strain of battle was beginning to wear them down. In this assault they suffered heavy losses from the defenders, men of 305th and 715th Divisions, who were able to put up a much more solid defence as their front contracted. Even so, Anders' men fought on:

> The operations of the II Polish Army Corps in the Emilian Apennines had needed strenuous effort by the men, who, battling in the hills or paddling in mud, fought, attacked and pushed back the enemy. There were no spectacular achievements; it was just a case of steady relentless fighting, and duty well done. The Army Corps losses in these battles amounted to 42 officers and 627 other ranks killed, 184 officers and 2630 other ranks wounded, and 1 officer and 32 other ranks missing.[10]

The Carpathians' efforts and their contribution to Eighth Army's advance in those winter weeks of 1944 were recognised by McCreery in a signal to Anders on 17 December:

> My best congratulations to you and 3rd Carpathian Division on your successful operations in difficult country, which have driven back the enemy to the Senio on a wide front with heavy losses. The mounting of this attack with the great lack of roads in your area was a fine achievement. Engineers and gunners deserve every credit. Well done indeed.[11]

The third element of Eighth Army's attack, that by V Corps, opened on the night of 3/4 December, having been delayed by bridge repairs along the supply routes. Once again the Hampshire Brigade was to the fore, leading 46th Division's assault crossing of the Lamone, about four miles from Faenza. The Hampshires were assisted by diversionary moves by the New Zealanders on the other side of Faenza. With the reconstituted 1st KRRC covering the brigade flank, 2nd Hampshires made their way across by wading and by a ladder bridge. On the far side they had to climb wet and slippery banks before engaging in battle. To their left 1/4th Hampshires were also across the river:

> The 2nd Hampshire, on the right, eventually gained their objective by a full-blooded bayonet charge on a two-company front, and the 1/4th, on the left, fought their way slowly forward up a series of ascending features. The 5th passed through but could make little progress. The rain returned, and the bridgehead was secured only by the frantic efforts of porterage parties and the combined ingenuity and per-severance of the sappers in launching an Ark bridge.[12]

Thanks to the sappers' work in providing that bridge, 2 Armoured Brigade tanks were able to cross the river after dark on 4 December. The bridgehead was then expanded by 138 Brigade which was joined on its right flank by 169 Queen's Brigade.* The latter belonged to 56th Division but was under command of 46th Division to compensate for the loss of 139 Brigade which had been airlifted to Greece.

The bridgehead thus created by 46th Division came under extreme pressure from the enemy. Von Vietinghoff, temporarily commanding German forces in Italy, had brought 90th Panzer Grenadier Division back to oppose Eighth Army's advance and, specifically, to wipe out the bridgehead which 46th Division had won from 305th Division. In spite of German pressure 46th Division inched its way forward until, on 9 December, a furious and determined counter-attack struck the bridge-head. Under a storm of fire from tanks and artillery, 90th Panzer Grenadiers assaulted the British positions. For all their efforts the Panzer Grenadiers were brought to a halt by the dogged resistance of 46th Division's troops. The only ground gained by the Germans was a feature that had been held by the carrier platoon of 6th Lincolns of 138 Brigade, under Captain J H C Brunt, MC. Three Mark IV tanks supported a body of infantry attacking Brunt's platoon position:

---

* Officially designated 169 (London) Infantry Brigade but generally referred to as a Queen's Brigade since it included 2/5th; 2/6th and 2/7th Queen's Royal Regiment.

The house around which the platoon was dug in was destroyed and two Sherman tanks knocked out. Captain Brunt rallied his remaining men, moved to an alternative position and continued to hold the enemy infantry, although he was heavily outnumbered. Personally firing a Bren gun, Brunt killed about fourteen of the enemy. When his Bren ammunition was exhausted he fired a Piat and 2-inch mortar, left by casualties. This aggressive defence caused the enemy to pause and enabled Captain Brunt to re-occupy his previous position and get away the wounded that had been left there.[13]

That did not end Brunt's gallantry: he continued to demonstrate aggressive and inspiring leadership during a further German attack later that day. Brunt, a 22-year-old, was killed next day by a chance mortar bomb as he lay waiting for his batman to bring him breakfast. He was posthumously awarded the VC.

The Lincolns, with 6th York and Lancaster on their right, had taken the brunt of the German attack and both battalions were, understandably, exhausted. Throughout most of 46th Division such a state of exhaustion prevailed and it was clear that the division had to be relieved. That relief began on the 10th with 25 Brigade of 10th Indian Division taking over from the Hampshire Brigade while the New Zealanders relieved both 138 and 169 Brigades. Brunt was one of the last casualties suffered by 46th Division in Italy for the remainder of the division would shortly join 139 Brigade in Greece and, although it would return to Italy before hostilities ceased, it would see no further action in the peninsula.

The counter-attack on 9 December had indicated the German determination to hold the Lamone line. On that same day they also attacked a position held by 27th Lancers near Ravenna:

Peniakoff came to their rescue with five jeeploads of his men. He took position on a flank and pumped bullets into wave after wave of heedless Jaegers. When at last the latter withdrew they left eighty dead behind them. The loss incurred by Popski's Army consisted only of their commander's [left] hand. In exchange he won the DSO.[14]

On the night of 10/11 December the Canadians launched another attack over the Lamone with two brigades, 3rd from 1st Division and 11 from 5th Armoured, some three miles apart. Both assault crossings were successful but the way ahead was dissected by several small rivers, each with the inevitable floodbanks. To make matters worse, a fresh German division, 98th, had just arrived to support 114th Jäger and 356th, both of which had seen much hard fighting; the three divisions were grouped together as LXIII Corps. This reinforcement meant that the Canadians had to fight for every yard of muddy ground and attacks across the Naviglio canal on the night of 12/13 December were fiercely contested. On the Canadian right 12 Brigade crossed the canal, created a lodgement and were hit by a series of determined counter-attacks which forced a withdrawal. However, on the left, 1 Brigade had more success: the Hastings, who had led the crossing, held out firmly against all that was thrown against them and established a bridgehead with the help of the Carleton and York Regiment. Slowly but surely the bridgehead was expanded as armour and artillery came to 1 Brigade's aid while fighter-bombers also played their part.

The bridgehead created by 46th Division was the jumping-off point for the next attack, by elements of 2nd New Zealand and 10th Indian Divisions, the following night. The attacking units, three battalions of 5 NZ Brigade, two of 10 Indian and two of 25 Indian, accompanied by tanks from 4 NZ and 7 Armoured Brigades, were supported by a tremendous preliminary artillery bombardment, the result of an assiduous rationing of shells to provide support when it was most needed.

> It was a great achievement of the sappers to have made the tracks and built the bridges to pack such strength into the wild, sharp-featured, and rain-drenched country beyond the torrent-prone Lamone, and the sudden eruption came as a shock to the enemy.[15]

Shocked or not, the Germans put up stout resistance with 10 Indian Brigade finding some of the toughest in their path. However, the attack's momentum continued and the objectives were taken: on the night of the 15th the enemy began evacuating Faenza. Next day the New Zealanders increased their total of prisoners to 300, mainly from 90th Panzer Grenadiers. Faenza was finally cleared of enemy troops on the morning of the 17th, on which day New Zealanders and Indians advanced to the Senio where an attempt to create a bridgehead over the river was beaten off and the advance halted. On the left flank, Anders' Poles also reached the Senio.

Another pair of attacks from Faenza, by 6 NZ and 43 Gurkha Brigades, reached the Senio as well. This was to be the Army's line for what remained of the winter and the Canadians came up to it with an attack by eight battalions on 21 December which gained Bagnocavallo. There were still German troops lodged south of the Senio and, although 15 Army Group was ordered to pass to 'offensive defence' at the beginning of January 1945, McCreery interpreted this order to allow operations to improve his positions for the offensive that would come with the spring.

At the turn of the year frost hardened the ground on the coastal plain sufficiently for armoured operations to take place: between 2 and 6 January 5th Canadian Armoured Division advanced on the Canadian Corps' right flank in a sweeping ten-mile move to the southern shore of

Lake Comacchio, a huge coastal lagoon; the Canadians also gained the base of the spit of land that lies between the lake and the sea. From Alfonsine, to the south-east, the Germans launched a counter-attack that was smashed by the weight of fire concentrated on it by the Perth Regiment, 1st KRRC and 12th Lancers; the latter pair of units formed part of another ad hoc force, under command of 9 Armoured Brigade, which was charged with holding the coastal sector. German losses came to almost a thousand.

South-east of Bagnocavallo, another Canadian attack, launched in conjunction with a 56th Division assault, brought an end to a further large German salient south of the Senio. On the night of 3 January the Canadian 2 Brigade, with the PPCLI forward, took the town of Granarolo and at dawn 56th Division launched its converging attack from the left

> led by the Shermans of the 10th Hussars and 2nd Tanks, with the 2/6th Queen's in close support, riding in sawn-off Shermans, which were named Kangaroos, manned by the 4th Hussars, and each filled with a section of infantry. Having disgorged their sections at the rear of houses, or on top of more open defences, the Kangaroos returned laden with prisoners, of whom 200 were swiftly netted. About the only price to be paid for such a gain was the revelation of the new conveyance. It had enabled McCreery to achieve an essential task of reduction with minimal loss of life and minimal drainage of his meagre stock of shells.[16]

Fifth Army was still stuck in the Apennines before Bologna. However, Eighth Army was now well positioned to strike behind the defenders of Bologna towards Ferrara and thereby cut the German line of retreat to the Po. With the terrain offering more opportunity for mobile operations, and the newly devised Kangaroo armoured personnel carriers providing more mobility for the infantry, there was a resurgence of enthusiasm in Allied headquarters about the chances of destroying totally the German armies in Italy.

Considerable changes in the Allied high command in the Mediterranean had been precipitated by the death in Washington on 5 December of Field Marshal Sir John Dill,* head of the British Military Mission in the USA. His successor was General Sir Henry Maitland Wilson, Supreme Commander

---

* The absence of Dill through illness earlier in 1944 had been an important factor in the American decision to go ahead with Operation ANVIL/DRAGOON. Had his advice been listened to in London and had he been present in the late spring and early summer of 1944 to advise the Combined Chiefs of Staff his diplomatic skills might well have led to the operation either being cancelled or reduced in scope. Either option would have benefitted the Allied Armies in Italy. [17]

Mediterranean; the natural choice to succeed Wilson was Alexander. Alex took up his new appointment on 12 December in the rank of field marshal with his promotion backdated to 4 June, the day on which Rome had fallen, to maintain his seniority to Montgomery, promoted to field marshal on 1 September, in the Army List. Monty's promotion had caused much resentment in Italy where it was perceived as a slight on Alexander and his soldiers. However, it had not been possible to promote the latter at the same time since Wilson, the Allied Supreme Commander, was a general and Alexander could hardly outrank his superior.

Alexander's promotion meant a vacancy at the head of Allied Armies, Italy which was filled by Mark Clark, although with no promotion in rank, while the former title of 15 Army Group was revived. Lucian Truscott, commanding VI Corps in Seventh US Army in France, was brought back to Italy to command Fifth Army thus giving Clark two cavalrymen as army commanders.

One of Alexander's responsibilities in his new position was the Greek situation and he paid a visit to Athens almost as soon as he was appointed. He was forced to send more troops to Greece and the remainder of 46th Division thus followed 139 Brigade, 4th British and 4th Indian Divisions. A corps HQ was also sent to Greece in the form of Tactical HQ, X Corps, under Lieutenant-General Hawkesworth, which had been in reserve in Italy.* Since all these formations had been due to be rested, Alexander's hope was that most would be back in Italy for the spring offensive. That hope was to be disappointed: only 46th Division returned to Italy before hostilities ended but too late to take part in active operations.

The German command in Italy had also seen changes. On 23 October Kesselring had been seriously injured in a road accident while visiting formations under his command.[18] He was succeeded as temporary commander of Army Group C by von Vietinghoff with Lemelsen, recently returned from sick leave, taking command of Tenth Army and von Senger taking over Fourteenth Army. At the beginning of 1945 Army Group C fielded twenty-one German divisions with a further two guarding the eastern approach to Italy. Although these divisions were of variable strength they still represented a considerable fighting force and the importance attached to the Italian front by the German high command was demonstrated in January 1945 when 710th Division was transferred into Italy from Norway: this occurred at a time when Allied troops had already crossed the German border at several points.

Kesselring returned to Italy at the beginning of February 1945, although not yet fully recovered, and resumed his visits to front-line units which he considered important morale boosters. At the same time he re-organised

* III Corps was subsequently formed to command the forces in Greece.

his armies in readiness for the Allied spring offensive. Under his command were four Italian divisions, three of which were deployed to guard the western flank under Graziani's Army Liguria while the fourth was in Fourteenth Army in an area where an Allied attack was considered unlikely. Although the Germans had a major internal security problem in occupied Italy, operations against partisans were not conducted by Kesselring's formations but by a separate command under SS General Karl Wolff with a strength equivalent to ten divisions and including Italians, Cossacks, Slovaks and even some Spaniards.

Reinforcements were still arriving in Italy for Army Group C, albeit in reduced numbers, as were supplies of ammunition. Kesselring's greatest shortages were in aircraft, the Luftwaffe in Italy had been almost entirely shot out of the sky, and petrol. The latter shortage had most effect on his five mobile divisions: 26th Panzer; 1st and 4th Fallschirmjäger; and 29th and 90th Panzer Grenadier.

By contrast Alexander's forces in Italy were reduced even further in early-1945. At the end of January, Alexander was summoned to Malta to meet the British and American Combined Chiefs of Staff who were travelling to the Yalta conference. There he was told that 1st Canadian Corps was to be transferred to north-west Europe to join Crerar's First Canadian Army. The loss of the Canadians, who had played such an important part in Eighth Army's operations in Sicily and Italy, was a tremendous blow to Alexander and to McCreery who had planned a major role for them in the new offensive. As if the transfer of the Canadian Corps was not enough, three other British divisions were to follow to north-west Europe. Fortunately, only one division did so: 5th Division, which had spent an almost unbelievable eight months in Palestine before returning to Italy in February 1945 to relieve 1st Division, was almost immediately transported to Naples whence it sailed to Marseilles and eventually entered operations in Germany itself in mid-April.*

Only seven British, Commonwealth and Imperial divisions remained in Italy for the spring offensive; there was little chance of any others returning from Greece. In total Alexander had seventeen divisions, including three armoured, against twenty-one, albeit weaker, German divisions. However, 15 Army Group was reinforced in early 1945 by the

---

* Fifth Division earned the soubriquet *The Cook's Tour Division* because of its wartime travels. Although warned of possible moves to either Finland or Norway the Division's travels began with the BEF in France in 1939-40 and, continued, after service in Northern Ireland, with a move to India in 1942. En route 5th Division took part in operations against the Vichy French in Madagascar. There had also been shore leave in South Africa and Kenya. After less than two months in India, 5th Division was then ordered to Persia which it reached via Iraq. Its next move was by road to Syria from where it moved to Egypt and thence to join Eighth Army in Sicily.

inclusion of four Italian groups, wearing British uniforms and equipped with British arms. These were the Cremona Combat Group, which included 21st and 22nd Regiments and had the support of 28 Garibaldi Brigade; Friuli Combat Group, with 87th and 88th Regiments; Folgore Combat Group, with Nembo and San Marco Regiments; and Legnano Combat Group, with 68th and 69th Regiments. There was also an Italian SAS unit. Of the Italian combat groups Cremona served with V Corps, Friuli with X Corps, and Folgore with XIII Corps, which returned to Eighth Army; Legnano served with II US Corps in Fifth Army.

Another new formation to join Eighth Army in January was the Jewish Brigade which included three battalions of the Palestine Regiment, created in Palestine during the British mandate. There had been a reluctance to accept a Jewish formation under British command because of the antagonism between Jew and Arab in Palestine and the prospect of the mandate ending.

> . . . Jewish proposals to create an independent body to fight against the Germans had been received with limited enthusiasm by British officials committed to the nearly impossible task of maintaining strict impartiality between Jews and Arabs. It was not therefore until August 1944 that the British War Office, after four years of discussion, had withdrawn all objections to the establishment of a Jewish Brigade.[19]

Churchill was enthusiastic about the creation of the Jewish Brigade, telling Roosevelt that the Jews 'of all people have the right to strike at the Germans as a recognisable body' and supporting their desire to fight under their own standard, the Star of David. As well as the Palestine Regiment, many recruits came from the Polish Army which included men who, although Polish citizens, were not ethnic Poles; these included Ukrainians and Jews. The Polish contribution to the Jewish Brigade was such that Moshe Dayan later described General Anders as the 'father of the Israeli army'. The Jewish Brigade was commanded by Brigadier E F Benjamin, a British regular officer with Canadian roots; his command included a variety of Jews from Russia, the Yemen, Poland, Hungary, Italy and France as well as Britain.

Freyberg's 2nd New Zealand Division had created a third infantry brigade by converting the divisional cavalry, the Motor and Machine-gun Battalions to infantry. The division also received reinforcements from home allowing the repatriation of those soldiers with three years' active service.* The divisional commander remained in place until the end of the

---

* Reinforcements included many men from 3rd New Zealand Division which had fought in the Pacific theatre but had been repatriated in February 1944. First New Zealand Division remained at home as a defence force.

war, thus achieving a record of five years' command in seven countries under nine superior commanders.

In February 2 Commando (formerly Special Service) Brigade rejoined Eighth Army with 2 and 9 Army Commandos, 40 and 43 Royal Marine Commandos and the Special Boat Service. The following month 2 Parachute Brigade, including 4th, 5th and 6th Parachute Battalions, returned from Greece in time to take part in Eighth Army's final operations in Italy.

During that final winter of war in Italy the Allied armies had a persistent morale problem. The worst was probably over by the beginning of February 1945 but it had been caused by the

> imminence of victory, the coming hard-to-imagine outbreak of peace, with the apparently subsidiary nature of the Italian campaign [which all] combined to depress. Desertions increased sharply. Survival looked more attractive than suffering, and the latter's value was questioned.[20]

Desertion had been a problem for some time, peaking in March 1944 due to the strain of service at Anzio, and again in June during the advance to Rome. However, it was at its worst in November and December 1944 with 1,200 British soldiers posted as absent without leave or deserters in each month. At its peak the problem was costing the equivalent of the infantry strength of a division that had been in the line for some time with another division needed to guard captured deserters. The highest number imprisoned in Italy at any time was 5,150.[21]

Deserters fell into three general categories: the two main types were straightforward cowards, 'those who will not take it', who could only have been deterred by the death penalty, which had been abolished for desertion in 1939; 'those that cannot take it',[22] men who had reached the limit of their personal quota of courage but could sometimes be rehabilitated by careful handling within their own units, although that might have an adverse effect on other men; and those who felt no sense of identity within a unit. The last category was a particular problem in Italy as the reinforcement system sent men to units unconnected to their parent regiments; these often included casualties returned from convalescence. Converting AA gunners, RAF men and some naval personnel into infantry could not always be guaranteed to be successful. In some instances, where the members of an AA battery were kept together as a company, there could be success in producing a good sub-unit. In other cases there was less of a problem: some LAA units had earlier been converted from infantry battalions and had maintained regimental distinctions, thus making the process of converting to infantry that much easier.

But discipline held for the majority of the troops whose

spirit was now immune to whatever the fates might do – like Wellington's men in the Peninsula, or Lee's or Napoleon's, or any others long together. I think it was Stonewall Jackson who said in Virginia, 'It is fortunate that war is so horrible . . . otherwise we might grow to like it.' Like it? Never – but our soldiers had grown accustomed to it, and some of us had forgotten what any other life was like.[23]

Good leadership at all levels counted for much, especially when soldiers knew about the many shortages that existed: 25-pounder ammunition was rationed to five rounds per gun each day; medium machine guns were restricted to 100 rounds per day and mortar crews to four bombs per day. The only exceptions were for defensive fire tasks.

And there was a swipe at Eighth Army's morale from an unexpected source: a member of parliament. The MP concerned was Lady Astor who was alleged to have called troops in Italy the D-Day Dodgers. Eighth Army's cartoonist, Jon, quickly produced a cartoon for the Army newspaper depicting his famous 'Two Types' sitting in a jeep festooned with names such as Salerno and Anzio and wondering which D Day they had dodged. One battalion commander, Bala Bredin of 2nd London Irish, decorated his jeep in like fashion, to the chagrin of some in higher quarters while songs and poems were produced on the same theme. The best-known of the latter was a ballad called 'D-Day Dodgers' (*see* Appendix V) sung to the tune of 'Lili Marlene', itself almost Eighth Army's anthem.

One version of the Lady Astor story is that she received a letter from soldiers in Italy signed 'D-Day Dodgers' which she, mistakenly, assumed to be a unit nickname and repeated either in a speech or in a letter. Fortunately little harm was done: the soubriquet was adopted almost as a badge of pride by Eighth Army in much the same fashion that the BEF of 1914 adopted the title 'Old Contemptibles'.

Richard McCreery's own handling of Eighth Army at this time did much to build confidence and morale. His use of dismounted cavalry regiments to hold sections of the winter line, allowing infantry units to rest and recuperate, was but one element of that. His preparation for the forthcoming offensive was another: without the showmanship of a Montgomery he imbued Eighth Army with a level of confidence probably as great as at any time in its existence. For McCreery was determined that Eighth Army would succeed while giving his soldiers the best possible chances of survival. He was, in the words of John Strawson, a veteran of the Italian campaign the greatest cavalry soldier of his generation and at the same time that rare coalition of a brilliant staff officer and higher commander.[24]

NOTES

1. Blaxland: *Alexander's Generals*, p.226
2. ibid
3. Fraser, *And We Shall Shock Them*, pp.356-357
4. Blaxland, op cit, p.226
5. Molony et al: *The Mediterranean and the Middle East, vol vi, Pt I*, pp.444-447
6. Williamson: *The Fourth Division*, p.284
7. ibid, p.289
8. Peniakoff: *Popski's Private Army*, pp.406-407
9. Supreme Allied Commander, Mediterranean: *Report on the Italian Campaign, Pt III*, p.87
10. Anders: *An Army in Exile*, p.235
11. ibid
12. Blaxland, op cit, p.232
13. Smyth: *The Story of the Victoria Cross*, pp.412-413
14. Blaxland, op cit, p.233
15. ibid, p.235
16. ibid, p.241
17. Danchev; *Very Special Relationship*, pp.77-78 et seq
18. Kesselring: *Memoirs*, p.218
19. Howarth: *My God, Soldiers*, p.198
20. Fraser: op cit, p.357
21. Blaxland, op cit, p.221
22. PRO: WO170/4466, *Morale*, notes by Brig TPD Scott
23. Horsfall, *Fling Our Banner to the Wind*, pp.212-213
24. Strawson, *The Italian Campaign*, pp.183-184

CHAPTER XVIII
The Final Blow: Spring 1945
Now thrive the armourers

In the three-month period between the ending of active operations by 15 Army Group and the opening of the spring offensive in April, continual engagements occurred between the protagonists. The Canadian historian[1] recorded that, in late December, Canadian soldiers found an order from Heidrich, the Fallschirmjäger Corps* commander which told the German paras that fighting should never cease and that 'The "leave me alone and I will leave you alone" attitude must be entirely absent'. German soldiers proved especially active in small-scale operations that allowed their opponents little chance to relax.

Eighth Army's soldiers were not to be intimidated and frequently took the fight to the enemy. Daily press communiqués related that

> 'patrols were active on the Italian front' and few but the front-line soldier knew what those words meant in danger, in toil and in the hardships of rain, mud, snow, and cold. The patrols supplied a steady stream of prisoners – and of information.[2]

In many ways conditions were similar to those of the Great War on the western front with their routine of patrols, raids and harassing small-arms and mortar fire. That similarity was accentuated by the proximity of the opposing front lines which were separated only by the width of the Senio, and sometimes not even by that as the Germans continued to hold some outposts on Eighth Army's side. Such positions were usually on the reverse side of the British-held floodbank. Those banks were often up to thirty feet high and about ten feet wide at the top, although the river itself was less than twenty feet across.

Along the Senio the Canadians carried out their last duties in Italy as part of Eighth Army.

---

* The two divisions which made up I Fallschirmjäger Corps had been brought up to a combined strength of 30,000 men and most of Army Group C's other remaining divisions were reinforced to almost full strength during the winter.

. . . until the end of their war in Italy, the Patricias engaged in static warfare along the Senio, patrolling and raiding. As one remarked, 'If it had not been for the weather, we'd have enjoyed it'. There were many successes and one notable disaster. Two platoons of C Company raided a group of buildings on the Fosso Vecchio after a heavy artillery concentration. The enemy fled and as the Patricias entered the first of the buildings, a delayed charge brought it down on their heads. When others ran to dig them out, the enemy brought down a devastating mortar concentration. The action cost thirty-seven casualties.[3]

Since the Senio meanders considerably, the river's many loops meant that each side could have the local advantage of being able to see behind the other's lines. Where the Germans held positions on the reverse side of a British-held floodbank, they constructed bridges or rafts to allow them to man or reinforce those positions. With the German bridges so close to British troops it was often impossible to bring artillery fire to bear on them but the infantry themselves devised a method of bombarding the bridges: by using the unloved PIATs as mortars.

During daylight opposing troops normally kept their heads down so as not to invite sniper fire. Darkness was the signal for an intensification of activity

when we kept up a continuous fusillade of small arms, grenades, 2 in mortars and a new use for the PIAT – fired as a mortar. The bomb made quite a noise falling and must have proved unnerving to the opposition.[4]

Amongst platoon weapons in constant use . . . was the 2" mortar. . . . In order to reduce the range . . . and bring targets 40-75 yards away into effective range, half the propellant charge from the cartridge . . . was removed. Mortar crews became very proficient at hitting close-range targets on the opposite bank. . . . On the Senio [the PIAT] was used as a mortar and fired at high angle. PIAT bombs exploding on the roof of a dugout could cause damage and severe shock waves underneath and its blast effect was quite considerable.[5]

The Germans launched frequent attacks on the British positions, some-times tunnelling through the floodbank to do so, although this was often reciprocated by the defenders. Newly arrived units were most at risk from German raiders as 56th Reconnaissance Regiment discovered when they relieved 44 Recce: less than an hour later German infantry attacked with grenades and machine guns while mortars bombarded the centre troop position. Three men were killed, four wounded and five taken prisoner in a short-lived raid.

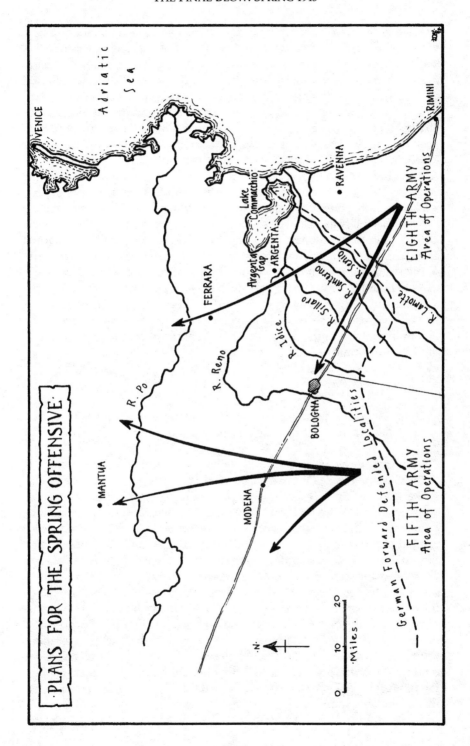

PLANS FOR THE SPRING OFFENSIVE

Another weapon favoured by the Germans was propaganda. Units holding the Senio line found themselves being bombarded with paper, the leaflets warning the British soldiers of the dangers that lay before them on the Po, a river, according to the propaganda, that was worse than all previous river crossings combined. Other leaflets suggested that American servicemen in Britain were making free with the wives and girlfriends of the British soldiers who manned the Senio line. There was even broadcast propaganda with specific mention of Eighth Army units. Recforce, 44 Recce and 12th Royal Lancers came in for some of this in early April. A broadcast which suggested that 'someone out of uniform at home is taking your job; they are not longing for your return so die quicker pal'[6] was brought to an end by a quick burst of artillery fire.

Such was the picture along the Senio as winter turned to spring in 1945. Behind the line preparations for Operation GRAPESHOT, the spring offensive, were gathering pace. Mark Clark had intended to give Fifth Army the major role in the forthcoming operations, assigning subsidiary tasks to Eighth Army which he believed to be worn out. He was dissuaded of this idea by his two army commanders. Both Truscott and McCreery had given considerable thought to renewed offensive operations and were determined that Fifth and Eighth Armies should have the destruction of the German armies in the field as their objective, whereas Clark's eyes were set, again, on a territorial objective: the capture of Bologna by US divisions of Fifth Army.

The final plan was not a compromise, a course invariably fatal, but contained the inputs of two highly professional army commanders.[7]

The 15 Army Group plan was for a double encirclement, a strategy known to the Germans as *Keil und Kessel*, or 'wedge and trap'. Fifth Army was to strike into the Emilian plain, west of Route 64, with IV Corps before sidestepping II Corps on to an axis west of Bologna. Truscott planned that one wing of Fifth would advance towards Verona; the other would strike north before swinging east behind Bologna and south of the Po. For Eighth Army, McCreery proposed to strike northwards to cross the Po but Clark, lacking confidence both in Eighth Army and its commander, ordered McCreery to strike eastwards on Route 9; he considered a breakthrough in Eighth Army's Adriatic sector unlikely and seems to have felt that the best McCreery could do would be to draw Army Group C's reserves away from Truscott. However, Eighth Army's operation, BUCKLAND, was to start on 9 April with the entire Allied air effort dedicated to its support until the 12th when Fifth Army was due to open its offensive, CRAFTSMAN. (On 6 February McCreery had requested maximum air support 'in view of the fact that the over-all striking power of my Army has been materially curtailed by recent decisions'.[8]) In the event McCreery and Eighth Army were to prove Clark entirely wrong with an operation that ranks as one of Eighth Army's finest.

McCreery's plan showed imagination and great care. Eighth Army's left flank was in the mountains with its right facing Lake Comacchio; the centre was barred by eastward flowing rivers, especially the Reno into which most of the others flow. Looping behind Bologna before sweeping east and then south into the Adriatic, the Reno was a formidable obstacle. Another obstacle had been created by the Germans who had flooded much of the low land west of Lake Comacchio. But there was one weak spot in the German defences: a corridor of land running north-west to Argenta carrying Route 16 was free of any obstruction by water between the Reno and Comacchio's southern shore. This Argenta Gap, surveyed by McCreery from an artillery spotter plane, became the fulcrum of his effort to destroy the enemy's defences.

Instead of obstructing Eighth Army's movement, Lake Comacchio would be used to assist that movement. McCreery had obtained enough armoured, tracked assault vehicles* to equip a brigade. Codenamed Fantails these vehicles would enable Eighth Army to use Comacchio as a route on which to attack the Germans; the lake would cease to be an obstacle to manoeuvre. Thus Eighth Army would throw a right hook at the Germans. The Fantails were added to the Kangaroos in the Army inventory as were Duplex Drive amphibious tanks, DDs, such as had been used in Normandy.

> Armoured regiments were re-equipped with flame-thrower tanks, up-gunned Sherman and Churchill tanks, and with tank-dozers. Some . . . tanks were fitted with widened 'Platypus' tracks to enable them to move over the soft fields of the Romagna. New armoured engineer equipment was also produced within the theatre for rapidly bridging ditches, canals and rivers. All these new equipments and devices needed specially trained crews to man them and new tactical techniques. In the rear areas, particularly round Lake Trasimene, intensive experimental work and training went on throughout the winter.[9]

Infantry divisions out of the line underwent concentrated training programmes and divisional battle schools were set up. Since McCreery's

---

* Landing vehicles, tracked, or LVsT, which had been developed by US forces in the Pacific and used in north-west Europe by the Canadians where they were known as Buffaloes.Their use had impressed McCreery and Alexander who sought 600 of the vehicles to carry three assault brigades in the Po valley. Only 400 were allocated to be divided between the two armies but 15 Army Group offered the loan of the American LVsT to Eighth Army. The codename *Fantail* was intended to hide the true nature of the vehicles for as long as possible.

plan involved a sharp, rapid thrust through the Argenta Gap with infantry carried in Kangaroos, the units selected for this operation had to undergo special training. The division tasked with the Argenta operation was 78th, now returned with XIII Corps from Fifth Army and re-allocated to V Corps, commanded by Charles Keightley, its former divisional commander. The Battleaxe Division was to be heavily reinforced for the operation with 2 Armoured Brigade under command while 4th Hussars, who had converted to Kangaroos, trained the infantry in operations with armoured personnel carriers.

Previous experience in crossing water obstacles, and the knowledge that many more such obstacles lay ahead, led to a proposal by Brigadier B T Godfrey-Fausett, Eighth Army's new Chief Engineer, that the existing assault engineer regiment be upgraded to a brigade. Thus 25 Army Tank Brigade was reformed as 25 Armoured Assault Brigade, Royal Engineers, bringing tanks and sappers together. The reconstituted brigade included flamethrowing Churchills, called Crocodiles, mine-destroying Flails, bridging tanks and dozers. Due to problems of supply from the UK, REME workshops in the Mediterranean theatre carried out local conversions to produce almost 200 specialised armoured vehicles to equip 25 Brigade which included 51 RTR and 1st and 2nd Armoured Engineer Regiments, previously 1st Assault Regiment, RAC/RE and 1st Armoured Divisional Engineers.[10](*See* Appendix III)

The artillery was well prepared for its task: 1,020 guns had been assembled and a supply of 2,000,000 rounds of ammunition was available. But, more than that, massive air support was also being provided which included not only fighter-bombers and medium bombers but USAAF strategic bombers based in Italy whose targets in Germany had been overrun by the Soviets. General Traugott Herr, commanding Tenth Army, decided to establish his main defensive line along the Santerno river, beyond the range of Eighth Army's gunners, while maintaining a forward line along the Senio. In so doing he unwittingly assisted in the success of McCreery's plan as the Allied strategic bombers were able to pound the Santerno line mercilessly while artillery bombarded the Senio line. The artillery had also produced a further aid to the assaulting infantry: searchlight regiments, mostly redundant in their original role, were deployed to provide artificial moonlight, first used in 1944, to assist the movement of troops during the hours of darkness; the glare of the searchlights also had a detrimental effect on the vision of the opposing troops.[11]

Air co-operation was improved with the Rover Control teams that provided direct links with the fighter-bombers of the aerial cab-rank service being increased in number and given added mobility with scout cars or tanks. Closer contact with battalion or brigade commanders would permit almost immediate strikes on targets as required. Light aircraft, which had been available to artillery observers in Italy for some time, also proved a valuable asset.

Once again a deception plan was used to convince the Germans that Eighth Army was preparing an amphibious attack north of Venice. Although that area of coast was entirely unsuitable for such an operation, both offshore and on land, and most Allied landing craft had already been withdrawn from the Mediterranean, the Germans accepted the possibility of such a landing and 29th Panzer Division was moved to cover against that eventuality. The deception was aided by a simulated concentration of II Corps behind Eighth Army's right wing and by naval operations in the Adriatic. With no experience of amphibious operations the Germans were not to know that they were guarding against an illusion. The deception plan had the added advantage of disguising preparations for the crossing of Lake Comacchio.

The Comacchio operation was to be entrusted to 56th Division with 2 Commando Brigade under command as well as 9 Armoured Brigade. The former included the Special Boat Service, as well as 28 Garibaldi Brigade of Italian partisans, in addition to its four commandos. All were part of V Corps, to which was entrusted the main attack: while 56th crossed Comacchio, 8th Indian and 2nd New Zealand Divisions were to attack across the Senio and Santerno; once a bridgehead over the latter had been established, 78th Division was to cross, strike rapidly to its right for the bridge over the Reno at Bastia, link up with 56th Division and clear the Argenta corridor. That would allow 6th Armoured Division to commence an armoured thrust, part of which would swing westwards to link up with Fifth Army. Once V Corps had split in two, HQ XIII Corps, under Harding, was to take command of the left wing. Eighth Army's direct thrust to Bologna on Route 9 would be undertaken by II Polish Corps, commanded by General Bohusz-Szyszko as Anders had been promoted CinC of Polish forces, and XIII Corps. But before operations began, McCreery had to resolve a major problem with the Poles.

The results of the Yalta Conference, at which Soviet intransigence over Poland's future eastern frontier had held sway over the western Allies, had been a bitter blow to the Polish soldiers, and to Anders himself. At one point Anders threatened to withdraw his men from Eighth Army,* suggesting to McCreery that they be made PoWs, but relented in the face of the latter's persuasion and query as to what might be done to fill the gap that the Poles' departure would leave in Eighth Army's line.[12] To demonstrate his confidence in II Polish Corps, McCreery assigned 7 Armoured Brigade and 43 Gurkha Brigade Group to it. Together with reinforcements already received, which allowed the formation of third

---

* Anders had earlier proposed the transfer of II Polish Corps to north-west Europe.

brigades within the Carpathian and Kresowa Divisions, this increased the size of the Corps to almost twice its strength at Cassino.[13]

During March Hitler decided to replace Gert von Rundstedt as commander of German forces in the west and his choice as replacement was Kesselring who left Italy to take up his new command on 23 March,[14] just in time for Operation PLUNDER, the Rhine crossing. Once again Kesselring's replacement in Italy was von Vietinghoff, recalled from the Baltic; Lemelsen returned to the command of Fourteenth Army with Herr commanding Tenth Army. It was von Vietinghoff who decided that Eighth Army might make an amphibious assault north of Venice and accordingly moved 29th Panzer Division there.

The Germans ranged against Eighth Army still represented a formidable foe. Tenth Army's LXXVI Panzer and I Fallschirmjäger Corps each deployed four divisions on Eighth Army's front; 305th Infantry Division of I Fallschirmjäger Corps was arrayed against II US Corps. The move north of Venice of 29th Panzer Division took it some eighty miles away from Argenta, and cost precious fuel, while Army Group C's reserve division, 90th Panzer Grenadier, was some sixty miles to the west, having been moved to counter a Fifth Army offensive in February.

Eighth Army's deployment at the beginning of April included V Corps on the right flank with 56th Division,* the Cremona Group, 8th Indian Division, 78th Division and 2nd New Zealand Division. In addition to brigades, such as the Commandos and 2 and 9 Armoured† which were assigned to some of these divisions, the Corps also included 21 Tank Brigade. Astride Route 9 was II Polish Corps with 3rd Carpathian and 5th Kresowa Divisions augmented by 7 Armoured and 43 Gurkha Brigades as well as 2 Polish Armoured Brigade. In a holding role from the Poles' left flank to south of Imola was X Corps, consisting only of the Jewish Brigade and the Friuli Group, while XIII Corps deployed from south of Imola to Monte Grande with the Folgore Group and 10th Indian Division. In reserve were 6th Armoured Division and 2 Parachute Brigade. The latter was to drop behind the German lines but, although some thirty different plans were drawn up, it was not deployed because of the strength of German anti-aircraft defences.

Easter Sunday fell on 1 April in 1945 and that evening the first element in McCreery's plan was put into operation. Men of 2 and 9 Commandos took to the waters of Lake Comacchio with the objective of eliminating enemy observation of Eighth Army's right flank from the spit that divides the

* The division now included 24 Guards Brigade in place of 168 Brigade.
† This brigade included 755 (US) Tank Battalion.

lake from the Adriatic. There was initial frustration as the Fantails foundered in slime but stormboats, twenty-foot long, flat-bottomed and plywood, were brought into use. Each carrying twenty men, these raced across Comacchio, following navigation lights laid out by M Squadron SBS under Major Anders Lassen; as dawn broke, the commandos landed on the spit and, in spite of an artillery bombardment, found the enemy unprepared for an assault. The noise of the stormboats' approach had been drowned by several measures: RAF bombers circled above the area; tanks drove up and down the lateral road behind the front line; and No. 40 Commando, at the spit's base, played Wagner over a loudspeaker.

Coinciding with the Army commandos' attack, 40 and 43 RM Commandos had attacked across the Reno to clear the spit's east side. No. 43 Commando made good use of 4th Hussars' Kangaroos in their operation to overcome resistance in a strongly fortified area.

> After two days, despite rifle, machine gun, mortar and artillery fire, and many mines, the whole spit was in our hands, along with nearly 1000 prisoners. Small enemy outposts on islands in the lake were also wiped out.[15]

The commando operations, ROAST (the main effort) and FRY (the seizure of the islands on Comacchio) included a series of outstanding actions. Nos 1 and 2 Troops of 9 Commando took one strongly defended post, codenamed 'Leviticus', by attacking across 150 yards of open ground against heavy machine-gun fire and led by a piper playing *The Road to the Isles*; the position was captured with nearly a hundred prisoners.

On Easter Tuesday, 2 and 43 Commandos were ordered to resume the advance with armour support. Moving off at 2pm, 2 Commando were pinned after 1,000 yards by heavy artillery and mortar fire; 43 went on to clear the village of Scaglioca and advanced towards the Valetta canal where C Troop, leading, came under heavy fire. At that point Corporal Tom Hunter

> who was in charge of a Bren gun section, offered himself as a target to save his troop. Seizing the Bren gun he charged alone across 200 yards of open ground under most intense fire towards a group of houses where three Spandau machine-guns were lodged. So determined was his charge that the enemy were demoralized and six of the gunners surrendered, the remainder fled. He cleared the house, changing magazines as he ran and continued to draw the enemy fire until most of the troop had reached cover and he was killed, firing accurately to the last.[16]

Hunter was posthumously awarded the Victoria Cross. The Commandos were relieved by 24 Guards Brigade who secured their gains and made some offensive moves against Porto Garibaldi.

A second posthumous VC was earned in the aftermath of Operation FRY, the clearance of the islands in Lake Comacchio, when Major Anders Lassen, MC (and two Bars) of M Squadron SBS began a series of raids on the German-held shore. On the night of 8/9 April Lassen led a raid on Comacchio town which came up against a blockhouse. This was engaged and the enemy soldiers surrendered, but as Lassen went forward to secure them, a Spandau on the other side of the causeway between Porto Garibaldi and Comacchio opened up. Lassen was among the wounded as a firefight developed, leading to further casualties. He decided to withdraw but it was impossible to recover the wounded due to heavy enemy fire. All those fit enough to pull back were ordered to do so but

> Lassen refused to allow his men to evacuate him as he said it would impede the withdrawal and endanger their lives. But he had certainly achieved his object; three enemy positions were wiped out, six machine guns destroyed, eight of the enemy were killed, several more wounded and two prisoners were taken.[17]

Lassen gave covering fire until he was killed. Two of the wounded managed to escape and Lassen, a Dane who had begun the war as a merchant sailor, was posthumously awarded the Victoria Cross.

On the night of 5/6 April, 167 Brigade of 56th Division, with 1st London Irish leading, crossed the Reno westwards from San Alberto. The objective was to drive a wedge between the Reno floodbank and the flooded area west of Lake Comacchio thus securing a slime-free launching point for the Fantails. Although the initial crossing was made without opposition, and two troops of 10th Hussars' Shermans were rafted over, Jägers of 42nd Division later went into action, firing from pillboxes and inflicting considerable loss, especially on 167 Brigade's accompanying sappers. Nonetheless the brigade succeeded in hammering in their wedge as planned and V Corps' right flank was secure.

All was now ready for Eighth Army to begin its offensive, Operation BUCKLAND. Morale was high and a sense of purpose pervaded the Army; the number of soldiers reported absent in April 1945 was the lowest for any month since the landing in Italy. McCreery had issued an order of the day in which he declared that the Germans

> must not be allowed to use his Armies in Italy to form a garrison for a Southern German stronghold. . . . We will destroy or capture the enemy south of the Po.[18]

McCreery's order of the day was short and to the point. The Army Commander knew his soldiers well and had earlier described Eighth Army as being like 'an old steeplechaser, full of running, but rather careful' and he intended to use its strengths to advantage. Alexander also issued an order of the day in which he pointed out that the turn of the armies in Italy to play their part in the final defeat of Germany had arrived; but he stressed that it 'would not be a walk-over' as a mortally wounded beast could still be dangerous.

At 1.50pm on 9 April an aerial bombardment by 825 Flying Fortress and Liberator heavy bombers of the US Fifteenth Strategic Air Force began. In the ninety minutes that followed they dropped 125,000 fragmentation bombs on the German artillery lines and reserve areas in front of Eighth Army's assaulting corps. Aided by carefully devised navigational aids, including a bomb, or marker, line of smoke shells fired by 3.7-inch heavy AA guns, they 'completely drenched' their target areas. At the same time over 600 medium bombers were attacking defensive locations and troop concentrations back towards the Santerno, to which river the heavies would turn their attention on the 10th, while the tactical air forces, the US XXII Air Support Command and the British Desert Air Force, deploying 720 aircraft, hit command posts, gun and mortar positions and strongpoints right on the forward edge of the enemy line. As many as fifteen planes might swoop on a single tank, thus emphasising the absolute supremacy of the Allies in the air.

The aerial attacks were followed by a tremendous artillery and mortar bombardment by 1,500 guns over a forty-two minute period. Naturally the defenders expected the ending of this bombardment to signal the opening of the attack. Instead the fighter-bombers returned to strafe the river banks before switching their attention to the area behind the river, at which point the guns and mortars opened fire again. This hurricane of artillery, mortars, bombs and rockets lasted for five-and-a-half hours during which the Germans experienced four 'false alarm' bombardments.

At 7.20pm there was another false alarm; but this time it came from the fighter-bombers which swooped down as if to strafe the riverbank. The aircraft did not open fire but Wasp and Crocodile flame-throwers opened their jets and poured flame across the river. It was a spectacular display and, although it probably did little physical damage to the German troops, it certainly sapped the morale of many; by contrast it was a morale-booster for the assaulting troops. After ten minutes of assault by fire, the leading troops of Eighth Army stepped forward to do battle.

In V Corps the assault divisions were 8th Indian and 2nd New Zealand, each attacking with four battalions across the Senio in what was now a purely infantry battle. Eighth Indian was on the right, separated from the New Zealanders by the five miles of river that curved around Lugo: its attack was led by 19 Brigade, on the right, with 1st Argylls and 6/13th Royal Frontier Force Rifles forward and 21 Brigade with 1/5th Mahratta LI and 3/15th Punjabis forward.

The leading companies took their objective, the smoke-shrouded forward floodbank, easily enough but, as the following companies passed through, defending soldiers of 362nd Division, recovering their poise, left their dug-outs to man weapons. The Frontier Force Rifles and Mahrattas, in the divisional centre near Fusignano, faced the most determined resistance but each battalion produced a heroic individual who ensured that the advance went ahead.

The Frontier Force company had dropped its assault boats and waded into the Senio, which was about fifteen feet wide and four deep at that point. Heavy machine-gun fire met them and only three men of the left platoon reached the far bank in a state to take cover and contribute to the battle. One of the three, Sepoy Ali Haidar, with covering fire from his two comrades, attacked a German machine-gun post.

> Having hurled a grenade, he was immediately hit in the back by a shell splinter from a German grenade. He lurched onwards, captured the machine-gun and four wounded Germans, and at once assailed another post, from which multiple automatic fire was coming. He was felled by two further hits, on an arm and a leg, and yet managed to crawl forward, hurl a grenade with his left hand and flop upon the post in a state of collapse, to receive the surrender of two unharmed and two badly wounded Germans.[19]

Incredibly Ali Haidar survived to receive the Victoria Cross he had so clearly earned. His efforts had allowed the remainder of his battalion to continue the attack and, as darkness deepened, they chased the enemy from his hides on both sides of the far floodbank.

The Mahrattas had also waded the river and Sepoy Namdeo Jadhao, a company runner, was the only man from his group to reach the enemy bank unscathed. There his first action was to carry a wounded man back across the river and up the east floodbank. He then returned and brought another wounded man to safety, all the while under enemy fire from both banks. Having rescued the wounded, which was valour enough, he returned singlehanded to the attack, determined to avenge his dead comrades, and

> made lone assault with a Tommy-gun, wiped out one post on the first bank, was wounded in the hand, and wiped out two more posts by hurling grenades. He then galvanised the remains of the company (whose commander had been wounded next to him in the initial crossing) by cheering them on [by shouting the Mahratta war cry] from

the top of the bank with mortar bombs falling fast around him.[20]

Namdeo Jadhao's actions not only saved many lives but also enabled the Mahrattas to secure their bridgehead and overcome all resistance in the area. He, too, was awarded the Victoria Cross and survived to receive it.*

By dawn 8th Indian had advanced a mile and a half beyond the river, although fighting had lasted all night in some places, while the sappers had put three bridges across the river which allowed Churchills of 21 Tank Brigade to join the infantry. Supported by the tanks, and with further efforts from the air forces, 19 and 21 Brigades were at the Santerno, almost four miles beyond the Senio, as day broke on the 11th. Lugo was liberated that day by 1st Jaipur Infantry who were welcomed by the mayor brandishing a bottle of wine and a white flag. Seven Brigade also moved up ready for the crossing of the Santerno. Italian soldiers were also in the picture: the Cremona Group had crossed the Senio and was advancing towards Alfonsine through Fusignano.

By then the New Zealanders were already across the Santerno which they had reached after nightfall on the 10th. At dawn next day, 25th and 24th Battalions, of 6 Brigade, crossed the Santerno and 28th (Maori) Battalion, of 5 Brigade, then pushed out the bridgehead on the right flank. In making their five-mile advance four New Zealander battalions, the fourth was 21st, of 5 Brigade, had eliminated three battalions from 98th Division and caused severe hurt to the remaining three. With fewer than 200 casualties themselves, some of them from Allied bombs which had fallen short at the Santerno, Freyberg's men had taken over 700 prisoners.

A crucial factor in the speed of the New Zealand advance had been the work of the divisional engineers. Colonel Hanson, Freyberg's CRE, had brought bridging equipment as far forward as possible and had then either built bridges on site and floated them across on rafts or had assembled girders, launched them on a raft and pushed them across as construction continued. With forty- to fifty-foot long bridges being completed in between thirty-five minutes and an hour, the New Zealand sappers had five tank bridges across the Senio by 6.30am on the 10th. By contrast, 8th Indian had one and the Poles none. The speed of the New Zealanders' advance, however, had exposed both divisional flanks: 8th Indian had yet to come up on the right flank while II Polish Corps was farther behind on the left.

---

* In Fifth Army two posthumous Medals of Honour were won by PFC Sadao S Munemori, a Nisei or Japanese-American, of 442nd (Nisei) Infantry, on 5 April and PFC J D Magrath of 85th Mountain Infantry on 14 April. These two Medals of Honour and the two VCs emphasise the multi-national character of 15 Army Group with awards going to a Hindu, a Muslim, a Japanese-American and an Irish-American.

On the Polish front the crossing of the Senio had been assigned to 3rd Carpathian Division using its original pair of brigades to which had been added 6 Lwow Brigade from Kresowa Division; the Corps' two new brigades were in a holding position astride Route 9. The Carpathians ran into difficulties even before they moved off: an American heavy bomber dropped its bombs on the Poles' forming-up positions, causing 160 casualties in one battalion. (Anders was watching the bombing with Clark and, in response to the latter's apology, commented that soldiers do not like to become casualties before entering battle.) Although this did not delay the time of the advance the Carpathians ran into uncleared German mines on their half-mile approach to the Senio, an area from which they had not previously cleared the Germans.

Undeterred, the Poles forced a crossing of the river and two brigades were over the Senio by the morning of the 10th. The Polish attack was directed at an inter-corps boundary: the junction between 98th Division of LXXVI Panzer Corps and 26th Panzer of I Fallschirmjäger Corps. Schlemm, the Fallschirmjäger commander, was forced to adjust his front to take the brunt of the Polish attack while General Graf von Schwerin, commanding LXXVI Corps and the first German general to fight in the desert, struggled to make a cohesive force from the remnants of 98th and 362nd Divisions. Against stiff resistance the Poles did not reach the Santerno until the night of 11 April, a day after the New Zealanders.

As the New Zealanders crossed the Santerno on the morning of the 11th, 169 Queen's Brigade of 56th Division were crossing Lake Comacchio in Fantails crewed by men of 27th Lancers and the US 755th Tank Battalion. Eighty Fantails, carrying 2/5th and 2/6th Queen's, were approaching the villages of Menate and Longastrino at the edge of the flooded area west of the lake.

> Launching problems delayed their departure, but a smokescreen, fired from guns mounted in the Fantails, successfully shrouded their arrival in full daylight. Few shots were fired at them as their great square hulks gradually rose out of the water and trundled through the slush to emit their loads. Each of the leading ones carried a small platoon, and its men leapt out with a machine-gun blazing from the Fantail's forward turret.[21]

The Fantails had given 169 Brigade the initiative over 42nd Jäger Division, of whom 300 men were captured with little loss from the two assaulting battalions. Believing the flooded area to be impassable the defenders were completely unbalanced by this new development and by an attack from an unexpected direction. Exploitation of these gains was assigned to 40 Commando who advanced towards a bridge north of Menate by wading along a ditch. However, the Germans were beginning to recover and, although the bridge was taken, the Marines suffered considerable losses.

When 8th Indian Division's 17 Brigade attacked across the Santerno on the evening of the 11th, they too met determined opposition and it was only with great difficulty and many losses that 1/5th Gurkhas and 1/12th Frontier Force each obtained a foothold on the far bank. Those lodgements were linked by 1st Royal Fusiliers upon whom the fury of a German counter-attack fell the following morning. The situation was grim with enemy tanks and infantry pressing upon the Fusiliers but relief arrived at 11.30am in the shape of Churchills from 21 Tank Brigade which had crossed the river by an Ark bridge. The Fusiliers went on to take what was left of Mondaniga; the bombing had reduced the village to rubble.

Throughout the 12th the New Zealanders fought hard and were in the outskirts of Massa Lombarda by dusk. Freyberg's men were now fourteen miles south of Argenta while their advance, with its axis parallel to Route 9, also threatened Bologna. They had

> succeeded both in gaining ground from which to make an outflanking attack on Argenta and in creating a diversion from it. Furthermore, the diversion could readily be switched to main effort if the drive on Argenta failed, and as GOC 13th Corps, Harding had already been warned that the New Zealanders might be transferred to his command, for operations in concert with 10th Indian Division.[22]

It was now time for 78th Division to pass through the bridgeheads created by the assaulting divisions. At the same time, Keightley planned to hit the enemy from the north as well, employing 56th Division and the Fantails to carry out a further outflanking movement over lake and flood. On this occasion 24 Guards Brigade were ordered to seize Argenta; their right flank would be protected by 2 Parachute Brigade who would be dropped around Bando. By the morning of the 13th, a Friday, 1st Buffs, who had taken the place of 5th Grenadiers in 24 Guards Brigade, were ready to move off in their Fantails.* The Buffs' objective was the Fossa Marina, two miles in front of 169 Queen's Brigade's foremost positions; the battalion was to seize the Fossa's banks with 9 Commando coming in from their right in another amphibious operation and 2 Para Brigade landing about a mile away.

But, as the para battalions had arrived to board their aircraft the night before, intelligence reports had been received that elements of 26th Panzer Division had been moved to the Fossa Marina. Those reports were confirmed by air reconnaissance which also indicated an increase in AA guns in the area. Since the tactical air forces were unable to divert enough

---

* The Battalion was accompanied by its padre, Rev. G Tyson.[23]

aircraft with Fifth Army's attack beginning at the time, McCreery ordered the cancellation of the airborne assault. Bad as this was, it was further discovered that 9 Commando's route was blocked by a high bank and no suitable diversion was available. The Buffs were to fight alone.

Although artillery support had been arranged for the battalion this was insufficient and the Buffs suffered heavily. C Company's four Fantails fell victim to enemy tanks.

> No opposition was met until the leading LVT was less than 100 yds from the landing point, when it became evident that the enemy was prepared, and determined, to contest the landing. What had appeared to be a house revealed itself as a MkIV Tk, opening up on the leading LVT at point-blank range, and at the same time the remaining vehs were engaged by at least two more Tks on the flank. All LVTs were hit, and, with one exception, all ramps jammed, men coming down under H[eav]y enfilade fire from MGs sited on the Left and Right, as they tried to leave the damaged vehicles.[24]

Of those who made the shore, another thirty-five were hit as they crossed the crest of the bank at the water's edge. The company was re-organised into a platoon and attempted to gain its objectives. Its OC, Major W S Riley, was subsequently ordered to abandon the attack and consolidate. The Germans later offered medical assistance to some of the badly wounded while Major Riley, with his strength down to fifteen to twenty men, decided to withdraw at last light. Thirteen men, with two American crewmen and a prisoner, made it back to their own lines that night.

The other attacking company also met enemy fire but this was less effective than that to their right and a bridge over a canal was taken by Sergeant Whitbread's No.3 Platoon. Lieutenant Aylett's No.2 Platoon cleared houses to Whitbread's flank and took nine prisoners. No immediate reinforcement was forthcoming as the American crewmen of the Fantails had been granted the right to decide where to land and the third company was, therefore, put ashore in safer territory although it still met opposition. A farm was captured, with about 100 Germans and Turcoman SS, and a link-up with the surviving forward company was made after dawn on 14 April although the troops holding the bridge had to wait until that evening when 2nd Coldstream, supported by 10th Hussars, finally reached them by which time Sergeant Whitbread, who had been an AA gunner, held thirty-four enemy prisoners as well as the bridge.

Enemy resistance was now hardening and reconnaissance reports indicated that 29th Panzer Grenadier Division was returning from north of the Po. An attempted crossing of the Fossa Marina by 9 Commando on the night of 14/15 April was repulsed and it seemed clear that there could be no approach to Argenta from the north. Meanwhile 167 and 169 Brigades of 56th Division were converging on Bastia, about five miles south-east of Argenta. On the 14th 2/5th Queen's reached Filo; to their left 9th Fusiliers broke through an extensive minefield.

Although von Vietinghoff had by now realised that he had fallen for a British deception plan and had ordered 29th Panzer Grenadiers back, it was really too late, although the attacking soldiers of Eighth Army were still to meet dour and determined resistance as they pressed on with their advance. Such had been the experience of 56th Division, an experience shared by 78th Division.

Passing through V Corps' bridgehead over the Santerno, 78th Division's task was to crack through the enemy defences and strike for the bridge over the Reno at Bastia, thus providing the southern arm of a pincer movement on that town; 56th Division was the northern arm.

> Experience had taught the Division the policy to lay down for the operations. There were to be no halts at night-fall, for instance, for we had learnt in 1944 that the enemy was often able to re-establish a line or a rearguard position during the night because of our failure to follow up with tanks or infantry during the dark hours.[25]

The division was to advance along the 'line of fewest water-obstacles', aiming at taking important canal crossings, since a captured bridge might save a day, or more. While 11 Brigade held a firm line, the division's other two brigades were to link up with armour and other arms in 'wedding' areas before striking out. The task of breaking out and exploiting was assigned to the Irish Brigade for which it was swollen almost to the size of an armoured division. Brigadier Pat Scott's command now included three elements: a break-out force of two battlegroups each built around a battalion of either Inniskilling or Irish Fusiliers with a squadron of Bays, a machine-gun platoon of 1st Kensingtons, a sapper recce party and either a scissors bridge, for the Irish Fusiliers' group, or a Crocodile squadron of 1 RTR for the Inniskillings';* a mobile force, dubbed *The Kangaroo Army*, under command of HQ 2 Armoured Brigade, with 9th Lancers, 4th Hussars, providing the Kangaroos, a troop of SPGs, an assault troop of sappers, and 2nd London Irish Rifles; and a reserve force for 'special roles' which included another squadron of Bays, an anti-tank battery, a troop of self-propelled anti-tank guns, an armoured sapper troop, a mortar platoon of 1st Kensingtons, a sapper field company and a field ambulance.

---

* After the Trasimene battles in June 1944, 6th Inniskillings had been disbanded and their place in the Irish Brigade had been taken by 2nd Inniskillings, transferred from 13 Brigade of 5th Division.

In immediate support the break-out force deployed two gunner regiments, 17th Field, and 11th (HAC) Regiment RHA.

The Kangaroo Army included more than 100 main tracked vehicles from 9th Lancers and 4th Hussars with each company of the Irish Rifles assigned eight Priest Kangaroos* while Battalion HQ had a further eight, two of which were to carry reserve ammunition and two for medical purposes. Each rifle company vehicle carried sufficient ammunition and food to allow forty-eight hours of independent operations.

The Irish Brigade moved off from its start line at 6.30am on 13 April, its move delayed from the previous evening because of congested tracks and bridges. To their left, 36 Brigade had struck out in the direction of San Patrizio and Conselice in order to provide elbow room and knock the Germans off balance. As the Irish Brigade headed north the Germans were undoubtedly foxed and C Company of the Inniskillings led the breakthrough.

> It was slow and stubborn fighting between the canal on the left and the river Santerno on the right; the road ran . . . up the middle of a triangle the apex of which was where canal and river met, just short of Bastia. There were many enemy strong-points, which became harder to overcome as the front narrowed, and there was particularly hard fighting for both battalions in the villages of San Bernadino and La Giovecca before the order came to consolidate short of Cavamento. The left flank of this main advance was now exposed, for there was a gap between them and the Royal West Kents, in front of Conselice, but this was not the only reason for halting the [Irish] Fusiliers and the Inniskillings; the thrust for Bastia was to be made by the composite Kangaroo Force.[26]

With the two fusilier battalions clearing the way, the Kangaroo Army surged forward at noon against opposition that was, initially, patchy and irresolute. Although there were *Panzerfausten* parties that caused trouble, and one tank was knocked out by an AA gun, the Germans appeared shaken and off balance; the normal determined and cohesive defence was missing.

> The objective of the mobile force was to take the crossings on the Conselice canal and then, if possible, exploit to the Reno. As the leading elements neared the canal the flanking rivers opened out and H Company with C Squadron, 9th Lancers was able to come up on the left of G Company. Some resistance was encountered in the village of La Frascata but this was by-passed. However, just as the leading tanks

---

* The Kangaroos were either de-turreted Sherman tanks or de-gunned Priest SPGs, known as 'de-frocked Priests'.

arrived at the Conselice canal the bridge was destroyed. H Company had also by-passed La Frascata and, quickly de-bussing on the canal banks, forced a crossing over what was left of the road and rail bridge. For this, they had the support of their tanks and got into the houses on the far bank so rapidly that they rounded up most of the defenders.[27]

While G Company cleared the area up to the canal bank, E moved up to clear La Frascata and assist H Company in holding and enlarging the bridgehead over the canal. The three companies had taken eighty prisoners and about ten Germans had been killed by 6.30pm. Soon afterwards the bridgehead was secure and the sappers set about building a new bridge over the canal ready for the morning. The Irish Brigade's other two battalions were holding positions at La Giovecca and west of the Fossatone to protect the divisional flank.

The Kangaroo Army had made a good start and Eighth Army, the old steeplechaser, was proving that it still had the skill and morale needed to inflict defeat on the Germans.

NOTES

1. Nicholson: *The Canadians in Italy, 1943-45*, p. 652
2. HQ, 15 Army Gp: *Finito! The Po Valley Campaign 1945*, p.5
3. Williams: *Princess Patricia's Canadian Light Infantry*, p.63
4. PJC Trousdell: letter to author
5. RJ Robinson: notes to author
6. PRO: WO170/4372, war diary 44 Recce, 1945
7. Graham and Bidwell: *Tug of War*, p.390
8. PRO: CAB106/441, *Operations of British, Indian and Dominion Forces in Italy 3 Sep 43 – 2 May 45; Pt IV The Campaign in Lombardy*
9. Jackson: *The Battle for Italy*, pp.293-294
10. Jackson: *The Mediterranean and the Middle East, vol vi, Pt III*, pp.402-403
11. Routledge: *Anti-Aircraft Artillery, 1914-55*, p.317
12. Anders: *An Army in Exile*, pp.251-254
13. Blaxland, *Alexander's Generals*, p.248
14. Kesselring: *Memoirs*, p.237
15. *Finito!*, op cit, p.12
16. *Register of the Victoria Cross*, p.160
17. Smyth: *The Story of the Victoria Cross*, p.427
18. Blaxland, op cit, p.249
19. ibid, p.257
20. ibid
21. ibid, p.259
22. ibid
23. PRO:WO170/4992, War diary, 1st Buffs, 1945
24. ibid
25. Ray: *Algiers to Austria*, p.201
26. ibid, p.204
27. Doherty: *Clear the Way!*, p.239

CHAPTER XIX
The Final Victory: May 1945
Sound all the lofty instruments of war

In 1965 Sir Richard McCreery, in an interview with Brian Harpur, an Eighth Army veteran, explained that the key to success in battle was simple, provided that four conditions existed:

> One, you must have good intelligence . . . in every sense of the word. . . Two, you must have good organisation – your troops must be well trained, well supplied, and well motivated. Three, you must always have up your sleeve an enormous element of surprise because this can fox the enemy, give you the initiative, save lives, and provide an unforeseen bonus which [it] is up to you to identify and exploit before it disappears. Four – you must never give the enemy any rest. Never let him rest. Always be doing something to which he has to re-act. If you don't then he'll be doing something to which you have to re-act and you have lost the initiative. No, never let him rest. And I mean that literally as well.[1]

To date, in this offensive, McCreery had demonstrated with Eighth Army the practical application of these thoughts. Intelligence, in every sense, had been demonstrated at the planning stage; the Army's organisation was good and morale was at a new high as shown by the desertion figures for April;* the element of surprise had been there, with the enemy fooled by the deception plan and then taken off balance by the deployment of Fantails on Lake Comacchio and the flood lands. And now the enemy was being given no rest.

On 14 April the Kangaroo Army resumed its advance, pushing on towards the Reno river. Near Lavezzola one of its two columns had to sweep to the right to avoid minefields but, although the entire area was heavily mined (and houses in Lavezzola were booby-trapped), the danger

---

* Brian Harpur suggested that the revitalisation of Eighth Army, and of the campaign in Italy, 'was the most unlikely miracle in military history since David slew Goliath'.[2]

was reduced by the fact that the Germans had not had time to remove their own warning signs and the Sherman Crabs were kept busy flailing the minefields to destroy their deadly crop.

At 9.40 that morning 2nd London Irish reached the Reno where, although the road and rail bridges had been demolished, there was sufficient rubble to allow a dryshod crossing. Two platoons crossed to establish a bridgehead but, as they moved forward from the river, they were hit by a counter-attack and over-run; following a fierce fight most were made prisoner. High floodbanks and the absence of a bridge meant that the tanks had been unable to help and, although a reconnaissance was made in preparation for a deliberate crossing, it was decided to hold positions on the near bank for the night. The battalion was later told to maintain those positions for the next two days.

In spite of this setback Keightley was determined to keep V Corps' operation moving. Irish Fusilier patrols moved out to clear the marshland up to the Sillaro river on the 15th, continuing that task until 36 Brigade took it over in the evening. With 56th Division passing across the front of the Irish Brigade towards Bastia and Argenta, bridging began across the Reno and the Irish Brigade was placed on four hours' notice to continue its advance on the morning of the 16th.

In the meantime the New Zealanders had continued their speedy advance with 24th Battalion crossing the Sillaro, seven miles on from the Santerno, on the night of 13/14 April. The Poles had also been pushing hard against the Germans on the road to Bologna and had taken Imola and drawn level with the New Zealanders whose objective was Budrio, some ten miles from Bologna and on an axis diverging from that of the advance on Argenta. From 6pm on the 14th McCreery transferred the New Zealanders from V Corps to XIII Corps which was now between the Poles and V Corps. Harding then moved 10th Indian Division into reserve behind Freyberg's command; the mountain sector had been handed over to X Corps.

Fifth Army had begun its assault that morning and was already making good progress spearheaded by 10th Mountain Division, 1st US Armored Division and the Brazilian Expeditionary Force. Mark Clark's 15 Army Group was now punching with both fists, and three river lines on which the Germans had depended had been breached within five days.

Having been thwarted in his plan to pinch out the Argenta Gap from both north and south, Keightley decided to bring 78th Division's 11 Brigade across the Reno on a Bailey bridge about three miles east of Bastia where the Cremona Group were firmly established. This was in preference to launching an assault across the river in front of the Irish Brigade. Eleven Brigade began its move before dawn on the 15th as 56th Division continued its advance on Bastia.

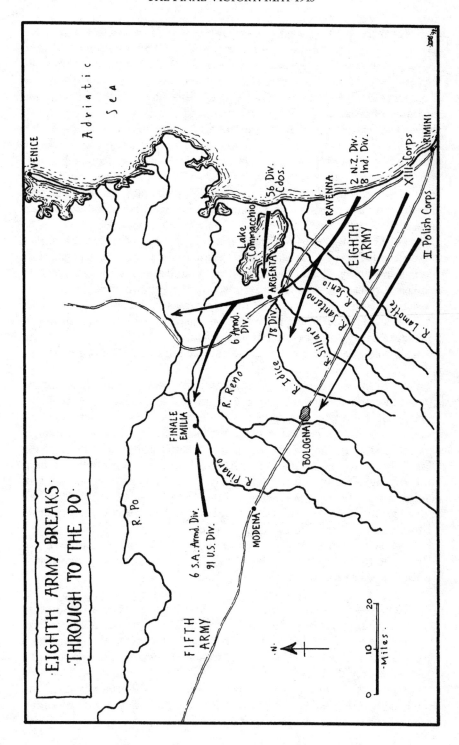

EIGHTH ARMY BREAKS·
·THROUGH TO THE PO·

Spearheading 56th Division's advance was 167 Brigade with 169 on the right flank. Already the two brigades' efforts had all but wiped out 42nd Jäger Division so that the most serious obstacles facing the brigades were natural rather than the work of their adversaries. At one stage 9th Royal Fusiliers, supported by a 10th Hussars' Sherman, attacked the ruined remains of a factory building. They found themselves wading almost knee-deep through a sticky glutinous mess; their objective was a treacle factory, the product of which was flowing from the building as a result of the bombers' attentions. One warrant officer almost drowned in the substance after falling into a treacle-filled shellhole, while the Sherman, its crew enjoying the WO's discomfiture, found itself bogged down in treacle. Fortunately the Germans had abandoned Bastia: otherwise the laughter might have been shortlived.

Major-Generals Whitfield and Arbuthnott, of 56th and 78th Divisions respectively, had decided to make the main breach of the German line across the Fossa Marina north-east of Argenta. A regiment from 29th Panzer Grenadiers was already ensconced in the fortified line of the Fossa and both generals agreed that the attack had to be made at speed if the line of retreat of the enemy's main body was to be cut. There was no time to wait for a heavy bomber assault. Instead 11 Brigade of 78th Division passed through 169 Queen's Brigade of 56th before daybreak on 16 April.

Two battalions, 1st East Surreys and 5th Northamptons, advanced across five miles of flat, wet and mined ground. Although mines were the main problem, there were pockets of German resistance, each of which received the attention of cab-rank fighter-bombers followed by an infantry attack. Churchill Flails of 51 RTR cleared a path through the mines for the Bays' Shermans to support 11 Brigade. As a result, it was a slow advance but, by nightfall, the Northamptons held the cemetery on the edge of Argenta. The Surreys were still short of the Fossa but renewed their advance under cover of darkness and soon gained a covering position through which 2nd Lancashire Fusiliers passed.

The Lancashires' CO was wounded by shellfire and the battalion lost contact with its Flails, but they pressed on under cover of a hastily arranged bombardment of the Fossa which they scaled

in haste and disorder, plunged across its chest-deep dyke, and launched assault with bayonet and grenade on such enemy groups as emitted fire from either bank. They spent two hours in silencing them and then came under heavy shellfire and were three times counterattacked. They stood firm and by daybreak had penetrated as far as a farm, 200 yards beyond the Fossa. They had three Shermans of the Bays with them, which had crossed on an Ark bridge most stoically launched under heavy shellfire. Prisoners numbered barely forty, but many more

Germans lay dead on the banks and in the dyke. It transpired that they had been caught by the barrage when making a relief.[3]

Although heavy enemy shelling knocked out two tanks and smashed the Ark bridge, a determined, co-ordinated effort was made to enlarge the endangered bridgehead. Arbuthnott assigned the infantry role in this to the Irish Brigade on the 17th and Brigadier Pat Scott sent 1st Royal Irish Fusiliers and 2nd Inniskillings to push out to the right and left flanks respectively. Both battalions were soon engaged in heavy fighting but succeeded in widening the bridgehead; the Inniskillings took objectives beyond Argenta and across the railway while the Faughs were almost up to the Scolo Cantenacci. At the same time 2 Commando Brigade was advancing along floodbanks through the inundated ground north-west of Argenta.

The town was cleared on the evening of the 17th with the Northamptons making considerable use of their supporting gun and flamethrower Churchills. Fighting continued throughout the night with a series of counter-attacks, one of which, at company strength with armour support, was beaten back into the arms of 2nd Inniskillings. Argenta had been pounded to rubble and the streets were littered with the corpses of Italian civilians, underlining the bloody cost of the war to the ordinary people of Italy. Perhaps thinking of this toll of human life, one soldier was heard making an announcement at Argenta station, where there was heavy fighting, that was typical of the black humour of the front-line soldier: 'The next train will be calling at Oxshott, Bagshot, Bloodshot and all the other bloody stations down the line'.[4]

With the bridgehead enlarged Arbuthnott sent 36 Brigade on a northward thrust during the night. The village of Boccaleone, less than three miles beyond Argenta, was taken by 6th Royal West Kents just after dawn; the Argylls pushed on for another two miles to take Consandolo with support from tactical aircraft, artillery and tanks. The airmen also lent their support to the Kangaroo Army, now racing ahead on 36 Brigade's right flank:

This was an unforgettable move. Through the orchards north of Argenta, in the narrow gap between Lake and Canal, moved a mass of armour, all passing over one bridge that had been constructed over the main water obstacle. Wrecked vehicles, equipment and enemy dead strewed the route, while machine-gun fire, from an Argenta already surrounded, crackled away on the left flank.[5]

Arbuthnott had been wise to keep this team intact, and by dash and fine cooperation they gleaned a tremendous haul, which included two bridges over the wide Fossa Benvignante, four tanks, twenty guns ranging in calibre from 150-mm to 88-mm, and 455 prisoners. It was a great achievement, far from lightly won, gained under the command of two officers who had fought the Germans in 1940 and had suffered wound and won decoration at regular intervals ever since, Price of the 9th Lancers and 'Bala' Bredin of the London Irish Rifles.[6]

On 78th Division's right 56th Division were also in action: 2/5th Queen's, in co-operation with Churchills of 12 RTR, took a bridge over the Fossa Benvignante before the Germans could demolish it. The fact that Churchill Crocodiles were belching flame across the Fossa may have helped secure the crossing intact. The Fossa Marina had been crossed by 1st Scots Guards whose bridgehead was exploited by 2nd Coldstream; an attempt to rush another bridge over the Fossa Benvignante came to naught because of a minefield.

The night of the 18th/19th was like a bonfire night: flames lit the sky as vehicles, houses and store dumps blazed around the Fossa Benvignante where pockets of German troops were being rounded up. But there was still forward movement: 5th Buffs, of 36 Brigade, passed through the Argylls at Consandolo to push as far as San Nicolo, ten miles beyond Argenta and a similar distance short of Ferrara. McCreery was preparing to loose his reserve, 6th Armoured Division, on the morning of the 19th and, to clear the way for the division's advance, Pat Scott of the Irish Brigade sought permission to co-ordinate 6th West Kents, 2nd Inniskillings and the Commando Brigade to secure the jumping-off area. Scott was concerned that the Germans were holding a position near the Reno from which they could launch a counter-attack to threaten 78th Division's rear area as well as creating problems for 6th Armoured.

At midnight the Commandos attacked under a heavy artillery programme. The Inniskillings and West Kents launched converging attacks at 1.30am and, although the Inniskillings suffered casualties from the Commandos' artillery support, the attack was carried through. The Inniskillings and West Kents closed the circle and cleared the floodbanks and houses; by dawn the Germans had withdrawn and the way was open for 6th Armoured. The Argenta Gap had been cracked open.

The pace of the advance was by this time causing heavy congestion on all the supply routes, and it was becoming increasingly difficult to bring forward the heavy and cumbersome bridging equipment which was so necessary in this canal-ridden country. To maintain the tempo of the advance it was essential that the infantry and armour be able to cross the wider canals with the minimum delay. No one realised this more than did the Royal Engineers, and they worked heroically to bring the equipment up despite the overcrowded and dust-laden roads. Dust, was there ever such! In many respects it was worse than sand. Nothing was safe against it – the troops ate dust-covered food and drank water that was heavily laced with the stuff.[7]

Freyberg's New Zealanders were still advancing east of Bologna. As they did so, crossing water obstacle after water obstacle, they drew numbers of Fallschirmjäger battalions, and 278th Division, against them. After the Poles took Imola and crossed the Sillaro on the night of 15/16 April, 43 Gurkha Brigade was transferred from Polish to New Zealand command and it was the Gurkhas who, in Kangaroos manned by 14th/20th Hussars, supported by 2 RTR, took Medicina on the night of the 16th/17th.

Both XIII Corps and II Polish Corps crossed the Gaiana river on the night of the 18th/19th after the Germans had rebuffed an earlier effort. For this assault crossing 10th Indian Division formed XIII Corps' right flank.

> Great slaughter was inflicted on the men of 4th [Fallschirmjäger], and there were signs that even their morale was beginning to wither, most of all under the flame cast upon them by Crocodiles and Wasps.*[8]

The New Zealanders were in Budrio early on the 20th, going on to cross the Idice river, upon which the Germans had bestowed the name 'the Genghis Khan line'. The Idice was a formidable obstacle with high banks and troops had been rushed to defend it. Although some of them had been resting with their boots off when the summons came they were ready for an assault by 1/2nd Punjabis of 10th Indian's 20 Brigade, who attacked on the New Zealanders' right. Two Punjabi platoons were caught in an ambush beyond the river near Mezzolara

> and when at last the battlefield was won after a night of furious fighting (20/21) the men of these leading platoons were found lying dead, many with blood on their bayonets interlocked with staunch opponents of the 278th Division.[9]

By now Bologna had become untenable. On the evening of the 20th, von Vietinghoff had sought permission from Hitler to withdraw from the city. Permission was refused but evacuation of the city's defences was carried out that night anyway. Soon after dawn on 21 April, 3rd Carpathian Division entered Bologna, the first Allied troops to do so, followed some two hours later by 34th (US) Division and by the Italian Friuli Group, of Eighth Army's X Corps. En route to Bologna the Poles had met with stiff

---

* German veterans of the Italian campaign told the author at a Fallschirmjäger reunion in Germany in 1990 that they would have shot out of hand any Crocodile or Wasp crew member who fell into their hands; they did not consider the flamethrower to be a 'fair' weapon of war.

resistance from Fallschirmjäger, especially on the Gaiana river where

> for the third time in the Italian campaign they encountered the 1st
> Parachute Rifle Division, the same one that had defended Cassino. An
> unrelenting and merciless night followed, but the enemy was at length
> defeated and forced to withdraw during the night of April 20, pursued
> by our infantry and tanks.[10]

Anders later wrote that Clark had 'with great kindness' indicated to the
Polish commander that he would be very glad if II Polish Corps were to
take Bologna and thus the Carpathians had been directed on the city.[11] It
was a 'thank you' from the American, as 15 Army Group commander, for
the sacrifice and effort made by the Poles as an army in exile and a
consolation of sorts for the fact that there would be no V-Day for Poland.

On 21 April Mark Clark took the salute at a parade of American, British
and Polish troops in the market-place in Bologna. Two days later
McCreery issued a special order of the day to II Polish Corps outlining
their recent achievements and concluding:

> You have shown a splendid fighting spirit, endurance and skill in this
> great battle. I send my warmest congratulations and admiration to all
> ranks, and I wish you all the best of luck as you continue the march with
> Eighth Army until the enemy's final collapse in Italy is achieved.[12]

At noon on 18 April 6th Armoured Division had passed from Eighth
Army Reserve to V Corps, thus bringing it once again under the command
of Charles Keightley who had first taken it to war in 1942. The division
was to prove true to its emblem, a clenched, mailed fist, for it was now to
launch an armoured blow on the retreating Germans. Major-General Nat
Murray's orders were

> to swing north-westwards through the left flank of 78th and with its
> own left flank by the River Reno to race for Bondeno, on the River
> Panaro, there to link up with Fifth Army and complete the encirclement
> of the remains of Armies 10 and 14, caught in the noose of Bologna's
> defence.[13]

Sixth Armoured moved to the fray through 78th Division on the afternoon
on the 19th with 8th Indian Division ordered to protect the left flank; 56th
and 78th were to continue the attack towards Ferrara and the crossings of
the Po north of that city. Nat Murray's division deployed four cavalry
regiments (16th/5th Lancers; 17th/21st Lancers; 2nd Lothians and Border
Horse, all in 26 Armoured Brigade; and 1st Derbyshire Yeomanry as
divisional reconnaissance regiment) as well as two motorised infantry

brigades, 1 Guards Brigade and 61 Brigade. While the Guards were held in reserve for assault tasks, each of 26 Armoured Brigade's regiments had a Greenjacket battalion from 61 Brigade assigned, forming three battlegroups.

The breakout from the Argenta Gap gave a rare opportunity for armour to carry out its role and 6th Armoured surged forward enthusiastically. That enthusiasm was dented when 26 Armoured Brigade ran up against the Po Morto di Primaro, their first water obstacle. On the right the Lothians and Border, with 2nd Rifle Brigade, found elements of 26th Panzer Division opposing them at San Nicolo while, on the left, 16th/5th Lancers and 1st KRRC met similar difficulty at Traghetto. During the night the KRRs managed to cross the Po Morto and establish a bridgehead while the tanks of 16th/5th Lancers crossed by Bailey bridge in the morning.

At this stage the Greenjackets were left to secure the bridgehead while 16th/5th swung right, across country that was ideal for anti-tank operations, to allow 17th/21st Lancers to come up on the left flank; this also allowed the Shermans to use better going by the Reno. By the end of the day 17th/21st were well ahead of 16th/5th, having pushed about four miles beyond Traghetto, while the latter were hindered by natural obstacles, such as ditches and thickets, as well as being assailed by *Panzerfausten* parties of infantry and anti-tank guns; such attentions cost the regiment five tanks.

Although there were shades of those days in the Gothic Line, in which 1st Armoured Division had become bogged down, the situation was distinctly different. McCreery was keeping a close eye on the battle and from him

> pungent and pertinent criticism descended, based on his assessment of the grouping demanded by the terrain – and as Keightley subsequently admitted, with admiration, McCreery usually observed the battle at even closer range than he did himself.[14]

The Guards Brigade was ordered forward through 16th/5th Lancers and, at 4am on the 21st, 17th/21st, with 7th Rifle Brigade, renewed their advance. As day dawned the Lancers and Rifles had travelled four miles and were entering Segni against some stiff opposition from Germans who, having blown the bridge, were dug in along the Fossa Cembalina which flows into the Reno at this point. Air support was called down and fighter-bombers swooped on enemy tanks, putting them to flight and allowing Lancers and Rifles to launch an assault which permitted the sappers to bridge the Fossa with an Ark.

By 4pm the position in Segni was consolidated and 17th/21st Lancers drove on in accordance with McCreery's exhortation to allow the enemy no rest. As they did so they fired into buildings, forcing many Germans to surrender. By 5.30 they had taken the bridge near Gallo, thus cutting the main road from Bologna to Ferrara, Highway 64. A message from Brigade HQ stating 'This is the chance of a lifetime' added impetus to their advance as, for the first time in the Italian campaign, the tanks could really charge; it was a cavalryman's dream.

Before darkness had descended the 17th/21st battlegroup had reached Poggio Renatico, blocked all exits from the town and cut the only alternative Bologna-Ferrara road. The Lancers and Rifles were now four miles beyond Gallo, seven from Segni and had advanced eleven from their starting-point.[15] They were faced with an almost surreal situation, by the light of haystacks burning 'particularly well',[16] as motley groups of enemy soldiers, including AA gunners, service and support troops, either fought with little cohesion or tried to surrender. The Greenjackets took on the task of tackling those who appeared to be most determined to fight on.

> At Corps and Army headquarters, the victory was now assured, but in the dark, under the walls of Poggio Renatico the Regiment felt very insecure. There had been heavy expenditure of ammunition on a large number of targets and possible enemy positions during the advance, petrol was down to below twenty-five miles, and there was no prospect of replenishment until the route was cleared of the enemy.[17]

The position of 17th/21st Lancers and 7th Rifle Brigade was causing concern at 6th Armoured HQ, especially as a company of 1st Welch Regiment which had crossed the Fossa Cembalina had been forced to withdraw in the face of a counter-attack by infantry and armour; the latter had included Tiger tanks. However, concern was eased when a further assault by the Welch after sunset met with success, to which a German platoon contributed by deserting their posts. The bridgehead was then enlarged by 3rd Grenadiers thus allowing the Lothians and Border Horse to move forward at dawn the next day.

> Charging with reckless daring, which caused the loss of eleven of their Shermans, they reached the key objective, Bondeno, in the late afternoon. Two of their tanks rushed the bridge over the Panaro, were followed across by two Tigers, and were thereupon cut off by a great explosion, under which the bridge disintegrated.[18]

As 17th/21st Lancers mopped up at Poggio Renatico, overcoming an 88mm flak battery and taking 200 prisoners, their fellow Lancers of 16th/5th, in the centre of 6th Armoured's sector, passed by their flank as they made for the second key objective along the Panaro, the town of Finale Nell Emilia, which was reached early on the 23rd. The Lothians and

2nd RB took Bondeno and exploited northward towards the Po. While 17th/21st and 7th RB were capturing San Augustino, 16th/5th and 1st KRRC were making contact with Fifth Army's II Corps at Finale. It was almost a disastrous contact.

The Lancers and Riflemen had intercepted a German convoy on which they had called down a devastating air strike when they learned that elements of Fifth Army were about to attack Finale. Contact was made in time to order the cancellation of a planned bombardment intended to cover 12 South African Motor Brigade's attack on Finale. Instead peaceful contact was made between the leading elements of 6th British and 6th South African Armoured Divisions. However, there was still mopping-up to be done, in the course of which the CO of 1st KRRC, John Hope, was shot while travelling in a 'sawn-off' Stuart with 16th/5th's CO. A corporal who went to give first aid was shot dead. Hope died some days later. He had served with the 1st KRRC since joining the battalion as a subaltern in the autumn of 1940. Highly decorated and respected by his riflemen, he was one of the very few veterans of the original Eighth Army to have survived to northern Italy.[19]

German troops were falling back to the Po, carrying out rearguard actions en route. For many there was no escape: five of the divisions that had been committed to the defence of Bologna had no form of transport and hence had been mopped up by the enveloping Allies. However, both 1st and 4th Fallschirmjäger Divisions were mobile and had checked both the New Zealanders and South Africans on the 21st. The rapid advance of Murray's 6th Armoured Division had jeopardised the Paras' withdrawal but the destruction of the bridge over the Panaro at Bondeno had allowed them to escape from the British armour. That escape was assisted by the efforts of 278th Division but neither that division, nor 362nd, were able to make a withdrawal to the Po. Much of Schwerin's LXXVI Corps had been destroyed.

Fifth Army was first to reach the Po with men of 10th Mountain Division arriving at San Benedetto on the evening of 22 April. Eighth Army's first contact with the mighty river came next day when Major-General Russell's 8th Indian Division reached it. Keightley had thrust Russell's division into the gap created by the diverging advances of 78th and 6th Armoured Divisions; with 21 Brigade in the van, 8th Indian had struck for Ferrara. German resistance proved strong there and 19 Brigade became locked against the defenders.

However, 21 Brigade was working its way round left of Ferrara with 1/5th Mahratta LI attacking the airport which was held by tenacious defenders. The Jaipur Infantry also moved forward, but it was 5th Royal West Kents who swept wide to the left of Ferrara where they found a gap and, supported by tanks of the North Irish Horse, made for the Po which they reached in the morning of the 23rd, St George's Day, taking over 150 prisoners with no loss to themselves. At much the same time the Derbyshire Yeomanry spearheaded 6th Armoured Division's advance to the Po.

German resistance continued at Ferrara and other points south of the Po but it was crumbling against the inexorable pressure of Eighth Army, whose war diary narrative for the 24th reads

CREMONA GP advanced in coastal sector and captured ARIANA 5296. Between them and FERRARA 56 DIV and 78 DIV continued to reduce the enemy's bridgehead South of the PO against stiff resistance from enemy infantry supported by quite a large number of tanks. By last light the enemy's line was beginning to weaken and our advances had brought us to within two miles of the river PO at several different points. Ferrara was occupied in the morning without opposition with the assistance of partisans who had taken over the city as the enemy withdrew. Resistance continued on the Northern outskirts. There was no change on the 6 Brit Armd Div sector, 2 NZ Div closed up to the PO on the left of 6 Brit Armd Div and patrolled across the river. Many prisoners have been taken in mopping up operations during the day.[20]

That evening the Jaipurs ran into stiff opposition from a panzer group at Pontelagoscuro and 9th Lancers, from the Kangaroo Army of 78th Division, deployed to attack the Germans from the right flank.

A tremendous battle developed across open marsh, which brought back memories of the Desert to many of the Lancers as they searched for folds in the ground from which to fire back at the dark forms belching tracer at them. There was the big difference that they wielded the heavier firepower, for the Tigers and Panthers had all been expended in isolated actions in support of the infantry, and only Panzer IVs were left to confront Shermans that were armed in many cases with high-velocity 76-mm guns. Only one Sherman was knocked out, and the blazes that raged long after the fall of darkness proved the loss they had inflicted.[21]

Next morning the Jaipurs took Pontelagoscuro without opposition and later that day, the 25th, the enemy front on V Corps' sector collapsed completely except for one small area in a bend of the Po 'where an enemy group continued to fight fiercely'.[22] Otherwise there was little resistance and no organised opposition. In the course of the day 27th Lancers captured Lieutenant-General Graf von Schwerin, commander of LXXVI Panzer Corps. When asked about the dispositions of his corps, von Schwerin replied simply: 'You will find them south of the Po'. Von Schwerin issued an order to his soldiers, which was printed on Eighth

Army leaflets dropped on what remained of his corps, advising his soldiers to surrender.

> It is now the duty of every officer, of every NCO and of every soldier bravely to look facts in the face and to realize that it is criminal to throw away more human lives.[23]

The rout of his command had been complete and the devastation which German propaganda leaflets had promised the Allies along the Po had been visited upon the Germans themselves. So rapid had been the Allied advance, and so wide the Po, that the river became the Dunkirk, without an evacuation, of von Vietinghoff's Army Group. For those British battalions that had endured the Dunkirk campaign this was satisfaction indeed.

Eighth Army headquarters had anticipated a major assault crossing of the Po and McCreery had ordered X Corps, under Hawkesworth, to plan for such an operation. On 21 April that order had been rescinded. Instead 6th Armoured Division was transferred from V to XIII Corps and the respective corps commanders were instructed to cross the Po wherever the opportunity presented itself. And so Eighth Army crossed, led by 56th Division and 6th armoured. The New Zealanders also crossed, allegedly over an American bridge having 'bought' the right to cross with three bottles of whiskey although New Zealand battalions also crossed in assault boats under cover of an artillery bombardment, after midnight on the night of 24/25 April. The Grenadiers of 6th Armoured crossed in Fantails with amphibious Shermans of 7th Hussars following in support. Some opposition was encountered on the far bank but was soon swept aside.

The brigades of 56th Division had no bridge to use and thus the division also had to use DUKWs and Fantails both for the initial crossing, by 169 Brigade, and for the subsequent supply of that brigade.

> As this method rather limited the number of men that could be employed forward, General Whitfield decided that the advance should be continued by 169th Brigade, and the 167th and the Guards Brigades were temporarily grounded.[24]

Eighth Army's next objective was the Adige river, some ten to fifteen miles from the Po, which was almost as impressive a barrier as the Po. Behind the Adige was the Venetian Line, a formidable series of fortifications that, had they been manned fully, would have been a tough proposition. But there were few German troops left and not enough to man the Venetian Line.

The troops surged onwards like hounds in full cry, jostling each other, blasting aside spasmodic opposition, and often speeding across bridges proudly preserved for them by partisans. Entering Rovigo late on April 26, the Queen's found that the German garrison had already been incarcerated in the gaol. But next day the 2/7th Queen's were strongly counterattacked after crossing the Adige and had a grim fight to retain a bridgehead.[25]

The Partisans' Committee of Liberation had called for a general uprising against the Germans on the 25th following the success of operations carried out by F Squadron SAS which, reinforced by volunteers from the Folgore Group, had been parachuted into German-held territory in groups of three or four on the night of 20/21 April. The operation had taken place on McCreery's orders. However, the hapless 2 Parachute Brigade remained on the ground and, as they studied plans for their thirty-second proposed operation on the 25th, they were informed that their services would not be needed.

Behind the advancing troops the sappers were ensuring that Eighth Army's advance could be sustained by putting bridges across the Po: a 1,110-foot-long Bailey pontoon at Ficarolo in XIII Corps' sector was carrying traffic early on the 27th and a similar bridge, at Pontelagoscuro in V Corps' sector, became operational at midnight that night.

Freyberg's New Zealanders, still with 43 Gurkha Brigade under command, crossed the Adige at Badia Polesine on the night of 26/27 April, meeting no opposition. However, Freyberg marked time in order to build up his divisional strength before moving against the Venetian Line with 12th Lancers acting as his reconnaissance regiment. The New Zealand advance began at dawn on the 28th and the Lancers drove through the day without meeting any substantial opposition.

> During the day rapid advances were made by our troops from the two bridgeheads across the Adige and by last light leading elements were reported at MONSELICE 2330 and ESTE 1529.[26]

Pausing to remove barriers 12th Lancers reached Este at 3pm where they were told to move on for Padua which was entered after midnight. There they found that partisans had again imprisoned a German garrison, this time 5,000 strong.

After knocking out a German rearguard party at Mestic, some miles west of Venice, 2/5th Queen's, of 56th Division's 169 Brigade, entered Venice on the 29th, beating 44th Reconnaissance Regiment which had recce'd at speed towards the city hoping to claim the distinction of being first there. That missed opportunity added to the sense of frustration felt by 44 Recce which had seen little action in the final phase of the war.

For us the break-through was disappointing, as the great number of blown bridges slowed us down so much that infantry often did the job faster, and consequently we were not employed as much as we should have liked.[27]

In the race for Venice the Queen's had been joined by elements of the New Zealand Division and by Popski's Private Army. Welcomed by an enthusiastic crowd in Venice they received some 3,000 German prisoners who had been rounded up by partisans. Next day a New Zealand officer went by boat to the Lido and the islands of Murano and Burano to take the surrender of the German garrisons there. Peniakoff achieved what he had described as his war's ambition: to drive a jeep around St Mark's Square; in fact he led a procession of jeeps which went around the square not once but seven times.[28]

It was clear that the end of the war in Italy was now in sight. As early as February, General Karl Wolff, SS commander in Italy, had contacted an American diplomat, Allen Dulles, later to head the CIA, in Switzerland to open negotiations for an armistice. Liaison continued through a German-speaking Czech who was working for the American OSS and who operated a wireless set from the top of the house in which Wolff had his headquarters. Although the Czech wore SS uniform, only Wolff and his chief of staff knew of the existence of the wireless. While Kesselring, as overall commander in the west, adopted a diehard stance, Wolff continued negotiations but these were pre-empted when von Vietinghoff learned of Hitler's death and immediately issued orders for his soldiers to surrender. Those orders preceded the time agreed for the surrender by one hour.

On the 29th an agreement for the unconditional surrender of all German and Axis forces in Italy and in the Austrian provinces of Vorarlberg, Tyrol, Salzburg and parts of Carinthia and Styria, some 230,000 men, was signed at Alexander's headquarters at Caserta in the presence of Lieutenant-General Sir William Morgan, Alex's chief of staff. All fighting was to cease by noon on 2 May.

There were celebrations in Eighth Army that night of 2 May but they were muted for it took time for men to appreciate that the war was really over. And there were so many thoughts, so many memories, and so many feelings of loss that it was difficult to absorb the news immediately. After all men were still dying of wounds and bodies of those killed earlier were still being discovered. Lieutenant Jim Trousdell, of 1st Royal Irish Fusiliers, summed up feelings which were probably typical of most members of Eighth Army.

That evening the end of the war was celebrated with a tremendous barrage of verey lights, parachute flares and everything else that was luminous and noisy. The opportunity to dispose of these items which had been carried for so long could not be missed. It was difficult to realise that the war really had ended and it took sometime to adjust to the unusual experience of peace. I had gone straight from school in 1939 into the Army and now a new life was about to begin . . .[29]

On the battlefields of the previous winter the scars of war were healing with the new growth of spring, and birds sang where mortar bombs had crashed down and machine-guns had screeched. But the scars of battle did not mend so quickly in towns, nor did they do so in people either. As Eighth Army's soldiers tried to comprehend what the end of the war might mean some were heard to remark that the D-Day Dodgers had beaten Monty to it.

Poor old 'D-Day Dodgers'; they had a long fight for their money.
What a long time ago it seemed since those early days in North Africa with the appalling discomforts of that campaign. It seemed a long time, too, since the epic battles of Sicily and Southern Italy.
How very few had seen them all.
How few in the Rifle Companies who had landed in North Africa were still with us to see the culmination of their efforts.
One's mind turned that evening to a lot of faces of old friends whom one would not see again. One hopes that they, too, were able to join in the feeling of satisfaction and thankfulness that the last shot had been fired.[30]

NOTES

1. Harpur: *The Impossible Victory*, pp.122-123
2. ibid, p.101
3. Blaxland, *Alexander's Generals*, p.265
4. Harpur, op cit, p.162
5. Bredin: *Account of the Kangaroo Army*
6. Blaxland: op cit, pp.266-267
7. Williams: *The Black Cats at War*, p.118
8. Blaxland: op cit, p.271
9. ibid
10. Anders: *An Army in Exile*, p.267
11. ibid
12. ibid, p.268
13. Blaxland: op cit, pp.267-268
14. ibid, p.268
15. PRO: WO170/4629, war diary, 17/21L, 1945
16. ibid
17. ffrench Blake: *History of 17/21 Lancers*, p.222
18. Blaxland: op cit, p.270

19. ibid
20. PRO: WO170/4180, war diary narrative, Eighth Army HQ, April 1945
21. Blaxland: op cit, p.275
22. PRO: WO170/4180, op cit
23. Scott; *Account of the Irish Brigade*
24. Williams: op cit, p.119
25. Blaxland: op cit, p.276
26. PRO: WO170/4180, op cit
27. PRO: WO170/4372, op cit
28. Peniakoff: *Popski's Private Army*, p.425
29. PJC Trousdell, letter to author
30. Scott: *Account of the Irish Brigade*

CHAPTER XX

Eighth Army's Final Days: An Uncertain Peace

Your deeds will gleam and glow

Wars can never end cleanly: while succeeding generations may look back and say that a war ended on a specific date this ignores the many issues which have to be resolved at the end of any war. Among such issues are territorial disputes, displaced persons, refugees, the detritus of battlefields with all the dangers of live ammunition, and the identification of those guilty of war crimes.

The end of the Italian campaign brought all these issues to the fore: there were territorial disputes with the Yugoslavs over areas of Italy and Austria and with the Soviets in Austria; there were tens of thousands of displaced persons and refugees – the two are not synonymous; munitions, weaponry and war debris to be made safe; and the perpetrators of horrendous war crimes to be hunted down. Many such matters became the concern of soldiers of Eighth Army as the days of fighting receded, turning the Army's role from a military to a political one virtually as soon as the shooting stopped.

The first element of Eighth Army to encounter a major territorial dispute was 2nd New Zealand Division. At Venice the New Zealanders were ordered to make for Trieste where a political imperative demanded the presence of Eighth Army soldiers. Supporting 2nd New Zealand Division were 12th Lancers and 1st Scots Guards. The city of Trieste had been part of the old Austro-Hungarian empire until 1915 when it had been ceded to Italy under a secret treaty signed in London. Although the majority of the city's population wanted Trieste to remain Italian, the city became a target for Marshal Tito's expansionist ambitions for Yugoslavia. Columns of partisans were evident to the New Zealanders after crossing the Isonzo; roads were festooned with portraits of Tito as well as posters proclaiming the area to be Yugoslav.

Near Monfalcone Freyberg met the partisan commander, General Drapsin, whom he informed that the New Zealand Division was only the advance guard of a powerful formation of infantry and armour. In spite of this bluff partisans entered Trieste on 1 May, a day before the leading units of Eighth Army. The sight of the latter must have been a tremendous relief to the remaining Germans in Trieste who had pulled back to the harbour area and had no wish to surrender to Yugoslavs. On the afternoon of the 2nd the Germans formally surrendered to Sir Bernard Freyberg and soldiers of Eighth Army occupied the port.

Eighth Army's soldiers found a situation in which the local population lived in terror of their Yugoslav 'liberators' who had closed shops, cafes and cinemas and were operating 'something in the nature of a reign of terror'.[1] Soldiers were called on to be diplomats and protectors while their commanders had to try to create good relations with the Yugoslavs. As a result of a meeting between General Harding and the Yugoslav General Drapsin, a football match was arranged between British and Yugoslav troops, followed by further sporting and cultural exchanges including a dance and concert organised by Freyberg's Maoris.

However, resolution of the Trieste problem was not in the gift of the soldiers on the ground, or their commanders. It lay much higher, on a political level, and involved the long-term ambitions of a number of politicians including the Soviet leader Josef Stalin to whom Tito still looked for guidance. Stalin's view was that Italo-Yugoslav frontiers, and the port of Trieste, did not justify friction with the British and US governments. When these views were communicated to Tito there was a visible warming in relations between British and Yugoslav personnel in the Trieste area.

So that the Yugoslavs would be in no doubt about British and American support for Italy over Trieste, Churchill suggested to Alexander that a strong force of troops, supported by aircraft, should be stationed in the area. Such a convincing demonstration of support would not only prevent any Yugoslav attempt to annex the area but would also undermine the Italian communists. Churchill was convinced that the average Italian cared more for Trieste than for communist ideals. The force in the Trieste area was reinforced with a US division in early-May in a demonstration of Allied solidarity. This was the first time that such a large US formation had served under Eighth Army command although the Fantail crews assigned to V Corps during Operation BUCKLAND had been US troops.

In 1947 Trieste became part of a free territory under United Nations protection and remained as such until 1954 when Italy and Yugoslavia agreed on frontiers. At that stage Trieste became part of Italy and British and US troops finally bade goodbye to the area.

Trieste was not the only area of friction between soldiers of Eighth Army and their former allies: Austria provided another source of potential conflict, even though the division of the country into occupation zones had been agreed by the Allied leaders who had, in 1943, accepted that

318

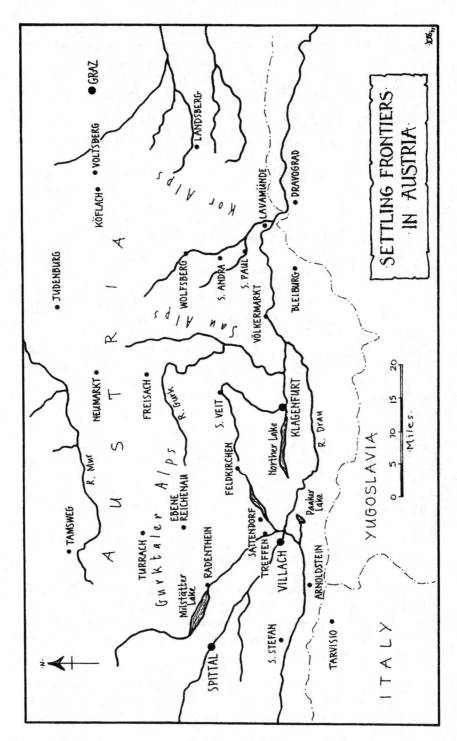

Austria should be re-established as a free, independent state after the war.

Soviet forces had occupied Vienna by mid-April and Austria was effectively conquered by Stalin's forces although they did not overrun all the country. Vienna was to be placed under the joint control of Soviet, British, US and French forces, in the same manner as was Berlin, while British troops were to occupy the provinces of Styria and Carinthia. Almost as soon as German resistance collapsed elements of Eighth Army, in this case UK units, began to move across the frontier from Italy into Austria.

> From drummer to general the contrast on entering the beautiful country of Austria was not unremarked. As we crossed the frontier the difference was before our eyes in one mile – just one mile. Where we had seen only mud and squalor, cleanliness now held sway. Where shattered barns and tank-blasted farms had been to us the norm there now lay red-tiled roofs, clean paintwork and gardens. Green fields, neat hayricks and soaring white mountains beckoned . . .[2]

Klagenfurt was surrendered on 9 May by a local official to an Eighth Army column commanded by an SOE officer, Lieutenant-Colonel Peter Wilkinson, who had served in Yugoslavia. The Yugoslav partisans with whom he had served were now to provide Wilkinson, and many other British officers, with one of the principal headaches of the immediate aftermath of war. Klagenfurt was placarded by posters emanating from the Yugoslavs.

> The Yugoslav Army has entered Carinthia in order to cleanse the land of Nazi criminals and bring liberty and democracy to Slovene Austrians. Complete victory over the Germans has now been attained by the Yugoslav partisans alone. It was also furthered by the help received from the Soviet Union, England and America. We hereby make known that throughout the whole of liberated Carinthia the military authority of the Yugoslav Army has been established . . . . The population and all branches of our administration are to extend every help to our Army and to obey unconditionally all published decrees.[3]

The situation was further complicated by the arrival of German troops who wanted to surrender to the British while Yugoslavs were trying to block the road east of Klagenfurt to prevent British troops travelling any farther. In the words of Brigadier Adrian Gore, of 61 Brigade, there were too few troops in the area.

> Other units of Eighth Army had reached Klagenfurt just in time, and in sufficient strength, to prevent Tito from taking over the province of Carinthia. Numbers of tanks at 'action stations' beside the Lindwurm,

and firmness by their infantry colleagues, soon dissuaded the Yugoslavs from pursuing their ideas any further.[4]

However, the Yugoslavs continued to try to take advantage of the unsettled situation in Carinthia and gave every appearance of wanting to extend Yugoslavia's borders at the expense of Austria. Both the British and US governments sent notes of protest to Tito's government in which it was made clear that the war had been fought to stop nations grabbing the territory of other nations; if necessary Britain and the US would continue fighting to uphold that principle.

The diplomatic notes were backed up by a show of strength involving a regrouping of forces: V Corps was aligned along the Austro-Yugoslav border with the Jewish Brigade taking over Tarvisio; two divisions from Fifth Army moved in south of them to cover the area of the Tarvis Pass while XIII Corps prepared to hold the line from there to Trieste. Brigadier Pat Scott's Irish Brigade Group, with a regiment of tanks under command, was deployed to Villach where it

> looked as if we might have to pull through our rifles once more, not for the first time during the last fortnight! It was hardly surprising that we had had no time for VE Day.[5]

Eighth Army's show of strength had the desired effect: on 20 May Tito issued orders for his forces to be out of Carinthia by 6pm the following day. Although units stood by for sweep and search operations in case some partisan groups did not get the message, this precaution proved unnecessary and the Yugoslavs withdrew from Carinthia during the 21st.

During the period of attempted Yugoslav infiltration of Carinthia the most serious problem arising from the presence of Tito's men had been the surrender of Croat troops to Eighth Army. On 14 May some 20,000 Croatians were discovered to be passing through Bulgarian lines in order to surrender to the British. Behind the Croat soldiers were about half a million civilians together with the survivors of some German divisions.

A Croat liaison officer arrived at the headquarters of 17th Field Regiment at Bleiberg with a request that Croat forces should be allowed to surrender to the British to whom they would give up their arms. Since 17th Field was part of the Irish Brigade Group the Croat liaison officer was sent on to Brigade HQ. It seemed that the Bulgarians had been prepared to allow the Croatians to pass through but Yugoslavs had arrived on the scene, pushed back the Bulgarians and opened fire on the Croats who, in spite of some casualties and the loss of some tanks, had fought off Tito's men to continue their march to the British zone.

Brigadier Scott was told that he could not accept the surrender of the

Croats: since the latter had fought for Germany against the Yugoslavs, and had declared themselves independent of Yugoslavia, the official position was that they would have to surrender to the Yugoslavs. Since the situation was bound to become even more difficult, Brigadier Scott asked what help he could expect if the Croats refused to co-operate. Manpower was very limited: at Bleiberg Scott's total resources were a battery of 17th Field Regiment, two troops from 46 Recce, some armoured cars from 27th Lancers and two or three tanks; two companies of 16th Durham LI under Major Alan Hay had already reached Bleiberg with the remainder of the battalion to follow;[6] 27th Lancers were also ordered to Bleiberg to join their few cars already there.

With such slim resources Scott was forced to play a game of bluff: a show of force was put on with guns drawn up in the most open area available, while another battery was deployed south of the Drau as a contingency measure. Scott conducted negotiations with both sides beginning with the Yugoslavs whose chief was a commissar called Milan Basta. Basta, who apparently held the rank of major-general although he was only in his early twenties, told Brigadier Scott that he intended to defeat the Croats in battle and that he had given orders for the battle to begin in thirty minutes. The latter told Basta that he was doing his utmost to 'prevent any more gallant Yugoslavs getting killed' and that he wanted to find an easier solution to the problem than a pitched battle.

> The Commissar eventually agreed that if I would be good enough to try and make the Croats surrender to them he would be very pleased, but if I did not mind he could only wait for quarter of an hour before he would have to give orders for the battle. I congratulated him on the excellence of communications which enabled him to launch such a mighty army from so many directions with such exactness.[7]

By contrast the Croatians were more orthodox. Led by General Herencic and a commissar, the ten-strong delegation stressed, through the same Yugoslav-American interpreter who had accompanied Basta's party, that they were all, soldiers and civilians alike, prepared to die rather than surrender to Bolshevists. They told Scott that the entire Croat nation was emigrating and wanted to speak to Field-Marshal Alexander as this was a political matter. Brigadier Scott asked what their eventual destination was but they appeared not to have given this matter much consideration and when he pointed out that most of Europe was 'already entirely disorganised and extremely hungry' they suggested that they might go to America or Africa. Told that the means to transport them were non-existent at that time and that they would probably starve wherever they went, they insisted that starving 'was an infinitely preferable course to surrendering to Tito'.

Herencic's commissar took the floor at every available opportunity to harangue Scott with political speeches while Basta was sending a series of messages to say that he could wait no longer and that battle must start. Basta's threats caused Scott to sum up the alternatives for the Croats: he told them that they had only five minutes in which to make up their minds.

> The alternatives were these. First: that they would surrender to the Yugoslavs. That I would use my influence, though unofficially, to try to ensure that they would be treated correctly. Second: that they stayed where they were and were attacked by the Yugoslavs. Third: that they endeavoured to advance into the British lines, when they would not only be attacked by the Yugoslavs, but by all the might of British and American air forces, land forces and everything else that I could get my hands on, in which case they would unquestionably be annihilated.[8]

Both Yugoslavs and Croats were brought together and an agreement was signed by both sides in the presence of Brigadier Scott, although Basta still insisted that, unless surrender had been signified formally to his side within an hour, battle would be joined. Although Scott argued for a longer period, the Yugoslavs were intransigent and the Brigadier had to remind the Croats that they were already over a week late in surrendering and thus could count themselves fortunate to be treated as prisoners of war at all. Within the hour the surrender had been made: its terms guaranteed that, except for political criminals who would be tried by Allied courts, Croatian soldiers would be treated as prisoners of war and civilians would be fed and repatriated by the most direct route.

Tito's officers proved not to be men of their word: thousands of Croats were massacred after crossing the border; some were even murdered in the grounds of the castle where the negotiations had taken place. Brian Clark, then Adjutant of 1st Royal Irish Fusiliers, recalled that two senior Croat officers shot themselves rather than surrender to Tito's Yugoslav Army of Liberation.[9]

A platoon of Clark's battalion was on duty at the Drau bridge when the Yugoslavs began herding their prisoners across to what, for many, was certain death. Although the Irishmen were unaware of the Croats' intended fate they felt a bitter loathing towards the Yugoslavs as they watched them herd their victims across the bridge. Lieutenant Colin Gunner was at the bridge as was the battalion machine-gun officer, Bob Hogan. When one Croat soldier collapsed, Hogan ordered two of his Faughs to lay the man at the side of the road and give him some rum. As they did so Hogan realised that the man wore the field-grey uniform of the German army and, almost immediately, he had a sign erected reading, in German, 'All German soldiers fall out here'. In Gunner's words:

Hogan must have seemed like Christ the Saviour to several as they fell out and were given a drink of water and a Woodbine. A Jug officer complete with whip clattered up on his pony and screamed at the resting Germans like a hysterical whore. The Germans turned their eyes to Hogan. The Jug then made the mistake of screaming at Hogan and brandished his whip. Hogan spoke to the gunner behind the Vickers. 'If this bastard lifts that whip blow him out of that fucking saddle.' The gunner elevated the Vickers to aim square at the Jug's belly and put his thumbs on the triggers. More hysterical screams then the Jug turned his horse and buggered off. Neither Hogan nor he understood a word of either's language but a machine gun at a range of ten feet needed no interpreter.[10]

As a result of Bob Hogan's intervention some eighty Germans were rescued from the Yugoslavs and were taken off to a British PoW camp.

The Croats were not the only former enemy personnel to attempt to surrender to Eighth Army. Some days before the crisis with the Croats began a Bulgarian officer had asked Lieutenant-Colonel M J F Palmer of 1st Royal Irish Fusiliers to take the surrender of a Cossack force which had fought for the Germans. It transpired that the Cossacks had refused to surrender to anyone other than the British; Palmer radioed his Brigadier, Pat Scott, who joined him at Lavamünde whence the two Irishmen set off, with Lieutenant Fred Lafferty and eighteen men, to accept the Cossacks' surrender. They had then to move the Cossacks safely across the Drau bridge without being attacked by the Bulgarians. This was achieved by the simple expedient of waiting until the Bulgarians were all drunk.

Thus it was that the Cossack column moved off at 3am on 12 May with Colonel Palmer and the Cossack commander, Prinz zu Salm, an Oberstleutnant of the Totenkopf Hussaren, at its head. The escort was bolstered by eighteen New Zealand ex-PoWs on horseback and the five-mile long column eventually cleared the Drau bridge, at which point the Cossacks decided to stop for a meal. Palmer's remonstrations with their commander were to no avail and the meal stop drew the ire of V Corps' commander, Lieutenant-General Keightley, when he arrived on the scene. 'He was very unhappy and he let me know it, even though I did explain that I couldn't have stopped them anyway.'[11]

The Cossacks had joined the German forces in large numbers when the German army had penetrated the Soviet Union as far as the northern Caucasus in 1942. They had never accepted communist rule and the German invasion gave them the opportunity to migrate westwards. Large numbers of Cossacks, including women, children and elderly had trekked across Europe to northern Italy where they settled near Friuli before moving to Tolmezzo near Udine. There they were joined by Cossacks from western Europe who had fled their homeland after the Russian revolution. Male Cossacks proved a valuable source of manpower for the German forces. Among the contingent that surrendered to 1st Royal Irish Fusiliers were other former Soviet subjects who had served under German command in Yugoslavia where they had been responsible for atrocities against civilians.

The subsequent fate of the Cossacks is well known. Under the terms of the Yalta agreement they were repatriated to the Soviet Union where many were brutally killed. Among those to die was the German General Helmut von Pannwitz who had been the Cossacks' corps commander.

> General von Pannwitz made a special journey to St Andrae where, in Murphy's [Lt-Col Murphy Palmer] absence, I received his thanks for the chivalrous manner in which the Royal Irish Fusiliers had accepted the surrender of his Cossacks. He voluntarily expatriated himself to stay with his men and was hanged on Red Square.[12]

For the soldiers who had the task of forcibly repatriating the Cossacks it was a traumatic experience. Harold Macmillan estimated the number of Cossacks and 'White' Russians at about 40,000 and noted that handing them over to Stalin's forces was condemning them to a horrific future, if not actually to death. However, he noted that a refusal to hand them over would be a contravention of the Yalta agreement and would deeply offend the Russians.

That political aspect was not something with which the men of 36 Brigade would have been familiar; but they were aware that they were participating in a human tragedy. Two battalions of the brigade were engaged in the task of getting the Cossacks on to transport to take them back to the Soviet Union: 2nd Royal Inniskilling Fusiliers and 8th Argyll and Sutherland Highlanders, the former temporarily detached from the Irish Brigade. The hand-over had to be conducted by force; officers and other ranks were separated and the officers were handed over first. However, that did not make the task any easier as a report to 36 Brigade HQ by Lieutenant R Shields of D Company, 2nd Inniskillings, indicates. Arriving at the entraining point, Shields was immediately asked to have a company of his battalion brought up to deal with the difficulties that had already begun. As he waited for the company to arrive he saw men lying outstretched on the ground with their chests bared and asking to be shot, as well as women in a state of frenzy. At a second entraining point Shields found the Cossacks formed up as if to move off.

> By this time Captain Campbell had arrived with the main body of A Company. Then the trouble started again! The minute we moved to remove them to the train they . . . sat down where they were with their

arms inter-laced, refused to move and demanded that we 'shot them where they lay'. Captain Campbell decided that this was no time to be gentle and try and coax them to move – it was case of move them by force. The troops fixed their bayonets, and started breaking the body into small groups. This proved no easy job. After 10 minutes of beating with sticks, rifles and even to the extent of bayonet points being used, and not too gently either.[13]

By this stage tempers on both sides were fraying and when someone opened fire with an automatic weapon the Inniskillings fired over the heads of the Cossacks and into the ground in front of them.

Scenes were pretty wild by this time and the big worry was that we might shoot up our own people, fortunately that did not happen. By this time quite a number had been moved to the trucks to embus for the train but the main body still would not move an inch despite the really rough handling they had received. One man in particular I thought he must have been the ringleader because he seemed to have all the control over them. He by the time he had been dragged to the trucks was bleeding from the blows he had received and [his] leather coat (which was a very good one too before the fight started) was in shreds, likewise the jacket and shirt underneath.[14]

The removal of this man, plus the effect of the firing, which Shields noted was 'becoming more erratic', resulted in the majority of the Cossacks beginning to move towards the trucks. However, about 200 broke away and tried to escape through nearby woods. They were met by warning fire from Bren guns sited for that purpose which stopped most of them, although there were some casualties. Those who made it into the woods were later rounded up by 6th Royal West Kents.

From then on the job was easy. We cleared the camp, collected the wounded and killed, which amounted to 3 killed and 4 wounded, 2 of them seriously who were sent to hospital.

All told it took the Company 2 hours to clear one camp which totalled some 800 Cossacks.[15]

Such scenes were repeated many times as the repatriation of the Cossacks was carried out. Many chose to commit suicide rather than face the wrath of Stalin. It was difficult for the average British soldier to understand the depths of the Cossacks' fears: although they knew that the Cossacks had fought against their homeland they could not appreciate the depths of fear that existed. To the British soldier Stalin was an ally who had been portrayed in wartime propaganda as the friendly *Uncle Joe* figure.

Some Cossacks managed to evade repatriation at that time and eluded Eighth Army's soldiers for some time. Those who managed to stay free until the end of May were the luckiest: from June all Cossacks captured were to be classed as 'Surrendered Enemy Personnel' and, as such, were not to be repatriated to Russia. Thus ended an episode which most of those involved would prefer to forget and which can cause considerable emotion even today.*

The experiences with the Cossacks and Croats were the most traumatic to befall British soldiers in the early days of peace in Austria. But there were many other tasks to be carried out, including the settling of boundaries between the occupying former Allies. This was achieved through a series of conferences including one at Wolfsberg on 14 May at which Keightley met his Soviet counterpart and reached a general agreement on boundaries; more precise local agreements were made as a result of other meetings at the same time. The Soviet delegation at Wolfsberg had been received with the full panoply of military honours; H Company 2nd London Irish provided a Guard of Honour.

There were surrendering enemy personnel to be dealt with: on the day of the conference at Wolfsberg one brigade alone held almost 25,000 prisoners ranging from SS men through Army Group E Headquarters personnel to Hungarian and Cossack troops. The task of accommodating and feeding such numbers was daunting but it was achieved efficiently and effectively by Eighth Army's logistic personnel.

As well as the PoWs there were also displaced persons who had to be looked after. Many of these were people who, for a variety of reasons not always of their own making, found themselves in the wrong country. A number of Arabs were among the DPs in the Irish Brigade area while the earlier experience of James Lucas of the Royal West Kents shows just how individuals can be tossed about by the storm of war. A German soldier had appeared with a surrender document and the company commander had asked Lucas, who spoke German, to bring the man in. Although wearing German uniform the man was oriental looking and belonged to the Turcoman Division. He was finally identified by two officers of an Indian division who were able to converse with him and ascertain that the prisoner was a Tibetan pedlar who

---

* One ex-Inniskilling, who asked for his name to be withheld, told the author in 1990 that he was ashamed to have been involved in the repatriation. He said that he and his comrades could not understand the enormity of what was happening but they knew that the Cossacks were terrified and they felt pity for them even as they forced them on to trucks. He saw a number of male Cossacks throw themselves at bayonets in an effort to commit suicide.

had a small caravan of animals. He was selling things near the Russian frontier when a group of men in brown uniforms seized him, gave him a brown uniform and he then found himself fighting against men in grey uniforms. They captured him and put him into a grey uniform and now he finds himself fighting in a grey uniform against a new lot of men in brown uniforms. He wants to know what is happening and he is very worried about his caravan of animals and asks how soon he can get back to them.[16]

In the early days of occupation much attention was given to seeking out Nazi suspects and patrols swept the countryside in search of such individuals as well as SS men who had gone on the run. Among the units engaged in such operations were the Lovat Scouts whose mountain experience was deemed suitable for such work. At Wolfsberg the new mayor, who had spent five years in a concentration camp, asked for help in rounding up Nazis. His request was met by 2nd London Irish Rifles who, with some of the older local police, arrested and jailed thirty-one leading Nazis on 11 May as well as nearly seventy SS officers and men while, on the 12th, the German ambassador to Croatia, Gauleiter Kache, and Feimtl, the Croatian war minister, were caught trying to slip through the town. On their arrest the pair were found to have 250 British gold sovereigns in their possession.

There were lighter moments as well. A German officers' drink store was 'liberated' by the Irish Brigade and the contents 'secured' by two battalions of that brigade, 1st Royal Irish Fusiliers and 2nd London Irish. Having 'secured' this treasure each battalion then used three 3-ton trucks to remove the contents to the respective battalion messes, which were spared expenditure on alcohol for almost two years. (The Inniskillings did not share in this booty as they had been detached to 36 Brigade.) Similar troves were uncovered by other units and German vehicles also proved quite popular as did horses. The 'liberation' of former German army horses, including some thoroughbred stock, allowed Eighth Army formations to run race meetings as the pace of life in Austria began to ease. These proved a popular attraction although expensive for many whose eye for a good horse was not perhaps as keen as they might have believed.

As life settled to a peacetime pace there was more time for all those things upon which a peacetime army thrives including inspections, sport and parades. There had been no time for a victory parade at the end of hostilities and the opportunity was taken of organising such parades at various levels. Perhaps the most spectacular was that held by one of Eighth Army's veteran divisions, 78th, at Spittal in the Drau Valley on 6 July. Since this was going to be the last time the Battleaxe Division would be together as a formation, much serious preparation went into the parade.

The preparation was time well spent for the parade was a tremendous success. Lieutenant-General Sir Richard McCreery, Eighth Army's commander, took the salute as the units of 78th Division marched past, led by 56th Reconnaissance Regiment. McCreery had earlier inspected the division and, at the end of his inspection, called for two minutes' silence in memory of those who had fallen in action. After the silence, which was almost palpable, the bugles of the Irish Brigade sounded Last Post and Reveille. Then, as the notes died away in the still air of the valley, the Highland pipes of 8th Argyll and Sutherland Highlanders struck up the lament, *The Flowers of the Forest*. It was a highly emotional occasion and, as Colin Gunner wrote, 'the ghosts fell in silently with the living. They had never been far away and are not far away even now'.[17] As the Division marched past the Army commander towards the dispersal point it passed under boards hung across the road and emblazoned with the names of battles from North Africa to northern Italy. There were few in the infantry battalions who had fought from North Africa to Austria and almost certainly none who had served with Eighth Army from its birth in North Africa back in September 1941.

Shortly after that parade, units of 78th Division began to disband or to transfer out of Eighth Army. The older soldiers were also being demobbed while leave convoys were departing every other day; each convoy took 300 officers and men of Eighth Army home to the UK for thirty-eight days' leave. Those convoys had been started by McCreery in June and proved immensely popular.

Another popular measure was the end of the ban on travel within Austria which came on 17 July when control posts were finally lifted. Some units were already looking forward to the winter and reconnoitring facilities for skiing but perhaps the most popular measure of all was the ending of the ban on fraternisation with Austrians. The latter, however, did not occur until September by which time Eighth Army had been transformed into British Troops Austria. General McCreery marked the demise of Eighth Army at the end of July with his last Special Message of the Day to all ranks of Eighth Army in which he wrote:

Today, the Eighth Army officially breaks up. At this time all will recall its great achievements in battle, but the cheerful, unselfish service which All Ranks of the Eighth Army gave throughout a long war must continue. Only hard work, a spirit of endurance and willing service for our King, our country and our families can make the Empire prosperous and secure. Each man has still to see the job through.

Formations and Units of Eighth Army will go on to solve the many new and urgent problems with which we have been faced since the enemy's unconditional surrender on the 3rd [sic] May, 1945. Right well have those problems been tackled. Wherever they have gone, from Pola to the Austrian Alps, the veterans of the Eighth Army have gained the respect and admiration of the civilian population, and have thus already helped to win the peace.

The Eighth Army was composed of many Nations; all worked together in true comradeship. This spirit of generous co-operation is a good augury for the future of the World. Eighth Army men will be playing a tremendous part if they continue in fresh fields to fight and work for right and justice with the same enthusiasm that won great victories from El Alamein to the Po.[18]

NOTES

1. Howarth: *My God, Soldiers*, p.215
2. Gunner: *Front of The Line*, p.138
3. PRO: FO371/48827, Yugoslavia file no. 24
4. Doherty: *Clear The Way!*, p.260
5. Scott: *Account of the Irish Brigade*
6. A Hay: letter to author
7. Scott: *Account of the Irish Brigade*
8. ibid
9. BDH Clark: interview with author
10. Gunner: op cit, p.146
11. MJF Palmer: interview with author
12. BDH Clark: notes to author
13. PRO: WO170/4461, war diary, 36 Bde, 1945
14. ibid
15. ibid
16. J Lucas: notes to author
17. Gunner: op cit, p.157
18. PRO: WO170/4465, war diary 38 Bde, 1945

CHAPTER XXI

Eighth Army in Retrospect

As gallant an army as ever marched . . .

Britain created eight field armies during the Second World War, starting with the British Expeditionary Force of 1939. Eighth, Ninth and Tenth Armies were next to be formed, in 1941, followed by First Army in 1942. Then came Second Army in 1943 as well as Fourteenth Army, the largest British field army of the war, and finally Twelfth Army in 1945. There were also British elements in First Allied Airborne Army and in the US Fifth Army. Of all these formations, Eighth was undoubtedly the best known, not only during the war but also in the decades immediately after the war. How and why did it achieve its image?

Perhaps the simplest answer to that question is that Eighth Army was Britain's sole ground formation engaged against the Axis powers for a long period in the early part of the war. From its formation in late 1941 until November 1942, when the spearhead elements of First Army landed in north-west Africa, no other significant body of British troops was fighting the Germans or Italians. But that is a simple answer and, while it may be part of the equation, it is not the entire solution. Where Eighth Army fought is also a significant factor; so too is the personality of its best-known commander.

When Eighth Army was formed by General Auchinleck in September 1941 it marked a strengthening of British forces in North Africa. For the public at home, however, the new army carried with it the image of the forces that had already been engaged in the desert campaign. Thus O'Connor's success in Operation COMPASS in December 1940 was transferred, at least symbolically, to Eighth Army which included in its formations and units many that had served as part of Western Desert Force. The latter had become XIII Corps which subsequently became one of the two foundation corps of Eighth Army and so it is understandable that the image of Western Desert Force should have settled on that Army.

Although Western Desert Force's gains were later lost this does not seem to have detracted from public perception of the Force. It had achieved its success at a time when British victories were few indeed. Western Desert Force gained a special place in public affection in Britain as 'Wavell's 30,000' and its defeat of Italy's Tenth Army became a fresh

David and Goliath legend. Although the RAF had defeated the Luftwaffe in the Battle of Britain in the late summer of 1940, there was little else for the British public and taxpayer to cheer about as far as the fighting forces were concerned: the BEF had been ejected from mainland Europe and the Royal Navy was engaged in a bitter struggle against the Kriegsmarine's U-boat fleet with the latter sending large numbers of merchant ships to the bottom. Thus success was to be greeted enthusiastically from whatever quarter and Western Desert Force's victory over the Italians was a morale booster at home. It mattered little to the British public that the bulk of the front-line soldiers of O'Connor's command hailed from the Empire or the Dominions rather from Britain itself.It was still a British force which had gained a British victory.

Even when Rommel snatched back the fruits of that victory, public interest in the North African campaign did not seem to diminish. If anything the charismatic German increased interest in the desert war. Cinema newsreels carried regular stories of the conflict with Rommel's Afrika Korps with the latter becoming an elite formation in the eyes of the British public. The only other source of pictorial images at that time was the printed media: while newsprint was rationed, thus restricting the size of wartime newspapers, these still managed to carry news, features and photographs from North Africa. Even today there are many who recall such newspaper or newsreel stories and who will readily identify any British soldier who served in North Africa as belonging to Eighth Army. Equally all German veterans of the campaign are deemed to have served in Afrika Korps.

As the war went on a form of romantic haze enveloped the desert war. For those who did not have to fight there, it was a clean war and both sides appeared to behave in a chivalrous fashion. Certainly there are few instances of anything approaching an atrocity in North Africa but that does not mean that men were not dying and being maimed in circumstances as horrible as any other theatre: Keith Douglas's description of the body of a dead German gunner 'how on his skin the swart flies move;/ the dust upon the paper eye/ and the burst stomach like a cave'* is proof of that.

This romantic haze may have owed something to Lawrence of Arabia, or even to the British army that had defeated Napoleon's army in Egypt. Whatever the reason, it placed the mantle of hero on the shoulders of desert veterans. Visiting relatives in the north-west of England, while on weekend leave from his battery in the Derby area in late-1944, Gunner Bertie Cuthbert went out for a beer. He was amazed to find that he did not have to pay for a drink at all: once the Africa Star ribbon with the figure 8 on his battledress blouse had been noticed by the patrons in the bar the

* from the poem *Elegy for an 88 Gunner*, also known as *Vergissmeinnicht*

young gunner became a hero and was plied with as much beer as he could drink.[1]

In Britain the desert war was seen as being very important since the security of the Suez Canal depended on British success in Egypt, irrespective of the fact that the canal, as the main route to India, was denied to British shipping by enemy air and naval action in the Mediterranean. Mussolini also perceived the desert war as being an important struggle but Hitler regarded it as a sideshow, a view that would be shared by many postwar historians. Winston Churchill was another who regarded the campaign in the Middle East as crucial and feared the possible loss of Egypt: he and his CIGS, Sir John Dill, disagreed over the relative importance of Egypt in British strategic thinking. (There was potential for a German southward strike through the Caucasus that would threaten Egypt and allow a link up with Rommel, a possibility that the latter recognised.) Thus Churchill's perception of the importance of Egypt played its part in shaping the British public's view of the theatre.

When Rommel took Tobruk in June 1942 it led to an attempt to censure Churchill in the House of Commons which was followed by the prime minister's visit to Egypt, the sacking of Auchinleck and the appointments of Alexander, as CinC Middle East, and, eventually, Montgomery as GOC Eighth Army. Initially the media identified Alexander as the saviour of the Middle Eastern situation, a view reflecting that of Churchill to whom Alexander was the ideal of a soldier, a veritable *beau sabreur*. As noted in Chapter V, Montgomery, although the preferred choice of Brooke, the CIGS, was appointed only after the death of General Gott. Before long, however, it was Montgomery who had gripped the public consciousness at home in Britain and it is with his name that the desert war, and Eighth Army, has been most closely identified ever since.

Bernard Law Montgomery became a household name in the months following the final El Alamein battle. That victory was lauded as an outstanding achievement by a British army, coming as it did after one of the blackest periods of the war for the Allies. The man perceived to be Germany's greatest general had been defeated by a British commander who, by definition, had to be greater than Rommel. Almost overnight, Montgomery achieved heroic status and became the modern-day equivalent of Wellington or Marlborough, an image which endured for decades after the war. Since Alamein was a major British land victory over Germany, and portrayed by some as the *first* British victory, the architect of that victory, marked by the ringing of church bells throughout the nation,* was certain to become a national hero. Subsequently, as it became

---

* On 15 November 1942 on the orders of Winston Churchill although he was careful to ensure that the Operation TORCH landings in French north-west Africa had been successful before the bells were rung.

clear that Alamein, with Midway and Stalingrad, was one of the turning points of the war, that status was enhanced.

Montgomery revelled in the adulation that he received. On a visit to England in May 1943, when the North African campaign had ended, he became aware of his popularity, although he had not been asked to attend a Thanksgiving Service for the end of the African war in St Paul's two days after his arrival.

> Yet to my delighted surprise, wherever I went I was followed by crowds. The incident made me realise that if I were pretty popular with a lot of people, I was not too popular in some circles. Perhaps the one explained the other.[2]

When Montgomery went to see a performance of *Arsenic and Old Lace* in a West End theatre the audience gave him, rather than the cast, a standing ovation at the end of the show. On leaving the theatre he was met by crowds of admirers, ten deep, who wanted to see, or even touch, the victor of Alamein. At his hotel a similar crowd of well-wishers awaited him. Such shows of adulation were alien to a senior Army officer of the period; but Monty thrived on them to the extent that he began to enjoy the hero worship so much that Brooke had to remind him brusquely of the need to return to Africa and the conference which the prime minister was convening in Algiers.

By contrast, Montgomery was unpopular with many of his peer group. That unpopularity was not so much due to envy of his success as to the belief that, in courting publicity, Montgomery was not behaving as a gentleman should. Gentlemen not only never sought publicity but actively shunned it: it was said that a gentleman's name should only appear in a newspaper on the occasions of his birth, engagement, marriage and death. Monty's penchant for publicity led to his being regarded as a 'bounder' by many. General Lumsden,* whom Monty relieved of his command of X Corps after Alamein, is reputed to have said in his London club that he had been sacked because there was room for only one shit in the desert; and that was Montgomery.

More than half a century later the type of public adulation which greeted Monty is almost an everyday phenomenon, accorded to popular music artists, film stars, media personalities, many of whose sole claim to fame is that they appear on TV screens as presenters or journeymen actors in soap operas, and members of the Royal Family. The cult of the

---

* Lumsden was subsequently given command of an armoured corps and was later knighted. In 1944 he became Churchill's liaison officer with General Douglas MacArthur and was killed in a kamikaze attack on board the US Navy's battleship *New Mexico* in January 1945.

personality has become such an integral part of late-twentieth-century culture that it is difficult to imagine that hero-worship of this kind was once confined to only a few. Bernard Montgomery was one of those few and the name of Eighth Army was intimately associated with his in the public mind.

Thus both Montgomery and Eighth Army crossed over that invisible line that implants individuals or organisations in the public subconscious. Winston Churchill had, of course, helped. His visit to Eighth Army at Tripoli in February 1943 and his famous comment that 'it will be enough to say: I marched and fought with the Desert Army', as well as his comment to King George VI that the men of Eighth Army were perhaps the finest troops in the world, all served to build and perfect the image of Eighth Army.

There are many accounts of how Monty related to the soldiers and of how his personality transmitted itself to the men under his command. Lieutenant-General Sir Brian Horrocks, noting how sceptical soldiers usually are of the 'brass', commented on how the ordinary soldiers responded positively to Montgomery's visits. Lieutenant-General Sir Sidney Kirkman likened Monty to a film star and compared his rapport with the troops with that which Wellington had enjoyed in the Peninsular War.[3] However, perhaps the most important testimony comes from Geoffrey Keating, who headed the Army Film and Photographic Unit, and Warwick Charlton, who was responsible for Eighth Army's newspapers.[4]

In his biography of Montgomery, Nigel Hamilton quotes both men at length on the way in which Monty fired up Eighth Army. Charlton recalled for Hamilton how Keating and John Poston, Monty's ADC (who had served under Cunningham, Ritchie and Auchinleck), stage-managed Monty's adoption of the black beret as his 'trademark'. He also told Hamilton that Montgomery ensured that he (Charlton), although only a 24-year-old journalist, would have the freedom to print what he wished in his newspapers, thus making Charlton's papers 'a powerful new weapon in the arsenal of Eighth Army's mounting morale'.[5]

Charlton described how Montgomery had changed attitudes in Eighth Army which had very little morale left when he arrived and in which the most popular general 'was probably Rommel'.

> Until Monty came. There was this extraordinary little man whom nobody knew anything about, really. And what he did was a sort of Wesleyan thing – in my view. It was a revival thing – to revive their spirits, revive their minds.[6]

Charlton's view was that Monty was a revolutionary general who created a revolutionary army. Thus began the legend of Eighth Army, the great sense of purpose that pervaded the Army and spread beyond its confines through the families and friends of its soldiers to infect the nation. Hamilton outlines it thus:

> To counter the morale of Rommel's army, Monty preached an Eighth Army gospel based on simple virtues, understandable by all: the infectious pride of belonging to a great and professional team, fighting for time-honoured principles, paramount among which were freedom and respect for the individual. There was no element of coercion: of a ruthless general imposing harsh discipline upon an ailing army.[7]

So it was that Eighth Army owed much of its special place in the British psyche to Bernard Montgomery. Its soldiers also maintained a special place in their hearts for Monty: the general they believed they could trust; the man they felt would not risk unnecessary casualties; the man who had made the individual soldier feel important. It was Monty's leadership that made this great army of civilian-soldiers, for by the time he arrived in the desert the bulk of Eighth Army's soldiers were wartime conscripts, swell its collective chest with pride, with a sense of purpose – the defeat of evil-and the belief that it could march to victory. Not for nothing was Monty described as the dynamo of Eighth Army.[8] The BBC's Denis Johnston wrote that Monty had turned Eighth Army from 'the shoulder-shrugging cynics they used to be into the confident, self-advertising crowd they now are'.[9] It had been the electrical charge from Monty that had brought about the change which Johnston described. One desert veteran, a member of a REME unit, recalled how Monty's

> arrival was a great moral[e] booster. He visited all units, and had a talk about what was going to happen. VICTORY that is, no more retreats etc.[10]

Monty himself recognised the phenomenon. In notes on morale written in August 1943 he compared a successful army to a large family in which everyone knew 'the form' and knew each other; above all they knew the head of the family, the army's commander. He wrote:

> Morale is based on confidence. The troops must have complete confidence in their higher commander; they must know that the battle is safe in his hands, that he will not sacrifice their lives needlessly, that success will always crown their efforts.[11]

He accepted that his style of leadership was not to everyone's liking.

> Some people would say, and I know do say, that I advertise myself. But I regard the state of affairs that exists in my Army as a pearl of very great

price, and as a battle-winning factor of the first degree. I have, by my methods, obtained the affection and loyal trust of my men; hero-worship is inherent in the British public, and because I have never failed to give them success my troops regard me as the sort of General they like, and they try to show it.[12]

Was the legend of Eighth Army a deserved one? In the aftermath of war the achievements of that army were regarded as among the greatest in British military history. The public continued to regard Montgomery as a national hero and when he retired from military life in 1958, after fifty years' service in the Army, he was quick to publish his memoirs, which proved a bestseller.* Publishing rights to the book were sold across the world and it was serialised in newspapers; the readership of the *Sunday Times* rose by 100,000 as a result of the paper obtaining the serialisation rights. The BBC also became involved in what was a media phenomenon by engaging Montgomery to present a series of live television programmes on his career.

Thus the memory of Eighth Army was kept fresh in the public mind and Monty's victory at El Alamein was generally considered to be on a par with Wellington's at Waterloo. In subsequent years, however, the status of Montgomery as one of Britain's greatest-ever generals has increasingly been questioned. This questioning began shortly after the publication of his memoirs with Correlli Barnett's book *The Desert Generals* which presented the first complete account of the North African campaign from June 1940 until May 1943. The five principal British commanders of the period were assessed in detail with Monty's version of the campaign being challenged by Barnett. The very necessity to fight the October battle of El Alamein is questioned by the author who suggests that the TORCH landings in early-November would have precipitated a German withdrawal from Egypt to avoid being trapped between two armies. Rommel, argues Barnett, would have been anxious to withdraw from the Alamein positions to defend his main supply base at Tripoli; the Allied troops landing in Algeria and advancing into Tunisia were closer to Tripoli than was Rommel's army. Why then was Alamein fought at all? Barnett's view is that

> It was the last purely British victory in the war against Germany; it was the swansong of Britain as a great independent power. After *Torch* the British war effort from Churchill and Montgomery downwards became subordinate to the American. Second Alamein was the last chance to

* The first edition, of 140,000 copies, sold out within two days and was swiftly followed by two further impressions, bringing the total to 200,000 within weeks of publication.

restore British prestige, shaken after a year of defeat, with banner headlines, with the ringing of church bells, and with any other means that might make the victory as famous as Blenheim or Waterloo. . . . The ultimate judgement of history may well be to record it as a political victory.[13]

Barnett is certainly right when he points out that El Alamein was the last purely British victory against the Germans. He is also right in suggesting that history may well record it as a political victory, notwithstanding the fact that all victories are, to a greater or lesser extent, political. But that is not to accept the argument, espoused by such writers as R W Thompson in *The Montgomery Legend*, that there was no need to fight the battle with its large toll of casualties. Michael Carver, in the foreword to the third edition of his book, *El Alamein*, comments that

> that was not the view that Churchill and the Chiefs of Staff took. They still pressed for a major victory over Rommel before the Operation Torch landings, primarily to influence Spain not to intervene and to divert Axis effort and attention from them, but also to show both the Americans and the Russians that Britain could gain a victory on her own.[14]

There was, therefore, a moral, as well as a military-political imperative in British minds for fighting the battle. Not only the self-esteem of Eighth Army but British national pride demanded that Rommel be defeated by a British army. As Arthur Bryant commented in *The Turn of the Tide*

> It was this that made Churchill stride up and down his room in the Embassy in Cairo crying, 'Rommel, Rommel, Rommel! What else matters but beating him!'[15]

At El Alamein, Eighth Army gave Churchill what he wanted: the defeat of Rommel. Not only that, but it removed from the Italo-German order of battle several divisions, tens of thousands of soldiers, about 1,000 artillery pieces and over 500 tanks. Had Rommel been able to withdraw from Egypt with his forces relatively intact, which must surely have been the case had the British not launched the October offensive, then the Axis strength ranged against the Allies in French north-west Africa would have been so great that it is doubtful whether those operations could have met with success.

The Allied forces in Tunisia had very long lines of communication: First Army had been shipped out from Britain and the US forces had been transported across the Atlantic; immediate reinforcement was, therefore, not practicable. In the early phase of the Tunisian campaign the Germans were able to hold the Allies and prevent a breakthrough to Tunis in spite of having only a small force in the country. Bearing this factor in mind, it is reasonable to argue that the final battle at El Alamein was a necessary engagement which had an important strategic outcome. It must therefore rank as one of Eighth Army's most significant and outstanding achievements.

There were further achievements in the course of the campaigns in Africa, Sicily and Italy and, of course, Eighth Army had already inflicted serious loss on Rommel in the CRUSADER battles of 1941. Although those battles represent Eighth Army's first victory, that victory was Pyrrhic in its outcome with the victor almost as badly mauled as the vanquished; indeed, when looking at the armoured struggle, the victor was arguably more mauled than the vanquished.

However, Eighth Army's last victory must also rank as its greatest achievement: its part in 15 Army Group's final destruction of German forces in Italy. Prior to the Army Group's spring offensive of 1945 Mark Clark had considered Eighth Army to be a spent force and had little faith in McCreery who had succeeded Leese as its commander in the autumn of 1944. Clark's original concept had been to relegate Eighth Army to a subsidiary role in Operation GRAPESHOT, but the two army commanders, McCreery and Truscott, had persuaded him otherwise and so Eighth Army was allowed to launch Operation BUCKLAND which proved to be an outstanding success with one of the war's best examples of all-arms co-operation.

But even before that, McCreery had wrought wonders with Eighth Army's morale, restoring its sense of purpose and determination to destroy the evil of Nazism to a level not seen since the departure of Montgomery. McCreery achieved this without the self-promotion that had been so much a part of Montgomery's style. And he did it at a time when the average soldier knew that the war was near its end and that the final destruction of the Third Reich was not going to take place in Italy. At home, public interest had become concentrated on what was happening in north-west Europe and the progress of 12 and 21 Army Groups, and, to a lesser extent, 6 Army Group, inside the Reich itself. Against that background McCreery's re-invigoration of Eighth Army must rank as an outstanding example of leadership and, when looked at in combination with what the Army achieved in April 1945, must make a very strong argument for proposing Richard McCreery as Eighth Army's greatest commander. And, of course

McCreery had perhaps the greatest personal ambition of them all [Allied commanders in Italy in 1945]. He had inherited the famous British Eighth Army whose line of brilliant commanders and unbroken successes since Alamein made it unthinkable that he should be the one to lead it shuffling into obscurity rather than marching to the matchless victory which its final days deserved.[16]

Eighth Army deserves to be remembered as an outstanding field army. It brought together soldiers from throughout the United Kingdom, the Commonwealth and Empire as well as from the occupied countries of Europe and from neutral Ireland to fight in campaigns from Africa to Austria's borders. One of its soldiers, James Lucas who served in 56th Division, summed up the esprit of Eighth Army when he wrote:

> During the Gothic Line offensive I lay upon a mountain peak (not on the sky line, naturally) and felt a glow of pride as I considered the 8th's order of battle. If one excluded the Yanks who lay on the Tyrhennian side, far beyond the mountains that run up the spine of Italy, then the rest of the peninsula belonged to us; 8th Army. And what a colourful variety of warriors formed that Army's battle line; New Zealanders, South Africans, a few Australians, Canadians, Indians, Nepalese, Scotsmen, Irishmen (from both sides of the border), Englishmen, Cypriots, Singalese and a miscellany of units of men drawn from all over the British Empire. It made me proud to be a member of a world-wide Empire and of a British Army whose fame had been born in the far-away deserts of Libya.[17]

James Lucas and his comrades were imbued with a common purpose: to fight and destroy Nazism. The choice of a Crusader's Cross as Eighth Army's badge was inspired for the Second World War was a crusade against evil and Eighth Army soldiers were among the many who participated in that noble crusade.

NOTES

1. Cuthbert: interview with author
2. Montgomery: *Memoirs*, p.183
3. Hamilton: *Monty, Master of the Battlefield*, p.294
4. ibid, pp.79-83
5. ibid
6. ibid, p.79
7. ibid, p.80
8. Sir Edgar Williams, quoted in Hamilton, op cit, p.263
9. ibid, p.481
10. L LePage, letter to author, Feb 1996
11. Brooks (ed): *Montgomery and the Eighth Army*, p.268
12. ibid, pp.269-270
13. Barnett: *The Desert Generals*, p.272
14. Carver: *El Alamein*, p.11
15. Bryant: *The Turn of the Tide*, p.365
16. Harpur: *The Impossible Victory*, p.102
17. J. Lucas: notes to author

Appendix I

Draft Order of Battle, Eighth Army, 1 November 1941
(compiled 5 October 1941)

HQ, Eighth Army
|
Armd Corps
|

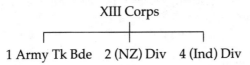

7 Armd Div   22 Armd Bde Gp   1 (SA) Div (less 1 Bde Gp)   22 Gds Bde

XIII Corps

1 Army Tk Bde   2 (NZ) Div   4 (Ind) Div

Under Army Cmd: Oasis Gp (29 Indian Inf Bde Gp)
2 (SA) Div (inc 1 Bde Gp LOB)
161 Inf Bde (less dets)
Matruh Fortress (Bde Gp 1 (SA) Div – LOB)
83, 86, 87 & 91 LoC Sub Areas
Army Troops

The following units came under Eighth Army command on formation:
RAC & Armd: KDG; CIH; Sqn, 6 SA A/car Rgt; 4 SA A/car Rgt; 3 SA
Recce Bn; Sqn 4H; 7H; 2, 8 & 44 RTR, Sqn 42 RTR; NZ Div Cav Rgt; 7 SA
Recce Bn
Infantry: 1/4 Essex; 1/5 Essex; 2/5 Essex; 1 KRRC; 2 RB; 1 Buffs; 1 R.
Sussex; 2 Camerons; 4/11 Sikhs; 4/16 Punjab; 2/5 Mahratta LI; 1/6 Raj
Rgt; 7 Indian Bde A/tk Coy; 11 Indian Bde A/tk Coy; 3 C. Gds; 2 S. Gds;
1 THR; 1 Worcs; 3/2 Punjab; 6 FFR; 18 -22 NZ Bns; 1 RNC; 1 TS; 1 DEOR;
1 NMR; 1/2 FF Bn; CTH; 1 SA Irish; 2 Rgt Botha; 3 TS; Rgt Pres Steyn
(MG); 1 ILH; 1 RLI; 1 RDLI; 2 UMR; 2 RDLI; Kaffir R; 2 TS; 1 SAP; 2 SAP

Appendix II

Order of Battle, Eighth Army, 23 October 1942 at El Alamein

HQ, Eighth Army –
    X Corps –
    1 Armd Div –
        2 Armd Bde: Bays; 9L; 10H; Yorks Dgns (Mot Bn)
        7 Mot Bde: 2 RB; 7 RB; 2 KRRC
        Hammerforce (from 8 Armd Div) 4/6 (SA) Armd Car
        Regt; 146 Fd Regt RA; 73 A/tk Regt; RA; 56 LAA Regt RA
Div Troops inc: 12 L; 2 RHA; 4 RHA; 11 RHA (SP); 78 Fd Regt RA; 76 A/tk
Regt RA; 42 LAA Regt RA; 1 & 7 Sqns RE; 1 Fd Pk Sqn RE; 572 A Fd Coy;
9 Fd Sqn (from 8 Armd Div); Div Sigs; X & Z Coys 1 RNF (MG Bn); 1 & 15
Lt Fd Amb RAMC
        8 Armd Div –
        Subordinate formations detached
        10 Armd Div –
            8 Armd Bde: 3 RTR; Notts Yeo; Staffs Yeo; 1 Buffs
            24 Armd Bde (from 8 Armd Div): 41 RTR; 45 RTR; 47 RTR;
            11 KRRC
            133 Lorried Inf Bde (from 44 Div): 2, 4 & 5 R Sussex; W
            Coy 1 RNF (MG)
Div Troops inc: Royals; 1 RHA; 104 RHA; 98 Fd Regt; 5 RHA; 84 A/tk
Regt; 53 LAA Regt; 2 & 3 Fd Sqns RE; 141 Fd Pk Sqn RE; 6 Fd Sqn RE; 571
& 573 A Fd Coys; Div Sigs; 3, 8 & 168 Lt Fd Ambs RAMC
Corps Troops inc: 570 Corps Fd Pk Coy RE; Corps Sigs; 12 & 151 Lt Fd
Ambs RAMC
        XIII Corps –
        7 Armd Div –
            4 Lt Armd Bde: Greys; 4/8 H*; 1 KRRC
            22 Armd Bde: 1 RTR; 5 RTR; 4 CLY; 1 RB
1Free French Bde Gp: 1 & 2 Bns FFL; 3 Bn Inf Marine Pacifique; 2 AA Coy
1 Fusiliers Marine; 2 FF A/tk Coy; 22 NA A/tk Coy; 1 FF Fd Coy Eng; 3

---

* A temporary amalgamation of 4th Queen's Own and 8th King's Royal Irish
Hussars which presaged the 1958 amalgamation of these regiments as the Queen's
Royal Irish Hussars.

Fd Regt RA (attd); 1 FF Flying Coln; Armd Car Sqn 1 Marocco Spahis; 1 FF Tk Coy; A/tk Tp 1 Marocco Spahis; AA Tp 1 Bn FFL

Div Troops inc: HCR; 11 H (in reserve); 2 Derby Yeo; 3 RHA; 4 Fd Regt RA; 97 Fd Regt RA; 65 A/tk Regt RA; 15 LAA Regt RA; 4 & 21 Fd Sqns RE; 143 Fd Pk Sqn RE; Div Sigs; 44 Recce Regt; 2 & 14 Lt Fd Ambs RAMC

      50 (Northumbrian) Div -
              69 Bde: 5 E Yks; 6 & 7 Green Howards
              151 Bde: 6, 8 & 9 DLI
              1 Greek Bde: 1, 2 & 3 Inf Bns; 1 Gr Fd Regt Arty; 1 Gr Fd
              Sqn Eng; 1 Gr MG Coy; 1 Gr Fd Amb

2 Free French Bde Gp: 5 & 11 Bns de Marche; 21 & 23 NA A/tk Coys; 2 FF Coy Eng; 2 FF Fd Amb

Div Troops inc: 74, 111, 124 & 154 Fd Regts RA; 102 A/tk Regt RA; 34 LAA Regt RA; 233 & 505 Fd Coys RE; 235 Fd Pk Coy; Div Sigs; Tac HQ and two coys 2 Cheshire (MG Bn); 186 & 149 Fd Ambs RAMC

      44 (Home Counties) Div –
              131 Bde: 1/5, 1/6 & 1/7 Queens
              132 Bde: 2 Buffs, 4 & 5 RWK

Div Troops inc: 57, 58 65 & 53 Fd Regts RA; 57 A/tk Regt RA; 30 LAA Regt RA; 11, 209 & 211 Fd Coys RE; 211 Fd Pk Coy; 577 A Fd Coy; Div Sigs; 6 Cheshire (MG Bn); 131 & 132 Fd Ambs RAMC

Corps troops inc: tp 4/6 SA Armd Car Regt; 118 & 124 RTR (dummy tks); HQ plus comp bty 4 Svy Regt RA; 578 A Fd Coy RE; 576 Corps Fd Pk Coy RE; Div Sigs

              XXX Corps –

4 Indian Div –
              5 Ind Bde: 1/4 Essex; 4/6 Raj Rif; 3/10 Baluch
              7 Ind Bde: 1 R Sussex; 4/16 Punjab; 1/2 GR
              161 Ind Bde: 1 A&SH; 1/1 Punjab; 4/7 Rajput

Div Troops inc: 1, 11 & 32 Fd Regts RA; 149 A/tk Regt RA; 57 LAA Regt RA; 2, 4 & 12 Fd Coys RE; 11 Fd Pk Coy RE; Div Sigs; 6 Raj Rif (MG Bn); 17 & 26 Ind Fd Ambs & 75 Lt Ind Fd Amb RIAMC

      51 (Highland) Div –
              152 Bde: 2 Seaforth; 5 Seaforth; 5 Cameron
              153 Bde: 5 BW; 1 Gordons; 5/7 Gordons
              154 Bde: 1 BW; 7 BW; 7 A&SH

Div troops inc: 126, 127 & 128 Fd Regts RA; 61 A/tk Regt RA; 40 LAA Regt RA; 274, 275 & 276 Fd Coys RE; 239 Fd Pk Coy RE; Div Sigs; 1/7 Middx (MG Bn); 51 Recce Regt; 174, 175 & 176 Fd Ambs RAMC

      9 (Aus) Div –

20 Bde: 2/13, 2/15 & 2/17 Aus Inf Bns
24 Bde: 2/28, 2/32 & 2/43 Aus Inf Bns
26 Bde: 2/23, 2/24 & 2/48 Aus Inf Bns

Div troops inc: 9 Aus Div Cav Regt; 2/6, 2/8 & 2/12 Aus Fd Regts Arty; 3 Aus A/tk Regt; 4 Aus LAA Regt; 2/3, 2/7 & 2/12 Aus Fd Coys Eng; 2/4 Aus Fd Pk Coy; 2/3 Aus Pioneer Bn; Div Sigs; 2/2 Aus Bn (MG); 2/3, 2/8 & 2/11 Aus Fd Ambs

Attd: 40 RTR (23 Armd Bde); 1 & 3 Secs 66 Mtr Coy RE

2 (NZ) Div –

5 Bde: 21, 22, 23 & 28 (Maori) Bns
6 Bde: 24, 25 & 26 Bns
9 Armd Bde: 3 H; R Wilts Yeo; Warwick Yeo

Div troops inc: 2 NZ Div Cav Regt; 4, 5 & 6 NZ Fd Regts Arty; 7 NZ A/tk Regt; 14 NZ LAA Regt; 6, 7 & 8 NZ Fd Coys Eng; 5 NZ Fd Pk Coy; Div Sigs; 27 NZ Bn (MG); 5 & 6 NZ Fd Amb; 166 Lt Fd Amb RAMC

1 (SA) Div –

1 Bde: R Natal Carabiniers; 1 DofE's Own Rif; 1 Transvaal Scottish
2 Bde: 1/2 Fd Force Bn; 1 Natal Mtd Rif; Cape Town Hldrs
3 Bde: 1 Imp Lt H; 1 R Durban LI; 1 Rand LI

Div troops inc: 3 SA Armd Car Regt; 1, 4 & 7 SA Fd Regts Arty; 1 SA A/tk Regt; 1 SA LAA Regt; 1, 2, 3 & 5 SA Fd Coys Eng; Div Sigs; Regt President Steyn (MG Bn); Coy Die Middelaandse Regt (MG); 12, 15 & 18 SA Fd Ambs

Attd: 8 RTR (23 Armd Bde)

1 SA Div Reserve Force inc : 8 RTR; 3 SA Armd Car Regt (less 2 sqns); 2 Regt Botha (from 1 SA Bde); plus one SA A/tk bty; one SA LAA Tp and a tp of Scorpions

In Corps Reserve: 23 Armd Bde Gp (less detd units) 121 SP Fd Regt RA; 168 LAA Bty 56 LAA Regt RA; 295 A Fd Coy RE; 7 Lt Fd Amb RAMC

Corps troops inc: Corps Def Sqn RAC; 3 tps 4/6 SA Armd Car Regt; 7, 64 & 69 Med Regts RA; comp bty 4 Svy Regt RA; HQ and 2 secs 66 Mtr Coy (Under Army Command) –

1 Army Tk Bde; 1 Armd Bde; 2 & 12 AA Bdes; 21 Ind Bde

Appendix III

Outline Order of Battle, Eighth Army, 9 April 1945

HQ, Eighth Army –
    V Corps –
    56 Div –
            167 Bde: 9 RF; 1 LS; 1LIR
            24 Guards Bde: 2 CG; 1 SG; 1 Buffs
            169 Bde: 2/5, 2/6 & 2/7 Queen's
    Cremona Combat Gp –
            21 (Italian) Infantry Regt
            22 (Italian) Infantry Regt
    8 Indian Div –
            17 Indian Bde: 1 RF; 1 FFR; 1/5 RGR (FF)
            19 Indian Bde: 1 A&SH; 3/8 Punjab; 6 RFFR; Bn of Jaipur
            State Inf
            21 Indian Bde: 5 RWK; 1MLI; 3/15 Punjab
    78 Div –
            11 Bde: 2 LF; 1 East Surrey; 5 Northants
            36 Bde: 5 Buffs; 6RWK; 8 A&SH
            38 (Irish) Bde: 2 Inniks; 1 RIrF; 2 LIR
    2 NZ Div –
            4 NZ Armd Bde: 18 Bn, 19 Bn & 20 Bn NZ Armd Regt
            5 NZ Bde: 21 Bn, 23 Bn & 28 (Maori) Bn NZ Regt
            6 NZ Bde: 24 Bn, 25 Bn & 26 Bn NZ Regt
            9 NZ Bde: 2 Bn (Cav), 22 Bn & 27 Bn (MG) Regt
2 Armd Bde: BAYS; 9 L
9 Armd Bde: 27 L (less 1 sqn); 755 (US) Tank Bn LVsT (Fantails)
21 Tank Bde: 12 RTR; 48 RTR; NIH
2 Cdo Bde: 2, 9, 40 (RM) & 45 (RM) Cdos
    II Polish Corps
    3 Carpathian Div –
            1 Car Bde: 1, 2 & 3 Car Rifle Bns
            2 Car Rifle Bde: 4, 5 & 6 Car Rifle Bns
            3 Car Rifle Bde: 7, 8 & 9 Car Rifle Bns
    5 Kresowa Div –
            4 Wolynska Bde: 10, 11 & 12 Wol Rifle Bns
            5 Wilenska Bde: 13, 24 & 15 Wil Rifle Bns

6 Lwowska Bde: 16, 17 & 18 Lw Rifle Bns
2 Polish Armd Bde: 1 Bn Pol Armd Cav Regt; 4 Bn Pol Armd Regt; 6 Bn Lw Armd Regiments
7 Armd Bde: 6 RTR; 8 RTR
43 Indian Lorried Inf Bde: 2/6 GR; 2/8 GR; 2/10 GR; 14/20 H; 2 RTR

X Corps
Jewish Inf Bde Gp: 1, 2 & 3 Palestine Regt
Friuli Combat Gp: 87 & 88 Italian Inf Regts

XIII Corps
Folgore Combat Gp: Nembo Regt; S. Marco Regt

10 Indian Div –
10 Indian Bde: 1 DLI; 2/4 GR; 4 Baluch; bn of Jodhpur Sardar Inf
20 Indian Bde: 2 Loyals; 3 MLI; 2/3 GR; 1/2 Punjab; bn of Nabha Akal Inf; Lovat Scouts; 2 HLI
25 Indian Bde: 1 KORR; 3/1 Punjab; 3 RGR; 4/11 Sikhs
Army Reserve

6 (Br) Armd Div –
26 Armd Bde: 16/5 L; 17/21 L; 2 Lothians
1 Guards Bde: 3 GG; 3 WG; 1 Welch
61 Bde: 1 KRRC; 2 RB; 7 RB
2 Para Bde: 4, 5 & 6 Para Bns

Appendix IV

VICTORIA CROSSES AWARDED TO EIGHTH ARMY

Some measure of the achievements of Eighth Army can be gleaned from the number of Victoria Crosses awarded to its members, thirty-four in all. Of these twenty were won in North Africa and the remainder in Italy; none was gained in Sicily. Almost half of the VCs were posthumous awards and two others died in action before their awards were announced officially; such a rate of posthumous awards was the norm during the Second World War.

Awards were spread among the armoured regiments, the gunners and the infantry and a wide range of nationalities was also represented: seven Indian Army soldiers were decorated, including two Gurkhas; Australia gained three, all from the same battalion and all posthumous; New Zealand claimed three, of which one was Charles Upham's bar to the VC he had earned in Crete and another was the first awarded to a Maori; Canada took two VCs; South Africa also provided the winners of two Crosses; Denmark's Anders Lassen won the VC posthumously in the closing weeks of the war; Ireland, a neutral country, also earned one posthumous VC; the remaining six included two Scots and five Englishmen, one of whom was born in India. The latter country therefore provided the greatest number of Eighth Army's VC winners.

Brigadier John Charles Campbell, Royal Artillery, commanding 7th Armoured Division Support Group; 21 November 1941 at Sidi Rezegh, Libya
Rifleman John Beeley, 1st Bn The King's Royal Rifle Corps; 21 November 1941 at Sidi Rezegh, Libya (Posthumous)
Second-Lieutenant George Ward Gunn, 3rd Royal Horse Artillery: 21 November 1941 at Sidi Rezegh, Libya (Posthumous)
Captain Philip John Gardner, 4th Royal Tank Regiment; 23 November 1941 at Tobruk, Libya
Captain James Joseph Bernard Jackman, 1st Bn The Royal Northumberland Fusiliers; 25 November 1941 at El Duda, Libya (Posthumous)

Lieutenant-Colonel Henry Robert Bowreman Foote, 7th Royal Tank Regiment; 27 May – 15 June 1942 at the Gazala line, Libya
Sergeant Quentin George Murray Smythe, The Royal Natal Carabineers; 5 June 1942 at Alem Hamza, Egypt
Private Adam Herbert Wakenshaw, 9th Bn The Durham Light Infantry; 27 June 1942, south of Mersa Matruh, Egypt (Posthumous)
Captain Charles Hazlitt Upham, 20th (The Canterbury Regiment) Bn 2nd NZEF; 14/15 July 1942 at El Ruweisat Ridge, Egypt (The only Bar to a VC of the Second World War)
Sergeant Keith Elliott, 22nd Bn 2nd NZEF; 15 July 1942 at Ruweisat, Egypt
Private Arthur Stanley Gurney, 2/48th Bn (SA) AIF; 22 July 1942 at Tel el Eisa, Egypt (Posthumous)
Private Percival Eric Gratwick, 2/48th Bn (SA) AIF; 25/26 October 1942 at Miteiriya Ridge, Egypt (Posthumous)
Sergeant William Henry Kibby, 2/48th Bn (SA) AIF; 23 – 31 October 1942 at Miteiriya Ridge, Egypt (Posthumous)
Lieutenant-Colonel Victor Buller Turner, 2nd Bn The Rifle Brigade; 27 October 1942 at El Aqqaqir (Kidney Ridge), Egypt

Lieutenant-Colonel Derek Anthony Seagrim, 7th Bn The Green Howards; 20/21 March 1943 at the Mareth Line, Tunisia (later killed in action; his brother, Major H P Seagrim was later posthumously awarded the George Cross in Burma, the only instance of a single family having both a VC and a GC winner)
Second-Lieutenant Moana-Nui-a-Kiwa Ngarimu, 28th (Maori) Bn 2nd NZEF; 26/27 March 1943 at Tobaga Gap, Tunisia (Posthumous) The first Maori VC
Subadar Lalbahadur Thapa, 1/2nd Gurkha Rifles; 5/6 April 1943 at Ross-es-Zouai, Tunisia
Private Eric Anderson, 5th Bn The East Yorkshire Regt; 6 April 1943 at Wadi Akarit, Tunisia (Posthumous)
Lieutenant-Colonel Lorne MacLaine Campbell, 7th Bn The Argyll and Sutherland Hldrs; 6 April 1943 at Wadi Akarit, Tunisia
Company Havildar Major Chhelu Ram, 6th Rajputana Rifles; 19/20 April 1943 at Djebel Garli, Tunisia (Posthumous)
Captain Paul Triquet, Royal 22ᵉ Regiment, Canadian Army; 14 December 1943 at Casa Berardi, Italy

Sepoy Kamal Ram, 8th Punjab Regt; 12 May 1944 at Cassino, Italy
Captain Richard Wakeford, 2nd/4th Bn The Hampshire Regt; 13 May 1944 at Cassino, Italy
Fusilier Francis Jefferson, 2nd Lancashire Fusiliers, 16 May 1944 at Cassino, Italy

Naik Yeshwant Ghadge, 5th Mahratta Light Infantry; 10 July 1944 in the upper Tiber Valley, Italy (Posthumous)
Major John Keefer Mahony, The Westminster Regt, Canadian Army, 13 July 1944 at the Melfa river, Italy
Lieutenant Gerard Ross Norton, Kaffrarian Rifles, South African Army, attd 1/4th Bn The Hampshire Regt; 31 August 1944 at Monte Gridolfo, Italy
Rifleman Sherbahadur Thapa, 1/9th Gurkha Rifles; 18/19 September 1944 at San Marino, Italy (Posthumous)
Private Ernest Alvia Smith, Seaforth Hldrs of Canada; 21/22 October 1944 at the river Savio, Italy
Captain John Henry Cound Brunt, The Sherwood Foresters, attd 6th Bn The Lincolnshire Regt; 9th December 1944 on the Lamone river near Faenza (killed before his award was gazetted)

Corporal Thomas Peck Hunter, 43 RM Commando; 2 April 1945 at Lake Comacchio, Italy (Posthumous)
Major Anders Frederik Emil Victor Lassen, attd Special Boat Service, No. 1 Special Air Service Regt; 8 April 1945 at Lake Comacchio, Italy (Posthumous)
Sepoy Ali Haidar, 13th Frontier Force Rifles; 9 April 1945 near Fusignano, Italy
Sepoy Namdeo Jadhao, 1/5th Mahratta Light Infantry; 9 April 1945 at the Senio river, Italy

An Eighth Army connection can be claimed for three further VCs. Just before the launch of Operation CRUSADER in November 1941 a commando raid was made at Beda Littoria in Libya in an attempt to take prisoner General Erwin Rommel. The raid was unsuccessful and the officer in command was killed. However, *Lieutenant-Colonel Geoffrey Charles Tasker Keyes*, 11th Scottish Commando (his own regiment was The Royal Scots Greys), was posthumously awarded the Victoria Cross; Keyes already held the DSO and the MC.

In October 1944 at Monte Cecco, Italy *Private Richard Henry Burton* of the Duke of Wellington's Regiment won the VC when, singlehandedly, he eliminated an enemy machine-gun post which was holding up an assault. At that time Burton's battalion was serving in XIII Corps which was under Fifth Army command but was normally part of Eighth Army.

Likewise *Rifleman Thaman Gurung* of 1/5th Royal Gurkha Rifles was under Fifth Army command when he won his posthumous VC for his gallantry while acting as a scout to a fighting patrol of his battalion during 17 Indian Brigade's operations against Monte San Bartolo. Seventeen Brigade was in 8th Indian Division of XIII Corps; Thaman Gurung's VC was actually won in Eighth Army's sector.

Appendix V

The D-Day Dodgers
(to the tune of 'Lili Marlene')

Oh, we're the D-Day dodgers, out in Italy
Always on the vino, always on the spree
Eighth Army scroungers, and our tanks
We live in Rome, amongst the Yanks
We are the D-Day dodgers in sunny Italy

We landed at Salerno, a holiday with pay
The Jerries brought the bands out to greet us on our way
Showed us the sights and gave us tea
We all sang songs, the beer was free
To welcome D-Day dodgers to sunny Italy

Naples and Cassino were taken in our stride
We didn't come to fight here, we just came for the ride
Anzio and Sangro were just names
We only came to look for dames
The randy D-Day dodgers in sunny Italy

On the way to Florence we had a lovely time
We ran a bus to Rimini, right through the Gothic line
Soon to Bologna we will go and after that we'll cross the Po
We'll still be D-Day dodging in sunny Italy

Dear Lady Astor, you think you know a lot
Standing on your platform and talking tommyrot
You, England's sweetheart and its pride
We think your mouth's too bleedin' wide
That's from your D-Day dodgers in sunny Italy

Look around the mountains in the mud and rain
See the scattered crosses, there's some that have no names
Heartache and sorrow are all gone
The boys beneath them slumber on
They are the D-Day dodgers who'll stay in Italy.

(Note: there are several versions of this ballad. This is the version best-
known to the author; it was also recorded by the Spinners at one time.)

350

Bibliography

Alexander, Field Marshal The Earl of Tunis and Errigal: *Despatch* (London, 1950)

Anders, Lieut-Gen. W, CB: *An Army in Exile: The Story of The Second Polish Corps* (London, 1949)

Barnett, C: *The Desert Generals* (London, 1960)

Bates, P: *Dance of War – The Story of the Battle of Egypt* (London, 1992)

Bateson, H: *First into Italy* (London, 1944)

Baynes, J: *The Forgotten Victor – General Sir Richard O'Connor* (London, 1989)

Blaxland, G: *The Plain Cook and the Great Showman – The First and Eighth Armies in North Africa* (London, 1977)

—— *Alexander's Generals – The Italian Campaign 1944-45* (London, 1979)

Blumenson, M: *Mark Clark* (London, 1985)

Borthwick, Capt. James: *The 51st Highland Division in Africa and Sicily* (Glasgow, nd)

Brookes, S (ed): *Montgomery and the Eighth Army* (London, 1991)

Brownlow, D G: *Checkmate at Ruweisat – Auchinleck's Finest Hour* (Massachusetts, 1977)

Bryant, A: *The Turn of the Tide* (London 1977)

—— *Victory in the West* (London,)

Butler, J R M: *Grand Strategy*, Vols II and III (London, 1957 and 1964)

Buzzell, N (compiler): *The Register of the Victoria Cross* (Cheltenham, 1988)

Carver, M: *El Alamein* (London, 1962)

Churchill, Sir Winston: *The Second World War* (London, 1951)

Connell, J: *Auchinleck – A Critical Biography* (London, 1959)

D'Este, C: *Bitter Victory – The Battle for Sicily 1943* (London, 1988)

Doherty, R: *Wall of Steel – The History of The 9th (Londonderry) HAA Regiment, RA(SR)* (Limavady, 1988)

—— *Clear The Way! – A History of the 38th (Irish) Brigade 1941-1947* (Dublin, 1993)

—— *Irish Generals – Irish Generals in the British Army in the Second World War* (Belfast, 1993)

—— *Only the Enemy in Front – The Reconnaissance Corps at War 1940-1946* (London, 1994)

Douglas, K: *Alamein to Zem Zem* (Oxford, 1979)

Farndale, General Sir M: *History of the Royal Regiment of Artillery: The Years of Defeat 1939-41* (London, 1996)

Forty, G: *Afrika Korps at War* (London, 1978)

Fraser, D: *Alanbrooke* (London, 1982)

— *And We Shall Shock Them* (London, 1983)

— *Knight's Cross – A Life of Field Marshal Erwin Rommel* (London, 1993)

Gaylor, J: *Sons of John Company – the Indian and Pakistan Armies 1903-91* (Tunbridge Wells, 1992)

Greacen, L: *Chink – A Biography* (London, 1989)

Graham, D & Bidwell, S: *Tug of War – The Battle for Italy, 1943-45* (London, 1986)

Greenwood, A: *Field Marshal Auchinleck* (Brockerscliffe, 1991)

Gunner, C: *Front of the Line – Adventures with the Irish Brigade* (Antrim, 1991)

Hamilton, N: *Monty – The making of a general 1887-1942* (London, 1981)

— *Monty – Master of the battlefield 1942-44* (London, 1983)

Hapgood, D & Richardson, D: *Monte Cassino* (London, 1984)

Harpur, B: *The Impossible Victory: A personal account of the Battle for the River Po* (London, 1980)

Hart, P: *To The Last Round: The South Notts Hussars 1939-1942* (Barnsley, 1996)

Hinsley, F H: *British Intelligence in the Second World War* (London, 1993)

Howarth, P: *My God, Soldiers – From Alamein to Vienna* (London, 1989)

Humble, R: *Crusader – The Eighth Army's Forgotten Victory* (London, 1987)

Ireland, B: *The War in the Mediterranean 1940-1943* (London, 1993)

Jackson, W G F: *The Battle for Italy* (London, 1968)

Joslen, Lt-Col H F: *Orders of Battle Second World War* (London, 1960)

Kay, R: *Italy – Vol 2: from Cassino to Trieste (Official History of New Zealand in the Second World War, 1939-45)* (Wellington, 1967)

Keegan, J (ed): *Churchill's Generals* (London, 1991)

— *The Second World War* (London, 1989)

Kesselring, Field Marshal A: *Memoirs* (London, 1953)

Lamb, R: *War in Italy 1943-1945 – A Brutal Story* (London, 1993)

Lucas, J: *Panzer Army Africa* (London, 1977)

— *War in the Desert – Eighth Army at El Alamein* (London, 1982)

— *Storming Eagles – German Airborne Forces in World War Two* (London, 1988)

— *Hitler's Mountain Troops* (London, 1992)

— *Hitler's Enforcers* (London, 1996)

Macksey, K: *Rommel – Battles and Campaigns* (London, 1979)

— *Kesselring – German Master Strategist of the Second World War* (London, 1978)

Majdalany, F: *The Monastery* (London, 1945)

— *Cassino – Portrait of a Battle* (London, 1957)

— *The Battle of El Alamein* (London, 1965)

Marrinan, P: *Churchill and the Irish Marshals* (Belfast, 1986)

Mead, P: *Gunners at War 1939-1945* (Shepperton, 1982)

Molony, C J C and Jackson, W: *The Mediterranean and the Middle East, Vols V-VI* (London, 1973-1988)

Montgomery, Viscount of Alamein: *El Alamein to the River Sangro* (London, 1948)

—*Memoirs* (London, 1958)

Moorehead, Alan: *The Desert War – The North African Campaign 1940-1943* (London, 1965)

Mowat, F: *And No Birds Sang* (Toronto, nd)

Nicholson, G W L: *The Canadians in Italy, 1943-1945 (Official History of the Canadian Army in the Second World War; Vol 2)* (Ottawa, 1956)

Neillands, R: *The Desert Rats – 7th Armoured Division 1940-1945* (London, 1951)

Nicolson, N: *Alex* (London, 1971)

North, J (ed): *The Memoirs of Field Marshal Earl Alexander of Tunis, 1940-1945* (London, 1962)

Orgill, D W: *The Gothic Line – the autumn campaign in Italy 1944* (London, 1967)

Pack, S C W: *Operation Husky – The Allied Invasion of Sicily* (Newton Abbot, 1971)

Parkinson, C N: *Always a Fusilier: The War History of the Royal Fusiliers* (London, 1949)

Parkinson, R: *The Auk – Auchinleck, Victor at El Alamein* (London, 1977)

Perrett, B: *Last Stand! Famous Battles Against the Odds* (London, 1991)

Phillips, N C: *Italy – Vol 1: The Sangro to Cassino (Official History of New Zealand in the Second World War, 1939-1945)* (Wellington, 1957)

Pitt, R (ed): *The Military History of World War Two* (London, 1986)

Piekalkiewicz, J: *Cassino – Anatomy of the Battle* (London, 1980)

Playfair, I S O: *The Mediterranean and the Middle East, Vols II and III* (London, 1956 and 1960)

Powell, Geoffrey: *The History of The Green Howards – Three Hundred Years of Service* (London, 1992)

Ray, C: *Algiers to Austria – The History of 78 Division 1942-1946* (London, 1952)

Raugh, H E, Jr: *Wavell in the Middle East 1939-1941 – A Study in Generalship* (London, 1994)

Roberts, O N: *31st Field Regiment RA: A Record* (Bristol, 1994)

Rosignoli, G: *The Allied Forces in Italy 1943-45* (Newton Abbot, 1989)

Routledge, N W: *History of the Royal Regiment of Artillery: Anti-Aircraft Artillery, 1914-55* (London, 1994)

Schmidt, H W: *With Rommel in the Desert* (London, 1951)

Senger und Etterlin, E von: *Neither Hope nor Fear* (London, 1963)

Smith, Claude: *The History of The Glider Pilot Regiment* (London, 1992)

Smith, E D: *The Battles for Cassino* (London, 1975)

Smith, P C: *Massacre at Tobruk* (London, 1987)

Smyth, Sir John: *The Story of the Victoria Cross* (London, 1963)

Stevens, G R: *Fourth Indian Division* (Toronto, 1948)

—— *The Tiger Triumphs* (London, 1946)

Strawson, J: *El Alamein – desert victory* (London, 1981)

—— *The Italian Campaign* (London, 1987)

Tedder, Lord: *With Prejudice* (London, 1966)

Trevelyan, R: *Rome '44 – The Battle for the Eternal City* (London, 1981)

Tuker, Sir Francis: *Approach to Battle* (London, 1963)

Verney, G L: *The Desert Rats – The 7th Armoured Division in World War II* (London, 1954)

Warner, P: *Horrocks – The General who led from the Front* (London, 1954)

—— *Alamein* (London, 1979)

—— *Auchinleck – The Lonely Soldier* (London, 1981)

Whiting, C: *The Long March on Rome* (London, 1987)

Williams, David: *The Black Cats at War – The Story of the 56th (London) Division T.A., 1939-1945* (London, 1995)

Williamson, Hugh: *The Fourth Division 1939 to 1945* (London, 1951)

ARTICLES

Alexander of Tunis, Field-Marshal the Rt Hon. The Earl: *The Battle of Tunis,* (The Basil Hicks Lecture delivered to the University of Sheffield, 1957)

Sadkovitch, J J: *German Military Incompetence through Italian Eyes.* (War in History, Vol I, No.I; pp39-52)

UNPUBLISHED SOURCES

The 8th Armoured Brigade, 1939-1945 (n.d.)

Battalion HQ, 2nd Seaforth Highlanders: *The 78th Highlanders in Sicily, July-August 1943* (Sicily, 1943)

Bredin, CB, DSO**, MC*, DL, Maj-Gen H E N (Bala): *An account of the Kangaroo Army*

Chavasse, DSO*, Col K G F: *Some Memories of 56 Reconnaissance Regiment* (n.d.)

Parsons, MC, Capt A G: *extracts from letters to his parents during the war*

Woods, MC*, Col A D: *A personal account of his service with 2nd London Irish Rifles in Italy*

HQ 15 Army Group: *Finito! The Po Valley Campaign 1945*

Supreme Allied Commander, Mediterranean: *Report on the Italian Campaign, Pts I – III*

Public Record Office, Kew

CAB44/97; 98; 99; 101; 108; 122; 123; 127; 128; 135; 136; 145; 146; 147; 148

(Official history narratives)

CAB106/441: Operations of British, Indian and Dominion Forces in Italy 3 Sep '43 – 2 May '45 Pt IV, The Campaign in Lombardy

FO371/48827: Yugoslavia File No. 24

WO169/996: War diary, Advance HQ, Eighth Army Sep-Dec 1941

— 4171: War diary, 51 (H) Recce Regt 1942

— 4230: War diary, 8 Armoured Brigade 1942

— 4994: War diary, 1st Buffs 1942

WO170/407: War diary, 4th Division 1944

— 474: War diary, 46 Recce Regt, RAC 1944

— 475: War diary, 46 Recce Regt, RAC, 1944 contd

— 605: War diary, 38 Brigade, 1944

— 4180: War diary, Main HQ, Eighth Army Apr 1945

— 4368: War diary, 56th Division, Mar/Apr 1945

— 4372: War diary, 44 Recce Regt, RAC 1945

— 4461: War diary, 36 Brigade 1945

— 4465: War diary, 38 Brigade 1945

— 4466: War diary, 38 Brigade 1945 contd

— 4488: War diary, HQ Jewish Infantry Bde Gp 1945

— 4629: War diary, 17/21 Lancers 1945

— 4992: War diary, 1st Buffs, 1945

WO201/355: General Auchinleck's account of the CRUSADER operation

— 358: Report of operations, Eighth Army Sep-Nov 1941

— 359: Report of operations, Eighth Army Nov-Dec 1941

— 391: 1st South African Division Operations Report 27 Jan – 14 Jun '42: Gazala Defensive Battle

— 423: Defensive Planning in Western Desert 24 Aug – 6 Nov '42

— 425: Battle for Egypt Oct/Nov '42

— 430: RE Notes, Benghazi to Tripoli

— 433: Operation LIGHTFOOT, Memorandum No.2 by Army Cmdr

— 449: Lessons on Operations, El Alamein to conclusion of Tunisian Campaign, ME Training Memorandum No. 8

— 452: Notes on Main Lessons of Recent Operations in Western Desert, 13 Jul '42

— 538: Lessons from Operations 10 Sep '41 – 25 Aug '42

— 542: Short Account of Operations, 8th Hussars 23 Oct – 13 Nov '42

— 545: 24 Armd Bde; Notes on AFVs on Operations 23 – 29 Oct '42

— 1812: Twelfth Army Op Order No.1

The Royal Irish Fusiliers' Museum, Armagh

Russell, Brig. N: *An Account of the service of The Irish Brigade,* Nov 1942-Feb 1944

Scott, Brig T P D: *An Account of the service of The Irish Brigade,* Feb 1944-June 1945

Index